The Most
Glorious
Fourth

The Most Glorious Fourth

Vicksburg and Gettysburg, July 4, 1863

Duane Schultz

W. W Norton & Company
New York London

For information about permission to reproduce selections from this book,
write to Permissions, W. W. Norton & Company, Inc.,
500 Fifth Avenue, New York, NY 10110

The text of this book is composed in Caslon, with the
display set in Chevalier Open and Copperplate 33bc
Composition by Sue Carlson
Manufacturing by The Haddon Craftsmen, Inc.
Book design by Chris Welch
Production manager: Leelo Märjamaa-Reintal

Library of Congress Cataloging-in-Publication Data

Schultz, Duane P.
The most glorious fourth : Vicksburg and Gettsburg, July 4, 1863 /
by Duane Schultz.
p. cm.
Includes bibliographical references and index.
ISBN 0-393-04870-5
1. Vicksburg (Miss.)—History—Siege, 1863. 2. Gettysburg (Pa.), Battle of, 1863.
3. Vicksburg (Miss.)—History—Siege, 1863—Personal narratives. 4. Gettysburg
(Pa.), Battle of, 1863—Personal narratives. 5. Fourth of July. 6. United States—
History—Civil War, 1861–1865—Personal narratives. I. Title.

E475.27 .S38 2001

973.7'349—dc21   2001031478

ISBN 0-393-32381-1 pbk.

W. W. Norton & Company, Inc., 500 Fifth Avenue, New York, N.Y. 10110
www.wwnorton.com

W. W. Norton & Company Ltd., Castle House,
75/76 Wells Street, London W1T 3QT

1 2 3 4 5 6 7 8 9 0

CONTENTS

Acknowledgments ix

CHAPTER 1 WHAT WILL THE COUNTRY SAY? *3*

CHAPTER 2 AND THEN CAME WAR *16*

CHAPTER 3 ROBERT WAS ALWAYS GOOD *41*

CHAPTER 4 THE GIBRALTAR OF THE WEST *67*

CHAPTER 5 HOW VERY SAD THIS LIFE *97*

CHAPTER 6 THE SUSPENSE WAS DREADFUL *134*

CHAPTER 7 TO FIND AND FIGHT THE ENEMY *169*

CHAPTER 8 WE NEED HELP NOW *199*

CHAPTER 9 THE BLOOD STOOD IN PUDDLES *232*

CHAPTER 10 THE SLAUGHTER WILL BE TERRIBLE *269*

CHAPTER 11 FOR GOD'S SAKE, COME QUICK! *295*

CHAPTER 12 THEY'VE BROKE ALL TO HELL! *318*

CHAPTER 13 THE MOST GLORIOUS FOURTH *348*

CHAPTER 14 A STRANGE AND BLIGHTED LAND *374*

Chapter Notes *409*

Bibliography *433*

Index *441*

Saturday, July 4, 1863

This was the most Glorious Fourth I ever spent.
—Isaac Jackson
Private, Eighty-third Ohio Regiment

This is a day of jubilee, a day of rejoicing.
—William T. Sherman
Major General of Volunteers
Army of the United States

Tuesday, July 14, 1863

*Now the opportune chance of ending this bitter struggle is
lost. The war will be prolonged indefinitely.*
—Abraham Lincoln
President of the United States

ACKNOWLEDGMENTS

It is a pleasure to acknowledge the assistance of the dedicated librarians, archivists, and photo researchers with whom I have been fortunate to work. I am grateful to the reference and interlibrary loan staffs at the Clearwater, Florida, Public Library, especially Candace McDaniel, for cheerfully filling my requests, many of which were for materials long out of print.

Also helpful were the personnel at the Prints and Photographs Division of the Library of Congress, and the Still Picture Branch of the National Archives. In addition, I wish to thank the U.S. Army Military History Institute (Carlisle Barracks), the Gettysburg National Military Park, the Adams County (Pennsylvania) Historical Society, the General Lee Headquarters Museum (Gettysburg), the Valentine Museum (Richmond), the Old Court House Museum (Vicksburg), and the Mississippi Department of Archives and History.

Finally, I would like to record my gratitude to Starling Lawrence and Drake Bennett of W. W. Norton & Company, for sharing their ideas and challenging me to consider most carefully the issues raised by the Gettysburg and Vicksburg battles.

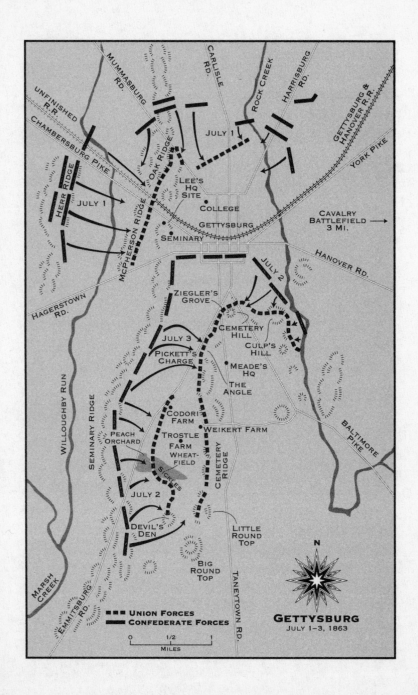

UNFINISHED R.R.

CHAMBERSBURG PIKE

MUMMASBURG RD.

CARLISLE RD.

ROCK CREEK

HARRISBURG RD.

GETTYSBURG & HANOVER R.R.

YORK PIKE

JULY 1

HERR RIDGE

JULY 1

OAK RIDGE

McPHERSON RIDGE

LEE'S HQ SITE

COLLEGE

GETTYSBURG

SEMINARY

CAVALRY BATTLEFIELD 3 MI.

HANOVER RD.

HAGERSTOWN RD.

ZIEGLER'S GROVE

JULY 2

JULY 3

PICKETT'S CHARGE

WILLOUGHBY RUN

SEMINARY RIDGE

CEMETERY HILL

CULP'S HILL

MEADE'S HQ

THE ANGLE

CODORI FARM

PEACH ORCHARD

TROSTLE FARM

WHEAT-FIELD

SICKLES

WEIKERT FARM

CEMETERY RIDGE

BALTIMORE PIKE

JULY 2

DEVIL'S DEN

LITTLE ROUND TOP

BIG ROUND TOP

TANEYTOWN RD.

MARSH CREEK

EMMITSBURG RD.

N

UNION FORCES
CONFEDERATE FORCES

0   1/2   1
MILES

GETTYSBURG
JULY 1–3, 1863

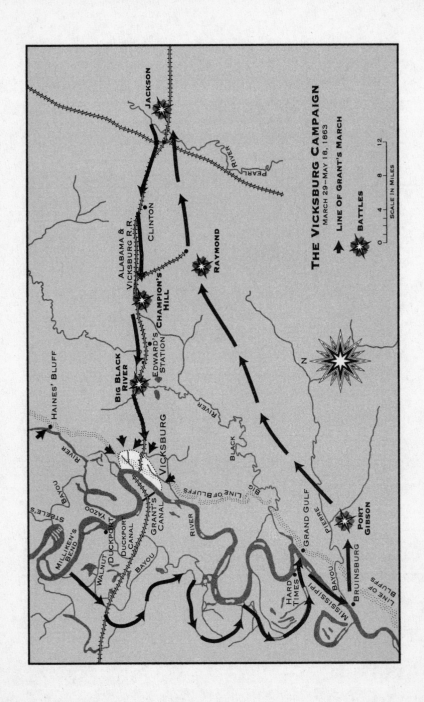

THE VICKSBURG CAMPAIGN
MARCH 29–MAY 18, 1863

➤ LINE OF GRANT'S MARCH
✴ BATTLES

SCALE IN MILES
0   4   8   12

JACKSON

PEARL RIVER

CLINTON

RAYMOND

ALABAMA & VICKSBURG R. R.

CHAMPION'S HILL

EDWARD'S STATION

BIG BLACK RIVER

HAINES' BLUFF

VICKSBURG

BIG BLACK RIVER

LINE OF BLUFFS

N

STEELE'S BAYOU

MILLIKEN'S BEND

YAZOO RIVER

WALNUT

DUCKPORT

DUCKPORT CANAL

GRANT'S CANAL

BAYOU

RIVER

GRAND GULF

ST. PIERRE

PORT GIBSON

HARD TIMES

MISSISSIPPI

BAYOU

BRUINSBURG

LINE OF BLUFFS

THE MOST
GLORIOUS
FOURTH

CHAPTER 1

WHAT WILL THE COUNTRY SAY?

July 2, 1863

BEFORE THE WAR, the room had been a library. The books were still there, stacked on glass-enclosed shelves in deep recessed alcoves between the five windows overlooking Pennsylvania Avenue. But the young men working in shifts around the clock had little time for reading. They were too busy sending and receiving messages to and from the Union army.

The room, now the War Department's telegraph office, was located on the second floor of the office building next to the White House at Pennsylvania Avenue and Seventeenth Street. Abraham Lincoln referred to it as his office, but it was really much more than that. It had become a sanctuary, a refuge. He liked to joke with the telegraph operators, his "boys," he called them. He told one, A. B. Chandler, "I come here to escape my persecutors."

Lincoln spent almost as much time there, escaping the constant parade of people who wanted something from him, as he did in the White House. Even when he was not awaiting telegrams informing him of the outcome of a battle, he would wander in from next door like a boy playing hooky from school.

He would sit at the large desk, opposite the man on duty at the telegraph key, and read through the yellow copies of messages received since his last visit. Then he would slump forward, perched on the very edge of the hard-backed chair with his right knee nearly on the floor, to read the more important telegrams a second time. Then he would straighten up and say, "Well, I guess I have got down to the raisins."

After hearing this for weeks, Chandler finally asked the president what he meant. Lincoln embarked on one of the folksy tales he liked to tell, this one about a girl who tended to overindulge when eating raisins. Now, that was not so bad by itself, Lincoln explained, but one day she ate too many raisins followed by far too many sweets.

The inevitable happened. The child became ill and began to throw up. Eventually the raisins reappeared and the girl, much relieved, said to her mother, "I will be better now, I guess, for I have got down to the raisins."

The president seemed more at ease at the telegraph office than anyplace else in the city. He enjoyed chatting with the operators when they were not occupied with their clicking keys. Sometimes he thought they were the only people in Washington who did not want some favor from him, and they appeared to enjoy his company, too. Maj. Thomas Eckert, who was in charge of the facility and who rarely left the room, liked to amuse Lincoln by taking one of the soft-iron pokers that stood in front of the fireplace and bending it double over his left arm.[1]

Occasionally Lincoln napped on an ancient horsehair-covered couch—until the day he found a bedbug on his lapel. He laughed and joked that he would have to stop using the couch. It had gotten a little too buggy! Usually he tilted back in a chair, feet propped on a table, and gazed out the window at the passing crowds on Pennsylvania Avenue. He seemed lost in thought; his boys stayed quiet so as not to break the mood.

Back in late spring of 1862, Lincoln spent hours hunched over the

---

[1] Eckert later became president of the Western Union telegraph company.

table by the window slowly putting words to paper. He wrote a line or two, stared out the window, and wrote some more. Whenever he left to return to the White House, he handed his unfinished work to Major Eckert, instructing him to lock it up and to not let anyone read it. The next day, Lincoln collected the pages from Eckert and laboriously wrote some more. The document was the first draft of the Emancipation Proclamation, crafted amid the clattering of the telegraph keys in the closest place the president could find peace.

But there were far too many nights in the telegraph room when there was no peace, when Lincoln's refuge became a place of pain and suffering, when the deciphered words on yellow tissue paper told of another battle lost, of greater casualties; of the failure of yet another army general in whom he had invested hope and trust. This had happened before, beginning at Bull Run in the summer of 1861, when Gen. Irwin McDowell let him down.

"If hell is [not] any worse than this," Lincoln said after hearing of that first Union defeat, "it has no terror for me." When Gen. George McClellan failed in the Peninsular campaign in 1862, Lincoln said, "[I was] as nearly inconsolable as I could be and live."

A few weeks later came Gen. John Pope's disaster at the second battle of Bull Run. Lincoln said he felt disposed to hang himself. And a few months after that, in December 1862, Gen. Ambrose Burnside presided over the loss of thirteen thousand men at Fredericksburg. When Lincoln received the news, the pain showed clearly on his face. He groaned aloud, paced the floor, and wrung his hands. His mood darkened and he succumbed to the blackest depression anyone could recall. He believed it was all his fault. He chose the leaders, but it seemed as though he would never find one who could win.

On May 6, 1863, another devastating loss occurred when Gen. Joe Hooker at Chancellorsville failed to live up to his nickname, "Fighting Joe." Lincoln sought out Edwin Stanton, the secretary of war. "My God!" Lincoln said. "Our cause is lost! We are ruined—we are ruined; and such a fearful loss of life! My God! This is more than I can endure!"

Noah Brooks, a newspaper reporter for the *Sacramento Union*, was a close friend of Lincoln's from their time in Illinois. Brooks recalled the moment they received the news about Chancellorsville.

> I shall never forget that picture of despair. [Lincoln] held a telegram in his hand, and as he closed the door and came toward us I mechanically noticed that his face, usually sallow, was ashen in hue. . . . Never, as long as I knew him, did he seem to be so broken, so dispirited, and so ghostlike. Clasping his hands behind his back, he walked up and down the room, saying, "My God! My God! What will the country say! What will the country say!"

And now, on the night of July 2, 1863, the uncertainty and agony gripped Lincoln again as he waited for news and worried about the country's reaction to another possible debacle. This time, the situation was even more painful because it was not one general and one battle on which the fate of the nation hinged, but two.

Out west was Gen. Ulysses S. Grant, the reputed drunkard everybody pressured Lincoln to get rid of. So far, Lincoln had resisted, continuing to put his trust in a man whom he had never met. For months Grant and his Army of the Tennessee had been trying to capture Vicksburg, holding the city under siege for the past six weeks. It seemed as if the rebels planned to hold out forever. Lincoln was beginning to think he had once more chosen the wrong general, that the Union would be denied this victory.

Vicksburg was the key. No matter how much success his armies in the east might have, though they had achieved none so far, the Confederacy could not be defeated as long as the South held Vicksburg. What irked Lincoln was that Grant did not keep him informed. Once, ten days had passed before Lincoln received any news. At that time, a frantic president telegraphed his other generals asking if they had heard from Grant. No one had. Lincoln scoured the Richmond newspapers, only to read that Grant's forces had suffered disastrous defeats, that

General Sherman had been grievously wounded, and that the Confederates were rushing up reinforcements to strengthen Vicksburg's garrison. The news reports were all wrong—wishful thinking or rebel propaganda—but Lincoln didn't know that at the time.

Although he heard nothing from Grant, he continued to receive complaints about Grant and demands that he be dismissed. The criticisms came in the form of letters, newspaper editorials, and delegations of irate citizens calling on Lincoln in person. The editor of the *Cincinnati Gazette* wrote, "Our noble army of the Mississippi is being wasted by the foolish, drunken, stupid Grant. He cannot organize or control or fight an army. I have no personal feeling about it; but I know he is an ass."

A group of clergymen echoed the familiar refrain that Grant was a drunk and must be fired. Baiting them, Lincoln asked if they knew where Grant got his liquor. Puzzled by the question, the ministers said they had no idea. "I am very sorry," Lincoln told them, "for if you could tell me, I would direct the Chief Quartermaster of the army to lay in a large stock of the same kind of liquor, and would also direct him to furnish a supply to some of my other generals who have never yet won a victory."

Lincoln loved that story and repeated it every chance he had, but beneath his laughter he was sorely worried about Grant. If he did not take Vicksburg, the North would blame Lincoln for keeping a bumbling, incompetent drunkard in command. Lincoln clung to his belief in Grant's proven courage, but as public attacks mounted, it sometimes seemed that Lincoln was the only friend Grant had left.

As if Vicksburg were not worry enough, Lincoln had a greater problem on hand with Robert E. Lee's audacious invasion of the North, which had begun two weeks earlier. Panic was widespread throughout the northeast as the Southern forces advanced into Maryland and crossed the border into Pennsylvania. When Lee's troops occupied Hagerstown, Maryland, they cut the telegraph line and toppled the poles. For two days, until another telegraphic connection could be routed through Hanover Junction, Pennsylvania, no one in Washington received any news of Lee or the whereabouts of his army. Even when the new line was established, communications were poor and intermittent, adding to the general unease in the capital city.

After Hagerstown, Lee went on to capture Chambersburg, York, and Greencastle, all north of the Pennsylvania line. And in each town, rebel troops seized the livestock and bought out the shops, politely exchanging worthless Confederate currency for shoes, socks, shirts, and pants. Some of the rebel soldiers had never been dressed so well. The South was outfitting and feeding its army on Yankee spoils.

During the day and late into the night, Lincoln would trudge over to the telegraph office, desperate for news. Where was Lee heading? Where would he strike next? No one knew. On June 21, some Washington residents reported hearing cannon fire from the direction of Manassas, no more than twenty-five miles away. It was rumored that Union supply wagons had been attacked within sight of the capital city and that rebel cavalry had been spotted not far from Georgetown. On June 28, Postmaster General Montgomery Blair brought his family into town from their country home at Silver Spring, Maryland, to escape the threat posed by Lee's army. Silver Spring was fewer than thirteen miles from the White House.

And still Lincoln could not find out what was happening. The news coming in over the single line from Hanover Junction was sparse and infrequent. Finally, late on July 1, the president learned of what seemed to be a major battle at Gettysburg, news that was confirmed the following day. Now, on the night of July 2, Lincoln was waiting again for word of the day's events on the battlefield and of how his newest general—the latest in that sad series of army leaders—was faring.

The outcome of the fight at Gettysburg depended on Gen. George Meade, to whom Lincoln had given command of the Army of the Potomac only five days before. The questions plagued Lincoln. Was Meade the right man for the job? Should someone else have been appointed to replace Joe Hooker? Why wasn't there a Union general who could best Robert E. Lee, who could have prevented him menacing Washington, Philadelphia, and New York? If Lee defeated Meade, the Confederate army could be advancing on Washington tomorrow, taking a victory march down Pennsylvania Avenue from the Capitol to the White House.

Independence Day was only two days away, and Lincoln knew that if Meade lost in Pennsylvania and Grant failed in Mississippi, the Union whose birth was celebrated on July 4 would forever be divided. The people would blame Lincoln. History would blame him, and he would blame himself until the day he died. The waiting was almost more than he could bear.

⊷⇒◉←⊷

LIBBY CUSTER, THE new bride of young George Armstrong Custer, thought the president looked terrible. She recalled him as the "gloomiest, most painfully careworn looking man I ever saw." Lincoln's old friend, Adm. John Dahlgren, who saw him frequently, remarked that Lincoln had become so downhearted that he seldom told his folksy stories anymore.

His appearance had changed under the unremitting pressures of the war. He looked like someone ravaged by a serious illness. His skin was pale, the circles under his eyes heavy and dark. His funereal black suit hung loosely on an emaciated body. "His hair was grizzled," the journalist Noah Brooks said. "His gait more stooping, his countenance sallow, and there is a sunken deathly look about his large cavernous eyes."

Mary Todd Lincoln worried constantly about her husband's health and safety, especially since he had taken to walking the city streets, talking to strangers, and crossing to the telegraph office by himself at night. She knew of the threats made against his life. She took them seriously, even if he did not.

The White House grounds were not fenced, and the house itself was open to the public. A doorkeeper was supposed to screen visitors, to keep out unsavory types, but he was elderly and could not cope with the hordes of people who wanted an audience with the president, regardless of the hour. Once outside the small private family quarters on the second floor, Mr. and Mrs. Lincoln frequently found themselves confronted by angry citizens seeking a word or insisting on delivering a message.

As the war dragged on and the casualty lists mounted, the number of threats against the president's safety grew apace. Lincoln issued orders that he not be shown such letters. He did not want to know the details, perhaps out of a sense of fatalism—or realism. He recognized that there was no way he could be completely safe. He had told Noah Brooks:

> I long ago made up my mind that if anybody wants to kill me, he will do it. If I wore a shirt of mail, and kept myself surrounded by a body-guard, it would be all the same. There are a thousand ways of getting at a man if it is desired that he should be killed.

The security detail did their best to protect Lincoln from harm, but he was often less than cooperative. Col. Charles Stone, in charge of security, hid armed soldiers behind the shrubbery around the house and stationed troops in the basement ready for action. Stone pressed for an armed escort to accompany Lincoln outside the White House, but the president liked to slip out unaccompanied. He did not relish the thought of armed soldiers trailing after him, and he was too impatient to wait for them to assemble whenever he decided to go for a walk.

He did allow the cavalry to escort him out the Seventh Street Pike to the Soldiers' Home, three miles beyond the city limits. The Lincolns often rode there in the summer to escape Washington's oppressive heat and humidity. But more often than not, he came back to town alone, on horseback or driving himself in an open carriage.

No wonder Mary Todd Lincoln was so worried. And she was particularly concerned about the frequent late-night visits to the telegraph office.

"Where are you going now, father?" she would ask, when he got ready to go out after dark.

"To the War Department, mother, to try to learn some news."

"But, father, you should not go out alone. You know you are surrounded with danger."

"All imagination," Lincoln would say. "What does anyone want to harm me for?"

Mrs. Lincoln was away from the White House on the night of July 2, when her husband prepared to visit the telegraph office. Earlier in the day, she had been driven out to Anderson Cottage, the small stone house on the grounds of the Soldiers' Home reserved for the president's use. Returning to the White House that afternoon, the carriage lurched and Mrs. Lincoln was thrown to the ground. Her head struck a rock. She sustained multiple bruises and lacerations and was confined to bed back at the cottage. The incident apparently had been a plot to kill the president. Someone, who was never identified, had deliberately unscrewed the bolts that secured the driver's seat to the carriage frame. When the seat broke free, the horses stampeded.

As much as Lincoln wanted to be at her bedside, he could not leave Washington, not on this night of July 2, when the fate of the Union hung in the balance. He walked alone in the dark to the telegraph office, sick with worry about his wife and desperate for news from Vicksburg and Gettysburg.

⟞⟐⟐⟞

JOHN CLIFFORD PEMBERTON came from a wealthy Philadelphia family. When he was growing up, two of his childhood friends were named George. One was George McClellan, the other George Meade. Now Pemberton was their enemy, a lieutenant general wearing the uniform of the Confederacy, many of whose citizens did not trust anyone born a Yankee. And they certainly did not trust him to command such an important Southern bastion as Vicksburg.

On the night of July 2, the forty-sixth day since the siege of the city began, General Pemberton summoned his senior commanders to his headquarters. It was a moment he had long anticipated—and dreaded.

A few days earlier, someone—he never found out who it was—had slipped a note under his door. Across the top was printed: AN APPEAL FOR HELP.

> If you can't feed us, you had better surrender us, horrible as the idea is, than suffer this noble army to disgrace themselves by desertion. . . . This army is now ripe for mutiny unless it can be fed.

Pemberton knew that their provisions could feed his troops for only a few more days, at most. He faced an agonizing decision. Should he surrender and face the shame of presiding over the largest capitulation to take place on American soil? Or should he try to fight his way out through the encircling Yankee forces that far outnumbered his own?

He put the questions to his four division commanders in a letter, asking if their men were in any condition to do battle. Their answers, delivered to Pemberton personally at the meeting the night of July 2, were unequivocal and unanimous. The men were too weakened from starvation, disease, exposure to six weeks of continuous shell fire, and the unrelenting heat and humidity of a Mississippi summer to march and fight their way to safety. Indeed, they were probably capable of defending the city only for a few days more. Pemberton was left with no alternative but surrender.

When his division commanders left, Pemberton drafted a note to "Sam" Grant, with whom he had served during the Mexican War. He dated the letter July 3 and arranged for it to be delivered by one of his officers, Maj. Gen. John S. Bowen, who had also been a friend of Grant's. Bowen would know how best to approach the Yankee commander. Pemberton also assumed that Grant would be so eager to take the surrender on the Fourth of July, that most fervently patriotic Union holiday, that he would be generous with his terms.

Ulysses S. Grant held no meetings that night of July 2, nor did he feel any urge to capture the city on Independence Day. Why spend more lives on a symbolic gesture when the prize was due to fall into his hands within a matter of days? He knew Pemberton was trapped. So Grant dispatched no telegrams to the waiting Lincoln that night. He believed he had nothing important to say. He was doing his job, and there was no point in sending a message about that.

⌁⌁⊙⌁⌁

Robert E. Lee's headquarters camp, situated in a grove of trees near the Chambersburg Pike on the outskirts of Gettysburg, was crowded with staff officers and generals. The talk was confident, all about the great victory they would achieve the following day.

It was true they had sustained heavy losses, but reinforcements had arrived, sufficient to more than make up for the casualties. Stuart's three brigades of cavalry were finally present, along with four additional independent cavalry brigades. George Pickett's division was in place, Virginians to a man. There would be no stopping them tomorrow.

"It is all well, general," Lee told A. P. Hill. "Everything is all well."

And, indeed, everything did look promising to Lee and most of his generals. Only Pete Longstreet disputed their rosy view, and he had chosen to stay away from headquarters that night. He did not share Lee's optimism, nor did he agree with Lee's plan of attack. But Lee and the others remained convinced of success. Troop morale was high. Many divisions, even exclusive of the reinforcements, had not yet seen battle or had suffered only modest casualties. They were fresh and eager to engage the enemy.

Lee had decided on his battle plan. On the first day, he had attacked the Yankees on the right side of their line. On the second day, he had moved against the left side. Although Lee had not been victorious, he reasoned that Meade would have weakened the center to shift troops to reinforce the left. So it would be at the center of the Union line where

Lee intended to attack. Pickett's rested division would spearhead the assault. Maybe they would even end the war as they took the crest of Cemetery Ridge.

--------◦◦==◦--------

LESS THAN TWO miles from Lee's camp, Gen. George Meade assembled his twelve corps commanders in the small frame house he used as headquarters. They convened in a room little more than twelve feet square. It was sparsely furnished, with a narrow bed in one corner, a small pine table, and several straight-back chairs. On the table were a wooden bucket full of water, a tin cup, and a candle.

A few of the officers sat down, a couple of them perched on the bed, and the rest stood. Gen. Gouverneur Warren, exhausted from the day's battle and suffering a wound to the neck, stretched out on the floor and fell asleep.

After the commanders had reported to Meade on the actions in their sector and the extent of casualties, their attention turned to speculation about the South's intentions the following day. What would Lee do, and how should they prepare for it?

Their answers were unanimous. Whatever Lee might do, the Army of the Potomac should hold its present position and wait for an attack. They should not consider taking the offensive themselves. Meade took no part in the discussion but made it clear that the opinions of his generals coincided with his own.

While his officers waited, Meade wrote a message to be telegraphed to the War Department in Washington; it was sent at eleven o'clock that night.

The enemy has attacked me about 4 P.M. this day, and after one of the severest contests of the war, was repulsed at all points. We have suffered considerably in killed and wounded. . . . We have taken a large number of prisoners. I shall remain in my present position tomorrow, but am not prepared to say, until better advised of the condition of the army, whether my operations will be of an offensive or defensive character.

This was the only message Lincoln received from the Gettysburg front that night. It left him with many nagging questions. Was the North winning or losing thus far? How heavy were their casualties? How many troops did Meade have left? Could he hold, or was Lee in position to break through and march on Washington? Lincoln knew only that he would spend another sleepless night wondering whether he could continue to hold the Union together through this Fourth of July.

CHAPTER 2

AND THEN CAME WAR

HIS GIVEN NAME was Hiram, but everyone in the small town of Georgetown, Ohio, where he grew up, used his middle name, Ulysses. He preferred that himself, even when other children deliberately mispronounced it and mocked him as "useless."

Hiram Ulysses Grant was an awkward and unsociable boy, with no real talents beyond being able to handle a horse. He appeared to have little ambition or direction in life, but if he did not yet know what he wanted to do when he grew up, he was certain of what he did *not* want to do. He would not work in his father's tannery with its bloody sights and sounds of death. He had to get away from the overwhelming stench of slaughtered animals, hides, rendering vats, and powerful acids.

If these aversions were not reason enough to avoid working in the tannery, the boy and his father had learned early on that Ulysses had no head for business. When he was about eight years old, he took a fancy to a neighbor's colt and begged his father to buy it. Jesse Grant offered the owner twenty dollars, but he held out for twenty-five.

Ulysses badgered his father to meet the man's price until Jesse finally relented, but he told his son that the horse was not worth the twenty-five dollars the man was asking. Jesse instructed his son to first offer twenty dollars. If the owner refused, Ulysses should offer twenty-two fifty. If that price was rejected, only then should Ulysses offer twenty-five—if he really wanted the colt that much.

Well, Ulysses did want the colt that much. In fact, he wanted it so desperately that when he reached the neighbor's house, he blurted out exactly what his father had told him. "Papa says I may offer you twenty dollars for the colt, but if you won't take that, I am to offer twenty-two and a half, and if you won't take that, I am to give you twenty-five."

Many years later Grant wrote,

> It would not require a Connecticut man to guess the price finally agreed upon. This transaction caused me great heart-burning. The story got out among the boys of the village, and it was a long time before I heard the last of it.

The boy became a laughingstock and never lost the sense of humiliation. The incident was a lifelong reminder that he had no ability for business dealings. Whatever combination of talent and temperament was needed in that world, Hiram Ulysses Grant did not have it.

When the boy was old enough to consider his future, Jesse Grant took charge. He knew how much his son hated the tannery while lacking the aptitude he had for business or for learning a trade or craft. The family did not have enough money to send Ulysses to college, so Jesse, shrewd man that he was, contacted his congressman and secured for the boy an appointment to the military academy at West Point. If Ulysses could not do anything else, perhaps he could be a soldier. At least the school was free.

"But I won't go," Ulysses said, when he learned what was in store for him. He did not want to be a soldier. As Grant later described the exchange, Jesse "said he thought I would [go], *and I thought so too, if he did.*" And so, at the age of seventeen, Ulysses Grant escaped from a future at the tannery and, in the process, changed his name.

The man who made the appointment was an old friend of Jesse's. Like everyone else, Congressman Thomas Hamer called the boy Ulysses and assumed that was his first name. Hamer also guessed, when completing the appointment form, that the boy's middle name was Simpson, his mother's maiden name. And that was why Ulysses found himself listed on the West Point cadet roster as U. S. Grant. He decided not to correct it. Inevitably, the initials led to the nickname "Uncle Sam," not a bad moniker for a soldier. His few close friends called him Sam.

Grant hated everything about life at the military academy. He eagerly followed the ongoing congressional debate about shutting the place down. That, he believed, would be his only honorable way out. He did not think he had the ability to complete the demanding program and he greatly feared returning home a failure.

The first year was every bit as difficult as he anticipated, but when Congress did not close the academy as he had hoped, he resolved to stick it out. By the second year, to his amazement, he was doing well in his studies, standing tenth in a class of fifty-three. Even with this unexpected achievement, however, Grant wrote that he "had not the faintest idea of staying in the army even if I should be graduated, which I did not expect." He planned to become a college professor after his obligatory tour of active duty following graduation—that is, if he managed to graduate.

Grant did graduate from the military academy. Although he did not get his first choice of branch of service, the cavalry (then called "dragoons"), and was selected for the infantry instead, he was proud of his new lieutenant's uniform. He was eager to show it off to his schoolmates back home, especially to the girls. Perhaps that visual symbol of success, the smart, well-cut uniform of an army officer, would ease the lingering humiliations of his childhood.

But it was not to be. Stopping in Cincinnati on his way home, Grant was taunted by a street urchin who made fun of his uniform, bringing to mind the teasing he took after his childhood horse trade. He was in for greater embarrassment at home. The barefoot, dull-witted stable boy took to mocking him, parading up and down the street wearing dark blue pants with a crudely made white stripe affixed to the outer seams. "The joke was a huge one in the mind of many of the people," Grant recalled, "and was much enjoyed by them; but I did not appreciate it so highly."

In February 1844, twenty-two-year-old Lt. Ulysses S. Grant's life changed forever when he began courting seventeen-year-old Julia Dent, the sister of a West Point classmate. She lived at White Haven, the Dent family estate, a few miles outside of St. Louis. It was in this city that, five months earlier, Grant had reported to Jefferson Barracks, the nation's largest army post. He first met Julia that winter when she returned home from boarding school.

One of Grant's biographers wrote, perhaps unkindly, that

Julia was no beauty. Even at seventeen her figure was stumpy, she had more neck than chin, and she suffered from strabismus. A malfunctioning muscle caused her right eye to move up and down involuntarily.

But she was lively and quick-witted, and loved to ride and roam the countryside with the attentive Lieutenant Grant. She set her cap for him early on, and got him, though she would have to wait four years for marriage.

The nasty little war with Mexico got in the way. Grant was on leave visiting his parents when his regiment was ordered south for service over the border. By the time he returned to St. Louis, his outfit had already moved out. He rode at once for White Haven to say goodbye to Julia. He had to cross a creek to reach the Dent estate. Ordinarily, that was easy enough on horseback, but that day heavy rains had left the creek swift and overflowing, and clearly dangerous. Revealing the determination that would lead to the Union's success at Vicksburg, Grant later wrote, "One of my superstitions had always been when I started to go anywhere, or to do anything, not to turn back, or stop until the thing intended was accomplished."

He plunged into the raging waters, clinging to his horse's neck while they were swept along with the current. He arrived at the Dent house so drenched that he had to borrow clothes from Julia's brother. That was the day Sam Grant and Julia Dent reached an understanding. She would wait for him and they would marry when he returned from the war.

Her power over him would always be stronger than anyone else's. He needed Julia Dent and depended mightily on her, as he revealed in a letter a year later.

> You can have but little idea of the influence you have over me, Julia, even while so far away. If I feel tempted to do anything that I think is not right I am sure to think, "Well now if Julia saw me would I do so" and thus it is, absent or present, I am more or less governed by what I think is your will.

⊷≡◦≡⊶

GRANT'S FIRST WAR was mostly waiting and boredom, impatience and routine. He spent his time drilling troops and playing cards with his friend, Pete Longstreet. When the American army finally crossed the border into Mexico, Sam Grant was made quartermaster. His duties included purchasing mules and loading them with supplies, acting more as a clerk than a soldier.

"I felt sorry that I had enlisted," Grant wrote. When he was left in command of a company whose officers were sent on a separate mission, Grant led the troops forward under fire at Resaca de la Palma, where he captured a few Mexican soldiers. His first exposure to enemy fire seemed to have left little impression on him, mirroring what he felt his own contribution to the battle had been. It "would have been won, just as it was, if I had not been there," he noted.

Three months later in a larger battle at Monterrey, Grant, acting against orders, rode to the front line.

My curiosity got the better of my judgment, and I mounted a horse and rode to the front. . . . I had been there but a short time when an order to charge was given, and lacking the moral courage to return to camp—where I had been ordered to stay—I charged with the regiment.

It was a bloody affair. The regiment lost one-third of its men and withdrew to a place of relative safety before charging anew. Grant was pressed into service to replace the regimental adjutant who had been killed. The following day Grant volunteered to ride through heavy enemy fire to bring up more ammunition. He hung over the side of his horse to shield himself from enemy bullets, and his mission was successful. The army captured Monterrey and Grant returned quietly to his quartermaster duties, while others in the regiment earned glory and promotions in ensuing victories.

Near the end of the war, in an attack on Mexico City, Grant again distinguished himself in combat. Leading approximately one dozen volunteers, he hauled a cannon to the belfry of a church that offered a clear and highly damaging field of fire. For his initiative and gallantry, Grant was commended in a report written by a young staff officer, Capt. Robert E. Lee. The commanding general, William Worth, was so impressed with Grant's accomplishment that he sent an aide to fetch him. The general wanted to congratulate Grant in person. The aide, Lt. John C. Pemberton, would meet Grant sixteen years later at Vicksburg.

⊷═◦═⊶

PETE LONGSTREET WAS the best man at the wedding of Ulysses Grant and Julia Dent on August 22, 1848. For the next four years, life was good for the Grants and the work was undemanding for an army quartermaster stationed in Detroit. Their happy times fell apart in

1852 when the regiment was transferred to the West Coast. Julia, with one child to care for and another one on the way, went to live with her parents. Grant was on his own, and that would be his undoing.

He spent two years at Fort Vancouver in Washington State. Life was dreary, depressing, and lonely. Grant longed for his family, but it was too costly to bring them out even on the salary that came with his promotion to captain. He tried to supplement his army pay with assorted and ill-conceived business ventures, but, typically, they all failed.

He invested his savings in a San Francisco store run by a friend, but it went bust; having lost Grant's money, the proprietor returned to the east. Grant considered the lumber business, then farming, but nothing worked out. When he tried to grow potatoes and oats on land beside the Columbia River, it flooded, drowning the entire crop.

In 1854, he was transferred to a bleak, isolated outpost at Fort Humboldt, on the California coast. He grew ever more morose. He carried with him a treasured letter from Julia on which she had traced the outline of his baby son's hand. He would smooth it out with trembling hands and show it to everyone who would talk to him, sometimes with tears in his eyes.

The commanding officer was a martinet. Grant despised him, a feeling that was returned in kind. He had been assigned few duties on the tiny post. With little to do and few people for companionship, he described the life as a nightmare. He wrote to Julia, "I do nothing but set in my room and read and occasionally take a short ride on one of the public horses. You do not know how forsaken I feel here."

In his despair and desolation, Ulysses Grant turned to drink. This was not unusual in the army; almost everyone drank to some degree or other. Old-timers liked to warn that you couldn't trust a man who did not drink. But Grant could not hold his liquor. Once he irritated a visiting officer named McClellan, and thus stories of his drinking spread beyond the post. He begged his commanding officer for a transfer back east, but the man refused. Grant was trapped, with no way out save the bottle.

Of course, there was another way out. He could quit the army and go home to his family. On April 11, 1854, while listed on the company roster as being sick, Grant submitted his resignation. He had reached bottom. Biographer William McFeely observed, "Grant did not leave the army because he was a drunk. He drank and left the army because he was profoundly depressed."

Grant was thirty-two years old with no savings, no business sense, and no prospects. His appearance was so dissolute that an army buddy in San Francisco felt ashamed to be seen with him in public. When Grant reached New York he was so destitute that Simon Bolivar Buckner, a friend from their West Point days, passed the hat among classmates and fellow officers to collect money for Grant's hotel bill and his train fare to St. Louis. His was not a triumphant homecoming.

"I was now to commence at the age of thirty-two, a new struggle for support," Grant recalled. He did not succeed. Indeed, he failed at every enterprise he attempted. Old Jesse Grant was so worried about his son's inability to survive outside the army that he wrote to the secretary of war, Jefferson Davis, pleading with him to reject Ulysses's letter of resignation. All he needed was a leave so he could spend some time with his family. Davis, who had heard the rumors about Grant's drinking, refused. In 1854, Grant's army career was over.

For seven years, Grant went from one disappointment to another. He tried to make a living as a farmer. Julia's father gave them sixty acres on the outskirts of St. Louis, and Grant's father gave them money to buy seed and horses. With his own hands, Grant built a house for his family. Though not much more than a crude cabin, Grant was proud of it. He named it "Hardscrabble." Julia called it primitive and ugly, a far cry from her parents' lavish home. "A black cloud fell around me," she said, "and I exclaimed (aloud, I think): Is this my destiny?"

Grant could not make a go of the farm. The crops were poor. He pawned his watch and was forced to cut cordwood to haul into town to sell on street corners. He looked like a derelict in his old blue army overcoat caked with mud and dirt. He saw embarrassment on the faces of his former army friends at Jefferson Barracks. After two years of this marginal existence, he begged his father for a loan, offering to pay 10 percent interest, but there is no record of the loan being made. By 1858, Grant auctioned off his remaining goods and sent Julia and the three children back to her parents. He could no longer support them.

His next business venture was selling real estate, but he was as inept at that as he had been at farming. He took mean lodgings in a room with no stove and walked twelve miles each way every weekend to be with his family. Renting a horse for the journey was too expensive. Because Grant had no talent for selling, he soon lost the real estate job.

He wandered the streets in search of work, hoping he might meet someone who could loan him a few dollars. One day he met a friend who had also left the service. The man was just as destitute as Grant. He, too, was unable to support his family and was desperately looking for any kind of work. The two men commiserated but then went their separate ways. They would meet again in a few years—Ulysses S. Grant and William Tecumseh Sherman—and they would make history together. But in the late 1850s, it appeared that neither man would amount to much.

Finally Grant traveled to Galena, Illinois, to take a clerk's job in the leather-goods shop run by his brothers. He failed at that, too.

⊷≡⊜⊂≡⊷

AND THEN CAME war. Ulysses Grant was saved. He returned to the only career at which he was ever any good: being a soldier. However, getting back in uniform was not easy. Rumors of his drinking persisted. At first, the best he could do was recruit volunteers for a new regiment being formed in Galena. Wearing his only suit and a slouch hat, working from a desk in the corner of an office, Grant looked like a clerk down on his luck. He was not even authorized to serve in the regiment himself.

Throughout North and South, Grant's fellow West Point graduates suddenly found themselves wearing the eagles of full colonel. George

McClellan, a plebe when Grant was a senior, now ranked as a major general. Meanwhile, Grant labored in obscurity and increasing frustration, unable to secure an appointment at any rank.

He wrote to the army's adjutant general in Washington but received no reply. He appealed to the veterans of the Mexican War with whom he had served, but each man rebuffed him. He called on General McClellan, sitting in his outer office, slouch hat on his lap, for two days, but McClellan would not see him. Grant knew the reason, of course. It was the awful stain on his reputation from being labeled a drinker. He grew so depressed that he worried about taking to the bottle again, something he had apparently not done since leaving California.

When Grant had almost given up hope, he returned to service, thanks to Elihu B. Washburne, the local congressman. For some reason (it may have been wishful thinking) Washburne sensed potential in Grant. Like most politicians of the time, Washburne desired to have high-ranking army officers in his debt. If they performed well and gained fame and glory on the battlefield, some of it would rub off on him.

And that was how and why Ulysses S. Grant received a commission as a colonel in June 1861, two months after rebel guns opened fire on Fort Sumter. That summer, Grant was ordered to take his regiment, the Twenty-first Illinois, to attack a rebel base in Missouri. Grant had been in combat before, but only as a member of a regiment. Now he was in command; the outcome would be solely his responsibility.

As they neared the rebel camp, Grant felt nervous.

[My] heart kept getting higher and higher until it felt to me as though it was in my throat. I would have given anything then to have been back in Illinois, but I had not the moral courage to halt and consider what to do; I kept right on.

To his immense relief, he discovered that the Confederates had retreated. He wrote:

My heart resumed its place. It occurred to me at once that [the rebel commander] had been as much afraid of me as I have been of him. This was a view of the question I have never taken before; but it was one I never forgot afterwards. From that event to the close of the war, I never experienced trepidation upon confronting an enemy. . . . I never forgot that he had as much reason to fear my forces as I had his. The lesson was valuable.

Not long after the incident, Grant was surprised to read in a newspaper that President Lincoln had requested Illinois congressmen to recommend state residents they considered worthy of appointment to the rank of brigadier general. The following day he learned that his name was on the list and had been submitted to the United States Senate for confirmation.

Ulysses S. Grant was a general in the army! He immediately communicated the good news to Julia and to his father. Julia shared his excitement, but his father felt compelled to remind him of his past failures. "Be careful, Ulyss," Jesse Grant wrote, "you're a general now; it's a good job, don't lose it."

⇥══◯══⇤

IN NOVEMBER 1861, General Grant led his troops against a Confederate force at Belmont, Missouri. Grant's men routed the rebels, but they quickly counterattacked, surrounding the Yankees. Some of Grant's officers panicked and urged surrender. Grant calmed them, rallied the troops, and led the fight out of the encirclement. The incident taught him two valuable lessons about himself: he need not fear the enemy, and he was capable of remaining cool and levelheaded even when a fight was going against him.

Immediately after the battle at Belmont, Grant learned a third important lesson: sometimes enemies can be found on your own side. A new commanding general took over the Army of the Missouri, the imperious, pedantic, formidable Henry Wager Halleck, known in the army as "Old Brains." Halleck was a Phi Beta Kappa from Union College and a West Point graduate. He spoke French fluently and was considered a military scholar, author of a highly regarded book on the tactics of modern warfare. He had resigned from the army and become an immensely successful businessman and lawyer in California. He also wrote two books on the law.

But now Halleck was back in uniform as Grant's superior. And he did not like Ulysses S. Grant. Halleck had met him once during Grant's difficulties at Fort Humboldt. As far as Halleck was concerned, Grant was an unreliable drunkard who had to be held on a short leash.

Halleck kept Grant out of battle, assigning him to the base at Cairo, Illinois, more quartermaster than combat commander. Grant was too impatient to wait out the war in Cairo. He wanted to fight, and he proposed to move his outfit by boat down the Tennessee River, capture Fort Henry, and invade the entire Tennessee River valley, ending up as far south as Mississippi and Alabama. He wrote to Halleck several times about his plan but received no reply. On his own initiative, acting without orders, Grant went to St. Louis to see General Halleck in person. The meeting did not go well; Halleck vigorously rejected Grant's idea.

Grant returned to Cairo, dejected and depressed. His spirits were revived by Flag Officer Andrew Foote, who, at age fifty-six, had spent forty years as a naval officer. He hated whiskey as much as he hated slavery, and he detested Halleck, calling him a "military imbecile who might just possibly make a good clerk." Foote did like Grant and his plans, and he overlooked the stories about Grant's drinking (or chose not to believe them). Together they badgered Halleck through numerous telegrams urging him to approve a combined army-navy campaign against Fort Henry. Halleck finally consented. Perhaps he thought the teetotaling Foote would keep Grant from drinking.

On February 3, 1862, Foote led seven gunboats and nine transports loaded with Grant's seventeen thousand troops down the Tennessee River. Three days later, part of Grant's army went ashore on the east bank of the river while the rest disembarked on the opposite shore. While the gunboats shelled the Confederate fort, Grant's soldiers attacked from the rear.

"Fort Henry is ours," Grant telegraphed triumphantly through channels to Halleck. McClellan, now general-in-chief of all the Union armies, was delighted with the victory and requested that Halleck pass along to Foote and Grant his personal congratulations. Halleck did acknowledge Foote's success, but in an act of pettiness sent no message to Grant.

No matter. Grant went on to win the Union's greatest victory yet. A few days after he took Fort Henry, Grant moved east to attack Fort Donelson, then under the command of Simon Bolivar Buckner—his old friend from West Point who had helped him when Grant was destitute in New York City. On February 16, ten days after his conquest of Fort Henry, Grant received a message from Buckner in the besieged fort, asking for an armistice to discuss surrender terms. Grant's response, reprinted in newspapers throughout the Union, made his a household name:

> Sir: Yours of this date proposing armistice and appointment of Commissioners to settle terms of capitulation is just received. No terms except an unconditional and immediate surrender can be accepted. I propose to move immediately upon your works.

Buckner surrendered.

Church bells rang in every city and hamlet in the Union. People built bonfires and danced in the streets to celebrate the first major northern triumph of the war. U. S. Grant became known as "Unconditional Surrender" Grant.

The victory at Fort Donelson took some of the sting out of the Union's humiliating defeat at Bull Run. Lincoln promoted Grant to major general, second in rank to Halleck in the western theater. The nation was ecstatic, Grant was thrilled, and Lincoln was delighted. The only person unhappy about Grant's achievement was Henry Halleck. Grant was becoming too dangerous a rival. Something would have to be done.

⊷═◉═⊶

HALLECK COMMENCED ALL-OUT war against Grant, who continued, on his own initiative, to move east through Tennessee toward Nashville. Halleck considered Grant insubordinate for not communicating frequently enough, and he feared that Grant was trying to establish an independent command. On March 3, Halleck dispatched an angry, spiteful telegram to McClellan.

> I have had no communication with General Grant for more than a week. He left his command without my authority and went to Nashville. . . . It is hard to censure a successful general immediately after a victory but I think he richly deserves it. I can get no returns, no reports, no information of any kind from him. . . . I am worn out and tired with his neglect and inefficiency.

It was a damning indictment, and McClellan took the charges seriously enough to authorize Halleck to arrest Grant, if the good of the service warranted it, and to replace him with Gen. C. F. Smith. But even that support from McClellan did not satisfy Halleck. The next day he wired McClellan again, noting that rumors had reached him that "General Grant has resumed his former bad habits. If so, it will account for his neglect of my often-repeated orders."

Halleck made his move. He relieved Grant of command and challenged him again to explain his alleged failure to keep Halleck informed of his position. Thus, two weeks after Grant's great victory at Fort Donelson, the national hero found himself out of a job.

Grant composed a restrained, respectful, and masterful reply to Halleck. He pointed out that he had regularly sent reports on troop strength and location to Gen. George Cullum, Halleck's chief of staff.

If Cullum had failed to pass that information on to Halleck, Grant argued, that was not Grant's fault. Grant offered several carefully reasoned points in his defense and asked to be relieved of all further duty in any capacity under Halleck.

But Grant went further. He sent a copy of this message to his sponsor, the powerful Congressman Washburne. Grant was quickly learning how the system worked, and how to work the system to his advantage. Washburne presented Grant's case to Lincoln and to Secretary of War Stanton; they decided in favor of Grant. Halleck was forced to scale back his campaign to get rid of Grant. On March 13, he sent Grant a conciliatory message.

> You cannot be relieved from your command. There is no good reason
> for it. I am certain that all which the authorities in Washington ask,
> is, that you enforce discipline and punish the disorderly. The power is
> in your hands; use it, and you will be sustained by all above you.
> Instead of relieving you, I wish you, as soon as your new army is in
> the field, to assume immediate command and lead it on to new vic-
> tories.

Grant thanked Halleck for his "justness." But although Grant had won a major political battle, his next fight, only three weeks later, did not go as well.

‹─══◯══─›

AT A PLACE called Shiloh Church, in the southwestern corner of Tennessee, more American soldiers were killed and wounded in two days (April 6–7) than in all the nation's previous wars, including the Revolutionary War, the War of 1812, and the Mexican War. The Confederate army lost 10,694 men. General Grant lost 13,047.

Grant was taken by surprise. He focused so intently on his plan of attack against the Confederate forces that he gave no thought to their own strategy. When his army made camp on the night of April 5, he issued no orders to dig in or to establish defensive lines. His few outly-ing picket posts were sited only a few hundred yards in front of the main Union camp.

When the rebels charged out of the woods the next day, yelling and firing, they pushed Grant's soldiers back with heavy losses. It was not until the following day, when fresh reinforcements arrived, that Grant's men were able to repulse the Confederates and force them to retreat.

The battle quickly tarnished Grant's reputation. The hero of Fort Donelson became a target of scorn and criticism. Rumors circulated that he had been drinking. Even though the army declared Shiloh a victory for the Union, Grant was pilloried in the press for sacrificing so many men.

A Pennsylvania Republican, A. K. McClure, denounced Grant as an incompetent alcoholic and a liability to the president. He urged Lin-coln to dismiss Grant at once. If Lincoln insisted on retaining Grant, McClure warned, it could jeopardize his presidency. The politician reported:

> Lincoln remained silent for what seemed a very long time. He then gathered himself up in his chair and said in a tone of earnestness that I shall never forget: *"I can't spare this man; he fights."*

◦━◦⊂━◦

GEORGE MEADE NEVER wanted to be a soldier. There was no mil-itary tradition in his family, no heroes to emulate. And although his mother sensed (correctly) that the army would not be a suitable career for him, she insisted that George attend the military academy. And so the dutiful son had gone off to West Point, even though he did not want to. It was all his father's fault for getting in trouble with the law and for dying too young.

The Meades were an old and wealthy Philadelphia family, active in the city's social and cultural life. Meade's father departed for Spain early in the nineteenth century and stayed seventeen years in Cadiz, working variously as a merchant, ship owner, and naval agent of the U.S. government.

The Meades' lavishly appointed home contained one of the finest art collections in all of Spain, paintings by Titian, Correggio, Rubens, Van Dyck, and Murillo, and family portraits painted by Thomas Sully and Gilbert Stuart. Richard Meade was so popular and influential in Cadiz society that he was offered Spanish citizenship. He declined the honor with thanks, saying that nothing would induce him to give up his American citizenship.

In a rapid change of luck, Meade received a two-year jail sentence for allegations of financial impropriety made against him and for his involvement with a British company doing business in Cadiz that turned out to be insolvent. Shortly thereafter, his son, George, was born. Two years later Mrs. Meade brought the family home to Philadelphia while Richard moved to Madrid to untangle his legal problems. He did not return for three years.

Young George was sent to a boarding school modeled after the military academy. When he was thirteen, his father died. The family's economic circumstances were reduced to genteel poverty. George's mother wanted him to attend college, as did he, to prepare for a profession, but they could not afford the expense. Although George's preference was to study law, his mother decided on West Point. The education was free and it was considered a proper school for gentlemen.

Once he satisfied his military obligation after graduation, George would be free to leave the army. Mrs. Meade was adamant about that. She did not intend for him to have an army career. And neither did he.

George Meade entered West Point in 1831 at the age of fifteen, having received his appointment from Andrew Jackson, president of the United States. (The Meades may have lost their financial status but not their social connections.) George was not the best of students, in part because the longer he stayed the greater was his desire to flee. He was careless about drill and failed to maintain his equipment and uniforms. His inattentiveness cost him heavily. By his third year he had accumulated 168 demerits, dangerously close to the 200 that would mean automatic expulsion.[1] Meade was also indifferent to his classroom studies but managed to earn average grades with little effort. He graduated in 1835, nineteenth in a class of fifty-six.

Even though Meade had stayed the course and received his commission, he had not developed any desire for an army career. He believed he had too much ambition to settle for assignment to a succession of dreary peacetime army posts, dull duty, slow promotions, and low pay. He considered resigning his commission immediately but decided that would be improper. With a three-month leave following graduation, he found work as a surveyor for the Long Island Railroad. He hoped to gain experience and make contacts in the booming railroad construction business. Perhaps, if he found a good job, he would not return to the army after all.

When his leave ended, however, Meade was unwilling to relinquish the secure, steady pay the army guaranteed. The world of civil engineering, though challenging and potentially lucrative, was risky, and he had seen how even a wealthy family such as his own could fall on hard times.

In January 1836, Meade joined his regiment at Tampa, Florida, to fight in the Seminole Indian War. He survived four months in the semitropical climate before being declared physically unfit to serve in the field. Reassignment to duty in cooler Massachusetts apparently did not suit him either, and Meade resigned from the army in October.

He embarked on a career as a civil engineer and surveyor, first back in Florida as assistant engineer on the Alabama, Florida, and Georgia Railroad. His next jobs were surveying the boundaries between the United States and the Republic of Texas, along the Mississippi River delta, and for the British provinces in the northwest.

Between these far-flung temporary positions, Meade would return

---

[1] In 1862, Meade's son received 200 demerits during his second year at West Point and was expelled.

to his mother's home in Washington, D.C., relying on her connections, as well as his own considerable charm and intelligence, to enter high social and political circles. At one such gathering he met Margaretta Sergeant, daughter of a wealthy Philadelphia congressman who, years earlier, had helped free Meade's father from a Spanish jail.

The couple married in December 1840. Meade continued to take the kind of short-term contract work he had done for the previous four years, since leaving the army. Apparently his new political connections were of little help in securing permanent employment. To make his situation worse, the U.S. Congress voted to stop contracting with civilians for survey work, turning over all such future jobs to the army's Corps of Topographical Engineers.

That decision was a disastrous blow for Meade, who now faced the loss of his livelihood if he could not secure a permanent position. He felt he had only one choice, to go back in the army. In May 1842, through the influence of his brother-in-law, a Virginia congressman, Meade was appointed a second lieutenant in the Topographical Engineers.

His first assignment involved building lighthouses and conducting coastal surveys in Delaware, with headquarters in Philadelphia. For the first time in his adult life, he could have his own home. Only a few years later, in August 1845, his blissful existence with his wife and three children was shattered. Meade received orders to report to Texas. The United States was going to war with Mexico.

Meade claimed to prefer the Topographical Corps rather than a troop command, yet in his letters to Margaretta, he revealed his growing depression and feelings of failure. On December 18, 1845, he wrote to his wife:

In a few days I shall be thirty years of age. Only think how old, what a dream has the last ten years been to me since I left West Point, what a waste of energy and time! I tremble sometimes when I think what I might have been, and remember what I am, when I reflect on what I might have accomplished if I had devoted all my time and energies to one object, an object where my exertions would have told in my advancement; but, alas, it is useless to speculate on what is passed! . . . It is the better part now to make the best of a bad bargain, and put the best face on it.

Even Meade's mother considered her son to be a failure and blamed herself for insisting that he attend the military academy. In a letter she wrote to him on his thirtieth birthday, which Meade told his wife "was in a melancholy tone, which drew tears to my eyes," his mother said:

Although in my ignorance I was cruel enough to send you to West Point, an act for which I never shall forgive myself, and never cease to regret, I did not dream that you would enter the army, my dear George.

There was nothing to be done about that now. Meade had chosen the army, even though, ten years after graduation, he was still a second lieutenant conducting surveys and making maps for an army at war with Mexico.

Meade learned that he did not like war; he was a reluctant soldier at best. Yet when he came under artillery fire and saw the dead and wounded after battles, he noted the "pleasant excitement of victory." But he added, in a letter to his wife,

Such is war and its terrible consequences. For my part I have no hesitation in saying I have no stomach for it. I trust I shall always do my duty, from a stern sense of the propriety of assisting in the defense of my country. . . . But I candidly acknowledge I have no penchant for it; nothing but a sense of duty would keep me at it.

He also complained to Margaretta of the hardships of life in the field, the terrible heat, the violent storms. He hated the deprivations, the long marches over the parched desert without food or water. Over a period of nine months of hardship, the routine was broken by only eight hours of actual combat. "No, soldiering is no play," he wrote, "and those who undertake it must make up their minds to hard times and hard knocks."

Margaretta was not happy either. She complained to George that she was mortified that she had not yet seen his name on the promotion lists published in the newspapers. He remained a second lieutenant while so many of his classmates, and even younger officers, were rising through the ranks. Meade said simply that he was not disappointed because he had not expected to be promoted. He noted that he could claim no distinction in the two battles in which his unit had participated. As a staff officer, there were few opportunities for him to perform the heroic feats that brought glory and promotion.

Then Meade suggested to his wife another, more questionable, reason for his lack of recognition and advancement. He said he did not have the requisite political influence in Washington! This was a strange grievance coming from a man whose father-in-law and brother-in-law were U.S. congressmen. Was Meade too proud to ask for help, or were his well-connected relatives reluctant to grant it?

The thirty-year-old Lieutenant Meade soldiered on as the army moved deeper into Mexico, and he poured out his frustrations in letters to Margaretta. He described the movements of the troops, the tribulations of everyday life, and the whereabouts of their old friends from Philadelphia such as John Pemberton, now a brevet major.

The war ended in a victory for the United States when a peace treaty was signed in Mexico City in February 1848. But by then George Meade had been stationed in Washington for nearly a year, ordered back to the States because of a surplus of officers in the Topographical Corps. Many young men won fame and glory in the Mexican War and came home hailed as heroes. Meade was thirty-three and still a second lieutenant.

In the peacetime army Meade returned to his surveying duties, charting coastlines and building lighthouses in Florida, Pennsylvania, and the Great Lakes. He was able to spend only limited periods of time with his wife and children. Finally, at the age of thirty-six, fully sixteen years after graduating from West Point, he received a promotion to first lieutenant. At forty-one he made captain. As he had written on his thirtieth birthday, when ruminating about what he might have become, he still believed that all he could do was make the most of his bad bargain with the army and put the best face on it.

But as the 1850s came to a close, it became increasingly difficult for Meade to do that. Anger deepened within him. The future held so little promise, so little hope beyond the dreary prospect of repeating the years that had already passed. More surveying, more lighthouses, periodic reunions with his family. It seemed dismal and depressing.

--=◦◦=--

AND THEN CAME war. Captain Meade was stationed at Detroit when Fort Sumter was fired on, and he was determined not to spend another war in the Topographical Corps. He resolved to have a fighting command and a rank more appropriate to his age. But these were not easy to obtain. Written requests to headquarters went unanswered. In June 1861, he went to Washington, D.C., to offer himself in the service of his country.

He was a West Point graduate and a veteran of the Mexican War. Surely there was a need for someone with his background. But in the confusion that gripped the capital city in the early weeks of war, no one heeded his plea. He returned to Detroit, fearing he would miss this one last chance to find some sense of accomplishment in his military career.

Meade's opportunity arose two months later. On August 31, 1861, he was given the single star of a brigadier general and command of a brigade of Pennsylvania volunteers. His wife was responsible for his instant rise from captain to general, though he may have been unaware of her intervention. She contacted on his behalf a prominent family friend who had the ear of a powerful Pennsylvania senator.

The volunteer brigade was Meade's first active troop command. He was determined to make it a success. But first, there was more building to be done. He was charged with the construction of a ring of defensive positions around Washington. Then came his chance to fight. He served under every commander of the Army of the Potomac, until he assumed that position himself. Meade performed well at Mechanicsville, Second Bull Run, Antietam, Fredericksburg, Chancellorsville, and in other campaigns, earning a reputation as a solid, dependable, if not brilliant, leader of men.

And yet he continued to complain to Margaretta that other men were promoted ahead of him because of their political connections. He wrote of his disapproval of one officer's advancement to the rank of major general.

> War is a game of chance, and besides the chances of service, the accidents and luck of the field, in our army, an officer has to run the chances of having his political friends in power. . . . A poor devil like myself, with little merit and no friends, has to stand aside and see others go ahead.

He did concede that "Upon the whole, however, I have done pretty well, and ought not to complain."

He continued to do pretty well until June 30, 1862, at one of the Seven Days' battles during McClellan's doomed Peninsular campaign. That day every member of Meade's staff was wounded. Meade was shot in the arm and side.

At first he thought the wound was not serious and he stayed at the front, but he became weak from loss of blood and had to relinquish command and make his way to a hospital. Doctors found that a bullet had pierced his forearm, entered his side, and exited his back, barely missing the spinal cord.

Meade was horrified when he heard the surgeon say he had been shot in the back. Throughout the night, recovering from the surgery, he moaned, "Just think, doctor, of my being shot in the back!" The thought of receiving such an ignominious wound carried obvious implications of being hit while running away. This worried him more than any physical damage. He was relieved when he learned that the physician's comment had been made after an initial hasty examination of his condition.

Meade was placed on leave and arrived home in Philadelphia on the Fourth of July 1862, one year to the day before his triumph at Gettysburg. He healed slowly and became anxious about being away from his command and missing the action. After forty-two days of convalescence, as soon as he was able to walk unaided, Meade left for the battlefield, against the advice of his physician.

In December, Meade led his troops in the bloody fiasco at Fredericksburg, Virginia. He survived the close fighting, but his horse was hit in the neck. He wrote that a bullet "passed through my hat so close, that if it had come from the *front* instead of the *side*, I would have been a goner." No one ever accused George Meade of leading from the rear. Shortly thereafter, Meade received his second star.

He also came close to death at the hands of one of his men, a soldier so dazed from the fighting that he refused to move when Meade ordered him forward. The man pointed his gun at Meade and was about to pull the trigger when Meade swung his saber and hit the soldier so hard with the flat of the blade that it snapped off. The blow apparently restored the man to reality.

However much he continued to pour out his self-pity to Margaretta, Meade, now a major general, was highly ambitious for further promotion. When President and Mrs. Lincoln visited the Army of the Potomac in its winter quarters opposite Fredericksburg, Meade tried to ingratiate himself. As he told Margaretta,

> I . . . have been making myself (or at least trying to do so) very agreeable to Mrs. Lincoln, who seems an amiable sort. . . . I have ventured to tell the President one or two stories, and I think I have made decided progress in his affections.

Several days later, Meade was delighted to receive a beautiful bouquet of flowers from Mrs. Lincoln.

At first I was very much tickled, and my vanity insinuated that my *fine appearance* had taken Mrs. L's eye and that my fortune was made. This delusion was speedily dissolved by the orderly who brought the bouquet. All the principal generals had been similarly honored.

At that moment, Meade was less than ten weeks away from taking command of the Army of the Potomac himself. Many of his fellow officers said that no one was better suited for the job. He was flattered, of course, but expressed doubt to his wife in a letter dated May 10, 1863:

I . . . do not believe there is the slightest probability of my being placed in command. . . . Having no political influence, being no intriguer, and indeed unambitious of the distinction, it is hardly probable I shall be called on to accept or decline.

In a letter dated June 25, Meade made a curious comment about the matter of promotion: "It remains to be seen whether I have the capacity to handle successfully a large army."

CHAPTER 3

ROBERT WAS ALWAYS GOOD

OBERT E. LEE had to be perfect. That was the only way to atone for the sins of his father. He had to excel, to erase the shame and disgrace the elder Lee left on the once proud family name. He would do it as a soldier, because it was in the army that his father had once known pride and honor. Thus the son's path, his road to destiny, was ordained. He had no other choice. His mother made sure of that.

Few heroes of the American Revolution were more romantic, more glamorous, more lionized than Robert E. Lee's father, "Light Horse" Harry Lee. The man's daring cavalry exploits under his friend George Washington were legendary, as were his audacious raids in the Carolinas under Nathaniel Greene. Some people said he would be the next president of the new nation, a worthy successor to Washington.

Harry Lee was elected to the Continental Congress, the Virginia House of Delegates, and the new Congress of the United States. He also served three terms as governor of Virginia. He wed his beautiful young cousin, Matilda Lee, who brought to the marriage an immense fortune, but the bride's bliss lasted only briefly before her glamorous husband's dark side surfaced. When Matilda Lee died, eight unhappy years later, her fortune was nearly gone.

Harry Lee ran through his wife's money with one bad business venture after another. He bought coalmines and ore fields, invested in interest-bearing loans and dubious currency transactions, and planned to build grandiose cities. Each scheme failed, and the money drained away to such an alarming extent that Lee even tried to pass a fraudulent bank note to George Washington.

After Matilda's death, Harry married well again. This time the bride was Ann Carter, daughter of the richest man in all Virginia, but even her fortune was doomed once Light Horse Harry gained control of it. By the time she was eight months' pregnant, he had sold off most of her possessions. Their mansion, Stratford Hall, was in ruins.

There were weeds in the fallow gardens, and the fields lay unworked. Barns were empty. . . . The overseer had left. Harry had sold the massive exterior staircase that ascended to the great hall, and had chained the doors against surprise from bill collectors. Most of the furnishings were gone, and the rooms were sealed off against the cold.

When Ann Carter Lee gave birth to the son she named Robert Edward, there was no money to pay the doctor or enough coal to heat more than one small brazier. Harry was away in Richmond, dodging his creditors and seeking easy marks to finance new moneymaking schemes.

Light Horse Harry spent a term in debtor's prison. The Lees were in disgrace. On a trip to Baltimore, Harry was caught in a political riot and severely beaten by the mob. He never fully recovered and spent five years wandering alone in the Caribbean islands in a vain effort to restore his health. He died in 1818 on his journey home and was buried on an island off the Georgia coast.

ROBERT EDWARD LEE barely knew his father. The boy was six when Light Horse Harry left for the Caribbean, and eleven when he died. Yet he spent the rest of his life striving to overcome the stain of his father's reputation. One biographer called it a "birth defect" that determined the course of Lee's life. Lee's mother devoted herself to ensuring that young Robert, a child she had not wanted, did not follow in his father's footsteps. Such was the legacy of Light Horse Harry Lee.

"Robert was always good," his father wrote a year before his death. The boy spent most of his childhood in Alexandria, Virginia, in homes provided by generous family members. By the time he was twelve, he had assumed considerable responsibility. He shopped for food, kept the keys to the pantry, and supervised the work of the household servants. He nursed his ailing mother, preparing her medicines and carrying her to the carriage for afternoon drives. In cold weather, he methodically stuffed paper into the cracks in the aging carriage to keep out the chill.

When he was thirteen, the Lees endured another scandal. Light Horse Harry's son by his first marriage (Robert's half brother, Henry) had an affair with his morphine-addicted wife's teenaged sister and stole money from her inheritance. Virginia society was shocked. Henry was disgraced. For the rest of his life he was known as Black Horse Harry.

To Robert's mother, it "showed what the flouting of codes of honor and comportment could bring." From the disgrace, she drew these lessons to teach young Robert. He must "practice self-denial and self-control." It would be his duty to restore the reputation of the Lees to its former place in Virginia society.

What was he to do with his life? There was no money for college and no land to inherit. To his mother there was only one answer. The boy had long been interested in the military, and West Point offered a free education and a proper environment for a gentleman.

To prepare for the rigors of the military academy, she enrolled him in a preparatory school located in a building next door to the Lee home in Alexandria. Robert performed extremely well. According to his teacher, he was an

> exemplary pupil in every respect. . . . He was never behind time at his studies; never failed in a single recitation; was perfectly observant of the rules and regulations of the institution; was gentlemanly, unobtrusive, and respectful in all his deportment to teacher and his fellow students. His specialty was *finishing up*.

His mother expected no less. Nor did he.

At West Point, Lee's classmates referred to him as the "marble model." Historian Gene Smith, who wrote a dual biography of Lee and Grant, described Lee as a perfect cadet who seemed to excel at everything.

> Always at the top of his class in every class, in four years he did not accumulate a single demerit. His buttons gleamed. His sword was spotless. He was never late for formation, never had his bed made up in less than perfect fashion, was never guilty of a sloppy salute, missed no bedchecks, was not cited for abusing a horse or for folding his towel incorrectly.

In addition, he was handsome, charming, well mannered, and skilled at swimming, skating, dancing, and riding. He was popular with the other cadets. They admired and respected him, and each succeeding year he was appointed to a higher rank in the Cadet Corps. As a senior he received the supreme accolade, the post of adjutant, reserved for the highest-ranking cadet.

The only honor Lee failed to achieve was to graduate first in his class academically. He placed second, but that plus his outstanding record put him among the elite chosen for the army engineers. Only the best and the brightest were selected for that branch of the service.

Robert E. Lee graduated in June 1829. He returned immediately to Virginia to attend to his dying mother. For the next month, he rarely left her bedside, nursing her as he had done as a boy. Whenever he had to leave the room, her stricken gaze never wavered from the door until he returned. And he believed that whatever he had accomplished in his life, whatever kind of man he had become, he owed everything to her.

After his mother's death he traveled south to barren Cockspur Island near Savannah for his first assignment as an army engineer. The job involved building a fort, laying out canals, embankments, and other defensive structures. Lee enjoyed Savannah, especially in the company of the sister of a West Point friend; he flirted outrageously, but with considerable charm and decorum. Such innocent pastimes (for that was what they always were with Lee) would continue throughout his life, for he truly enjoyed the company of attractive young women.

But soon the shadow of the past that hung over the Lee name reappeared. Black Horse Harry, Robert's half brother, had found work with Andrew Jackson in Tennessee. When Jackson became president in 1829, he nominated Harry to an ambassadorial post in Morocco.

The senate confirmation hearings for the post brought to public attention his notorious past. Newspapers across the nation covered the story, trumpeting the name of Lee. The vote against him was unanimous. Black Horse Harry left the country in disgrace, and he died, impoverished, in Europe.

Being related to such a reprobate, and being the son of the notorious Light Horse Harry Lee, did not make Robert E. Lee welcome in many homes as a serious suitor. Casual flirtations were tolerated—he was, after all, handsome and charming—but he could not be considered an acceptable or desirable son-in-law. The only families that might welcome him were those already related to the tarnished Lees.

--=◦=--

MARY ANNA RANDOLPH CUSTIS was Robert's twenty-one-year-old distant cousin; Robert had known her all his life. He had admired her family's home for just as long. Mary was the heiress of George Washington Parke Custis, grandson of Martha Washington and adopted son of George Washington. Custis worshiped Washington's memory and had owned many of his personal possessions. He had dedicated his life to promoting Washington's reputation and to pampering Mary, his only child.

Mary grew up at Arlington House, one of the grandest estates in the country, high on a hill overlooking the city of Washington across the Potomac River. General Lafayette had described the view from the great portico as the finest in the world. Construction of the house began in 1802. This estate comprised some fifteen thousand acres and 250 slaves, but Custis also owned two other estates in Virginia. The family was immensely wealthy, and Arlington was the jewel in their crown.

More than one biographer has commented on the Lee tradition of marrying money. One suggested that Lee was "as much enamored of Arlington as he was of Mary."

Though the Lees were distantly related to the Custis family, Mary's father was not happy when the relatively penniless army lieutenant, son of Light Horse Harry and half brother of Black Horse Harry, came calling. He did not encourage the match, but Mary's mother managed to do everything possible to bring the couple together. She knew that despite her family's wealth and landholdings, Mary had few gentlemen callers and opportunities. She saw in Lee "a brilliantly handsome and prepossessing young man, bright, animated, charming, whose concern for his late mother had been extraordinary." That was quite sufficient for her. And, apparently, for Mary as well.

Mary was a plain woman—austere, some said. Others described her as unpleasant, outspoken, opinionated, spoiled, imperious, tempera-

mental, and accustomed to lavish living and the constant doting attention of her father. She was intelligent enough, all agreed: well-read,
proficient in Latin, Greek, French, and mathematics, and adept at the
piano. She was slim, even frail in appearance, and deeply religious. She
reminded people of Lee's mother, somber and reserved, quite a contrast
to Lee's exuberant, outgoing personality.

The wedding took place on June 10, 1831, at Arlington House,
which Mary would never be able to leave for long, until forced out by
circumstances. Following custom, the marriage celebrations lasted for
two weeks; then the newlyweds, accompanied by Mary's mother,
embarked on a series of visits to family members throughout the state.
When both women became ill, Lee nursed them, as he had done for
his own mother.

In August, Robert and Mary left for his new post at Fortress Monroe, Virginia. She was homesick, unhappy, and depressed. She disliked
the social life, was bored by Robert's fellow officers and their wives, and
failed to make friends. She did not understand why he insisted on living solely on his army pay and was less than gracious about the two
barracks rooms in which she now lived. She occupied herself by staying
at home and reading her Bible.

Only one thing would make her happy: a return to Arlington. After
Mary and Robert went home for the Christmas holidays, he returned
alone to Fortress Monroe. When Mary finally joined him six months
later, she brought along her mother for company.

This became their pattern from year to year, from one assignment to
another. Lee was sent to survey the boundary between Ohio and
Michigan; to St. Louis, Fort Hamilton, and the North Carolina coast;
to New York City for construction projects at Staten Island and Brook-
lyn. More often than not, he left for each duty station alone while his
wife remained at Arlington with their growing family.

They had seven children in all. During the first fifteen years of their
marriage, Mary was either pregnant or recovering from childbirth,
which, of course, was best done at Arlington House. With each child,

she grew increasingly weak and "went steadily downhill toward an invalidism more complete than that which [Robert's] mother had known. It did not improve her temper."

By her early thirties, she had become an old woman, ill with what her doctor diagnosed as rheumatic disease. She lay bedridden for months at a time, suffering painful abscesses and arthritis. She insisted that only at Arlington could she properly rest and receive care and help with the children. Obviously an army post was no place for someone in her condition.

When the Lees were newly married and living at Fortress Monroe, it was apparent to many people that he became more relaxed and sociable whenever Mary left for Arlington. When she was present, he turned down invitations to parties and dances in deference to her wishes. To a few friends Lee had expressed his pleasure that his wife was away. "I am as happy as a clam at high water," he confessed.

Lee's good looks and charming manners continued to attract the ladies. With Mary away so often, he found it easy to conduct flirtations. In his mid-thirties he wrote to a friend, "You are right in my interest in pretty women. It is strange that I do not lose it with age. But I perceive no diminution." He exchanged letters with several women for many years. To twenty-eight-year-old Martha Custis Williams, a cousin to both Robert and Mary, he teased, "Oh Markie, Markie. When will you ripen?" Their correspondence continued for twenty-six years.

But as he grew older, Lee frequently wrote long letters to Mary, professing his increasing loneliness and telling her how much he missed her and the children. At home he was a devoted husband and father, but when he was away from them, which was much of the time, he grew irritable, sad, restless, and bored. He wrote to his wife:

> I am conscious of having lost a great deal that is desirable and what I value more than anything else, the society of you and my children.

He even considered resigning his commission. By 1846, he realized that the children had grown up without him. He was thirty-nine years old and only a captain after seventeen years of military service. But he resisted the impulse. His first duty was to his country, and his country was going to war.

⊷⇒◉⇐⊷

ROBERT E. LEE welcomed the opportunity the war provided. He was eager for his first chance at combat, and perhaps he envisioned glory and promotion. He was barely ashore at Veracruz when he came under fire—from one of his own men.

Lee and Lt. Pierre Gustave Toutant Beauregard were returning from a patrol when a nervous sentry challenged them. He scarcely waited for them to identify themselves before he opened fire, sending a ball between Lee's upper arm and his body, so close that it singed his uniform. Things improved after that.

Working on the staff of Old Fuss and Feathers, the legendary six-foot five-inch, three-hundred-pound General of the Army, Winfield Scott, Lee became known for daring feats of reconnaissance. In the mountainous terrain between Veracruz and Mexico City, the formidable artillery of General Santa Anna of Mexico stopped the U.S. Army. Scott sent Lee forward to seek a way to outflank the Mexican position.

Lee was almost captured. He evaded the enemy by hiding beneath a log for hours while Mexican soldiers sat nearby smoking. One nearly stepped on him. He fled at nightfall and reported back to Scott that he had found a way up the mountain, which Santa Anna had declared unscalable. Thanks to Lee, the Americans were saved from having to make a costly frontal attack.

Approaching Mexico City, Lee, now a major (and soon to be a colonel), scouted on horseback for thirty-six hours with no sleep and little food, tracing a path for American artillery through a lava bed considered impassable by the Mexicans. Once the soldiers crossed the lava field and opened fire, the enemy troops fled. In the final assault on the heavily defended Mexico City gate at Chapultepec, Lee worked through the night building supports for the heavy artillery. Aided by Lt. George McClellen, Lee toiled forty-eight hours straight until he dropped from exhaustion.

General Scott heaped praise on Lee, calling him the best soldier he had ever seen and insisting that he could not have won the stunning victory over Santa Anna's army without Lee's assistance. Suddenly Robert E. Lee was a national hero.

His homecoming, after the two-year absence, was not a happy one. He missed the carriage Mary had sent across the river in Washington to fetch him home. He rode instead on horseback up the long hill to Arlington House. The family expected the carriage and no one but the dog recognized the solitary rider approaching the mansion. Lee greeted them all with hugs and picked up his three-year-old namesake, only to find that he was cradling the wrong little boy. The child was his son's playmate. Little Robert long remembered his feeling of humiliation at his father's mistake. The older children were distant and reserved, and Mary seemed more sickly and frail.

Lee was assigned to Baltimore, for the monotonous work of constructing harbor defenses. He found this frustrating duty, a comedown after the glory of war. His next assignment did not seem to offer any improvement. He was ordered to West Point to serve as superintendent of the military academy, a job he approached with reluctance.

It turned out to be a pleasant three-year interlude during which, to his surprise, Mary and some of the children joined him. The superintendent's house offered space and luxury not unlike Arlington House, and Mary gladly and actively undertook the social duties a superintendent's wife was expected to perform.

She enjoyed working in the garden, despite her arthritis, and forced herself to take long walks in the hills. She entertained the faculty and their wives and took extra care, as did Lee, to make nervous cadets feel welcome and at ease at the traditional Sunday open house. She developed a particular fondness for one handsome cadet from Virginia. James Ewell Brown Stuart, destined to become known by his initials, JEB, greatly enjoyed the hours he spent at the Lee home.

Lee devoted much time and worry to the cadets, and he was considerate of those who had to be discharged for failing grades or excess demerits. To most, he offered the chance for resignation rather than dismissal, urging them not to dwell on their leaving but to pursue other careers.

Lee was amused by one cadet who seemed to have more of an artistic than a martial inclination. The others called him Curly, but his given name was James Abbott McNeill Whistler. His father had been a graduate of West Point. Despite Lee's best efforts to save him, Curly Whistler had to be dismissed. He was always in some sort of trouble. He liked to include human figures in his sketches of bridges and fortifications, even though the instructor repeatedly warned him not to.

Whistler failed chemistry when he incorrectly, and rather flippantly, identified the element silicon as a gas. He later said, with his characteristic lack of modesty, that if silicon had been a gas, he undoubtedly would have become a major general.

Most of the cadets—those who stayed and those who did not—had only positive memories of Lee as a soldier who always tried to be fair. They admired him greatly. Once Lee had to admonish a cadet who had been caught fighting. He asked the young man whether it would not be better if the cadets lived together in peace. "Yes, colonel," the cadet replied. "And if we were all like you, it would be an easy thing to do."

Being superintendent eventually wore Lee down. The demanding schedule, the paperwork and correspondence, meant long, tiring days and nights. He suffered digestive disturbances and eyesight problems and became irritable and short-tempered. His mood was further dampened by the death of Mary's mother, whom he had loved as his own. His letters began to reflect the notion of death and of meeting loved ones in the afterlife. It was clearly time for a change.

LEE AND HIS family left West Point in 1855. He wept openly as he bid good-bye to the cadets and the staff. The band played "Carry Me Back to Old Virginny." Mary and the children were indeed returning to old Virginia, to the home at Arlington, but Lee was going west, almost two thousand miles from the house on the hill that overlooked the nation's capital. In an even greater departure, he was transferring from a staff position to one of the line. After twenty-six years in the army, Lee would finally have command of troops in the field.

Jefferson Davis, the secretary of war, himself a graduate of the U.S. Military Academy, had established two new cavalry regiments to deal with the growing Indian problem in the west. The First Cavalry Regiment would be headed by Col. Edwin V. "Bull" Sumner, with Joe Johnston serving as second in command. The Second Cavalry would be led by Albert Sidney Johnston; Lee was appointed his second in command.

The Second Cavalry Regiment was headquartered in San Antonio, Texas, where half the regiment were stationed. Lee's command—12 officers and 226 men in four companies—was located at a barren, isolated post near what later became the town of Abilene, in northwest central Texas. Life there was primitive, physically demanding, and devoid of the creature comforts to which Lee had been accustomed. Officers and men were housed in tents during the freezing winter and the brutally hot summer.

Lee led his men on long, grueling campaigns across the trackless deserts in pursuit of Indians and Mexican bandits. One mission required more than a thousand miles of hard riding over two months. In time he grew to appreciate the wilderness, the open spaces, and the rugged beauty of the landscape.

He wrote to Mary that he had adapted well to the austere lifestyle and no longer viewed the conditions as a hardship. For companionship Lee had a pet snake and a chicken he trained to hop up on his camp table, where it habitually overturned his inkwell.

He decided that he liked being in command. He enjoyed the camaraderie with his junior officers, most of whom would fight for the South in the coming war. He liked the banter and good fellowship. The younger men came to regard him like a father. Lee's nephew, Fitzhugh Lee, served in the regiment along with Earl Van Dorn, Edmund Kirby-Smith, and the irrepressible John Bell Hood, who had been a West Point cadet during Lee's superintendency.[1]

The good times for Lee out west ended abruptly in October 1857, when Mary's father died. Lee took a two-month leave and headed back to Arlington. He arrived home a month later and was stunned to find that in his absence, Mary had become an invalid. She could no longer walk, had only limited use of one arm, and suffered constant pain, all attributed to her worsening arthritis. A second shock for Lee was that his father-in-law had left his estate in deplorable condition.

Custis had run up extensive debts and let his valuable properties deteriorate. Arlington House, the once beautiful white mansion on the hill, was decaying. The roof leaked and the walls and furnishings were water-stained. Weeds choked the lawns, and fences had collapsed from neglect. The other landholdings, Romancoke and the White House, were also in disrepair. Because none of the land was being farmed, no income had been generated. The slaves had been rented out to other farmers scattered throughout the state. The creditors were impatient and at first it seemed to Lee that Mary's inheritance would have to be sold off to avert financial ruin. Three other men had been named coexecutors with Lee, but they declined the honor, leaving the responsibility to him. Although he had no business experience, his duty was to save what he could.

The first task was to restore Arlington House. Lee pored over his father-in-law's ledgers. He hired and supervised a small army of workers who replaced walls, fixed the roof, and shored up the sinking foun-

---

[1] Hood had been stationed at Fort Vancouver, Washington, when Ulysses S. Grant had been post quartermaster and had started drinking seriously to escape his loneliness.

dation. Fences were mended, sagging stables and a grinding mill rebuilt, fields fertilized and corn planted, walls painted, draperies and pictures hung.

The work took far longer than Lee's original two-month leave. He appealed to General Scott for one extension after another, all of which were granted, until two years had passed and the job was still not finished. Lee might never have returned to active duty had not one of his favorite West Point cadets appeared at Arlington House on October 17, 1859, carrying sealed orders from the War Department.

The courier was Lt. Jeb Stuart, and the message ordered Lee to report to the secretary of war immediately. There had been some sort of uprising at the Federal Arsenal at Harper's Ferry, Virginia, and Lee was expected to quell it.

After meeting with President James Buchanan and Secretary of War John Floyd, Lee commandeered a B&O locomotive and headed for Harper's Ferry. He was dressed in civilian clothes; there had been no time to change into his uniform. Jeb Stuart volunteered to come along, to help end what the president had described as an armed insurrection.

Lee did not know the proclaimed purpose of the uprising or how many people were involved. He had been told that he had ninety U.S. Marines at his disposal, along with their commander, a lieutenant. They were the only troops who could be spared from the nation's capital. The marines had been sent ahead, but Lee and Stuart caught up with them outside of Harper's Ferry later that night. They could hear gunfire from the direction of the arsenal.

Some local residents reported to Lee that a strange man named Smith and some of his followers had taken over the arsenal, which had a large supply of weapons. They had taken hostages and barricaded themselves inside. The town militia had gathered and peppered the brick building with hunting rifles and shotguns to no effect. When Lee arrived the situation was a standoff.

The mysterious Smith was actually John Brown, a notorious zealot and abolitionist, known to have brutally murdered five proslavery settlers in Kansas. With a band of five black men and seventeen white men, including three of his sons, Brown had seized the arsenal at Harper's Ferry, intending to distribute its guns to the hundreds of slaves he expected to join his cause.

Lee, Stuart, and the marines surrounded the building. At daybreak, Lee sent Stuart, bearing a white flag, to the arsenal's door to demand Brown's surrender. Brown opened the door slightly and trained his rifle on Stuart. Brown refused to surrender, demanding instead safe passage out of town. The two men argued for a short time, then Brown declared he would die on the spot rather than give up.

Jeb Stuart stepped clear of the door and waved his hat in the air, the prearranged signal to attack. The marines swept forward with fixed bayonets and a battering ram. To protect the hostages, Lee had ordered that no shots be fired. Within three minutes, one marine and two abolitionists were dead. The insurrection was over.

Six weeks later, on December 2, 1859, John Brown was hanged in Charleston in what later became the state of West Virginia. Lee witnessed the death, as commanding officer of several thousand troops and militia assembled to prevent any bloodshed from Brown's ardent supporters in the abolitionist movement.

Among the motley assortment of units in Lee's charge that day was the entire cadet corps from the Virginia Military Institute. They were led by one of their teachers, Thomas Jackson, a thin, awkward, ungainly man who believed the left side of his body was withering because of poor nourishment. He sucked lemons to correct the condition. Lee had known him in the Mexican War and had recommended him for his post at VMI. In later years he would meet Jackson again, when he had acquired the nickname "Stonewall."

The Richmond Grays, a socially elite militia unit from the city, were also present. Among their number was a handsome young visitor to Richmond who was curious about military life. He was given a uniform and allowed to come along with the troops. He watched John Brown mount the scaffold and die at the end of the rope. John Wilkes Booth turned pale at the sight and lost his desire to be a soldier. He never forgot that day.

⊷⇒◯⇐⊷

LEE RETURNED TO full-time active duty in February 1860. He made the long journey back to Texas to rejoin the Second Cavalry Regiment at Fort Mason. He was becoming moody and sad, fearing that he had been a failure. He was fifty-three years old, once again away from those he loved. What had he to show for thirty-five years of army service?

He grew increasingly dissatisfied, "rent by a thousand anxieties," he said, his mind and body "worn and racked to pieces." He was deeply troubled, believing that he had also failed as a father and husband by being away so frequently. He foresaw no hope for change.

His letters were self-critical, revealing a sense of inadequacy, and he repeatedly spoke of repenting for sins and asking forgiveness for all the errors of his ways. When a grandson was born that year, Lee wrote to the boy's father, "I wish I could offer him a more worthy name and a better example" to help the boy "avoid the errors I have committed." And a year later, he told a daughter, "You see what a poor sinner I am, and how unworthy to possess what was given me; for that reason it has been taken away."

He might well have sunk deeper into his personal despair had his attention not been diverted by his concern, even alarm, for the country. The United States was being torn by the dissension over slavery and states' rights. In some states there was talk of seceding from the Union and of the possibility of war between North and South. The thought of such a split was intolerable to Lee. He wrote to his son:

> I can anticipate no greater calamity for the country than a dissolution of the Union. I am willing to sacrifice everything but honor for its preservation. Secession is nothing but revolution.

The situation deteriorated with the election of Abraham Lincoln to the presidency. South Carolina moved dangerously close to secession. Other states were sure to follow. Some of Lee's brother officers resigned from the army, unwilling to serve a nation their home states had abandoned.

Lee stood firm, calling the states that seceded "selfish" and "mad." He made his position clear. "I wish for no other flag than the Star Spangled Banner." Lee knew that as long as Virginia—the most powerful Southern state—remained loyal to the Union, there would be no large-scale war between the sections. If Virginia held firm, so would most of the South.

On February 4, 1861, Lee received an urgent dispatch from the War Department ordering him to report to General Scott. As Lee was about to leave for Washington, one of his officers asked the question that was on the minds of all who knew him.

"Colonel, do you intend to go South or remain North?"

"I shall never bear arms against the Union," Lee said.

That seemed to put the matter to rest. But Lee said more, indicating the true focus of his loyalty: "But it may be necessary for me to carry a musket in defense of my native state, Virginia." Should Virginia decide to secede, Lee was worried about the consequences not only for the country, but also for his own financial circumstances. Secession could be economically ruinous to the state and to investments made for himself and his wife's estate.

Three days after Lee left Fort Mason, he arrived in San Antonio to find secessionists preparing for war. Armed rebels filled the streets. That morning, the Union commander had surrendered Texas to the Confederates and turned over all government firearms. The American flag had been pulled down. Lee was shocked and moved to tears. His voice shook as he asked a friend, "Has it come so soon as this?"

Lee called on General Scott as soon as he returned home. They spoke privately for three hours about the possibility of war, but nothing was resolved. There was no war yet, as far as Virginia was concerned, and delegates to the state convention seemed opposed to the idea of secession.

But a single shot changed everything. In Charleston, South Carolina, on April 12, Pierre Gustave Toutant Beauregard, who had been with Lee at Veracruz and who was now a major general in the new Confederate army, gave the order to fire on Fort Sumter. The war between the sections had begun.

In Washington, the influential power broker Francis Preston Blair recommended to the president that Lee be appointed to lead the Union army. Lincoln agreed. On April 18, Blair invited Lee to meet at Blair's townhouse across the street from the War Department. Blair offered Lee the rank of major general and command of a 100,000-man army. Lee declined. He would not take part in any invasion of the Southern states. Lee crossed the street to inform General Scott of his decision. The old warrior received the news with sadness.

"Lee," Scott said, "you have made the greatest mistake of your life; but I feared it would be so."

⊷⊜⊷

THE COMING OF war may have spared Lee from wondering whether he had accomplished anything worthwhile with his life—as it did for Grant and for Meade—but it did not have an immediate effect. During the early days of the conflict, many Southerners considered Lee to be a failure as a soldier. Some even thought he was a traitor to the cause.

Lee spent the first months of the war in a tiny office in Richmond, working twelve-hour days performing the kind of clerical work he had always detested. His job was to recruit, process, organize, and supply thousands of would-be soldiers and make of them an effective army. It was a frustrating task, made worse by several factors. First, Lee had to deal with the individualism and eccentricities of the Confederate volunteers. Second, there was a severe shortage of weapons, ammunition, and other materiel needed to wage war. Third, the Southerners' bravado had the soldiers convinced that they would beat the Yankees in a month or two. After all, one Confederate soldier was worth at least ten Union men.

Lee did not share their optimism. He somberly and openly predicted a hard, bloody fight, lasting perhaps as long as ten years. He insisted that all recruits enlist for the duration of the war, not just the prescribed twelve months. Such sentiments were not what Southerners wanted to hear, and people began to ask what was wrong with a general whose thinking was so negative, so contradictory to the prevailing euphoria. Rumors began to spread about Lee's loyalty. Influential Confederate figures complained, "At heart Robert E. Lee is against us— that I know." Another argued that "General Lee will surely be tried for a traitor."

Lee spent day after day at his desk trying to create a fighting force when he didn't even have enough ammunition for target practice, and he worried about Mary and the children. They had sent the silver, paintings, and George Washington's papers and books to Richmond for safekeeping. Washington's bed and other personal items were stored in the attic and cellar of Arlington House. Mourning the loss of her beloved home, which she suspected she would never see again, Mary took the girls south to spend the war years boarding with various relatives and friends.

Union troops took possession of the house because of its commanding view of the Potomac River and the capital, confiscating it for nonpayment of taxes, based on a legal technicality. The army used the fences and trees for firewood, appropriated the family possessions, and eventually turned the garden and grounds into a Union cemetery.

◆══◉══◆

TOWARD THE END of that summer, Jefferson Davis appointed Lee military adviser and gave him his first commission. Lee was sent to the mountains of northwest Virginia to resolve differences among three

Confederate politicians who had been appointed to the rank of general. Their behavior was proving as antagonistic toward one another as it was toward the enemy.

Things went badly from the start. The generals refused to cooperate in joint military actions and Lee was too tactful to issue direct orders, preferring to offer polite suggestions—all of which were ignored. The rugged terrain made maneuvers difficult, there were no railroads to move troops or supplies, and the few roads turned to thick mud after twenty days of constant rain. The soldiers were poorly trained and lacked discipline, and the officers were ineffective. And the local population was strongly pro-Union. Then the troops were struck by epidemics of measles and diarrhea; they also lacked warm enough clothing for the cold spell that settled over the mountains.

When Union forces swept over the region, the three Confederate armies retreated in disarray. Four days later the local inhabitants voted to secede from Virginia to establish the new Union state of West Virginia. Lee returned to Richmond roundly condemned by the Southern press, derided as "Granny Lee" and "Evacuating Lee." People expected more from the son of Light Horse Harry Lee, a hero of the Revolutionary War. The criticism was hard for Lee to bear, and he wondered whether he would have any future in the Confederate army.

Jefferson Davis believed in him, however, and in November gave him an assignment to strengthen the coastal defenses around Charleston and Savannah. When the civilian and military leaders of those cities heard the news, they petitioned Davis to send someone else. They did not want Robert E. Lee. John Jones, a clerk in the War Department, observed Lee's mood. He noted in his diary that "Gen. Lee in the streets here bore the aspect of a discontented man, for he saw that everything was going wrong."

However, Lee's project on the coastal fortifications went well. It was primarily an engineering job, the kind of work Lee had been doing most of his career, although there was some grumbling among the

troops who considered digging and other forms of manual labor
beneath their dignity. After four months of intensive effort, Lee considered his work done. He took leave to visit his father's burial place on
Cumberland Island off the Georgia coast. He placed a flower on the
grave, observed a few minutes of silence, then left, never to return.

Lee also acquired a new horse, a young gray that had come to his
notice in western Virginia. The horse was called Greenbriar. When its
owner was transferred to Lee's new command, Lee admired the animal
and offered to purchase it for two hundred dollars.

The strength and endurance of this fine animal won him the reputation of being a "fine traveller" and ere long his old name was dropped
and he became simply Traveller.

Lee was recalled to Richmond in early 1862 to resume his duties as
military adviser to Jefferson Davis. He was not pleased with the assignment, telling Mary that he found neither advantage nor pleasure in it.
Yet, as always, he did his duty, quietly and self-effacingly.

Lee's fortunes changed the following June after Gen. Joe Johnston
was wounded during the Peninsular campaign launched by the Union
general George McClellan. In March 1862, McClellan landed 120,000
troops at Fortress Monroe and advanced slowly and methodically
toward Richmond. Johnston, whose father had fought in the Revolutionary War with Light Horse Harry Lee, kept withdrawing his vastly
inferior force until the Union army was within five miles of the Confederate capital. Jefferson Davis ordered his wife and children evacuated, a signal for hundreds of other civilians to jam the trains and roads
south, fleeing the Yankee advance. The Confederate gold reserves were
also shipped away.

On May 30, while Lee and Davis were visiting the front, General
Johnston was hit by a musket ball and a shell fragment and carried off
the field. His second in command was incapable of taking over, so

Davis (with reluctance, it was said) gave the command to Lee. Lee renamed his new army the "Army of Northern Virginia" and set about to change the course of the war.

Lee's first order, to dig trenches and rifle pits, was not well received by his troops, who objected to doing the work of slaves. They revived the nickname "Granny Lee" and dubbed him "the King of Spades." They were eager to attack and bristled at having to remain on the defensive. Lee too would have liked to attack, but his strategy was to deceive McClellan into thinking that the Southerners were preparing for a siege. When Lee did finally take the offensive, he sent Jeb Stuart's cavalry on a long reconnaissance ride around McClellan's right flank and found it vulnerable. Then on June 25, Lee massed his forces and unleashed them, beginning a series of deadly battles that came to be called the Seven Days. When they were over, McClellan was in retreat. The Richmond newspapers, once so critical, even contemptuous, hailed Lee as the Confederacy's savior, one of the most audacious, bold, and daring military leaders in history.

Lee was less pleased. He had not destroyed the Union army, which was his intention, and he had lost twenty thousand men. He wrote to Mary that victory had not been as complete as he had hoped, but it was all up to the will of God. Lee may not have accomplished the task he had set for himself, but he had saved Richmond and forced an army superior in numbers to withdraw. No one called him "Granny Lee" again.

⋆═◦═⋆

DURING THE NEXT two years Lee defeated Union generals almost as fast as they could be appointed. In July, Lee's Army of Northern Virginia met Gen. John Pope at Bull Run, the same battlefield where the Union army had been beaten so badly the previous year. Stonewall Jackson was there, sucking on his lemons, along with Pete Longstreet. In a daring action, Lee divided his much smaller army into two parts and attacked. The Union troops fled back to Washington. In less than three months, Lee had defeated two larger and better-equipped armies. Despite the Confederate losses, Lee could do no wrong in the eyes of the Southern public and press.

Lee was not content with merely subduing the Northern armies. He wanted to destroy them and the government that dared to invade Virginia's sacred soil. On September 5, three days after his victory at the second battle of Bull Run, Lee led his soldiers across the Potomac River to invade the North. He got as far as Sharpsburg, Maryland, on Antietam Creek. The enemy forces, led by McClellan, numbered ninety thousand. Lee had half that number. When the day was over, the casualties for both sides numbered more than twenty-three thousand. Lee's losses for that campaign exceeded thirteen thousand of his most experienced troops.

Both sides claimed victory, but in reality it was a standoff. Lee took his men back to Virginia, where the anticipated follow-up attack from McClellan never came. Abraham Lincoln dismissed McClellan and tried Ambrose Burnside next.

Burnside intended to attack Fredericksburg, Virginia, on the Rappahannock River, and then advance on Richmond. He did attack the town but waited far too long to do so, allowing Lee ample time to position men and artillery behind strong defensive fortifications. On December 13, Burnside sent wave after wave of Union troops across an open field to charge a stone wall behind which rebel infantrymen stood four deep, with men in the rear loading rifles for those in front. At day's end, thirteen thousand Union soldiers had fallen. Lee watched the slaughter and was overheard to say, "It is well that war is so terrible, else men would learn to love it too much."

The futility and stupidity, the staggering, horrible, senseless cost of marching men in perfect formation across an open field to take a well-fortified position was made perfectly clear that cold winter day in Fredericksburg when so many Yankees died. But seven months later, on July 3, 1863, the last day at Gettysburg, Lee himself would commit the same error. He would come to believe that his troops were invincible, that they would succeed where others failed and that nothing could stop them. But that was later. First, there was another Union general to defeat.

⤐═◉═⤏

"FIGHTING JOE" HOOKER had done a remarkable job of restoring the Union army that Burnside had shattered at Fredericksburg. In the spring, newly outfitted and provisioned, with morale high and miles of supply trains to equip and support them, Hooker moved 140,000 men south. Lee had only 60,000 troops to meet them, and they were short of food and supplies. Even shoes were hard to find. Some men suffered from scurvy and most were so thin that their ribs showed. Rations comprised four ounces of meat and a pound of flour per man per day—when they could find any meat and flour.

Lee, too, was suffering. "Old age and sorrow is wearing me away," he wrote, "and constant anxiety and labour, day and night, leave me but little repose." There would be less repose in the future, for by April 30 Hooker was on the march and coming for Lee. Lee had been experiencing severe pains in his chest, back, and arm—the symptoms of angina—that left him enfeebled, but he roused himself to meet the attack.

Hooker was clever. He sent 40,000 men across the river at Fredericksburg, east of his main point of attack, hoping that Lee would leave his army there to counter them. Lee gambled that Hooker's move was a feint and left only 10,000 men at Fredericksburg. He moved the rest of his troops west toward the area known as the Wilderness, a tangle of forest and dense undergrowth that stretched for miles—exactly where Hooker's main force was heading.

By May 1, Hooker's advance units were beyond the Wilderness, out in the open, forcing skirmishes with Lee's men. Hooker's main army was like a juggernaut, rolling along the forest trails, ready to break out onto the plain where they would have been unbeatable. Historian

Bruce Catton described how Hooker lost his nerve and stopped, paralyzed by overwhelming despair.

> He had planned his campaign like a master and had carried out the first half of it with great skill, and then, when the pinch came, he had simply folded up. There had been no courage in him, no life, no spark; during most of the battle the army to all intents and purposes had no commander at all.

Hooker ordered his soldiers back into the Wilderness to dig in and form a defensive line. Lee took advantage of Hooker's panic. He split his small army again, sending Jackson on a forced march to the poorly defended end of Hooker's right flank, leaving only 18,000 troops to face the Union's main force should Hooker recover his nerve. Lee's second major gamble of the campaign succeeded. Jackson's surprise attack on Hooker's flank shocked the Union troops, causing them to scatter and retreat.

On May 2, Lee was sitting astride Traveller near a burning house called Chancellor, from which the village of Chancellorsville took its name, when a courier rode up with devastating news. Stonewall Jackson had been wounded accidentally by his own men and his left arm had to be amputated. Lee commented that Jackson may have lost his left arm, but he had lost his right, as he had come to depend so greatly on Jackson. When Jackson died a week later, Lee wept openly.

⋯⊙═⋯

AT THE WILDERNESS Lee had won yet another battle, a major victory that stunned the North, but he knew he was still in danger of losing the war. The Confederacy was running out of men and materiel. Lee could not afford the losses sustained in many more victories like Chancellorsville. For the South, this was a war of attrition. It could not replace its troops, whereas the North seemed to have a limitless supply.

Lee believed that a final bold venture, a sustained invasion of the North, was the only way to win a decisive victory. He proposed to lead the Army of Northern Virginia deep into Pennsylvania, and from there turn on Baltimore or Washington. Faced with such a threat, Lincoln would have to withdraw his Army of the Potomac from Southern territory. He might even have to bring his western armies back east to defend the capital. That move would ease the pressure on the Southern stronghold at Vicksburg, now under attack from that tenacious Yankee general, U. S. Grant.

Lee intended to feed his men and replenish his supply of horses from Pennsylvania's lush fields and barns and full stables. He expected to spread terror throughout the North when he loosed his army in Pennsylvania. Their presence would embolden the Union peace activists who desired to end the war and could help recruit others for the cause. Lee hoped this would force Lincoln to sue for peace and let the Confederacy go its own way.

On May 14, 1863, Robert E. Lee presented his plan to Jefferson Davis and the Confederate cabinet. There was opposition from politicians who wanted Lee to send some of his troops to relieve the pressure on Vicksburg, but Lee disagreed. Virginia was the most important battlefield, as far as Lee was concerned, and it had to be preserved. It was in Virginia, not Vicksburg, that the fate of the Confederacy would be decided. Virginia was the heart and soul of the Southern cause. If it were lost, the South would be defeated.

Lee offered the government two choices. Either the army could retreat to Richmond, dig in, and prepare for a prolonged, and ultimately doomed, siege; or they could take the war to the people of the North. The cabinet members acquiesced. Vicksburg would have to fend for itself. Lee's army would go north.

CHAPTER 4

THE GIBRALTAR OF THE WEST

VICKSBURG MAY NOT have been so important to Robert E. Lee, but it mattered a great deal to Ulysses S. Grant and Abraham Lincoln. The president considered Vicksburg the key to the eventual Union victory. The war would not end as long as the Confederates held that vital point on the Mississippi River, a major supply line for the rebels. The Red, the White, and the Arkansas Rivers all flowed into the Mississippi, transporting cattle and hogs, corn, hominy, and cotton, as well as manpower from the western states for transshipment by rail throughout the Confederacy. Capture Vicksburg and that flow of goods would be choked off.

Grant recognized the city's strategic value but he may also have had a personal reason for choosing to take it. Since Shiloh, back in April 1862, his career had been stalemated. His prospects, once promising after so many failures, were dismal again and he was wondering if he had any future in the army.

Grant's old nemesis, Henry Halleck, was again the cause of his despair. Halleck never liked or trusted Grant and effectively prevented him from participating in the everyday conduct of the war. Four days after the battle of Shiloh, on April 11, Major General Halleck arrived at Grant's headquarters to assume direct overall command of the three armies: Don Carlos Buell's Army of the Ohio, John Pope's Army of the Mississippi, and Grant's Army of the Tennessee.

But Halleck did more than that. He relieved Grant of command of his army and gave him a meaningless position as second in command of the western armies—in effect, second in command to Halleck himself. Halleck froze Grant out of all duties and responsibilities to make sure he would have no active role in Halleck's coming military campaigns.

After all Grant had accomplished, this isolation deeply hurt him. He wrote in his memoirs, "Although next to [Halleck] in rank, I was ignored as much as if I had been at the most distant point of territory in my jurisdiction." Halleck even moved Grant's camp some distance from headquarters. When Halleck met with other high-ranking officers, he took them aside and whispered so that Grant would not overhear them. Such actions were petty and cruel, but they were also effective.

Whenever Grant made a suggestion, Halleck made it obvious to all within earshot that Grant's opinion was of no interest. Grant recalled,

> I was little more than an observer. Orders were sent direct to the right wing or reserve, ignoring me, and advances were made . . . without notifying me. My position was so embarrassing in fact that I made several applications . . . to be relieved.

Halleck refused Grant's requests for transfer. He was determined to deprive Grant of authority, responsibility, and even knowledge of the movements of the army.

Grant became increasingly depressed. His position was humiliating and he saw no way out. Even Lincoln was having second thoughts about Grant because of the high casualty figures at Shiloh. Grant passed his days sitting around a campfire at his headquarters reminiscing about the Mexican War. Whenever the conversation turned to Shiloh, Grant—perhaps deliberately, perhaps not—doubled the size of the rebel force he had faced, in his retelling of the battle, and halved the size of his own, thereby inflating the magnitude of his victory, at least to himself.

He told others he wished for a small command in some distant place like New Mexico, away from the press, which accused him of being drunk at Shiloh. Finally, he asked Halleck to be relieved of all duty with the army. His situation was no better than being under arrest. Grant felt so desperate that he was prepared to resign his commission.

Grant—and the Union—were saved by one man, William Tecumseh Sherman, who recognized the magnitude of the loss should Grant be allowed to resign. When he overheard Halleck say that Grant would be leaving the next morning, Sherman rode to Grant's camp. He found the staff packing Grant's gear. Grant was tying bundles of letters with red tape.

Sherman recorded the meeting in his memoirs. He pulled up a camp stool and asked if it was true that Grant was leaving the army. Grant allowed that it was, and Sherman asked why.

"Sherman," Grant said, "you know that I'm in the way here. I have stood it as long as I can and can endure it no longer."

Sherman pleaded with him to stay. He reminded Grant that if he left, his achievements would be forgotten, whereas if he stayed, "fortune might turn and lift him to his true place." In the end, Grant agreed to stick it out awhile longer.

-◦→▷═◁←◦-

GENERAL HALLECK WAS in the process of sending his 100,000-man army twenty-one miles from Shiloh to attack a Confederate camp at Corinth, Mississippi. The troops moved out on April 30. They encountered no large-scale Confederate resistance, but it took them a month to reach their destination. Halleck covered approximately one mile a day and insisted on digging extensive fortifications each time the army stopped. Thus, the men spent more time digging than marching; and by the time they reached Corinth, the Confederates had long since gone. They left behind a large sign welcoming the Union army—and nothing else.

Halleck proclaimed the Corinth campaign to be a major victory. He telegraphed the War Department to report that "The result is all I could possibly desire." Halleck was summoned to Washington where Lincoln appointed him general in chief of all the Union armies, east and west.[1]

Grant may have played a role in that selection. Shortly after Halleck left Corinth, and long before he reached the capital, Grant wrote to Congressman Elihu Washburne. "I do not know the object of calling Gen. H. to Washington, but if it is to make him Sec. of War, or Commander-in-Chief, Head Quarters at Washington, a better selection could not be made."

Washburne was known to be a close friend of the president, and Grant may have hoped that the congressman would pass along his recommendation to Lincoln. Whether he did or not, Grant was at last rid of the daily presence of Henry Halleck.

As second in command, Grant settled his headquarters in Memphis, but the war continued to pass him by. Halleck assigned him no duties beyond guarding communication lines and dispatching troops to assist units elsewhere. He was always warned not to accompany them himself. In the east, Robert E. Lee was winning battle after battle. Grant read newspaper accounts of Second Manassas, Antietam, and Fredericksburg, and felt, not without justification, that he was being denied his chance to participate in the war.

What kept Grant in the shadows was the unforgotten stain of

[1] Lincoln had become tired of operating as his own general in chief. Also, his annoyance with McClellan had reached the point where he needed someone else to take over. Halleck wasn't the perfect answer, but Lincoln hoped he would be an improvement.

Shiloh and the stories of his drinking that the press periodically circulated. Lincoln and Secretary of War Stanton had grown hesitant about Grant and their doubts may have been reinforced by the tales Halleck told when he arrived in Washington. Stanton decided to plant an informer in Grant's camp to help the president decide whether Grant was fit for further command.

The person Stanton chose to spy on Grant was Charles A. Dana, the forty-four-year-old former managing editor of Horace Greeley's *New York Tribune*. Appointed assistant secretary of war, Dana was asked by Stanton in March 1863 to undertake a secret mission out west. Dana recalled:

> He wanted someone to go to Grant's army to report daily to him the military proceedings, and to give such information as would enable Mr. Lincoln and himself to settle their minds as to Grant, about whom at that time there were many doubts, and against whom there was some complaint.

Dana reached Grant's camp on April 6, 1863, and was warmly welcomed by the general, against the advice of some staffers who urged him not to cooperate with this interloper from Washington. Dana told Grant he was there to investigate payroll problems. Grant suspected that Dana's real mission was to spy on him and he decided to make Dana's job easy, and to use him for his own benefit. Dana said:

> I think Grant was always glad to have me with his army. He did not like letter writing, and my daily dispatches to Mr. Stanton relieved him from the necessity of describing every day what was going on in the army.

Grant realized that with Dana's reports, his name would now appear daily in briefings read by Stanton and Lincoln. If Dana was impressed with him, so would they be. This could be Grant's way of getting back in the war and of undertaking the new campaign he had been planning. And in fact, within a few hours of their first meeting, Charles Dana sent Stanton an outline of Grant's plan to capture the fortress on the hill known as Vicksburg.

⤙⟚◉⟛⤚

CHARLES DANA WAS impressed with Grant from the outset and was soon sending laudatory dispatches to Washington. He told Stanton that Grant was extremely modest, had a great deal of courage, and was "the most honest man [he] ever knew." Dana appreciated, as did the troops in Grant's command, the absence of any "superfluous flummery" of rank about the man.

Grant dressed in a plain uniform without a sword or trappings of finery. With his worn black felt hat pulled low over his eyes and a cigar stuck in his mouth, he could have passed for an old farmer who had seen better days. He was a no-nonsense, get-the-job-done sort of fellow. Nor was he physically imposing. Weighing about 135 pounds, he stood five feet eight inches tall but seemed shorter because he slouched when he walked. One eye was slightly lower than the other, giving his face a lopsided look. His close-cut brown beard exaggerated his square jaw, and his full head of dark hair, combed back from his forehead, was so thick on the sides that it covered the tops of his ears.

Grant lived simply. He preferred plain food with no garnishes, sauces, or dressings. He insisted that his meat be cooked well-done, almost burned. He could not tolerate anything bloody, a reminder from childhood of his distaste for the sights and smells of his father's tannery. He never ate chicken, saying that it did not seem right to eat anything that ran around on two legs.

Grant was a plain and simple man. That was how he lived and that was how he planned to conduct his campaign against Vicksburg if he ever got the chance to unleash it. Making a good impression on Charles Dana was the key to that.

Dana liked most of Grant's staff, particularly the man others called the general's "keeper," thirty-three-year-old Col. John A. Rawlins, the chief of staff. Like most of Grant's aides, Rawlins had no military training or background. Before the war he had been an attorney in Galena, Illinois, where Grant was a clerk in his brothers' leather goods store. Rawlins liked Grant well enough to follow him into the army. He soon proved to be indispensable.

Rawlins was a superb organizer and expediter, which Grant needed, and he also became Grant's conscience. John Rawlins had a fanatical hatred of whiskey. His father had been an alcoholic and he was determined that Sam Grant would not be brought down by drink. That became his crusade. He watched Grant like a zealous nursemaid, visiting fits of fury on anyone, regardless of rank, who offered Grant a drink. He had even cursed Grant and made it clear that he would resign if Grant took to the bottle again. Grant believed him.

Rawlins had good reason to be vigilant, because Grant still had a problem with alcohol. Sylvanus Cadwallader, a Chicago reporter who spent more than two years in almost daily contact with Grant, wrote that

> The truth was Gen. Grant had an inordinate love for liquors. He was not an habitual drinker. He could not drink moderately. When at long intervals his appetite for strong drink caused him to accept the invitation of some old classmate, or army associate, to take "just one glass before parting," he invariably drank to excess unless some one was with him (whose control he would acknowledge), to lead him away from temptation.

Civil War historian James McPherson suggested that Grant "may have been an alcoholic in the medical meaning of that term. He was a binge drinker. For months he could go without liquor, but if he once imbibed it was hard for him to stop." Thanks to Rawlins's continuing concern, Grant's drinking was minimal; he never drank when it might affect the outcome of a battle.

Charles Dana was a shrewd and perceptive observer. He passed on his comments to Stanton and to President Lincoln and in the process rehabilitated Grant's reputation in Washington. Thanks to Dana, Grant would be back in the war.

❖═◉═❖

GRANT HAD HAD a Vicksburg campaign in mind for some time, but now that he had been restored to command of the Army of the Tennessee he faced a competitor for the honor of capturing the city. In late fall of 1862, Grant learned that Maj. Gen. John McClernand, a political general from Lincoln's home state of Illinois, had persuaded the president to let him organize a separate army under his independent command. McClernand wanted his own outfit for the sole purpose of taking Vicksburg, which he boasted he could accomplish in one week's time. He was to report not to Grant or even to Halleck (who had not been told of the arrangement) but directly to Lincoln.

McClernand had high postwar political aspirations. As the conqueror of Vicksburg, he believed he would go far, perhaps all the way to the White House. And there was more. The fifty-year-old McClernand was about to marry the twenty-six-year-old sister of his late wife. What better way to impress his new bride than a honeymoon on the Mississippi River, culminating in his glorious capture of a major Southern stronghold?

McClernand recruited dozens of regiments in Illinois and sent them to Memphis to await the assembling of the full complement of his new army. Grant was irate to find another general with a private army in his area of jurisdiction. He asked Halleck to clarify the command situation, to identify who was in charge of this force McClernand was recruiting. Halleck still had his doubts about Grant but trusted McClernand even less. Also, Halleck resented not having been informed of McClernand's appointment. Halleck notified Grant that all units in his department were under his command. He further instructed McClernand to divide his army into two corps and turn one of them over to Sherman.

McClernand protested directly to President Lincoln about losing half the men he had recruited, but the president supported Halleck's decision. Nevertheless, McClernand intended to take his remaining corps to Vicksburg. But when he reached Memphis on December 28, he found that his entire army had disappeared. Grant had ordered Sherman to act quickly and take all of McClernand's troops downriver toward Vicksburg.

—⊶◦⊷—

No one could take Vicksburg, it was said. The city was impregnable. Jefferson Davis himself, whose plantation lay twenty miles south of the city, called it the Gibraltar of the West. It was a citadel, a fortress, rising two hundred feet above the Mississippi. The steep hills and bluffs on which the city was built were hard enough to climb on a pleasant day with nobody shooting down at you. How could anyone think of sending heavily laden troops to ascend the bluffs in the face of withering fire? Who would imagine that Yankee ships could land troops at the docks with Confederate artillery above them? They would surely be blown out of the water.

It would also be difficult to approach the city by land. The only dry ground firm enough to bear troops and wagons was to the east, but Grant, coming from Memphis, was approaching from the north. The town had natural defenses there from the winding rivers and swamps, some fifty miles across and two hundred miles long. No army could slog its way through that. Even though a large Yankee fleet had sailed through the previous summer, Vicksburg's five thousand citizens felt safe and secure.

Vicksburg was a gracious town, worldly, cosmopolitan, and sophisticated, catering to the needs and desires of many wealthy people. Before the war, it had been a major port of call for passengers and cargo on the run between St. Louis to the north and New Orleans to the south. Fast, luxurious riverboats from New Orleans, Memphis, St. Louis, and Louisville docked in Vicksburg daily. Three times a week, boats departed Vicksburg for Memphis and New Orleans. Every half hour, a ferry crossed the river to the Louisiana side, linking the Vicksburg, Shreveport and Texas Railroad on the west with railroads on the east.

Visitors had their choice of elegant hotels, including the Washington, which reminded many of a British tavern, and the Commercial, built higher up the hill. There was a Parisian dressmaker, fine groceries stocked with imported foods, expensive shoe stores, tailors, jewelers, pharmacies, confectioneries, gunsmiths, and liquor dealers.

Vicksburg supported six newspapers—more papers than churches—a large public school, several private academies, two hospitals, and a bookstore that carried the latest novels from London and New York. The resident troupe at the playhouse specialized in Shakespearean tragedies and comedies, and the Vicksburg Lyceum presented visiting lecturers from around the world. To satisfy musical tastes, the city boasted its Philharmonic Society.

Overlooking it all was the grand courthouse, completed three years before the war. The large square building was surrounded by verandahs and gleaming white pillars. Built to last, its thick walls were made of brick with sugar added to reinforce the mortar. And its impressive cupola, the locals bragged, rivaled in height the dome of Saint Paul's Cathedral in London. Magnificent clock faces adorned all four sides, the proud achievement of a German watchmaker who lived down the hill from his masterpiece.

Vicksburg, being a port town, had its low side as well. Below the bluffs, where the town met the river, stood a string of seedy hotels and boardinghouses, noisy and dangerous saloons, and dingy but profitable warehouses and loading docks. The bordellos were always full. The most famous was Mollie Bunch's, which a few months before the war shocked the citizenry up the hill by staging a dazzling prostitutes' ball. The proprietress had the audacity to send formal invitations to the most prominent homes in the city, even to the ministers.

The consensus was clear: Mollie Bunch's bunch had gone too far. They would have to be taught a lesson. As soon as the ball commenced, fire alarm bells rang and a posse of respectable but irate citizens guided the fire engines to Mollie's place. They dragged the hoses to the ballroom and turned them on full force, drenching the elegantly dressed dancers and sending them reeling to the floor. In their zeal, they even hosed down the array of fine foods on the banquet tables.

The ball was over but the mob's sense of justice was not yet spent. They moved on to a tavern where they soaked the patrons, broke up the bar, and smashed bottles and kegs. The owner shot one man, but that did not stop the crowd from destroying his saloon. As they dispersed, they could be heard congratulating themselves on a good night's work. One resident described the events of the evening as "a quiet but determined way of correcting an evil."

—⇒◎⇐—

ALTHOUGH THE WAR had brought change to Vicksburg, its citizens did not experience privations or the real threat of danger for some time. The men joined volunteer regiments and local militia units and held grand parades with martial music for the cheering crowds. Ministers delivered exhortations from pulpits to speed the new soldiers on their righteous way. Everyone knew it would not take long to defeat the North, a region of tradesmen, factory laborers, and immigrants. But when the men did not return after a few months, or even a year, Vicksburg's reaction to the war became more serious.

Vicksburg women banded together to do their part for the noble cause. They formed sewing societies to make clothing and blankets for the troops. The Ladies Military Association collected money from wealthy planters for military supplies; some bolder women dared to solicit donations from people on the street. Some younger women felt frustrated at not being able to participate more directly. "Oh! To see and be in it all," wrote Kate Stone. "I hate weary days of inaction. Yet what can a woman do but wait and suffer?"

Still, there had been no direct threat from the Yankees. The closest the townswomen came to war was to tend sick soldiers in the hospital. Mahala Roach joined the Ladies Hospital Association and, at the end of March 1862, recorded these thoughts in her diary: "Went early to the hospital—nursed the sick all day . . . had many pleasant moments." Things became less pleasant two weeks later, on April 11, when train-loads of badly wounded soldiers from Shiloh reached Vicksburg. The men were filthy, moaning in pain. Many were dying. "It was a sad sight," Mahala Roach wrote, "and makes us realize that the war is near us indeed."

In May 1862, Commodore David Farragut sailed up the Mississippi River from recently conquered New Orleans. With a force of three thousand troops under the command of Brig. Gen. Ben Butler, Far-ragut easily took Baton Rouge and Natchez, but he considered the prize to be Vicksburg. On May 18, he trained his massive complement of more than two hundred naval guns on the city and sent its leaders an ultimatum demanding surrender.

Col. James Autry, the military governor, replied. "Mississippians don't know, and refuse to learn, how to surrender to an enemy. If Com-modore Farragut or Brigadier General Butler can teach them, let them come and try." And so they did.

At five o'clock on the afternoon of May 26, 1862, Farragut's sailors commenced firing. They shelled Vicksburg for two days, damaging several homes and the Methodist church, sending some people fleeing to the countryside. Confederate gunners chose to ignore the bombard-ment, saving their own ammunition and keeping their artillerymen fresh in case of an enemy landing. They knew Farragut's gunboats could not take the city alone, and that reinforcements of Yankee troops posed a greater threat.

Farragut was embarrassed that the rebels would not return fire. It was as though they considered his fleet to be insignificant, little more than a nuisance. Then, to his dismay, drought conditions caused the river to fall and he was forced to send the deep-draft transports and five of his eleven gunboats back to New Orleans to avoid being trapped. The Navy Department in Washington was furious and ordered Farragut back up the river. He was to sail beyond Vicksburg and link up with naval forces north of the city.

This time Farragut brought barges loaded with heavy mortars. His naval guns had done little physical damage but the mortars were more powerful. They fired larger, heavier shells that fell almost straight down, leaving craters up to seventeen feet. The renewed bombardment destroyed buildings and tore up streets but had little impact on the rebel guns and fortifications. Its greatest effect was to force most of the population, civilians and soldiers, to dig shelters and caves on the eastern slopes of the hills and ravines, away from the river.

In terms of casualties, however, the Yankee mortars killed only two Confederate gunners and wounded three others. But the Union fleet sustained forty-five casualties as it sailed upriver past Vicksburg's deadly batteries on the heights.

Once the Union fleet had cleared the city limits, the galvanized Confederate authorities began bringing more troops and guns into town and enlarging the fortifications. With this expansion of the defenses, the residents grew more confident of their ability to survive any renewed Union shelling. Caves and shelters were deepened and reinforced, and people returned to their homes, taking pride in their resilience and daring the Yankees to return.

Farragut was ordered downriver again to avoid being trapped by falling waters. In late July, his ships pulled up anchor and started south. They were attacked by a ramshackle, homemade steam ram, the *Arkansas*, which damaged and sank half the fleet. The people of Vicksburg cheered when they got the news. At the close of summer 1862 it appeared that they might beat the Yankees after all.

--◦=◦--

LT. GEN. JOHN C. Pemberton, commander of the Army of the Mississippi, was charged with keeping Vicksburg safe from the Yankees. Born in Philadelphia in 1814, Pemberton was from a wealthy, well-connected family. As a child he was taught Latin, Greek, and the social amenities. He grew up to be a handsome man, popular with the ladies despite his haughty demeanor.

He entered the military academy at West Point in 1833 and graduated with an average record—neither excelling as Lee did, nor being the class goat, as George Custer and George Pickett would become. Instead, Pemberton, like Grant, finished in the middle of his class. And like Grant, he excelled in only two areas, mathematics and horsemanship.

Pemberton stayed in the army through the Seminole Indian Wars in Florida. He served with distinction in the Mexican War. Twice wounded, he participated in every major assault. Sam Grant remembered Pemberton as conscientious, honorable, and resolute.

Grant liked to recount an episode in the Mexican campaign, when an order was issued that junior officers could no longer do the long, arduous treks on horseback. They were to set an example for the enlisted men by marching alongside them. That inspired considerable grumbling, as junior officers were not used to walking. Many were unable to stand the pace and eventually most of them remounted. But not Pemberton.

As Grant told it,

> Pemberton alone said, no, he would walk, as the order was still extant not to ride, and he did walk, though suffering intensely the while. This I thought of all the time he was in Vicksburg and I outside of it; and I knew he would hold on to the last.

After the Mexican War, from which Pemberton earned a higher rank than Grant, Pemberton was sent west to fight Indians. In 1847, he was stationed at Fortress Monroe, Virginia, and a year later, at age thirty-four, married Martha Thompson, a twenty-two-year-old Southerner.

As tension escalated between North and South, it would be clear where Pemberton's sympathies lay. At West Point, his closest friends had been Southern cadets, and he was a passionate believer in the rights of states to govern themselves. With the coming of war, his mother noted that her son's "heart and views are that the South is right and we are wrong."

After Fort Sumter was fired on, there was no question of Pemberton's loyalty or which color uniform he would wear. He resigned his commission and joined the staff of Joe Johnston before being sent to Charleston to serve under Robert E. Lee. If Lee had been an unpopular choice to South Carolinians, Pemberton was intolerable. This was an affront; the man was a Yankee. Mary Chesnut, the Richmond diarist, wrote that "born Yankees are awfully unlucky . . . commanders for the Confederacy. In high places, they are dangerous, indeed."

Pemberton's aloof manners and stiff bearing were considered an abomination by Southern gentlemen and contrary to the accepted code of behavior. The man was brusque, often rude. He was seen as "wanting in polish . . . too positive and domineering . . . to suit the sensitive and polite people among whom he had been thrown."

Despite his lack of popularity, Pemberton was placed in charge of Charleston's coastal defenses when Lee was recalled to Richmond. He further insulted the local residents when he ended the clandestine sale of cotton to Northern mills, a highly lucrative if illegal practice for Charleston growers and brokers. Of course they demanded that he be replaced, and Jefferson Davis obliged. In October 1862, he transferred Pemberton to Mississippi with instructions to deny Vicksburg to the enemy.

⋯≡⊂≡⋯

PEMBERTON'S COMMANDING OFFICER, Gen. Joseph E. Johnston, was a Southerner, born in Virginia in 1808. He entered West

Point in 1825 and was commissioned a second lieutenant four years later. He fought gallantly in the Seminole Indian Wars in Florida. Twice wounded, he once found a total of thirty bullet holes in his uniform. In another engagement, Johnston took command after all the other officers had been killed and thus saved the outfit from panic. The story was recorded in the flowery language of the day by Capt. William P. Snow.

> [Lieutenant Johnston] laid hold of a small tree with one hand, and, standing boldly out in face of the whole fire of the [Indians], called upon the men to rally and form upon him. They immediately returned to their duty and resumed the action, a perfect volley of balls sweeping around. At least one struck Johnston immediately above the forehead and passed backward over the skull, without fracturing the brain.

Following Johnston's example, the troops rallied and drove the Indians away.

He also fought with distinction in the Mexican War, demonstrating again his penchant for stopping enemy bullets when he sustained five wounds. Appointed quartermaster general, Johnston resigned from the Union army shortly after the firing on Fort Sumter. He accepted a commission from Jefferson Davis as a senior general and was instrumental in the Confederacy's victory at the first battle of Bull Run.

Although his career in the new army had gotten off to a solid start, that changed quickly in August 1861. Jefferson Davis had named Johnston and four others to the rank of full general, including Albert Sidney Johnston, Samuel Cooper, Beauregard, and Lee. Joe Johnston was outraged to learn that he was in fourth place on the list and he expressed his displeasure in a letter to Davis, protesting this gross insult to his honor.

He pointed out that in the Union army he had outranked all the others; therefore, a position of primacy was his due. He went on to accuse Jefferson Davis of having tarnished his "fair fame as a soldier and a man, earned by more than thirty years of laborious and perilous service": "I had but this [and] the scars of many wounds, all honestly taken in my front and in the front of battle." He felt humiliated and degraded, and he reminded Davis that he had already demonstrated his importance in battle, while others, presumably referring to Lee, had not yet shown courage or competence in the field.

Davis was insulted in turn by the accusatory tone of Johnston's letter. His reply was cold. The animosity in their relationship thereafter was obvious, though a level of civility was maintained thanks to the efforts of their wives. Davis never forgave anyone he felt had slighted him. Nor did Johnston. Despite their personal feelings, however, they had to accept their responsibilities as the war continued.

Johnston was not again offered a command anywhere near Richmond. In November 1862, after sufficiently recovering from wounds received in the Peninsular campaign, he was sent to Tullahoma, Tennessee, to command the Department of the West. Far from the power and glory of the Army of Northern Virginia that he had briefly led, Johnston knew he had been shunted aside. He considered his assignment "a nominal one merely, and useless."

To complicate matters for Johnston, he did not share the view of Pemberton, his subordinate, concerning his mission at Vicksburg. When Johnston arrived at his Tennessee headquarters, he began bombarding Pemberton with dispatches ordering him to conduct campaigns against Grant's forces. This approach completely contradicted Davis's orders to Pemberton.

The president had instructed Pemberton to defend Vicksburg at all costs and not to jeopardize the city's safety by moving his troops away to do battle with Grant. But Johnston believed the army's goal was to destroy the enemy's forces, not to cling to territory that could always be recaptured. He told Pemberton to prepare to lead his soldiers out of Vicksburg to link up with other Confederate units, thus forming a force of sufficient size to defeat Grant. Pemberton found himself caught in the middle of the personal hostilities that existed between Johnston and Davis.

⤙⟦◎⟧⤚

GENERAL GRANT WAS not unduly concerned about the opposition he faced from Pemberton and Johnston. He was confident that he had sufficient men and resources to deal with whatever threat might come. His more immediate and pressing problems with the Vicksburg operation were caused by terrain and weather. He could not attack the city from the river because the rebel artillery on the heights was far stronger than it had been when Farragut passed it. Grant would have to approach over land.

His army would be moving from the north, from Memphis, and the extensive swamps provided a natural barrier against the passage of a large military force. Although it seemed to many an impossible task to move troops, artillery, and supply wagons through that terrain, Grant was determined to accomplish it.

Grant's men spent months trying to force their way through the marshes. First they tried shovels. The Mississippi coiled back and forth, forming loops and bends. If a canal could be dug to connect two lengths of the river, troops could be shipped downriver by boat without having to pass the city's defenses. But the digging failed. Torrential rains overflowed riverbanks and collapsed the canal walls. And the damp, unhealthy conditions spread pneumonia, typhoid, and dysentery among the men.

The newspapers seized the opportunity to mock Grant once again, depicting him with derision and scorn. Inevitably, speculation circulated freely that he had been drinking. A Cincinnati newsman called Grant a "jackass in the original package": "He is a poor drunken imbecile. He is a poor stick sober, and he is most of the time more than half drunk, and much of the time idiotically drunk." Lincoln stubbornly continued to stand by Grant, keeping him in command despite renewed entreaties to fire him.

With the collapse of the canal, dubbed "Grant's ditch" by the press, Grant set his men to dredging a channel north of Vicksburg for passage of the gunboats and transports. The troops carted out tons of viscous black mud and felled thick trees deep underwater to force a route through the swamp. M. Sgt. Charles Wilcox, of the 33rd Illinois Infantry, recorded their daily progress:

> Began to dig on the canal . . . every able-bodied man used a shovel or spade. Saw [engineers] sawing off stumps six feet under water. This is done with a cross-cut saw which is attached to a frame. The frame is sunk deep into the water as deep as it is wished to cut the stump off under water. . . . It is slow work, however, one such saw only cutting from ten to fifteen stumps, a foot in diameter, in ten hours.

This effort also failed. Grant's next plan was to send the gunboats and transports through the bayou, following the path of two long narrow abandoned barge canals. The expedition began 140 miles north of Vicksburg, where engineers blew a hole in a levee to provide water deep enough to float the boats through the maze.

But low-hanging branches of cypress and cottonwood trees snapped smokestacks and swept lifeboats overboard. Snakes and wildcats shaken loose from the trees fell on the decks, where they were attacked by vigilant sailors manning brooms. Rebel troops built barricades of downed trees and harassed the naval crews with gunfire day and night. The channels left no room for the boats to turn around. The two expedition commanders feared they would be trapped; one collapsed from nervous exhaustion.

A second expedition with Sherman's men also got stuck. The boats could no longer advance or turn around, and Confederate troops were fast converging on them. The infantry, in transports at the rear of the column, was ordered forward through waist-deep water to beat back the rebels.

Grant justified the early attempts to traverse the swamp as a way of keeping the soldiers from getting bored during the rainy season. It was to enhance morale, he wrote, because soldiers needed to be kept busy. He described the maneuvers as "a series of experiments to consume time, and to divert the attention of the enemy, of my troops and of the public generally. I, myself, never felt great confidence that any of the experiments resorted to would prove successful." He was right.

The rains finally stopped in April and Grant proceeded with what he claimed had always been his real plan. He intended to march most of his army down the west bank of the river on the Louisiana side to a point well below Vicksburg. (The heavy rains had prevented them from doing so sooner because the bank had flooded.) Once the troops assembled south of Vicksburg, they would cross the river and head inland, approaching the city on firm, dry land from the east.

The only problem was getting the army across the mile-wide, fast-flowing Mississippi. Grant's solution was simple. Adm. David Porter would take his fleet of gunboats and transports downriver past Vicksburg's guns. The transports would carry supplies to the waiting army and then ferry the soldiers to the other side.

Porter immediately agreed to try. However, he warned Grant that if the ships did get past Vicksburg safely, they could not return upriver. Because the boats had insufficient power to counter the swift current, they would be unable to travel upriver fast enough to avoid the Confederate artillery. Many more rebel guns were trained on the river now than when Farragut had come the previous summer.

The operation was a gamble. The entire Northern fleet could be destroyed, and with the exception of Rawlins, everyone on Grant's staff argued against the plan. Even the loyal Sherman disapproved. In a long letter to Grant he described the idea as the riskiest of any war anywhere. Charles Dana also opposed it. The political general, McClernand, supported it, but he was the man in whom Grant had the least confidence.

Grant refused to budge. While the preparations were underway, the people of Vicksburg remained convinced that they were no longer in danger. They had heard how the Yankee boats got stuck in the bayous, and they knew that the Union troops were no longer digging uselessly through the swamps. On April 11, Pemberton notified Joe Johnston that Grant was giving up the campaign and returning to Memphis.

On April 16, the *Vicksburg Whig* newspaper reported that the Union troops were completely demoralized. Readers were assured there was no immediate threat to the city. In celebration, Vicksburg society chose that night to host a grand ball. The Confederate officers in town were all invited. No one knew that General Grant had chosen that same night to send his ships down the river.

--→=◦⊂=←--

GRANT WATCHED THE battle from his chair on the upper deck of the riverboat *Magnolia*, his headquarters ship. Julia and their twelve-year-old son, Fred, sat at his side. Ulysses Junior, age ten, perched in the lap of a staff officer. It was ten o'clock on the night of April 16, 1863, time to find out whether Grant's gamble would pay off. If Grant was apprehensive, no one around him noticed. He sat quietly, smoking and holding Julia's hand, as calmly as if they were awaiting the annual Fourth of July fireworks display.

The *Magnolia* was anchored just beyond the range of the rebel guns, surrounded by a flotilla of more than two dozen skiffs, yawls, and tugboats from which other Union officers and their wives had assembled to view the excitement. They stared at the lights of the city high up on the bluffs. Admiral Porter aboard his flagship headed a single-file column of eight heavily armored gunboats. Three transports fully loaded with supplies followed. The boats were strung out at fifty-yard intervals.

The fleet boasted a total of seventy guns. Defenses against small-arms fire included logs and wet hay bales packed tightly around exposed wheelhouses and boilers. Barges heaped with coal were lashed to the sides of the gunboats. All the big guns were trained on the lights of the city.

Some time between 11:30 and midnight—accounts are not clear on the precise time—the Confederate lookouts spotted the Yankee fleet. The first to see the dark shapes bearing down on them were the nightly pickets patrolling the river in rowboats. A few of the men made for shore to raise the alarm for the city. The rest dashed for the opposite shore, the Louisiana side, to set afire several abandoned houses, the railroad station, and stacks of wood soaked in pitch. The fire blazed up quickly, the bright flames clearly illuminating each Yankee ship as it passed by.

A signal flare arced high above the river as Vicksburg's gunners commenced the attack. Cannon roared from the bluffs. Porter's sailors instantly returned fire. The hillsides and the river itself seemed to be ablaze. Shells whistled, and explosions ripped the night. Many witnesses recalled that the battle dwarfed any Independence Day fireworks they had ever seen.

Grant watched it all calmly, holding Julia's hand and smoking his cigar. In his memoirs he wrote, "The sight was magnificent, but terrible." It was much too terrible for young Ulysses who shut his eyes and buried his face in the chest of the colonel on whose lap he sat. Grant ordered the boy taken to his cabin.

A shell hit Porter's flagship, slicing through armor plate and forty inches of oak, wounding one man and chopping the leg off another. The gunboat crews cut loose the coal barges so they could maneuver better and gain a few precious knots of speed. Behind them, the army transports bearing their volunteer crews of soldiers spun about in the current. Some tried to retreat but an old captured Confederate gunboat bringing up the rear got them back in line and on course. A transport loaded with cotton bales and forage was hit and set afire. The crew abandoned ship. Sailors on other boats remember hearing a tremendous cheer from rebel artillerymen, who believed they had hit a gunboat.

The firing put a quick end to Vicksburg's celebration ball. One young woman dancing with a general when the first shells exploded asked where they should go. The officer urged her to leave the city as fast as she could run. The women guests fled through the darkness, dropping to the ground every time they heard gunfire. Their gowns were torn and muddied, the heels of their shoes broken. They ran inland for a mile until they found a house where the owners would take them in.

Mary Loughborough had arrived in Vicksburg the day before to visit friends. She had traveled from Jackson, forty miles to the east. Too tired to attend the ball, she was asleep when the battle began. Then she awoke and went out onto the verandah.

> The river was illuminated by large fires on the bank and we could discern plainly the huge black masses floating down with the current, now and then belching forth fire from their sides, followed by loud reports, and we could hear the shells exploding in the upper part of town. . . .
>
> We could hear the gallop, in the darkness, of couriers upon the paved streets; we could hear the voices of the soldiers on the riverside. The rapid firing of the boats, the roar of the Confederate batteries, and above all, the screaming, booming sound of the shells as they exploded in the air and around the city, made at once a new and fearful scene to me.

To all those watching the battle, on both sides, it appeared that the Union ships were doomed. Aboard the *Magnolia*, Annie Wittenmyer, a nurse, talked with Julia Grant. "'Our men are all dead men.' 'No one can live in such a rain of fire and lead,' we said to each other."

They were wrong. After an hour and a half, the Union ships, except for the one abandoned transport, passed safely through Vicksburg. Every ship had sustained damage but all remained seaworthy. Only a handful of casualties could be counted among the crews—a dozen sailors wounded and none killed. So far Grant's gamble had worked. His army and navy were below Vicksburg. It was time to take the next big chance.

—⸱≡◦⸱—

PEMBERTON'S FORCES, AND all of Vicksburg, were chagrined and disappointed to see most of the Yankee ships slip by their formidable guns. Some wondered aloud whether the city was as impregnable as everyone had been saying. With the Union fleet to their south, they were concerned that goods and supplies shipped from that direction would be cut off. The flow had already been restricted by the capture of New Orleans.

Still, a 240-mile stretch of the river below Vicksburg had remained open to the Confederates after New Orleans fell. There, the vital Red River flowed into the Mississippi, allowing the shipment of pork and beef, flour, salt, and sugar from Texas and Louisiana. There would be no more deliveries now that Union gunboats controlled the river. The railroad line east to Jackson remained the only source of supply. If that were disrupted, the city would be cut off.

Newlywed Dora Miller, who with her lawyer husband was among the few Unionists in town, worried about the future. "I never understood before the full force of those questions—What shall we eat . . . and wherewithal shall we be clothed?"

General Pemberton had a more immediate concern. What would be Grant's next move? At first, it seemed obvious: the Union army would march directly north to Vicksburg. Pemberton was determined to be prepared. He moved troops south of the city, ordering them to dig in and hold the line. However, Grant had a different idea. He was not heading for Vicksburg yet. He planned to move on Jackson so he could sever the railroad line that connected Vicksburg to the rest of the Confederacy.

Grant had learned that Joe Johnston in Tennessee was trying to organize an army in Jackson. Grant had to prevent that force from gathering strength. If he ignored it, he might suddenly find a large rebel army on his rear or his flank when he began his attack on Vicksburg.

In the meantime, his objective was to confuse Pemberton so he would not know for certain where an attack might come from. To this end, Grant sent seventeen hundred cavalrymen on a marauding expedition through Confederate territory east of Vicksburg. On April 17, Col. Benjamin Grierson's cavalry headed south from Tennessee. Ironically, Grierson, a former music teacher, had hated horses since childhood and still bore the scar from when one had kicked him in the head. But his troopers made a daring sweep over six hundred miles of territory, tearing up railroad track, burning trains and depots, and causing havoc among the civilians.

At the same time, Grant ordered Sherman to make a diversionary feint toward Haines' Bluff, some thirty miles north of Vicksburg. Sherman off-loaded his men from their transports and marched them through a forest out of sight of the rebels. Once in the woods they circled back, reboarded the transports and landed again. And again. The Confederate commander counted ten Yankee regiments coming ashore. Then he counted ten more. And ten more after that! There seemed no limit to the supply of Yankees. He sent an urgent dispatch to Pemberton pleading for reinforcements.

Pemberton did not know for certain which was the greatest danger, Grant to the south, Sherman to the north, or Grierson to the east. He dispatched troops in one direction, changed his mind, and sent them elsewhere. The result was chaos. The troops marched back and forth in such frenzy that many collapsed, unable to keep pace. Vicksburg's residents rushed out in their carriages to aid the exhausted soldiers, driving them on to Haines' Bluff. By the time they got there, Sherman was gone.

By April 30, Grant had part of his army, twenty-three thousand men, across the Mississippi and ready to head inland. The next day he contacted Sherman's force and the other units that had remained north of Vicksburg, ordering them to come south and cross the river. These new units would give Grant a total of forty thousand men. Pemberton had thirty thousand troops, but they had been scattered, trying to cover all the threats he thought he faced. In reality, there was only one significant threat and that was Grant's force—and Grant was headed for Jackson.

Grant knew he had to cover that distance quickly, before Joe Johnston could assemble a force against him. Because he had no time to waste, Grant deliberately cut himself off from his base of supply, forcing the men to live on the countryside. This risky move violated a basic rule of war as taught at West Point: an army had to stay linked to its supply base.

Grant expected Halleck to object to his unorthodox plan and knew that he would probably forbid Grant to proceed. Grant had to act before Halleck had time to protest. In his memoirs Grant recalled,

> I knew well that Halleck's caution would lead him to disapprove of this course, but it was the only one that gave any chance of success. The time it would take to communicate to Washington and get a reply would be so great that I could not be interfered with until it was demonstrated whether my plan was practicable.

Grant would already have succeeded, or failed, by the time Halleck would ever have a chance to stop him.

Sherman thought the plan was madness and told Grant so. How could he expect forty thousand men on a fast march to be supplied with food, ammunition, and other necessities of war? Grant's answer was that they would find all the food they needed in enemy territory. They would simply take it from the rebels.[2]

---

[2] Two years later Sherman adopted the same tactic—living off the land—in his march through Georgia and South Carolina.

And he was right. There was plenty of food. The men consumed great quantities of ham, chicken, corn and other vegetables, milk, and honey. Their own quartermaster had never fed them so well. Some Union soldiers were not averse to liberating a Southern family's silver or valuables, and their officers did nothing to stop them. One angry plantation owner astride a mule confronted a Union officer, complaining that the general's troops had taken everything he owned. The general replied that surely they could not have been *his* men. If they had, they would not have let the man keep his mule.

The only item Grant's army carried with it was ammunition. To transport the bullets, shells, and gunpowder, the soldiers requisitioned every wheeled vehicle they could find. They gathered an assemblage of fine carriages, buckboards, surreys, stagecoaches, and wagons drawn by horses, mules, and oxen.

There was whiskey available, too, some of which Grant discovered on the night of May 12. Neither Rawlins nor Charles Dana was with him, which was probably why he took the risk of drinking. Around midnight, Grant visited the tent of Col. William Duff, his artillery commander. Grant said he was tired and asked for some whiskey. Duff handed the general his canteen, from which Grant filled his standard-issue tin cup and drained it. Three times.

Present in Duff's tent at the time was Sylvanus Cadwallader, the *Chicago Times* reporter and the only newsman Grant trusted. When Grant left, Colonel Duff pledged the reporter to secrecy. Cadwallader noted the next morning that Grant was sharp and alert, showing no ill effects from the drink.

The army moved rapidly, easily brushing aside small detachments of Pemberton's men that crossed its path. The Confederates were growing desperate. Secretary of War Seddon ordered the still-convalescent Joe Johnston up from Alabama to personally take charge in Jackson. Wounded or not, he would have to stop Grant.

Johnston wired back to Seddon: "I shall go immediately, although unfit for field-service." It took Johnston four days to make the trip.

When he arrived on May 13 he was so exhausted that he took to his bed at the Bowman House, Jackson's finest hotel. Later, after being briefed on the military situation, he telegraphed to Richmond that Grant's army was already on the move between Jackson and Vicksburg. "I am too late," Johnston concluded.

But Johnston felt compelled to take some action. He wrote a dispatch to Pemberton, sending copies by three different riders in the hope that at least one would get through. Johnston advised Pemberton to combine his troops with Johnston's; the conjoined force could then attack Grant. He told him that if Pemberton could impose a force between Grant's army and the Mississippi, then the Yankees would be forced to fall back for lack of supplies. He did not know that Grant had no supply line. Nor did he know that one of his couriers was a Union spy who took his dispatch directly to Grant.

The next day, Pemberton received conflicting orders from Jefferson Davis and Secretary of War Seddon, who expected him to hold Vicksburg, and from General Johnston, who expected him to lead his men out of the city and attack the Yankees. Pemberton wanted Johnston to come to his aid and help him defend the city, but Johnston was asking Pemberton to come to him instead, some forty miles away, leaving the city defenseless.

Pemberton refused to abandon Vicksburg. He fashioned a compromise. He would leave some of his troops to defend the city and lead the rest about fifteen miles east and dig in, thus forcing Grant to attack him with an army that had no supply base. Johnston would be on his own in Jackson, where he had only six thousand troops to defend the capital city.

Grant captured Jackson on May 14, the day after Joe Johnston arrived. When Grant and his staff rode into town, they were directed to the Bowman House and Grant was given the same room Johnston had occupied the night before. The citizens of Jackson were outraged to see the Union flag hoisted atop the capitol. They blamed Pemberton for their fate and accused him of selling out the state of Mississippi to the Yankees. After all, he was one of them. No one blamed Johnston, even though he was the senior Confederate officer and had left the city before it fell. The people considered Johnston to be blameless; he was from Virginia.

Some people who had gone home to Jackson after visiting Vicksburg the night the Union gunboats passed through decided to return to Vicksburg where they would presumably be safe. Mary Loughborough wrote in her diary, "Ah! Vicksburg, our city of refuge. Yet, is there any place where one is perfectly safe in these terrible times?"

Jackson was burned to the ground that night. Grant and Sherman had strolled around town in the afternoon, noting much that was vital to the Confederate war effort: there was the railroad with its tracks, depots, freight yards, and standing trains; along with foundries, machine shops, warehouses, factories of various kinds, and arsenals.

They visited a textile mill and found women at work making gray cloth for Confederate uniforms. At Grant's suggestion, Sherman told the women to shut down their looms, take as much fabric as they could carry for their own use, and go home. Minutes later, the mill was ablaze. Leaving Sherman's men to complete the destruction and serve as a rear guard, Grant headed west toward Vicksburg and what he hoped would be a decisive battle with Pemberton.

The two armies met on the morning of May 16 at Champion's Hill, fifteen miles from Vicksburg. Pemberton had twenty-three thousand men assembled on the 140-foot high, heavily wooded hill. Grant attacked with a superior force of thirty-two thousand. When the battle ended five hours later, Grant had sustained twenty-four hundred casualties and Pemberton thirty-eight hundred. Pemberton's forces were in full retreat. The city appeared to be Grant's for the taking.

It had been just two days since Robert E. Lee in Richmond had persuaded Jefferson Davis and his advisers to support a planned invasion of the North rather than send troops to save Vicksburg. Now the city was cut off and surrounded, with Grant's large victorious army bearing down.

Emma Balfour, a forty-five-year-old resident of Vicksburg, spoke for many as she wrote in her diary. "Oh, will God forsake us now?"

CHAPTER 5

HOW VERY SAD THIS LIFE

May 17, 1863

MARY LOUGHBOROUGH SAW the beaten Confederate troops as they filed into Vicksburg after the defeat at Champion Hill. On her way back from church she had heard the unmistakable sound of cannon fire east of the city. She stopped an officer to ask what was going on. His answer stunned her. Pemberton had been beaten. The army was in full retreat. By evening, the Yankees could be in the city with no forces left to stop them.

Before long the first soldiers ambled down the street. These were the skulkers, the deserters, the men who had thrown away their weapons and abandoned their units and their friends. They slouched, fear and shame etched on dirty gaunt faces. Most would eventually reclaim their pride and return to their duties; but on that bright Sunday morning, they no longer had the will to fight.

Another disorderly column passed Mary. Other women emerged from their houses to join her and to stare, to speculate on the fate of Vicksburg and to cast blame.

"Where on earth are you going?" one woman shouted.

"We are running," a soldier said.

"From whom?"

"The Feds, to be sure."

"Shame on you!" the women cried.

"It's all Pem's fault," another insisted, trying to shift the shame of defeat to their Northern-born commander.

"It's all your own fault," a woman replied. "Why don't you stand your ground? Shame on you all."

By the afternoon, the remnants of regiments, brigades, and divisions had reached the city. The men seemed stunned and scared. They did not know where to go or what might be their fate. Would they be declared prisoners before the day was out or be ordered to stand and fight? Was there still a chance they might escape the Yankee encirclement?

Emma Balfour watched the defeated army. She wrote:

> I hope never to witness again such a scene as the return of our routed army. As the poor fellows passed, every house poured forth all it had to refresh them. . . . It made my heart ache to see them, for I knew from all I saw and heard that it was want of confidence in the general commanding that was the cause of our disaster.

Pemberton could not overcome the curse of his Northern birth. It was inevitable that he would be cursed as the cause of the catastrophe. The men had fought as bravely as soldiers anywhere: they were Southerners, after all. The rumors quickly spread that Pemberton had been paid a huge sum of greenbacks to turn over Vicksburg.

Dora Miller, a Unionist who longed for the Confederacy's defeat, nevertheless felt immense sympathy for the beaten soldiers who passed by her house. She recalled:

> Wan, hollow-eyed, ragged, footsore, bloody, the men limped along unarmed, but followed by siege-guns, ambulances, gun carriages, and wagons in aimless confusion. At twilight two or three bands began

playing "Dixie," "Bonnie Blue Flag," and so on, and drums began to beat all about; I suppose they were rallying the scattered army.

She was correct. By evening, order was being salvaged out of chaos. Men who had known the shame of retreat were being reorganized and reequipped to join the line being formed in an arc around the city's eastern rim. And though some broken, demoralized units continued to move west through the city, fleeing the advancing Union forces, fresh troops from north and south of Vicksburg were heading east to take up defensive positions. By nightfall, many citizens had been reassured that the Yankees might not be marching into town unopposed after all.

Throughout the night and into the next day, ambulances and wagons rumbled down the streets, bearing the dead and wounded from Champion Hill. The sad convoys left trails of blood behind them. After them came refugees from the territory being overrun by Grant's troops. Poor and rich, overseers and slaves, plantation owners and their families trekked into the city, swelling the population. Some rode in wagons and carriages full of possessions; others shuffled along with only what they could carry on their backs. All would mean more mouths to feed in the coming weeks.

But by the next day the Yankees had not arrived, and a procession of a different sort wound its way along the city's streets. Rearguard troops had been ordered to round up whatever they could find from the surrounding countryside to sustain a city under siege. What could not be transported had to be destroyed so it would not be left for the enemy. Confederate soldiers filled wagons with chickens, turkeys, corn, rice, sugar, hams, and bacon, and headed for town. Others rounded up cows, pigs, sheep, and mules and herded them all to Vicksburg. Emma Balfour wrote:

From twelve o'clock until late in the night the streets and roads were *jammed* with wagons, cannon, horses, men, mules, stock, sheep, everything you can imagine that appertains to an army—being brought hurriedly within the entrenchment.

It looked to some residents as if enough supplies were being hauled in to last for months, but in reality there would be only enough food for six weeks.

The soldiers taking up defensive positions were told to shoot sparingly. Bullets and shells were in short supply and not to be wasted. But although ammunition was scarce, few believed the siege would last long—Joe Johnston and his army were no more than fifty miles away. The defeated troops were rallying, and everyone had faith in Vicksburg's impregnability.

⟶≡⊙≡⟵

THE UNION ARMY had been delayed by the Big Black River, ten miles east of Vicksburg. Pemberton's men were well entrenched on the river's west bank facing the planked railroad bridge. To attempt a crossing would be suicidal, so General Grant decided to wait while Sherman and his three divisions crossed five miles upstream to outflank Pemberton.

One of McClernand's brigade commanders grew tired of waiting. On his own initiative, he ordered his men through the waist-deep bayous above and below the bridge to charge the rebels. They took 199 casualties but broke the Confederate line. Pemberton withdrew and ordered the bridge destroyed to delay the main Union army from crossing. Since no wagons or artillery could traverse the swamp, a new bridge would have to be constructed. When Grant sized up the situation, he ordered three bridges to be put in place as quickly as possible so that the three corps could cross simultaneously. His plan was to advance on Vicksburg with a three-pronged assault.

The troops took advantage of the materials at hand to span the Big Black River. Some used bales of cotton for pontoons, with lumber stolen from houses, fences, and cotton gins to lay the roadway. Others felled trees on the riverbanks, which landed with their branches intertwined, providing support for planks laid across them. Sherman's men had India-rubber boats to use as pontoons, linked by planks of wood.

Sherman encountered some of his men drawing water from a well near a small log dwelling. The house had been vandalized and its contents were strewn about the yard. Sherman was unconcerned about the depredations committed by his men. His attention was on the well; he was thirsty. He recalled:

> I rode in to get a drink, and, seeing a book on the ground, asked some soldier to hand it to me. It was a volume of the Constitution of the United States, and on the title-page was written the name of Jefferson Davis. On inquiry of a Negro, I learned that the place belonged to the then President of the Southern Confederation.

On the night of May 18, Sherman's men started across one of the new bridges. Sherman wrote:

> After dark, the whole scene was lit up with fires of pitch-pine. General Grant joined me there, as we sat on a log, looking at the passage of the troops by the lights of those fires; the bridge swayed to and fro under the passing feet, and made a fine war-picture.

The next day, Grant's entire army moved on, three columns advancing inexorably, destroying everything in its path. The drums beat, the bands played, and the men marched smartly, knowing they would be victorious. Tomorrow or perhaps the day after, they would make history and be another battle closer to the end of the war—and to returning home.

⊷⟞⟝⊶

GENERAL PEMBERTON GREW increasingly depressed as he neared Vicksburg. He rode in silence with his chief engineering officer, Maj.

Samuel Lockett, who thought it best not to intrude on his commanding officer's brooding silence. Finally Pemberton said, "Just thirty years ago I began my military career by receiving my appointment to a cadetship at the U.S. Military Academy, and today, the same date, that career is ended in disaster and disgrace."

Lockett tried to be encouraging. He pointed out that the situation was not as bad as it might seem. Two fresh divisions had been held back, ready to occupy the entrenchments Lockett himself had designed. The retreating, demoralized units could be reorganized. Lockett reminded Pemberton how important Vicksburg was to the Confederacy. Jefferson Davis had insisted that the city be held. Lockett noted that Davis had promised to send help if Vicksburg were ever besieged.

But Pemberton was not persuaded or heartened by Lockett's arguments. He said he did not believe his troops would be able to withstand an attack by the Union army. His mood was further dampened by a dispatch from Joe Johnston. Pemberton had warned Johnston the day before that if he could not hold his position on the Big Black River, then he would have to abandon Haines' Bluff. And if Haines' Bluff were taken (which it was by Sherman on the morning of May 18) there would be no passage in or out of Vicksburg. Any relief force Johnston sent would have to fight its way through the Union encirclement. The capture of Haines' Bluff would also give Grant a supply base on a river that flowed into the Mississippi. Johnston's reply to Pemberton's assessment of the situation came as a shock.

If Haines' Bluff is untenable, Vicksburg is of no value and cannot be held. If, therefore, you are invested in Vicksburg, you must ultimately surrender. Under such circumstances, instead of losing both troops and place, we must, if possible, save the troops. If it is not too late, evacuate Vicksburg and its dependencies, and march to the northeast.

But it was too late. With Haines' Bluff in Union hands, the only option was for the army to fight its way out. And even if there were an escape route, Pemberton could not abandon the city that Jefferson Davis had ordered him to defend, regardless of the cost.

Once Pemberton returned and saw that his two fresh divisions occupied the strong entrenchments, he became convinced that he could save the city. To abandon it would mean ceding control of the Mississippi River and cutting the Confederacy in two. He was determined not to be responsible for that fate.

He summoned his generals, apprised them of Johnston's dispatch, and asked whether they considered it possible to follow Johnston's order to evacuate the army. Their answers were unanimous. The troops could not fight their way out through the rapidly tightening Yankee noose without abandoning all artillery and supplies. In addition, even if the army should succeed, it would incur such high casualties and damage to morale as to render it ineffective as a fighting unit. Pemberton made his decision. He notified Johnston:

I have decided to hold Vicksburg as long as is possible, with the firm hope that the Government may yet be able to assist me in keeping this obstruction to the enemy's free navigation of the Mississippi River. I still conceive it to be the most important point in the Confederacy.

⊸⊱══⊰⊶

TOGETHER, GRANT AND Sherman rode the last few miles to Vicksburg. Ulysses S. Grant was confident of victory. He knew he had fought one of the greatest campaigns of the war. In only seventeen days he had marched his army 180 miles through enemy territory, cut off from his base of supplies. On the face of it, such an act appeared doomed to failure, but Grant had succeeded beyond all expectations. His troops had won five battles, killing or wounding more than seven thousand enemy troops; the cost was forty-three hundred casualties of their own. And now Grant faced what was surely a defeated, demoralized army fleeing in disarray. How could they stop him?

Grant had every right to feel pride in his accomplishment and for the major victory apparently within his grasp. In time he would receive many accolades for the Vicksburg campaign, but none meant more than the words of Sherman as they neared the city. As Grant recalled it,

[Sherman] turned to me, saying that up to this minute he had felt no positive assurance of success. This, however, was the end of one of the greatest campaigns in history, and I ought to make a report of it at once. Vicksburg was not yet captured, and there was no telling what might happen before it was taken; but whether captured or not, this was a complete and successful campaign.

Grant planned to crown this success by capturing the city immediately. He pressed his troops forward, expecting Vicksburg to be his by the following day. He did not yet realize the extent of the Confederate fortifications, nor the determination of Pemberton's fresh troops to hold them.

The terrain alone was forbidding. Grant later conceded,

The ground about Vicksburg is admirable for defense. On the north it is about two hundred feet above the Mississippi River at the highest point, and very much cut up by the washing rains; the ravines were grown up with cane and underbrush, while the sides and tops were covered with a dense forest. Farther south the ground flattens out somewhat, and was in cultivation. But here, too, it was cut by ravines and small streams.

The line of fortifications constructed by Major Lockett followed the crest of a long ridge for eight miles. It began north of the city at the river's edge, formed a semicircle three miles distant from the city proper, and ended south of the city at the river. All along the line, ragged, rugged fissures and ravines defaced the ground.

Lockett had erected substantial forts to provide cover for each of the six roads leading to Vicksburg from the east, as well as for the railroad line. Smaller forts and gun batteries were sited at strategic points. In front of each fort, soldiers had dug ditches eight feet deep and fourteen feet wide, potential killing grounds covered by overlapping fields of fire. All trees and structures that might provide shelter for the enemy were cleared in front of the defenses. In addition, firing points along the line were connected by rifle pits and trenches, allowing men to move unseen from one position to another.

Pemberton's defense force numbered thirty-one thousand. Although Grant would eventually have three times as many, he would be forced to place some of his troops facing east to repulse an expected attack from Johnston. Also, Pemberton's men were well protected for a battle, whereas Grant's troops would be out in the open.

The Confederates had 102 cannon, but it seemed like more to the Union soldiers. The rebels had mounted logs painted black, disguised to look like artillery pieces. Dubbed "Quaker guns," they fooled many a soldier.

Vicksburg's defensive line would be tough to breach, a fact that became increasingly obvious to Grant's men, the closer they came to the city. One Union officer described the sight:

A long line of high, rugged, irregular bluffs, clearly cut against the sky, crowned with cannon which peered ominously from embrasures to the right and left as far as the eye could see. Lines of heavy rifle-pits, surmounted with head logs, ran along the bluffs, connecting fort with fort, and filled with veteran infantry. In front, on the slopes, was a tangle of fallen timber, tree-tops interlaced to make an almost impenetrable abatis. . . . The approaches to this position were fright-ful—enough to appall the stoutest heart.

The sight was not threatening enough to cause Grant to call off the attack. Convinced that the Southerners were so demoralized by their recent defeats that they would not put up much of a fight, he ordered the assault to begin at two o'clock on the afternoon of May 19.

The attack failed. Union troops charged toward the ridge, yelling and cheering, confident of victory. The Confederate line exploded in a firestorm of bullets and shells, cutting the Yankees down. Some soldiers pushed on to the base of the fortified ridgeline and started climbing the slopes against the hail of fire. And that was as far as most of them got before going to ground, searching for concealment while rebel bullets whizzed over their heads.

"My troops reached the top of the parapet," Sherman reported, "but could not cross over. The rebel parapets were strongly manned, and the enemy fought hard and well. My loss was pretty heavy."

Mary Loughborough and several other women watched from the verandahs of their homes. Some climbed to the balcony that encircled the cupola of the courthouse, but all they could see were rising clouds of dense smoke. They waited throughout the afternoon, watching and listening to the sounds of battle.

Many Union soldiers were trapped in the ravines. Those who tried to withdraw were cut down. They remained under enemy fire until darkness, when they could return to their base. The operation was costly; Grant lost 942 men. The Confederates, enjoying the defender's advantage, lost fewer than 200.

Pemberton was as surprised as the Northerners were by the day's events. He sent a dispatch to Jefferson Davis announcing that the outcome of the Yankee attack had boosted the morale of Vicksburg's defenders considerably. One young woman, Lida Lord, observed that "Men who had been gloomy, depressed, and distrustful now cheerfully and bravely looked the future in the face. After that day's victory . . . one spirit seemed to animate the whole army, the determination never to give up."

Pemberton put his troops to work strengthening the defenses. The men had to improvise because of a shortage of shovels, but they fashioned tools out of wood and used bayonets for picks. They had taken a measure of revenge and it was sweeter for having been so long in coming.

Three days later Grant ordered an all-out attack to commence at ten o'clock on the morning of May 22. The assault would be preceded by a continuous mortar bombardment from the fleet beginning the night before. At dawn, all two hundred of Grant's artillery pieces would join in. After such a pounding, little enemy resistance was expected.

But among those making the assault, views differed. Many were not so sanguine about the outcome. Sgt. Charles Wilcox of the Thirty-third Illinois Regiment noticed that his officers looked "sad when talking of these orders, and are opposed to them." As for himself, Wilcox wrote, "my heart is much depressed when meditating upon our duty for the morrow. The men don't want to charge and yet they say they will do it when ordered."

At precisely 10:00 A.M., all three corps advanced toward the enemy line. They did not get far. The Union's artillery bombardment had generated a lot of noise and rearranged a lot of dirt, but it had not caused many casualties or lessened the defenders' determination to repulse the Yankee assault. Sherman watched from two hundred yards away.

> I could see every thing. The rebel line, concealed by the parapet, showed no sign of unusual activity, but as our troops came in fair view, the enemy rose behind their parapet and poured a furious fire upon our lines; and, for about two hours, we had a severe and bloody battle, but at every point we were repulsed.

The men were pinned down at the base of the ridgeline as they had been during the first attack, unable to advance or retreat without being cut down. A twenty-one-year-old private, Isaac Jackson of the Eighty-third Ohio Infantry, recalled:

It was the hottest place for men to be in that I ever seen. Our men get right up to the fort, some get in the ditch. The rebels dare not poke their heads up to shoot so they hold up their guns and pull their triggers. Sometimes they get their hands shot off. . . . Our boys could throw crackers over in the fort, so close they were.

But that was as close as they got. Then they were forced to hug the ground while bullets churned the earth around them, waiting for sundown and the chance to escape. Sergeant Wilcox's outfit took shelter in a rutted wagon road.

We lay there about eight minutes and yet it seemed an age to me for showers of bullets and grape were passing over me and not a foot above me, and on my right and left were my comrades dying and dead as well as living. What an awful eight minutes that was.

All along the line the Union soldiers could make no breakthroughs, though General McClernand claimed that his men had seized a rebel parapet. He sent an urgent message to Grant insisting that he was now in position to break through the line and capture the city, if only Sherman and James McPherson, the other corps commanders, would order their men to renew the attack in their sectors. "I don't believe a word of it," Grant said.

Sherman considered McClernand's dispatch and urged Grant to press the attack, if only for political reasons. How would it look, Sherman argued, if McClernand told the press that he would have won the battle for Vicksburg had not Grant refused his request for support? Reluctantly, Grant agreed and ordered the men forward, knowing they had little chance of succeeding.

The troops renewed the charge. Some reached the rim of the rebel parapets but no one came back. Grant watched his men die atop the awful ridge. He saw the dirt turn red with their blood. And it was all for nothing, a useless sacrifice. As Grant suspected, McClernand had lied. The reporter Sylvanus Cadwallader was a witness. He later told Grant and Rawlins that McClernand had never taken a rebel parapet and that the few of McClernand's soldiers who had actually reached the crest of the ridge had been shot or taken prisoner. Cadwallader vowed he would never forget the "fearful burst of indignation from Rawlins, and the grim glowering look of disappointment and disgust which settled on Grant's usually placid countenance, when he was convinced of McClernand's duplicity, and realized its cost in dead and wounded."

Grant vowed to get rid of the politically well-connected McClernand as soon as he had something substantial, in writing, on which to base his action. Not long after, McClernand handed Grant all the damaging evidence he needed. McClernand wrote an address to his troops, praising their courage in the assault. He disparaged the inaction of the other corps commanders, Sherman and McPherson, implying that they had deprived McClernand's men of their rightful victory.

That was McClernand's first mistake. His second was to send copies of his remarks to the newspapers in direct violation of War Department policy that forbade the publication of official army reports. The penalty was dismissal, which Grant was only too happy to implement.

The cost of the second failed Union attack was high, more than three thousand dead, wounded, and missing in action. The Confederates lost fewer than five hundred. Grant later confessed that he regretted only two decisions he made during the war. One was the charge against a heavily fortified line at Cold Harbor on June 3, 1864, which brought seven thousand casualties and no victory. The other was the second assault on Vicksburg. But he had learned his lesson about trying to storm the rebel line at Vicksburg. He knew now that it could not be done. "I now determined upon a regular siege," he wrote, "to 'out-camp the enemy,' as it were, and to incur no more losses."

THE MOOD MAY have been grim at Grant's headquarters, but it was downright funereal at the camp of Gen. Joe Johnston north of Jackson, Mississippi. He had assembled eleven thousand troops, sixteen cannon, and one fork.

A British visitor to the Confederate front, twenty-eight-year-old Lt. Col. Arthur James Lyon Fremantle of the Coldstream Guards, had made his way to Johnston's headquarters just prior to Grant's second assault on Vicksburg. Fremantle reported that Johnston

lives very plainly, and at present his only cooking utensils consisted of an old coffeepot and fryingpan—both very inferior articles. There was only one fork (one prong deficient) between himself and his staff, and this was handed to me, ceremoniously, as the "guest."

Fremantle found Johnston and his staff pessimistic about Vicksburg's future and quite suspicious of Pemberton.

I now heard everyone speaking of the fall of Vicksburg as very possible and its jeopardy was laid at the door of General Pemberton, for whom no language could be too strong. He was freely called a coward and a traitor. He has the misfortune to be a Northerner by birth, which was against him in the opinion of all here.

Johnston would soon receive reinforcements, enlarging his command to twenty-five thousand, but he told Fremantle that would still not be a force of sufficient size to attempt to save Vicksburg. Johnston seemed vague about just how large a force he would need before he could mount an attack on the Union army, and he was equally noncommittal with Pemberton about when he might be given relief. Messages took days to pass between the two commanders; they had to be smuggled through the Union lines.

Pemberton reported to Johnston on his successful repulse of Grant's first attack, but he emphasized that his troops were short of ammunition and urgently needed assistance from Johnston. "Am I to expect reinforcements?" Pemberton wrote. "From what direction and how soon? Can you send me musket-caps by courier? . . . The men credit and are encouraged by a report that you are near with a large force. They are fighting in good spirits."

After Grant's second assault on the city, Johnston hinted to Pemberton that his troops at Vicksburg might be relieved. Johnston told him to hold on; help was coming. "You may depend on my holding the place as long as possible," Pemberton replied.

Nine days later, having received no further communication, Pemberton wrote again to Johnston. "When may I expect you to move, and in what direction?" And three days later: "I am waiting most anxiously to know your intentions. . . . I shall endeavor to hold out as long as we have anything to eat." Johnston did not reply.

⋆⟿◉⟾⋆

IN THE WAR Department's telegraph room in Washington, Abraham Lincoln was waiting for a reply from General Grant. The last message was dated May 11, a cryptic telegram notifying the president that "you may not hear from me for several days." Two weeks had passed and Lincoln had no idea where Grant's forces were. The president had wired other commanders in the western regions but no one had any news about Grant.

Then on May 24, a telegraph operator received an astonishing communication. He wrote in his log,

> I have just finished copying, and having delivered to the Secretary of War, the dispatch telling us of the capture of Vicksburg. The President, Secretary Seward, Senator Doolittle, and Judge Whiting have just come in and are all talking so loudly I can hardly write.

The president was ecstatic, but the news turned out to be false. Whether a deliberate hoax or wishful thinking on someone's part remains unknown. The following day, an official dispatch arrived from Grant's headquarters giving the nation a legitimate reason to rejoice. Lincoln's faith in Grant, long maintained against fierce opposition, had been justified. Grant announced that he had won five significant battles, captured the state capital of Jackson, divided the Southern forces under Pemberton and Johnston, and stood on the threshold of Vicksburg. A gratified Lincoln pronounced the campaign "one of the most brilliant in the world."

⋯⊶◉⊷⋯

BY THAT SAME day, May 25, the battlefield at Vicksburg had become intolerable from the overwhelming stench of death and putrefaction. The dead from the two Union assaults lay where they had fallen. Some of the bodies had been on the ground for nine days since the first attack. Corpses had swollen and burst in the unforgiving Mississippi heat. Wounded soldiers remained untended, although there were fewer of them each day, each hour, but the gut-wrenching cries for help were agonizing. Mary Loughborough wrote:

> I was distressed to hear of a young Federal lieutenant who had been severely wounded and left on the field by his comrades. He had lived in this condition from Saturday until Monday, lying in the burning sun without water or food; and the men on both sides could witness the agony of the life thus prolonged, without the power to assist him in any way. I was glad, indeed, when I heard the poor man had expired on Monday morning.

Pemberton and Grant refused to ask each other for a truce to bury the dead and tend the wounded lest the request be taken as an admission of weakness. Each general waited to see who would give in first. It was Pemberton, mercifully, and Grant agreed to a truce of two-and-a-half hours beginning at six o'clock on the evening of May 25.

Oddly, while Yankee burial parties and medics went about their grisly tasks, a holiday atmosphere prevailed over the killing ground. "Now commenced a strange spectacle in this thrilling drama of war," wrote twenty-one-year-old Sgt. Willie Tunnard of the Third Regiment, Louisiana Infantry:

> Flags were displayed along both lines, and the troops thronged the breastworks, gaily chatting with each other, discussing the issues of the war, disputing over differences of opinion, losses in the fight, etc. Numbers of Confederates accepted invitations to visit the enemy's lines, where they were hospitably entertained and warmly welcomed. They were abundantly supplied with provision, supplies of various kinds, and liquors. . . . The members of the Third Regiment found numerous acquaintances and relatives among the Ohio, Illinois, and Missouri regiments, and there were mutual regrets that the issues of the war had made them antagonists in a deadly struggle.

Officers from both armies also fraternized. Major Lockett, Pemberton's chief engineer, was invited to meet General Sherman. After exchanging pleasantries, Sherman said he had asked to meet an officer in the hope that he might pass along some letters that had been given to him by Northern friends of some Confederate officers in Vicksburg. Sherman said, "I thought this would be a good opportunity to deliver this mail before it got too old." "Yes, General," Lockett teased, "it would have been very old, indeed, if you had kept it until you brought it into Vicksburg yourself."

The two men sat on a log and enjoyed what Lockett described as a cordial conversation. The war was suspended for the moment. But when the interlude ended, Lockett recalled, the sharpshooters immediately resumed their deadly work.

⋆⇒◉⇐⋆

SIEGE WARFARE IS a dull business. There are no sweeping envelopments to plan, no grand flanking maneuvers, no thrilling charges.

There is not much movement of any kind, and progress is measured in feet or yards. On June 6, Grant traveled up the Yazoo River on a steamer bound for Satartia, thirty miles northeast of Vicksburg, for an inspection tour. And because Grant was bored and missed Julia, he got drunk. Also, he was making the trip without John Rawlins, his "keeper."

The day before, Rawlins had found a case of wine outside Grant's tent. He had arranged for it to be destroyed, over Grant's protest that he was saving it for the celebration when Vicksburg surrendered. Rawlins noticed that some of the bottles were empty and he was sure he knew why. That night he penned a letter, which he handed to Grant before he boarded the steamer. The general put it in his pocket and, unfortunately, did not read it until three days later, when he sobered up.

Rawlins had written:

The great solicitude I feel for the safety of the army leads me to mention what I had hoped never again to do—the subject of your drinking. I find you where the wine bottle has just been emptied, in the company with those who drink and urge you to do likewise, and the lack of your usual promptness of decision and clearness of expression in writing tended to confirm my suspicion.

You have the *full* control of your appetite and can let drinking alone. Had you not pledged me the sincerity of your honor early last March that you would drink no more during the war, and kept your pledge during your recent campaign, you would not today have stood first in the world's history as a successful military leader. Your only salvation depends upon your strict adherence to that pledge. You cannot succeed in any other way.

Then Rawlins issued a warning: If Grant drank again, Rawlins would leave.

Two men had accompanied Grant on the inspection trip, either of whom could have ended Grant's career and left his name disgraced.

One was Charles Dana, whom Secretary of War Stanton had sent to report on Grant's behavior. The other was the journalist Sylvanus Cadwallader, who could have had a sensational exclusive story of national importance. Both kept Grant's secret. Dana did not reveal Grant's occasional drinking episodes until after Grant's death. Cadwallader reported nothing about Grant's drunken escapade on the steamer trip until he wrote his memoirs in 1896, which were not published until 1955.

As Cadwallader described the incident, Grant transferred to a second riverboat that was equipped with a well-stocked bar. Its captain was an old friend. The reporter recalled that after Grant made numerous trips to the bar, he became "stupid in speech and staggering in gait. This was the first time he had shown symptoms of intoxication in my presence, and I was greatly alarmed by his condition, which was fast becoming worse."

Cadwallader tried to persuade the captain and Lieutenant Towner, an aide to Grant, to take the general to his cabin and keep him there until sobered up. Neither man would intervene. It was up to Cadwallader to protect Grant's reputation. He wrote:

> I then took the general in hand myself, enticed him into his stateroom, locked myself in the room with him (having the key in my pocket), and commenced throwing bottles of whiskey which stood on the table, through the window.

Furious, Grant ordered him out, but Cadwallader refused to leave. Finally he calmed the general down enough for him to go to sleep.

As the boat neared Satartia, two naval officers warned the captain that it was unsafe to proceed. The captain insisted that Grant be consulted. Charles Dana told them that Grant was asleep and should not be wakened. But when the naval officers insisted that the boat turn back, Dana knocked on Grant's cabin door, explained the situation, and asked for instructions. Grant said he was feeling too poorly to think and left the decision to Dana. Dana ordered the boat to turn around and make for Haines' Bluff.

In the morning Dana was astonished to see Grant appear at breakfast, looking "fresh as a rose, clean shirt and all, quite himself."

An hour later Cadwallader found that Grant had "procured another supply of whiskey . . . and was quite as much intoxicated as the day before." When Grant regained his faculties this time, he ordered the captain to proceed to Chickasaw Bayou, a port for Union supplies. There Grant made his way to a sutler boat where Cadwallader caught him with a glass of whiskey. Cadwallader escorted Grant off the boat and onto a horse for the five-mile ride back to his Vicksburg headquarters.

The horse was aptly named Kangaroo, because it reared on its hind legs and plunged forward whenever it was mounted, as it did to Grant. The winding road passed over a number of guarded bridges, but Grant rode hell-for-leather as though the path were perfectly straight, ignoring sentries or other obstacles. Cadwallader recalled that Grant

> went at about full speed through camps and corrals, heading only for the bridges, and literally tore through and over everything in his way. The air was full of dust, ashes, and embers from campfires; and shouts and curses from those he rode down in his race.

When Cadwallader finally caught up with him just past the last bridge before camp, Grant had slowed to a walk and seemed very unsteady, apparently the effects of the whiskey. The reporter was amazed that the general had not accidentally killed himself on his wild ride. Grant's cavalry escort had long since lost sight of him. Cadwallader persuaded Grant to take shelter in a thicket and sleep off the drink before showing himself in camp.

While Grant slept, Cadwallader flagged down one of the escorts and sent him on to headquarters with a message for Colonel Rawlins. The escort was to speak to no one else and to tell Rawlins to send an

ambulance with a careful driver. When it arrived, Grant refused to get
in until Cadwallader agreed to go with him. They arrived at headquarters around midnight to find a grim-faced Rawlins and a second staff
officer, Colonel Riggin, waiting for them.

Cadwallader stepped out of the ambulance followed by Grant, who

shrugged his shoulders, pulled down his vest, "shook himself
together," as one just rising from a nap, and seeing Rawlins and Riggin, bid them goodnight in a natural tone and manner, and started to
his tent as steadily as he ever walked in his life.

The next morning, Rawlins engaged Grant in what Cadwallader
described as an impetuous and stormy conversation and roundly chastised the general for his behavior. Rawlins said he would no longer
serve Grant if he continued to drink. Grant took his scolding amiably
and "with the utmost good humor said that he had quit drinking; and
so disarmed Rawlins by his confessions, his open sincerity, and
promises of amendment, that the latter was induced to pass the matter
over for that time."

Grant did not take another drink for the remainder of the long
Vicksburg campaign. Rawlins saw to that.

SIEGE WARFARE WAS also boring for the soldiers, but their routine
was enlivened by being shot at day and night, and by the frequent digging of new trenches. Grant had his 220 cannon firing constantly.
Although Pemberton usually kept his 102 cannon silent to conserve
ammunition, his men devised other ways to harass the Yankees.

One clever and awesome weapon the rebels improvised to compen-
sate for their shortage of artillery shells was the thunder barrel. The
device was fashioned from large hogshead barrels filled with powder
and fuses passed through the bungholes. Soldiers lit the fuses and

rolled the barrels down the hills into the Yankee trenches. They made similar rolling bombs out of Union naval shells that had failed to explode, recycling the North's own weapons against them.

The rebels also fabricated new weapons from hand grenades, of which they had none. They refilled the ones tossed at them that had not exploded. Sometimes they caught them in midair and threw them back. Sgt. Willie Tunnard of the Third Regiment, Louisiana Infantry, wrote about the effectiveness of the grenades:

> These missiles weigh about a pound, are an oval-shaped iron shell, a little larger than a hen's egg, and filled with powder. These shells were thrown [back] in immense quantities. Numbers struck the men, exploding, and making frightful wounds.

Union soldiers also improvised. They did not have mortars as the sailors did, so they made them out of trees. They cut thick logs and bored out the centers wide enough to hold six- or twelve-pound shells and bound the logs with iron bands. The wooden mortars did their job well, hurling shells up and over the rebel parapets to reach targets that the cannon, with their lower trajectories, could not hit.

The Union shelling from the land forces and the fleet rarely paused. Pvt. Isaac Jackson of the Eighty-third Ohio Infantry wrote to his brother on June 15:

> It has been four weeks since we have been here and during that time there has been a constant firing of cannon. There has not been an hour hardly but we can hear the report of a gun along the line somewhere. We have become very much used to it.

That same day, Brig. Gen. William Orme of the Ninety-fourth Illinois Regiment wrote to his beloved wife, Nannie. "While I am writing you the bombardment is going on very briskly all around the line and I have got so that I scarcely notice the sound of the cannon."

Five days later Orme told his wife about his narrow escapes from a rebel shell and a sharpshooter.

> A day or two ago I was out to the front with several of my officers and after remaining in a position several minutes, I remarked to them that I thought it was not prudent to remain longer there; and we walked back some 15 or 20 feet; and just as we reached a large tree a shell exploded just exactly where we stood, but we found safe cover behind the tree. Yesterday afternoon I was again out and took a fine position for observation behind a large tree on a hill but within reach of the enemy's sharpshooters, and remained there some ten minutes examining their work with my glass. I had scarcely left there when some soldiers came and occupied the same place and one of them was immediately shot.

Not all casualties were attributable to the enemy. Sgt. Charles Wilcox of the Thirty-third Illinois recorded in his diary for May 24 how Sergeant Besse,

> my dear friend, had both his arms cut off by a piece of one of our own shells. Scarcely a day passed without two or three of our Brigade being killed or wounded by our own guns. . . . Both of [Besse's] arms will have to be amputated. Poor armless fellow! How I mourn over his loss!

When Sergeant Besse died on June 1, Wilcox wrote, "One more noble heart, brave soldier and true man has gone to rest. Good friend, true patriot, hail and farewell!"

Many soldiers died of their wounds and several of the rebel casualties were killed in their hospital beds. Union gunners did not deliberately target Confederate hospitals, but artillery fire was so notoriously inaccurate that some hospital tents were bound to be hit. Because land was scarce within the besieged city, the dead were buried in common graves, usually trenches three feet wide and up to fifty feet long. There were few coffins available. Most of the bodies were swathed in blankets and laid under the earth.

⋅⟫⊙⟪⋅

THE LIVING, TOO, lay in trenches, hiding from enemy bullets and digging, always digging. The Yankees were constantly extending their lines, zigzagging closer to the rebel positions, approaching the Confederates like moles. Each new trench line had to be covered with logs. Sandbags were heaped along the side facing the enemy, with just enough space between the bags to poke a rifle through. Some trenches were deep and wide enough for men to march four abreast from one point of the line to another.

As Union soldiers inched toward the Confederate lines, the Southerners were slowly being forced back. One night Union diggers looked up from their work to find Confederate pickets staring down at them with amusement. The rebel soldiers told the Yankees they were trespassing, but they were reluctant to shoot because surely the Yankees had not done so intentionally! Officers on both sides called a meeting and it was agreed that Confederate pickets would be repositioned so that the Union troops would not have to do any extra digging.

At one spot on the Union line, soldiers invented a mobile shield behind which they could dig trenches in safety. They called this shield a sap roller; to sap means to approach an enemy position by digging deep trenches ever closer to it. The Yankees' sap roller was built on the frame of a railroad flat car piled high with bales of cotton. The men rolled it forward as work on the trench progressed.

Confederate soldiers were furious that the Yankee diggers had this shelter from their rifle fire. Sgt. Willie Tunnard wrote that the sap roller was "a perfect annoyance to the regiment." An inventive young lieutenant, W. M. Washburn, is said to have come up with an infernal device to destroy the sap roller.

Washburn filled musket balls with cotton soaked in turpentine. A wad of the cotton protruded from a cavity in the ball. When the rifle was fired, the cotton ignited and the ball became a crude incendiary bullet. But after several flaming balls fired at the sap roller had no effect, the men lost interest. Then, as Willie Tunnard described it,

> the attempt was abandoned amid a general disappointment. The men, save those on guard, sought repose, and all the line became comparatively quiet. Suddenly someone exclaimed, "I'll be damned if that thing isn't on fire!"

Bright flames engulfed the Yankees' mobile safety shield. Quickly rebel soldiers peppered it with bullets to keep their enemies from dousing the fire. All that remained were the railroad car's wheels.

⊷═◉═⊷

THE WAR WAS a test of ingenuity and endurance, but men can only go so long without adequate nutrition. The contrast between the diets of the two sides is noteworthy. The Union army ate well, always better than the Confederate army did. Union Pvt. Isaac Jackson wrote to his sister on June 15:

> I have just finished my dinner. It consists of hard crackers and two or three pieces of fried mess pork. For breakfast we had coffee and crackers and supper is boiled beef, coffee, and crackers. Sometimes we get potatoes and codfish, but seldom.

Such meals were feasts compared to the rebels' provisions. By June 12, most foods were scarce. Willie Tunnard wrote in his diary that "fresh beef had long since been used up, and also, a large number of sheep, and the troops were now living on rations of bacon." Soon, the Southern troops had only a couple of biscuits, two rashers of bacon, a few peas, and a handful of rice to sustain them through the day.

The wounded in the hospitals received hard black pea bread made of ground peas and corn. It was heavy and difficult to digest, but it was all that was available. The soldiers looked gaunt and haggard and were often found begging for food in Vicksburg's streets, but there was little to be had. Pemberton's men were starving.

Although the Northern soldiers were better nourished than their enemies, they were much more bothered by the unrelenting heat, humidity, and insects. The men sweltered in their heavy woolen uniforms. On June 6 Sgt. Charles Wilcox noted in his diary: "Yesterday the Themometer [sic] stood 100 degrees Fah. In the shade in a hollow, and I believe it was 5 degrees hotter today than it was yesterday."

General Orme wrote to his wife on June 18:

The variety of bugs here would astonish you. At night my tent is full of all kinds of bugs, insects, spiders, &c. I am covered all over my body with large red lumps occasioned by the bite of some kind of a bug said to be the "jigger." The bumps itch me very much and make me feel very uncomfortably.

For all its grim reality of heat, hunger, suffering, and death, life in the trenches occasionally had its lighter moments. The men enjoyed games and liked to play practical jokes on the soldiers in the opposing trenches. They would wave their caps in the air on the end of a stick or a ramrod and take bets on the number of bullet holes they would find. It was great sport to trick the enemy sharpshooters with these empty caps.

Along many parts of the line, the trenches were near enough to toss objects back and forth. A Union soldier lobbed a hardtack biscuit with "starvation" written on it. A Confederate wag threw a message back thanking the sender for the gift of forty days' rations.

The banter was similarly good-natured.

"Yank, why don't you all make a general assault and end this thing?"

"Oh, don't be impatient, Johnny, we are in no hurry. We are just guarding prisoners and it would be inhuman to fire on them unless they undertake to break out."

At night, if no officers were around, Northerners and Southerners would climb out of their trenches and mingle. Visitors were welcomed cordially. Union men treated their guests to food and drink. They exchanged real coffee for Southern tobacco and traded knives, canteens, and other items. Sometimes soldiers happened on relatives and friends. The reunions were often joyous.

But at dawn they returned to their own defense lines with handshakes and good wishes. And with admonitions to keep their heads down and warnings that they did not aim to miss.

⋆⇒○⇐⋆

THE CIVILIANS OF Vicksburg were also suffering the torments of war, the same privations, dangers, hunger, and death. The Union bombardment rarely abated. Billy Lord, Jr., son of the Princeton-educated rector of Christ Church, described the array of weapons that terrorized the population around the clock.

> Bombshells in the form of huge iron spheres weighing nearly three hundred pounds and filled with gunpowder flew through the air, their burning fuses leaving a trail of smoke by day and fire by night. . . . Fire-shells containing tow [flax or hemp fiber] saturated with oil kept the fire brigade constantly busy in extinguishing the flames of burning houses. Chain shot, cannonballs linked in deadly union by iron chains, swept the streets from wall to curb. Canisters, like big vegetable cans, but filled with grapeshot, which were solid iron balls about the size of hickory nuts, say a hundred or more to a canister, scattered their contents far and wide. All these, together with shells filled with scrap iron, links of chain, rusty nails, and even bits of tin, were among the many kinds of missiles thrown into the city.

Vicksburg was soon a desolated city. Many buildings and homes had been blown apart or burned to the ground, and it was hard to find any structure that had not been damaged in some way. Even the animals were disturbed by the constant bombing. Horses reared, pulled their halters taut, and whinnied, making what Mary Loughborough was sure were cries of terror. Maddened dogs ran in frenzied circles when shells whistled through the air. Others cowered and howled.

The people sought refuge in the caves. The Reverend Doctor Lord and his family moved into a large communal cave holding approximately two hundred people. The place had a long central gallery with five smaller galleries running off it. The entrances at both ends of the main hall were for cooking and for housing the servants. Everyone else lived deeper within the cave, with families separating themselves from others by building flimsy wooden partitions or hanging blankets.

For many people, this sort of existence was primitive compared to the luxury, comfort, and privacy they were used to. Before long, according to Billy Lord, the

> squalling infants, family quarrels, and the noise of general discord [plus] the odor of stale food in the heavy, earth-laden atmosphere of the overcrowded cave so offended my mother's sensibilities that, persuaded by her, my father caused a private cave for the exclusive use of his own family to be constructed.

The reverend's family's new shelter was L-shaped with a front and a rear entrance. It was vital to have two escape routes in case an exploding shell sealed off one entrance.

A brisk business in cave construction quickly developed, with costs ranging up to fifty dollars for the larger caves. Black men who had access to picks and shovels made more money than they had ever seen before. Real estate agents did well whenever cave dwellers desired to move to larger or safer locations. Caves were available for sale or rent; the average rental was fifteen dollars a month.

Mary Loughborough and her daughter moved into a T-shaped cave. She wrote in her diary:

In one of the wings, my bed fitted; the other I used as a kind of dressing room. In this the earth had been cut down a foot or two below the floor of the main cave; I could stand erect here; and when tired of sitting in other portions of my residence, I bowed myself into it and stood impassively resting at full height.

Mary had the ceiling of her cave arched and well braced. The stout wooden supports took space away from her living area but she hoped that the reinforcement and the five feet of dirt above her head would protect them even from a direct mortar hit. The Loughborough family slave, George, slept at the cave's entrance. He was armed with a revolver to protect the family against intruders. Loyally, he vowed that if anyone tried to enter the cave, they would have to "go over his body first."

Some shelters had been made comfortable with luxuries brought from home. Beds, dressers, chairs, and tables had been transported. Planks laid across dirt floors provided flooring for fine carpets. Other rugs were fastened to the dirt walls to help control the dampness. Pictures and mirrors were set in place and children's toys scattered about. Occasionally the good crystal and china were brought out to boost morale.

No matter how imaginatively the residents decorated their caves or how deeply they were embedded into the hillsides, the people were always aware that death could come at any moment. The very real dangers of war could not be covered over with a fancy carpet.

Like most families, the Lords had their share of close calls. On May 21, in the lull between the two failed Union attacks on the Confederate line, they were still living in their house. While the family gathered around the dining room table for the evening meal,

> a bombshell burst in the very center of that pretty dining room, blowing out the roof and one side, crushing the well-spread tea-table like an eggshell, and making a great yawning hole in the floor, into which disappeared supper, china, furniture, and the safe containing our entire stock of butter and eggs.

Following that frightening incident, the Lord family moved into the church basement, thinking it would be safer. One afternoon, while Dr. Lord sat on a barrel smoking his pipe, a string of shells exploded directly outside the building. Mrs. Lord and the two children huddled on the coal pile. The little girl started to cry. Her mother tried to comfort her saying that God would protect them. The child replied that she was afraid God would be killed, too. Dr. Lord decided it was time to head for the caves.

Shortly after they were established in their first cave, a large shell exploded directly overhead, dislodging a huge chunk of earth, which fell on Lucy McRae, whose cot Dr. Lord had just put in place. In an instant Lucy disappeared under the dirt. Her mother, Dr. Lord, and others used their hands to dig her out. Lucy later wrote,

> The blood was gushing from my nose, eyes, ears, and mouth. A physician who was then in the cave was called and said there were no bones broken, but he could not then tell what my internal injuries were. Just here I must say that during all this excitement there was a little baby boy born in the room dug out at the back of the cave; he was called William Siege Green.

A shell exploded outside one of the entrances, sealing it off. The caves' occupants bolted for the other entrance. Another shell burst overhead. People screamed and turned to race back inside. The terror was complete. The young Lord boy narrowly escaped death. He wrote about it later, after his mother had described the incident to him. The threat had come

> from a spent shell which passed so near the top of my head as to stir my hair, and fell close behind me. So far had the force of propulsion left this shell that my mother, standing not far distant, distinctly saw the missile just escape hitting my head. I had, fortunately, stooped for the moment to gather something from the ground.

Others were less fortunate. During a lull in a bombardment, one mother foolishly allowed her three-year-old son to play near the entrance to her cave. Yankee cannon fire resumed without warning. The mother ran to grab her child but the boy sped away, thinking his mother was playing a game. She clutched at his hand but he pulled away and fell sprawling and laughing on the grass.

> In that very instant a shell exploded where he had stood a moment before, and it shattered his mother's outstretched arm and hand. This woman refused to call the loss of her hand and arm a misfortune because, as she explained, if she had retained her hold upon the child he surely would have been killed.

Another woman put her child to bed and sat down to rest near a cave entrance. A mortar shell struck the ground directly above the sleeping child. It sliced through several feet of earth and crushed the child's head. Another youngster discovered a spent shell on the ground and began to play with it. She turned it around, placed it upside down, and pounded on the fuse. The explosion left only shredded pieces of flesh.

A shell fragment caught another little girl playing outside her cave. Mary Loughborough recalled the child's screams. The girl ran into her mother's presence, sinking like a wounded dove, the life blood flowing over the light summer dress in crimson ripples from the death wound in her side, caused by the shell fragment. A fragment had also struck and broken the arm of a little boy playing near the entrance of his mother's cave. This was one's day's account.

Reminiscing years later about the siege, Mary wrote, "The screams of the women of Vicksburg were the saddest I have ever heard. The wailing over the dead seemed full of heartsick agony."

Even without the continual bombardment from the Union's guns, life in the caves was difficult. The heat and humidity were oppressive. Opportunities to bathe were rare; the usually fastidious women went for weeks without changing their clothing. Diseases affected civilians and soldiers alike; many were struck down with malaria and dysentery and suffered from malnutrition. Lice, mosquitoes, and other insects could not be controlled. Worse, the vines and thickets that wrapped themselves around the hillsides in which the caves had been dug were alive with snakes. It was not uncommon to awaken in the morning and find rattlesnakes beneath the mattresses.

Aggravating the effects of the heat and humidity was a water shortage. The heavy rains of May ended and the sun baked the earth solid as the siege dragged on. Counting soldiers and civilians, about thirty-five thousand people were consuming water from a system adequate for five thousand. People carried water from mud holes and ditches; others charged exorbitant prices for fresh water from their own underground cisterns.

Profiteers took full advantage of the growing food shortage. People willing to pay astronomical prices could buy beef, ham, flour, molasses, and sugar on the black market. But anger festered against the merchants who were making money from other people's misery. A group of civilians, thin and weak from hunger, set fire to several grocery stores whose owners were known to be speculators. The fire could not be contained and ultimately it destroyed an entire block of buildings downtown along with the food stored in the basements of the shops.

Sometimes people missed meals even when sufficient food was available. Cooking was only permitted outside the caves, which meant waiting for the lull between bombardments. Often the shelling went so long without interruption that people were forced to fast. But even so, there was less and less food to prepare. Lucy McRae wrote,

> Our provisions were becoming scarce and the Louisiana soldiers were eating rats as a delicacy, while mules were occasionally being carved up to appease the appetite. Mother would not eat mule meat, but we children ate some, and it tasted right good, having been cooked nicely. Wheat bread was a rarity, and sweet-potato coffee was relished by the adults.

Mary Loughborough recalled that "most of us lived on corn bread and bacon, served three times a day."

It wasn't long before the citizens of Vicksburg began running out of everything. Clothing became threadbare, shoes worn and patched. The newspapers, which were still doggedly being published, ran out of newsprint. J. M. Swords, publisher of the *Citizen*, improvised and produced a paper, but the size and type of paper varied daily. A page of the June 13 issue measured eighteen inches long and six inches wide. Later he had to print the daily edition on the paste side of pink-and-green patterned wallpaper. One enterprising subscriber read the paper, turned it over, and then hung it up, with the colorful side brightening the walls of his underground home.

The one continuing hope in news, rumor, and gossip was that Joe Johnston was coming to save them. Only a few days more, people said, and surely Johnston would be tearing through the Union lines with his 30,000 men. Or was it 40,000? Or 100,000? They must be on their way. Within twenty-five miles of the city? Or ten? If Vicksburg could just hang on a few days more.

The *Citizen* reported, "The undaunted Johnston is at hand. Ho! For Johnston. The most agreeable news nowadays is to hear from General

Johnston." Sgt. Willie Tunnard of the Third Regiment, Louisiana Infantry, noted the daily rumor in his diary for June 13. "General Johnston was at Clinton, Miss., with 25,000 troops, and positively asserted that he was approaching to succor the garrison." Old Joe was coming soon and Vicksburg would be saved. The story lifted morale. The people needed to believe they would be rescued.

And there was every reason to believe it, because Johnston himself had said it was so. "I am trying to gather a force which may attempt to relieve you," he said in one message. "Hold out," he commanded. On May 25, he sent another message asking Pemberton for information on the disposition of Grant's forces and advice on the best route to take to relieve Vicksburg.

But Johnston was not moving. He remained encamped with thirty-one thousand men more than fifty miles to the northeast, where he continued to wait for reinforcements that were not coming. On June 15, he sent a telegram to Richmond, to Secretary of War Seddon, that sealed Vicksburg's fate. "I consider saving Vicksburg hopeless," Johnston wrote. Seddon replied immediately. "Your telegram grieves and alarms us. Vicksburg must not be lost without a desperate struggle. The interest and honor of the Confederacy forbid it. I rely on you still to avert the loss."

Johnston took three days to formulate his reply. He suggested that Seddon did not appreciate the difficulties facing Johnston's army. Johnston's communications with Vicksburg were poor; messages had to be smuggled in and out, making it impossible to coordinate troop movements with the other commands. Besides, Grant had superior numbers. Johnston reiterated his gloomy conclusion that he could do nothing to save Vicksburg. He hinted to Seddon that he might attempt to rescue Pemberton's men, but he gave no indication of how that task might be accomplished.

Seddon tried to impress on General Johnston that it was time for bold initiatives despite the great risks. He reminded Johnston that the eyes and hopes of the whole Confederacy are upon you with the full confidence that you will act, and with the sentiment that it were better to fail, nobly daring, than, through prudence even, to be inactive. . . . I rely upon you for all possible means to save Vicksburg.

There would be no attempt to save the city. Johnston was unwilling, against such daunting odds, to "fail, nobly daring." On May 19, he had dispatched a courier to Pemberton in Vicksburg bearing the awful truth, but it was not delivered until June 13. Johnston had written, "I am too weak to save Vicksburg. Can do no more than attempt to save you and your garrison."

Pemberton sent message after message to Johnston, hoping they would get through. On June 15, Pemberton wrote, "Our men are becoming much fatigued, but are still in pretty good spirits. I think your movement should be made as soon as possible. . . . We are living on greatly reduced rations, but, I think, sufficient for twenty days."

On June 20, Pemberton ordered Capt. George Wise through the Yankee lines carrying a written message for Johnston. He gave Wise additional information verbally to pass on to Johnston, which he did not put in writing in case Wise was captured. Pemberton did not want Grant to learn how desperate the garrison's situation really was.

"I hope you will advance with the least possible delay," he wrote to Johnston. "My men have been thirty-four days and nights in trenches, without relief, and the enemy within conversation distance. We are living on very reduced rations, and, as you know, are entirely isolated. What am I to expect from you?"

Privately Pemberton told Captain Wise to inform Johnston that he could not hold out longer than about July 10 and that his men were too feeble to fight their way out. The city and its defenders could only be saved if Johnston launched an attack at once. When Wise reached Johnston's headquarters and delivered his messages, he was told to report back to Pemberton that Johnston lacked sufficient troops, horses, and supplies to mount a relief operation.

Wise was also to say that if it became necessary to surrender Vicksburg, then Pemberton should be the one to do it. Johnston insisted that for him to propose surrender to Grant "would be an impolitic confession of weakness." The orders were clear. Pemberton and his men were on their own, but Pemberton never knew of Johnston's last communication. Captain Wise was captured trying to return to Vicksburg.

Colonel Fremantle, the Coldstream Guards officer whose travels had taken him to Richmond, wrote on June 17 of having "the gloomiest forebodings with regard to the fate of Vicksburg. The fortress is in fact *given up*, and all now despair of General Johnston's being able to effect anything towards its relief." Two days later he noted, "I hear everyone complaining dreadfully of General Johnston's inactivity in Mississippi, and all now despair of saving Vicksburg."

❖══◎══❖

AT THREE O'CLOCK on the afternoon of Thursday, June 25, a powerful explosion ripped apart a key fort on the Confederate defensive line. A tunnel dug by Union soldiers deep beneath the fort had been packed with 2,200 pounds of powder. When it blew up, the entire fort and its surrounding trenches were pulverized, leaving a crater twelve feet deep and fifty feet across. Even before the dirt and debris and the remains of the bodies settled back to earth, every Union artillery piece along the line opened fire in a sustained bombardment accompanied by the rifle fire of fifty thousand Union soldiers.

An assault force charged into the crater intending to cut the rebel line in two, but the attack failed. The Southerners had been expecting an underground explosion and had already moved most of the fort's troops back to a second line of fortifications. They had established a commanding field of overlapping fire on the crater. They easily slaughtered the Yankee soldiers, trapping them there until dark.

When the civilians heard the explosion and artillery barrage that afternoon, they greeted the noise with cheers and renewed hope. They believed it signaled the advance of Joe Johnston's forces, shelling Grant's men and breaking through the Union line. Glory hallelujah! They were saved. The disappointment when they learned the truth was shattering, unnerving many who had reached the limit of their endurance. For the first time, people began to surrender their hopes.

Dora Miller, still a Union sympathizer, wrote in her diary: "June 25—Horrible day. The most horrible yet to me, because I've lost my nerve." The Millers had taken shelter in the cellar of their house, when a shell burst through the roof and came to rest beside them. Mr. Miller nearly lost his leg. A neighbor's leg was crushed; the same shell sheared off the arm of her servant. "For the first time I quailed," Dora wrote. She screamed at her husband: "You must get me out of this horrible place."

"How very sad this life in Vicksburg," Mary Loughborough wrote in her diary. "How little security we can feel, with so many around us seeing the morning light that will never see the night. . . . How blightingly the hand of warfare lay upon the town!" Vicksburg had become a ghost town. The only signs of life were the fearful eyes peering out from darkened caves.

⊰⊱

THE WAR WAS coming to an end for the people of Vicksburg. At the same time, a thousand miles to the northeast, the war was beginning for the residents of another town. This one was called Gettysburg.

CHAPTER 6

THE SUSPENSE WAS DREADFUL

"IT IS A SAD story," said Fannie Buehler of Gettysburg, Pennsylvania. "It was in the early month of June, 1863. How well do I remember the year and the month. I was then in my 37th year. I am now in my 71st; but in looking back it seems but as yesterday, so well do I recall the coming and the going of 'the Rebels' whom we had so long expected."

The rebels were coming. The Army of Northern Virginia—that invincible legion of Antietam, Fredericksburg, and Chancellorsville—was on the move. The army of Robert E. Lee that no Union general had defeated was heading north from Virginia. Like a juggernaut it marched relentlessly, an unstoppable force overpowering everything in its path.

It forded the Potomac River, moved across the narrow western strip of Maryland, and stormed into Pennsylvania. Where would it stop? Harrisburg, the state capital, a mere sixty miles from the border? Baltimore, Philadelphia, even Washington? Perhaps New York? Suddenly all of those cities seemed vulnerable.

No one knew the whereabouts of Joe Hooker and his Army of the

Potomac. "Everyone is asking, 'Where is our army that they let the enemy scour the country and do as they please,'" wrote thirty-year-old Sallie Broadhead in her diary on June 25. "It is reported that Lee's whole army is this side of the [Potomac] river, and marching on Harrisburg; also that a large force is coming on here."

All she and the other Gettysburg residents knew for certain was that Lee's army was coming from the southwest and getting closer to their homes every day. Fannie Buehler recalled that "frightful rumors were afloat, many citizens were leaving the town, taking with them all their treasures. The banks sent away their money, stores were closed, merchandise was shipped away, individuals chartered [railroad] cars in which were packed household goods and valuables of all kinds, and the cars were sent to some distant part of the North for safety."

Sallie Myers, a twenty-one-year-old Gettysburg schoolteacher, described how "people did little more but stand along the streets in groups and talk. Whenever someone heard a new report all flocked to him. The suspense was dreadful."

It was the same elsewhere in the North, the uncertainty, fear, and panic. Long columns of civilian refugees flooded the roads in advance of Lee's army. With their possessions piled high in farmcarts, wagons, and carriages, wilting in the awful summer heat, while their livestock dragged along behind them, the refugees headed north, not knowing where they would end up. Anyplace was better than watching their homes and farms being taken over by the rebels. And who knew what those devils would do to helpless women and children?

The free blacks living in the path of the Confederate army knew all too well what would happen to them. They would be shipped south and sold into slavery, no matter that they carried papers showing they were free. They, too, became refugees, carrying huge bundles of clothing, bedding, and pots and pans—whatever they could heft on their shoulders or drag behind them in the dust. Lee's army was on the move, creating chaos and pandemonium in the North.

ABRAHAM LINCOLN PACED the length of the telegraph office at the War Department, as ignorant of Lee's location and destination as any Pennsylvania farmer. He traced what he believed were Lee's movements on a large map tacked to the wall, but he knew that the route was no more than a guess. The information he received was conflicting and was hours, if not days, late. Outside on Pennsylvania Avenue, crowds milled about, watching the light streaming from his window as if it could tell them what they longed to know. Where were the invaders? Were they coming here?

Lincoln and Secretary of War Stanton rarely left the telegraph office. They read and reread every message that arrived, straining their eyes in the glare of the oil lamps and swatting away the insects that buzzed around them.

The telegraph key chattered with startling information that gave the president a glimmer of hope. Lee's cavalry, if this report could be believed, was not with his army. The dispatch said that Jeb Stuart was leading his troopers on a raid somewhere east of where the Army of Northern Virginia was supposed to be. This meant that Lee had no reconnaissance capability, so he probably had no idea of where Hooker's forces were. Lee may indeed have been an overwhelming force plunging deeper and deeper into Pennsylvania, but without Stuart he was operating blindly.

Lincoln was encouraged. Now was the time for Hooker to attack Lee. And, Lincoln added, "it appears to me he can't help but win." But it was a vain hope, and surely the president knew it. Hooker was too much like McClellan; he lacked the audacity to attack Lee, even when he outnumbered him and had him at a disadvantage. "Hooker may commit the same fault as McClellan and lose his chance," Lincoln said quietly. And he was right.

In the meantime, however, Lincoln had to take some action. On June 15, he issued a proclamation calling for a militia force of 100,000 volunteers to defend against the invaders. He requested 10,000 men from Maryland, 50,000 from Pennsylvania, 30,000 from Ohio, and 10,000 from West Virginia.

That same day, Charles Coffin, a newspaper reporter, arrived at Harrisburg, Pennsylvania. He was appalled at what he saw.

The city was a bedlam. A great crowd of people—excited men, women, wringing their hands, and children crying, all with big bundles—were at the railroad station, ready to jump into the cars to escape northward or eastward. Merchants were packing up their goods. There was a great pile of trunks and boxes. Teams loaded with furniture, beds, and clothing rumbled through the streets; wagons were crossing the bridge over the Susquehanna; farmers . . . were hurrying their cattle, horses, sheep, and pigs in droves across the river.

On the following day Coffin traveled to Baltimore and watched black workers building hasty fortifications and barricades on roads leading to the west. They felled trees, filled barrels with dirt, and piled up wagons, carts, logs, and hogsheads of tobacco, anything that might stop the rebel bullets.

Lee was coming. Perhaps today, perhaps tomorrow, maybe here, maybe there, but he was on his way. Who was to stop him? Not the 100,000 men Lincoln had asked for. The response was disappointingly low, about half the number needed. They were poorly led and trained, scattered over hundreds of miles, equipped with obsolete weapons. There was little they could be expected to do against Lee's battle-hardened veterans. Still, they could dig, and many were put to work in Harrisburg, and as far west as Pittsburgh, carving out rifle pits and building breastworks.

Lee was coming. Proclamations were issued, each one more urgent and strident than the last.

"Philadelphia has not responded," thundered the governor of Pennsylvania, A. G. Curtin. "Meanwhile the enemy is six miles this side of Chambersburg, and advancing rapidly. Our capital is threatened, and we may be disgraced by its fall. . . . The enemy is approaching."

"Jerseymen!" the governor of New Jersey, Joel Parker, cried, "the state of Pennsylvania is invaded! A hostile army is now occupying and despoiling the towns of our sister State. She appeals to New Jersey . . . to aid in driving back the invading army."

Governor Curtin made a second appeal for volunteers. "A people who want the heart to defend their soil, their families, and their firesides, are not worthy to be accounted men." And from Maj. Gen. N. J. Dana, headquartered in Philadelphia: "Arise now in your might. Shake off your apathy, and show, by rallying rapidly and arming yourselves to meet the enemy and drive him back, that you deserve the blessings of a home. To stand idly now would invite suspicion either of treachery or cowardice."

Lee was coming. But despite impassioned appeals to patriotism, charges of cowardice, or fear of the advancing rebel hordes, neither Lincoln nor the governors of the threatened states could induce 100,000 men to band together to defend their homes. Instead, many packed their belongings and fled, or stayed only to dig ditches and erect barricades—or simply to wait and pray.

On the night of June 16, the people of Gettysburg believed Lee's forces had closed to within ten miles and were torching everything in their path. Sallie Broadhead was awakened after midnight by sounds of shouting in the street. From her bedroom window she saw a huge fire raging in the distance. Some people panicked and headed out of town, but the residents soon learned that they were witnessing an accidental fire in Emmitsburg, ten miles away. (Out of control, the blaze consumed twenty-seven houses.) Fannie Buehler wrote that "we were in a condition to believe anything, either good or bad, and the whole town was in the streets all night long discussing the probabilities and possibilities."

On the morning of June 17, the townspeople gathered again, this time to send eighty-three more sons, husbands, and brothers off to war.

The local militia, the Gettysburg Blues, responded to the president's appeal. Those who remained behind suddenly felt less secure. Not only were the able-bodied young men gone, but also they had taken with them most of the town's weapons and ammunition.

That night the residents gathered in the courthouse to talk about forming a home guard unit, but before anything could be decided, two strangers burst into the hall shouting that the rebels were coming. They had already set Hanover afire, and that was only thirteen miles away. Gettysburg was next. The report turned out to be another false alarm, but everyone knew that one day soon, the warning would be real.

Though no one believed Lee had come all that way just to sack Gettysburg, they knew that whatever his goal, he would have to pass through their town. Gettysburg was a crossroads for no fewer than ten major highways. Roads fanned out to Carlisle, Harrisburg, York, Hanover, Baltimore, Emmitsburg, Fairfield, and Chambersburg. Any destination in southeastern Pennsylvania would take the Confederate army through Gettysburg.

But where were they? Sallie Broadhead recorded the uncertainty in her diary.

> *June 20.* The report of today is that the rebels are at Chambersburg and are advancing on here, and refugees begin to come in by the scores. Some say the rebels number from twenty to thirty thousand, others that Lee's whole army is advancing this way. All day we have been much excited.
>
> *June 21.* Great excitement prevails, and there is no reliable intelligence from abroad. One report declares that the enemy are at Waynesboro, twenty miles off; another that Harrisburg is the point; and so we are in great suspense.

⊷═◉═⊶

ROBERT E. LEE believed he had no choice. He had to carry his war to the North. The invasion was his only option, his only chance to win the war and the only way to feed his men. The farms and fields of northern Virginia had been so fought over and trampled that they were barren of spring harvests and stripped of livestock. Lee had to take his men north to the lush, fertile fields of Pennsylvania to find adequate provisions. The South could no longer feed its army.

And he had to take the war to the enemy, to "those people," as he called them, to fight the war on their land. The alternative was to continue to hold the defensive line along the Rappahannock River, beating back the next Union attack and the one after that, the way he had in May at Chancellorsville.

But each victory was costly to the Confederacy—Lee lost 21 percent of his army at Chancellorsville—and after every such triumph, the South found it increasingly difficult to replace its losses. The Confederacy was running out of manpower, which meant that eventually, inevitably, even someone like Joe Hooker would be able to break through the line and force Lee back to Richmond. Lee could not afford to wait for that to happen. He would seize the initiative and gamble that he could destroy the Army of the Potomac in one quick surprise blow.

Now was the time to strike, while Hooker's army was discouraged and demoralized following the latest in a string of defeats. Not only was Yankee morale low, but the strength of the Union army was reduced. During May, it lost twenty-five to thirty thousand men whose terms of enlistment had expired. Lincoln ordered a draft to replenish the ranks, but it would take weeks before the replacements would be fit soldiers.

Lee had other reasons for taking his army into Union territory. From the information he had received, he knew that Vicksburg would probably be lost. Even if he sent troops to try to save it, he believed the outcome would be the same. So if Vicksburg did fall, and if the Union army managed to force Lee's line back to Richmond, these twin blows to Southern morale would be intolerable.

On the other hand, if Lee could smash Joe Hooker again, and do so on Yankee soil, Southern spirits would soar. The increasingly powerful antiwar movement in the North, whose thousands of active supporters were known as "Copperheads," would win even more supporters. Their demands to end the war, bring the troops home, and let the Confederacy remain a separate nation appeared to many Southerners to be their only hope. The more battles Lee could win, the stronger these antiwar protests would become. In addition, a stunning defeat of the Army of the Potomac could lead, finally, to formal recognition and support from England and France.

These prospects were appealing. Lee and his men were confident of victory, especially after their brilliant successes at Fredericksburg and Chancellorsville only a few months apart. Lee told his friend Gen. Isaac Trimble that when Union troops came looking for him in Pennsylvania, he would "throw an overwhelming force on their advance, crush it, follow up the success, create a panic, and virtually destroy the army." Then, Lee added, "the war will be over."

Lee communicated that overwhelming confidence throughout the ranks, down to the newest private. Colonel Fremantle of Her Majesty's Coldstream Guards was struck by how certain the Confederates were of their victory. After meeting Gen. Joe Johnston near Vicksburg, the resolute Fremantle, determined to see as much as possible of the American civil conflict, had made his way to Virginia and followed Lee's army northward. He wrote,

> The [Confederate] staff officers spoke of the coming battle as a certainty, and the universal feeling was one of contempt for an enemy whom they had beaten so constantly, and under so many disadvantages.

They were so optimistic of success that they made no effort to conceal their plans. For several weeks before Lee's army headed north, Southern newspapers carried articles about the invasion. Some debated the relative advantages of different routes of march. By the end of May, it had become common knowledge. Joe Hooker sent a message to Lincoln describing the South's planned invasion as inevitable. Lee was coming and he was invincible. It was not only men in gray who believed that.

The invasion plans were simple. Gen. Richard Ewell would lead the army north with his Second Corps plus a cavalry brigade. They would move up the Shenandoah Valley on the western side of the Blue Ridge Mountains. Marching in three columns, they would cross the Potomac and then spread out, with some heading for Hagerstown, Greencastle, Chambersburg, and Carlisle and others moving toward Frederick, Emmitsburg, Gettysburg, and York farther east. In addition to spearheading the invasion, their goal was to round up horses and livestock and to empty the stores and barns of all the provisions they could carry, sending them back for the rest of the army.

Gen. A. P. Hill's Third Corps and Gen. James Longstreet's First Corps would follow in Ewell's path. Jeb Stuart was to lead his cavalry into Pennsylvania on the right flank of the Confederate forces and keep Lee informed of the location of Hooker's army. All was in readiness. Lee was coming. Now.

⊷══◉══⊶

ON JUNE 10, one-legged Richard Ewell, known fondly to his men as "Old Bald Head," led the Second Corps north. He headed up the Shenandoah Valley and in rapid succession chased thirteen thousand Yankee soldiers out of Berryville, Winchester, and Martinsburg. Three days later he crossed the Potomac River and captured Hagerstown and Sharpsburg along Antietam creek. In less than three weeks, the Second Corps advanced more than two hundred miles and captured twenty-eight Union cannon and close to four thousand troops. They appropriated five thousand barrels of flour, three thousand head of cattle, a trainload of ordnance and medical supplies, and hundreds of horses. They also stripped the countryside of cherries.

Ewell ate as much fruit as the next man. Unable to pick cherries because of his disability, he had others climb the trees for him. One [young man] assigned this duty watched in amazement as the general devoured branchful after branchful of the fruit, marveling that "so small a man could hold so many cherries."

The Confederates paid for much of what they took, although Union shopkeepers and farmers did not think they were receiving a fair price. And the only way their Confederate currency would have any value was if the rebels won the war.

Lee insisted on observing the proprieties. He did not want his army accused of looting and thievery. He wanted the world to know that his soldiers did not behave the way Union troops did in the South, simply taking whatever they wanted, sometimes at gunpoint. Lee told General Trimble, "I cannot hope that Heaven will prosper our cause when we are violating its laws. I shall, therefore, carry on the war in Pennsylvania without offending the sanctions of a high civilization and of Christianity."

On June 21, Lee issued General Orders Number 72, which directed that "No private property shall be injured or destroyed by any person belonging to or connected with the army, or taken, except by officers hereinafter designated." The orders specified that any and all goods requisitioned by Confederate forces should be paid for at the market price.

For the most part, Lee's men lived up to his high standards. There were some instances of civilians being robbed of watches, boots, money, and other valuables, but they were almost always committed by stragglers, not by regular soldiers. There were very few acts of plunder or vandalism when officers were present.

The only item stolen in quantity by Ewell's men were hats. The men needed hats for protection from the searing summer sun and they found large and ready supplies in every Northern town. When residents came out of their houses to line the streets and watch the rebels pass by, hands often reached out to snatch hats off unsuspecting male heads. The suddenly hatless civilians yelled and pointed but the soldiers were marching too fast to identify. Their officers, charged with keeping the columns in motion, had no time to stop and search for missing hats.

As Lee's troops advanced through Maryland and into Pennsylvania, they were increasingly astonished by the richness of the farms, the flourishing towns, fine homes, and well-dressed, well-fed people. For men who had grown to maturity believing unquestioningly in the superiority of a slave society, these sights were shocking. Historian Joseph Glatthaar examined letters and diaries written by the Virginia soldiers and described their reaction to the Northern countryside.

> Soldier after soldier wrote home of stunning landscape, with hardwood forests atop hills and lush pastureland and tidy fields scattered along the gentle slopes and valley floors. In Pennsylvania, the soil was rich and the livestock fat. Impressive stone homes and enormous barns dotted the panorama. Evidently, these middle-class farmers in a free labor society did quite well for themselves.

The rebel soldiers were also surprised at the large numbers of young men not in uniform. Back home, their wives, children, and younger brothers were working the farms; most of those families had no slaves. The South had few young men left on the land but the North seemed to have many to spare. The sight of so many potential replacements for Yankee soldiers was downright worrying.

Some Confederate officers asked a Chambersburg, Pennsylvania, man how long he thought the war would last. Another twenty years, he said, assuming the rebels could stand it that long. Jacob Hoke, a local resident, witnessed the exchange.

You, gentlemen, must have seen for yourselves since you have come North that there are any number of able-bodied men yet to draw upon, and the people here have scarcely yet awakened to the fact that there is a war upon their hands; but this invasion will open their eyes to the fact, and if it were possible for you to annihilate the whole of our armies now in the field, that would only bring out another and larger one to take you some morning before breakfast.

One Confederate officer looked at the others and said quietly, "There is more truth than fun in what he says."

⊷═◉═⊶

LEE CROSSED THE Potomac River into Maryland on June 25 and was greeted by a group of ladies bearing flowers. Some of the women were Southern sympathizers; others were simply curious to meet the legend. They welcomed him from under their umbrellas. Rain would not prevent them from the chance to meet Robert E. Lee.

After the women introduced themselves to the general, Lee presented Generals Longstreet and Pickett. Gracious speeches were made, the flowers offered and accepted. Then the ladies produced a wreath for his horse, Traveller. That was altogether too much fuss. Who did these women think he was—Jeb Stuart? It would not do for the head of an invading army to enter enemy territory with his horse wreathed in flowers. After some discussion, a compromise was reached. An aide would carry the wreath for the general's horse.

All along his route, people waited for hours in the rain to catch a glimpse of the famous rebel general. They were not disappointed, for Lee was still a majestic figure, with a full beard, almost white now, and his hair fluffed over his ears. He wore dark blue trousers, highly polished black Wellington boots, and a gray double-breasted jacket open at the neck to reveal a white linen shirt and black bow tie. The three stars of his rank formed a wreath on his collar.

Colonel Fremantle of the Coldstream Guards described Lee as

the handsomest man of his age I ever saw. He is fifty-six years old, tall, broad-shouldered, very well made, well set up, a thorough soldier in appearance; and his manners are most courteous and full of dignity. He is a perfect gentleman in every respect.

On those first few days in Maryland, as he rode through Hagerstown toward Pennsylvania, women continued to cluster on the road to greet him. One asked for a lock of his hair. He demurred, gracefully and gallantly, pointing out that nature was claiming too much of it already. And so it went as Lee led his army north—adulation, admiration, and fawning devotion from the people of Maryland, many of whom were Southern sympathizers. But even the young woman who defiantly waved a Union flag at Lee and his entourage was heard to exclaim, "Oh, I wish he was ours."

As the Army of Northern Virginia moved on, Lee's mood darkened. He continued to acknowledge those who came to greet him but he was growing increasingly worried. He had not heard from Jeb Stuart and the cavalry in more than ten days, so he had no idea of the location or movement of Joe Hooker's Union army. For all Lee knew, the Yankees could be marching on Richmond. He asked couriers, aides, and other officers about Stuart. Where is my cavalry? he inquired of startled generals, who also began to worry at the implications of the question. The absence of answers plagued Lee incessantly as he drove deep into enemy territory, leaving the Confederate capital ever more vulnerable.

As far back as June 15, ten days before he crossed the river, Lee had complained to Longstreet: "I have been waiting for the arrival of Stuart, or of information from him, but as yet have received none." Two days later he wrote again. "I have heard nothing of the movements of Gen. Hooker." On June 22, Lee sent a courier to try to find Stuart. His message read: "Do you know where [Hooker] is and what he is doing?"

The general's concern and uncertainty filtered down to the men. Lt.

John Dooley, a shy, sensitive twenty-one-year-old Virginia aristocrat whose nickname at Georgetown University had been Gentleman Jack, was marching with Pickett's division. He wrote in his diary about the "seven to ten thousand cavalry who should be with us but who, under the command of their dashing general, are far away toward Washington City, leaving our infantry and artillery unguarded in flank and rear."

A few days later, when a Pennsylvania physician visited Lee to ask if his blind mare could be exempted from conscription, he was shocked by Lee's appearance and manner. The man's worry and disturbed state of mind were obvious. The doctor wrote,

> Never have I seen so much emotion depicted upon a human counte-
> nance. With his hand at times clutching his hair, and with a con-
> tracted brow, he would walk with rapid strides for a few rods and
> then, as if he bethought himself of his actions, he would with a sud-
> den jerk produce an entire change in his features and demeanor and
> cast an inquiring gaze on me, only to be followed in a moment by the
> same contortions of face and agitation of person.

Oh, where was Stuart? And where was Hooker and the Union army?

⋆⇒◉⇐⋆

JOE HOOKER WAS across the Potomac heading north on a course roughly parallel to Lee's. He had crossed the river on June 23 and moved into Maryland, marching from Poolesville to Frederick, keeping his army between Lee's forces and Washington, D.C. On June 28 he left Frederick on a route east toward Taneytown, five miles from the Pennsylvania border. The first town across the border was Gettysburg.

Hooker was not happy to be shadowing Lee's army. When he heard that Lee was coming north, Hooker had wanted to march on Richmond but Lincoln had forbidden it. The president reminded him that

Lee's army was the objective, not the Confederate capital. Lincoln ordered Hooker to hound Lee, to "fret him and fret him."

But Hooker was the one who was fretting. The strength of his army had been reduced because of expiring enlistments and a growing sick list. He begged for reinforcements from the troops guarding Washington and other nearby garrisons, but Army Chief of Staff Halleck denied all requests. Hooker would have to confront Lee with what he had.

In addition, Hooker was almost as blind as Lee was. Although he had a general idea of the whereabouts of the Confederates, he had no notion of their objective. He was confused and perhaps a little fearful about meeting the man who had whipped him so thoroughly at Chancellorsville. He was also discouraged about what he perceived as a lack of support from Halleck and the president. On June 24, Hooker wired Halleck that he did not know if he was standing on his head or his feet!

Neither did the Maryland residents living in the path of Hooker's soldiers. Those farther west were more fortunate. The Confederate troops marching through their towns were courteous and well disciplined. But people on the Union route of march contended with hordes of unruly stragglers and drunken deserters who stole everything of value and terrorized civilians who got in their way.

A newspaper reporter witnessed the chaos in the wake of Hooker's army:

Take a worthless vagabond who has enlisted for the thirteen dollars a month instead of patriotism, who falls out of ranks because he is a coward and wants to avoid the battle, or because he is lazy and wants to steal a horse to ride on instead of marching, or because he is rapacious and wants to sneak about farmhouses and frighten or wheedle timid country women into giving him better food and lodging than camp life affords; make this armed coward or sneak thief drunk on bad whiskey, give him scores and hundreds of armed companions as desperate and drunken as himself; turn loose this motley crew, muskets and revolvers in hand . . . let them swagger and bully as cowards and vagabonds always do, steal or openly plunder as such thieves always will, [and] you have the condition of the country in the rear of our own army, on our own soil today.

These were the dregs of Hooker's force—far too many of them—but they did not represent the majority of the Army of the Potomac. Most soldiers, like those of the First Minnesota Volunteers, shouldered their weapons and marched on, accepting their responsibility to one another and to their country.

It was an awful march, hour after hour in the scorching sun that taxed even the Minnesota veterans of almost every campaign the Union fought in the east. Charley Goddard had enlisted in the regiment two years before at the age of fifteen, passing himself off as eighteen. On June 20, he wrote to his mother: "Since I last wrote we have been doing some 'Tall' marching. There has been no less than 70 men fell dead out of this Corps . . . caused by hard marching and excessive heat. There has been a great many disabled, also, about 1200 disabled and dead." And the campaign was just beginning.

"It was one of the most heartbreaking marches of our experience," wrote Sgt. James Wright, a former Hamline University student. "Many men wilted in the scorching heat and dust like mown grass. . . . There were a number of cases of fatal sunstroke, and some dying almost as quickly as if struck by a bullet." Matthew Marvin wrote, "I came darned near going under two or three times. I thought sure I was a gone duck."

Francis Donaldson, a twenty-two-year-old captain in the 118th Pennsylvania Volunteers, also had good reason to remember the march.

We have lost a dozen men or more in the brigade from sunstroke, and yesterday Lt. Col. Gleason of the 25th New York was overcome and died from the sun's effects, and as soon as we halted was buried in a little churchyard hard by. The dust was most appalling and a fearful looking set we are anyway. By keeping wet leaves in my hat and boughs carried overhead I continued to keep off the sun, and when I could do so I thoroughly wet my head and neck. It was a novel sight to see the mass of men carrying boughs and branches of trees. Truly we looked not unlike a walking forest.

The Minnesota Volunteers passed through Centreville in northern Virginia and crossed the battlefield at Bull Run where two years before the regiment had undergone its baptism by fire. Many of the dead from the first and second Bull Run battles had not been buried deeply, just covered over with dirt. Hands and skeletons reached out to the marchers, as though beckoning from their shallow graves, grim reminders of the trials that awaited them.

Some corpses had not been buried at all. Capt. Sam Fiske of the Fourteenth Connecticut Volunteers said he was

much shocked to find such great numbers of bodies . . . lying still unburied. Their skeletons, with the tattered and decaying uniforms still hanging upon them, lie in many parts of last year's battlefield, in long ranks, just as they fell; and in one place, under a tree, was a whole circle of the remains of wounded soldiers who had been evidently left to die under the shade to which they had crawled, some of them with bandages round their skeleton limbs.

Someone with a macabre sense of humor had placed atop a tree stump a skull with its skin intact and a bullet hole through one side and out the other. It appeared to be guarding the dead. The soldiers grew quiet as they passed it. He could have been a rebel, or one of their own. It made no difference anymore.

Near Haymarket, Virginia, the regiment skirmished with Jeb Stuart's cavalry, which was in the process of riding the perimeter of the Union army in a glory raid. They did not linger long enough to do serious battle, but they threw a scare into the bunch of sutlers, chaplains, surgeons, and other noncombatants who had thought they would be safe by sticking with the Minnesota regiment bringing up the rear.

The regiment crossed the Potomac River at ten o'clock on the night of June 26 and trudged on through Maryland, knowing, fearing, and hoping that they were closing in on Lee and his rebel army. The sooner they trounced the Confederates, the sooner they could go home. Sgt. Henry Taylor voiced their thoughts: "I presume we will meet the enemy in battle ere long."

⊷⇒◎⇐⊷

AT ELEVEN O'CLOCK on the night of June 15, the brigade of two thousand cavalry scouting ahead of Ewell's Second Corps thundered into Chambersburg, Pennsylvania, fewer than twenty miles from Gettysburg. Led by Brig. Gen. Albert Jenkins, they quickly occupied the town, shouting for the mayor to make an appearance. Suddenly, a horse stumbled on a pile of stones, throwing its rider and causing his carbine to fire. No one was hit, but one resident opened the shutters of his second-floor window and leaned out to see what had happened.

Some troopers, hearing the shot and glimpsing a figure in a darkened window, assumed the local man had opened fire on them. Angrily they pounded on the man's door, yelling threats to hang him. He slipped out the back door disguised in one of his wife's dresses and a sunbonnet. And so the war came to the people of Chambersburg.

Most of the troopers did not stay in town. By morning, the majority of them had ridden out about a mile to block off the roads in case Yankees turned up. General Jenkins and his staff established headquarters in town and ordered the citizens to bring all weapons to the courthouse within two hours' time. Most people complied; the alternative was a house-by-house search. The Confederates confiscated the usable guns and bashed the others to pieces on the courthouse steps.

General Jenkins ordered that every shop be opened for two hours so his men could purchase whatever they wanted. The merchants had little stock left, having hidden most of their goods or shipped them out of town. The soldiers carted off almost everything else, paying with their Confederate promissory notes and scrip.

The Confederates generally observed the proprieties about paying fair market value. But one soldier who stole a pile of ladies' dresses made the mistake of walking past Jenkins's headquarters carrying his loot. The general dragged the man back to the store, waving his sword and threatening to lop off the trooper's head. "Sell my men all the goods they want," Jenkins told the shopkeeper, "but if any one attempts to take anything without paying for it, report to me at my headquarters. We are not thieves."

A week later General Ewell arrived in Chambersburg with his Second Corps, accompanied by a military band playing "The Bonnie Blue Flag." The whole town turned out to watch the spectacle. A resident, Jacob Hoke, described the event.

> Their dress consisted of nearly every imaginable color and style, the butternut largely predominating. Some had blue blouses, which they had doubtless stripped from the Union dead. . . . Many were ragged, shoeless, and filthy, affording unmistakable evidence that their wardrobes sadly needed to be replenished. They were, however, all well armed and under perfect discipline. They seemed to move as one vast machine. Laughing, talking, singing, and cheering were not indulged in. Straggling was rarely seen.

The Confederate army was much in evidence in Chambersburg for several days. John Dooley, who marched through with Pickett's division, recalled, "we found the people very sullen and maliciously disposed, and not a few maledictions were hurled at us from garret windows by croaking crones; and many young but frowning brows and pouting lips we saw in doorways."

Colonel Fremantle of the Coldstream Guards rode through Chambersburg with Longstreet's corps. "All its houses were shut up; but the natives were in the streets, or at the upper windows, looking in a scowling and bewildered manner. . . . The women (many of whom were pretty and well dressed) were particularly sour and disagreeable in their remarks." General Ewell said that "The people look as sour as vinegar and I have no doubt would gladly send us all to kingdom come if they could."

Fremantle recalled a husky woman who draped a large American flag across her ample bosom as John Bell Hood's ragged, irreverent Texans ambled by. "Take care, madam," one of them yelled, "for Hood's boys are great at storming breastworks when the Yankee colors is on them!" Fremantle said the woman hastily retreated indoors.

General Ewell levied a huge requisition of supplies, enumerating his requirements for the town's leaders:

- 5,000 suits of clothing
- 100 saddles and bridles
- 5,000 bushels of grain
- 10,000 pounds of sole leather
- 10,000 pounds of horseshoes
- 6,000 pounds of lead
- 400 pistols
- 50,000 pounds of bread
- 100 sacks of salt
- 30 barrels of molasses
- 500 bushels of flour
- 11,000 pounds of coffee and sugar
- 25 barrels of sauerkraut

Ewell also asked for the town's supply of neat's-foot oil (a lubricant and a dressing for leather) and large quantities of vinegar, potatoes, beans, and dried fruit.

It was impossible to meet Ewell's demands, since most goods had been hidden or shipped elsewhere. The local merchants furnished the minimum they thought they could get away with. They told Ewell that even if he threatened to torch the town, no more supplies would be forthcoming.

Ewell's men, and later Longstreet's, were more successful in the countryside, where they seized horses, hogs, and cattle. When a farmer's wife protested to General Longstreet about the loss of her livestock, he replied, "Yes, madam, it's very sad, very sad; and this sort of thing has been going on in Virginia more than two years."

General Lee arrived in Chambersburg on June 27 and set up his headquarters less than a mile from town in a grove of trees known as Shatter's Woods. In happier days, it had been the local picnic ground. Now it held six tents and a Confederate flag.

Concerned about reports of looting by some Confederate soldiers, Lee ordered that no one below the rank of general be allowed to stay in Chambersburg. The less contact the army had with civilians, the fewer opportunities there would be for thievery and other kinds of behavior Lee found unacceptable for his army.

He issued General Orders Number 73, praising his men for their conduct on the march north. He complimented them on their fortitude and exemplary behavior but chastised the minority who had disobeyed his admonition against improper behavior toward civilians:

> It must be remembered that we make war only upon armed men, and that we cannot take vengeance for the wrongs our people have suffered without lowering ourselves in the eyes of all whose abhorrence has been excited by the atrocities of our enemies, and offending against Him to whom vengeance belongeth, without whose favor and support our efforts must all prove in vain.

He concluded his appeal by enjoining his officers to arrest and punish anyone who committed offenses against civilians or their property.

The civilians wasted no time in besieging Lee with complaints about the privations that they were suffering. He listened courteously and patiently while they talked about eggs stolen from a henhouse and

soldiers trampling down their fields. Mrs. Ellen McLellan asked for
the return of some flour that had been requisitioned, because so many
families in town were running out of bread. He told her to send one of
the millers to see him so that he could find out how much flour the
townspeople needed. As she was about to leave, Mrs. McLellan asked
Lee for his autograph. Jacob Hoke recorded the woman's recollection
of Lee's response.

> He replied: "Do you want the autograph of a rebel?" I said: "General
> Lee, I am a true Union woman, and yet I ask for bread and your
> autograph." The general replied, "It is to your interest to be for the
> Union, and I hope you may be as firm in your principles as I am in
> mine." He assured me that his autograph would be a dangerous
> thing, and that he only desired that they would let him go home and
> eat his bread there in peace. All this time I was impressed with the
> strength and sadness of the man.

Lee had reason to be sad and to be worried about the direction of his
campaign. He still had no news from Jeb Stuart and thus had no
knowledge of Hooker and the Union army. Were they advancing on
Richmond or staying near Washington to protect it from a Confederate attack? Or were they assembling just over the horizon waiting for
him? Lee also considered the possibility that Hooker, too, was at a disadvantage and might not know for certain where the Confederates
were. Both armies might be groping in the dark.

He did find some reason for optimism, however. The Southern
troops were well fed and better equipped than they had been in a long
time, and their morale and fighting spirit were high. And Joe Hooker
had demonstrated in the past that he lacked aggressiveness and staying
power when challenged. Perhaps this time Lee would defeat him even
more decisively.

Lee was further encouraged by comments from his friend Gen. Isaac
Trimble, who had lived and worked as a railroad engineer in that part

of Pennsylvania before the war. He told Lee that the country to the east of Chambersburg was perfect for maneuvering a large army and waging battle. Lee was pleased to hear that news and offered Trimble his own assessment of the situation. "Our army is in good spirits, not overfatigued, and can be concentrated on any one point in twenty-four hours or less. I have not yet heard that the enemy have crossed the Potomac and am waiting to hear from General Stuart."

Lee was still assuming that if Hooker had crossed the river and was heading north toward him, Stuart would surely be aware of it and would have warned him. He discussed this with Trimble:

When [the Union troops] hear where we are, they will make forced marches to interpose their forces between us and Baltimore and Philadelphia. They will come up, probably through Frederick, broken down with hunger and hard marching, strung out on a long line and much demoralized, when they come into Pennsylvania. I shall throw an overwhelming force on their advance, crush it, follow up the success, drive one corps back on another, and by successive repulses and surprises, before they can concentrate, create a panic and virtually destroy the army.

Trimble told Lee what he knew Lee wanted to hear, and what he believed himself, that the plan would succeed because the morale and spirit of the men had never been higher. Lee placed his hand on a map and pointed to a small town on the other side of South Mountain. "Hereabout," Lee said, "we shall probably meet the enemy and fight a great battle, and if God gives us the victory, the war will be over and we shall achieve the recognition of our independence." Trimble looked at the map. Lee's finger pointed to Gettysburg.

✦

"ON THE 26TH of June they came in considerable force." That was how Fannie Buehler remembered the arrival of the rebel cavalry in

Gettysburg at about 2:30 that afternoon. It was Jenkins's brigade, once again spearheading Ewell's Second Corps. Sallie Broadhead said, "They came with such horrid yells that it was enough to frighten us all to death. They came in on three roads, and we soon were surrounded by them." The soldiers raced through town, shouting and firing their revolvers in the air, easily intimidating the residents.

One of the most intimidated was Fannie Buehler's husband. As the town postmaster, a government job, he feared the rebels would transport him to Richmond as a prisoner or kill him on the spot. At the first sign of the enemy he stuffed a satchel with his official papers and stamps and raced out of town, one step ahead of the cavalry. Fannie saw him go and wondered if she would ever see him again. She did, but not until the battle was over.

Sallie Myers recorded the day's events in her diary:

> At last we have seen the rebels, and such a mean looking lot of men I never saw in my life. . . . I am not afraid of them and did not believe they were coming as I stood on the corner until two of them rode by furiously brandishing their sabres and pointing pistols.

Fifteen-year-old Tillie Pierce was in class at the Young Ladies Seminary when she and her schoolmates heard the shouts. The rebels were coming! Their teacher told the girls to run home at once. Tillie covered the two blocks to her house as fast as she could and as she reached the front door, she saw the men on horseback. She wrote, in her breathless, adolescent prose,

> I scrambled in, slammed shut the door, and hastening to the sitting room, peeped out between the shutters. What a horrible sight! There they were, human beings! Clad almost in rags, covered with dust, riding wildly, pell-mell down the hill toward our home! shouting, yelling most unearthly, cursing, brandishing their revolvers, and firing right and left.

Others also recalled the ragged condition of the rebels. Michael Jacobs, a professor at the Lutheran Theological Seminary, said they were exceedingly dirty and that some had no shoes. Fifteen-year-old Albertus McCreary said one cavalryman had spurs strapped to his bare feet. Fannie Buehler wrote,

> I never saw a more unsightly set of men, and as I looked at them in their dirty, torn garments, hatless, shoeless, and footsore, I pitied them from the depth of my heart. They excited my sympathy, and not fear, as one would suppose. I wondered what this coming meant; what they were going to do; and how long they were going to stay.

One reason why Jenkins's brigade looked so unkempt was that it was always the first to enter a town and the first to leave to set up the defensive perimeter on the outskirts. Consequently, the men rarely had the opportunity to participate in shopping expeditions the way the infantry did.

Jenkins's brigade was followed by the infantry, some five thousand men of Gen. Jubal Early's division, part of Ewell's Second Corps. They made camp in the open area in front of the courthouse, almost across the street from Fannie Buehler's house, then set out to explore their new territory.

Gettysburg was a prosperous community of twenty-four hundred people with fine homes and some 450 buildings. About 8 percent of the town's population were blacks, mostly runaway slaves; Gettysburg was a stop on the Underground Railroad, which led hundreds of slaves to freedom in the North.

The thriving economy provided jobs at the iron works, foundry, stove factory, brickyard, tanneries, blacksmiths, and carriage makers. Shops catered to nearly every need. There were nine law firms (Gettysburg being the county seat), three weekly newspapers, and two colleges—Pennsylvania (later Gettysburg) College and the Lutheran Seminary. With ten highways and the Gettysburg Railroad, the town was a regional commercial center. It even had paved sidewalks. To poor Southern boys, this was another reminder of how overwhelmingly wealthy the Yankees seemed to be.

As usual, the rebels quickly tried to requisition some of those riches for themselves. Shortly after Jubal Early arrived on the afternoon of June 26, he submitted his requirements to the local leaders. He desired sixty barrels of flour, seven thousand pounds of pork or bacon, twelve hundred pounds of sugar, one hundred pounds of coffee, one thousand pounds of salt, forty bushels of onions, one thousand pairs of shoes, and five hundred hats. Or, Early noted, he would accept ten thousand dollars in cash.

He received few of the supplies he wanted and no cash. The town council replied with a brusque note: "The requisitions asked for can not be given, because it is utterly impossible to comply. The quantities required are far beyond that in our possession." The only concession made was the offer to open the stores and ask the merchants to supply what they could.

Early did not press the matter, and his men went on only a modest shopping spree, buying up whatever had not already been shipped out of town or hidden. There was precious little available, and more than one Confederate soldier said he had trouble understanding how such a prosperous place could have so few goods in the shops. Nevertheless, the Southerners were always courteous in their dealings, paying the prices asked with their own currency. When one proprietor objected to the Confederate bills, his customer replied confidently, "In two months our money will be better than yours."

Ten-year-old Charles McCurdy gazed enviously through the window of Philip Winter's sweetshop as the rebels bought all the remaining goods. One soldier walked out with his upturned hat full of candy. He stopped when he saw McCurdy, pulled out a handful of treats, and gave them to the boy.

A few horses were stolen, including one belonging to Tillie Pierce's family, and some cellars were broken into and ransacked, but overall the rebels followed Lee's orders and behaved properly. They committed no major indignities, at least not to the white residents. Blacks were fair game. Albertus McCreary watched as some black residents were forced to line up and march out of town, to be returned to the South and sold into slavery.

Most of Gettysburg's black citizens had fled before the Confederates arrived, but some who stayed managed to avoid capture. A woman who worked for the McCreary family, for example, slipped away from the line of captives and hid in a church belfry for two days without food or water. Some white families hid black men and women until the crisis passed. One black farmhand stayed under cover in a wagon for three days while the farmer's son supplied him with food. Others were sheltered in attics and closets, despite the families' fears that rebel soldiers would search their homes.

For the most part, relations were satisfactory, even cordial, between the occupied and the occupiers. However, the townspeople did not appreciate the rebels' band concert. They did not like hearing "Dixie" and other Confederate songs. The soldiers enjoyed them, of course, and knowing that they were causing discomfort for the Yankees may have added to their pleasure.

Fannie Buehler was sitting on the front steps of her home across from the courthouse one evening when several soldiers asked if they might join her. "We had a pleasant talk," she recalled, with "no bitterness expressed by them or me." They told her how amazed they were by the North's prosperity and by the sight of so many men not in uniform.

Fannie explained that the Union army already had all the soldiers it required and that thousands of other men were ready to fill the ranks if needed. She added that the sooner the Confederates accepted the superior strength and wealth of the North, the better it would be for all of them. The soldiers fell silent for a moment. Then one said:

"Well, we haven't as many men left in the South as you have and not as much money, for look at these ragged clothes, but we will get better ones after we have been North awhile."

"Oh, I replied, how long are you going to stay?"

"Why, all summer, of course."

Fannie was alarmed at the thought that the rebels planned to occupy Gettysburg for months, so she was greatly relieved the next morning to find that all the soldiers had departed. By nine o'clock Gettysburg had returned to being a peaceful little town.

Elsewhere in Pennsylvania the war was spreading. Jubal Early proceeded from Gettysburg to York, where the town fathers foolishly agreed to pay him a ransom of twenty-eight thousand dollars. The rebel force moved on toward Wrightsville, with the intention of launching an attack on Harrisburg, the state capital. The rest of Ewell's Second Corps captured Carlisle. His forward units were also within striking distance of Harrisburg.

Joe Hooker seemed to be doing little to stop the Confederates' advances. Reluctantly he had crossed the Potomac River and moved his force north, but only after repeated prodding from President Lincoln. When another officer asked Hooker what his plans were, he replied that he did not know or care. He would simply do what Washington instructed—and no more. If there was to be another Union defeat at Lee's hands, let it be someone else's fault, not Hooker's.

General Marsena Patrick, the Union's provost marshal, wrote in his diary that Hooker, "acts like a man without a plan, and is entirely at a loss what to do. He knows that Lee is his master, and is afraid to meet him in fair battle."

The troops also lacked confidence in Hooker. Capt. Donaldson of the 118th Pennsylvania Volunteers wrote to his aunt that "There is a good deal of grumbling about Hooker and the men are convinced he is not competent to handle them." A homemade concoction of whiskey, water, sugar, and nutmeg became famous throughout the Fifth Corps; it was known as Hooker's Retreat, a reference to his behavior at Chancellorsville.

Hooker bombarded the War Department with requests for additional troops. He demanded control of all the units in the Washington,

D.C., area as well as the 10,000-man garrison at Harpers Ferry. He needed more troops, he said, because Lee's army was over 100,000 strong. Hooker grossly exaggerated the size of the rebel force. One of Hooker's staff officers noted that Hooker's "only salvation [is] to make it appear that the enemy's forces are larger than his own, which is false, and he knows it." Lincoln and Stanton knew it as well and refused Hooker's requests.

At one o'clock on the afternoon of June 27, Hooker sent a telegram officially requesting to be relieved of command. If Lincoln and Stanton had hoped for Hooker's departure, their wish was granted, but apparently they had given no thought to his replacement.

<hr />

THE PRESIDENT AND secretary of war met in Stanton's War Department office. Lincoln looked gloomy and sat silently while Stanton reviewed the list of candidates to replace General Hooker. Stanton described the qualifications of each officer of sufficient rank to command the Army of the Potomac. With each name, he offered little praise and much criticism. This was not an impressive group.

After a lengthy discussion, Stanton finally, albeit reluctantly, focused on Meade as the best of the group. He had certainly demonstrated competence, though not brilliance, as a commander. He had avoided political infighting and intrigue. And he was a native of Pennsylvania, where the battle was likely to take place. That seemed to be the deciding factor for Lincoln. "He will fight well on his own dunghill," Lincoln said.

And so it was settled. The fate of the nation would rest with George Gordon Meade, a man who had never wanted to be a soldier in the first place. But once the decision was made, it had to be implemented immediately. Since no one knew where Lee planned to strike next, the change of command would be made that night.

The orders were written and signed. A special locomotive made ready to leave the capital, and cash was assembled for expenses. Col. James A. Hardie of the War Department staff was summoned and charged with finding General Meade as quickly as possible. Hardie was reluctant to undertake the assignment, since he was a friend of both Hooker and Meade, but a colonel does not refuse orders from the president and the secretary of war.

Hardie changed into civilian clothes in the hope of eluding capture in case Jeb Stuart's cavalry stopped his locomotive. He boarded the engine and took off northwest to cover the forty miles to Meade's headquarters at Frederick, Maryland. He arrived after midnight to find drunken soldiers in command of the streets. In his civilian clothes he could exert no authority over them or secure army transportation to Meade's camp. He could not even requisition a horse.

Hardie was finally able to hire a civilian driver and buggy, but his problems were far from over. The roads were clogged with caravans of army wagons and rowdy soldiers ill disposed to give way to a civilian conveyance. Worse, no one seemed to know exactly where Meade's headquarters was located.

When they finally found the Union army headquarters, at almost three o'clock in the morning, Meade's staff at first refused to awaken him. After considerable argument, Hardie was shown to Meade's tent. He woke the general, said he had been sent by the War Department, then made what he thought was a joke: he told Meade he had come to give him trouble.

Meade's first reaction was to suspect he was being placed under arrest. He told Hardie that his conscience was clear and that he was prepared to deal with whatever charges had been levied against him. When Hardie told him the real purpose of his visit, Meade protested vigorously. He insisted that Gen. John Reynolds should be given command, instead. Meade said he was unprepared for such a difficult assignment and would telegraph the War Department asking that his orders be rescinded. Hardie persuaded him that he had no choice.

Meade's reaction was not encouraging. He said, "I've been tried and condemned without a hearing, and I suppose I shall have to go to execution."

Meade dressed and asked that his son George, who had joined his staff as a captain a few weeks ago, come to his tent. They stepped outside and a newspaper reporter, aware that Hardie's late-night visit indicated something of importance, recorded his observations of the general's appearance in the glow of the campfires. "He was standing with bowed head and downcast eyes, his slouched hat drawn down, shading his features. He seemed lost in thought. His uniform was the worse for wear from hard service; there was dust upon his boots."

Colonel Hardie and the Meades walked to Hooker's tent. Hooker had been expecting them. He received them in his dress uniform and impassively read the orders relieving him of command of the Army of the Potomac and reassigning him to an insignificant post in Baltimore.

The two generals discussed the military situation. Meade was distressed to learn that his army was scattered over a wide area. Then they wrote general orders to be distributed to the troops. Hooker referred to Meade as "a brave and accomplished officer, who has nobly earned the confidence and esteem of the army on many a well-fought field. Impressed with the belief that my usefulness as a commander of the Army of the Potomac is impaired, I part from it; yet not without the deepest emotion."

In his statement accepting command, Meade was equally effusive in praising Hooker. Then he spoke of the ordeal ahead.

The country looks to this army to relieve it from the devastation and disgrace of a hostile invasion. Whatever fatigues and sacrifices we may be called upon to undergo, let us have in view constantly the magnitude of the interests involved, and let each man determine to do his duty, leaving to an all-controlling Providence the decision of the contest.

⤙⟶◉⟵⤚

GEORGE MEADE LOOKED older than his forty-eight years. His hair was flecked with gray. Lines of worry streaked his face and deep creases flared alongside his nose. He was tall, scrawny, and unattractive. His men called him "a damned old goggle-eyed, snapping turtle." The oversize glasses that magnified his bulging eyes added to this impression. He always seemed to be angry and ready to explode. A staff officer suggested that Meade was like a firecracker whose fuse was constantly lit.

Meade seemed more like a scholar than a soldier, and his irascibility and uninspiring personality did not motivate or endear him to his troops. He was far from being a charismatic leader. He received few cheers from his men, the way Hooker and McClellan had in the past. And although some of the soldiers may have respected Meade, they did not revere him.

Given all that, it was no surprise that his appointment was received with little enthusiasm. Assistant Secretary of War Charles Dana, out west in Vicksburg with Grant, wrote:

> As a commander, Meade seemed to me to lack the boldness that was necessary to bring the war to a close. He lacked self-confidence and tenacity of purpose. . . . As soon as Meade had a commander over him he was all right, but when he himself was the commander he began to hesitate.

The soldiers far down the line wondered what Meade had done to merit the promotion. Capt. Sam Fiske said that Meade's appointment was "most unlooked for by us all, and one not likely to inspire the greatest amount of confidence." For a time following the announcement, morale plummeted. Among the Minnesota Volunteers, the "intelligence that 'Fighting Joe' is superseded by Gen. Meade falls on us 'like a wet blanket.'" The men believed they were doing their damnedest to put down the rebellion despite a series of incompetent generals. Now it looked like they were getting another one.

One of the few people who had anything good to say about Meade was the man who selected him for the job. When President Lincoln read a note Meade had sent to General Halleck, promising to give Lee a battle, the president seemed pleased. "I tell you," Lincoln said, "I think a great deal of that fine fellow Meade."

Meade faced an awesome task. He inherited an army whose units were dispersed. In addition, no one could tell him exactly where the units were located. There seemed to be no operations or procedures for Meade to implement. Hooker had left no present or future plans for the Army of the Potomac—for the simple reason that he had never formulated any.

In short, Meade did not know the whereabouts of his army or that of the enemy, and he had no idea what operations might be in progress. He later testified before the U.S. Congress,

> My predecessor, General Hooker, left the camp in a very few hours after I relieved him. I received from him no intimations of any plan, or any views that he may have had up to that moment, and I am not aware that he had any, but was waiting for the exigencies of the occasion to govern him.

Meade demonstrated immediately that he would not wait for the exigencies of the occasion to govern his initial actions. At 4:45 that afternoon he telegraphed the War Department to announce that the next day he would march his army northeast, toward York, Pennsylvania. That much done, with dispatch and resolution, Meade wrote to his wife.

> Dearest, you know how reluctant we both have been to see me placed in this position, and as it appears to be God's will for some good pur-

pose—at any rate, as a soldier I had nothing to do but accept. . . . I am moving at once against Lee.

-→═◉═←-

AT TEN O'CLOCK that night Lee received alarming news. He was in his camp at Shatter's Woods outside Chambersburg when Maj. John Fairfax called on him. Fairfax was an aide to Longstreet and was known to begin each day basking in his metal tub, reading his Bible, and drinking whiskey, all before breakfast. Fairfax told Lee that Henry Harrison, one of Longstreet's civilian scouts, had just returned from a mission behind enemy lines and reported that the Union army had moved north of the Potomac.

Lee was stunned. How could this have happened? How could they have crossed the river without Jeb Stuart knowing and reporting it to Lee immediately? Maybe it wasn't true. Lee had never trusted spies, but he knew he could not dismiss the information. If correct, then his army, now scattered over many miles, was in grave danger.

"I do not know what to do," Lee told Fairfax. "I cannot hear from General Stuart, the eye of the army. What do you think of Harrison? I have no confidence in any scout, but General Longstreet thinks a good deal of Harrison."

Major Fairfax ventured no opinion about the scout, though he likely knew that Harrison was paid $150 a month, which he insisted on collecting in greenbacks rather than Confederate currency. Fairfax left Lee alone to ponder the situation. Some time later, Lee decided that he should talk to the scout in person. Harrison arrived, "dirt-stained, travel-worn, and very much broken down" from his exhausting and dangerous mission behind enemy lines.

Harrison had traveled from Culpeper, Virginia, to Washington, D.C., where he spent freely in the bars and taverns, picking up gossip and rumor. That was where he first heard that the Union army had crossed the Potomac River and was moving north. He realized the significance of this intelligence and how vital it was to verify it in person. He would have to find the Union army for himself, not merely take the word of some drunken soldiers in a Washington saloon.

He made his way on foot to Frederick, and he spied a large contingent of the Army of the Potomac more than twelve miles north of the river. He told Lee he had seen two infantry corps on the outskirts of Frederick and that there was a third corps nearby, though he had been unable to see it. On his way to Chambersburg to report to Longstreet, Harrison crossed paths with two additional corps of Union troops considerably north of Frederick, close to South Mountain. And, he added, George Meade had been named to replace Fighting Joe Hooker.

The more Lee analyzed Harrison's report, the more disturbed he became. The Yankees were not only across the river but dangerously close to his position. And he had no cavalry to track them and determine where they were heading.

Lee's army was scattered. He would need to concentrate his forces, bringing all the units together, and move them as an army east of South Mountain. Meade would surely interpret such movement as a thrust toward Philadelphia or Baltimore, or perhaps Washington.

Meade would then be forced to pursue Lee to protect the great Northern cities. And Lee would then be able to catch the Yankees while they were in motion, strung out along the roads for miles, exhausted from a forced march in the awful summer heat. Lee could attack them piecemeal and obliterate them.

Orders went out to recall Ewell's Second Corps from York and Carlisle, and to cancel Longstreet's and Hill's advance northward. All three corps were ordered to assemble east of Chambersburg near Cashtown on the road to Gettysburg.

CHAPTER 7

TO FIND AND FIGHT THE ENEMY

June 28, 1863

"STILL IN THIS dreary cave," wrote Margaret Lord in her diary. "Who would have believed that we could have borne such a life for five weeks? The siege has lasted 42 days and yet no relief. Every day this week we have waited for the sound of Gen. Johnston's guns, but in vain."

The people of Vicksburg, soldiers and civilians, were running out of everything, including hope. The city was dying. Sgt. Willie Tunnard of the Third Regiment, Louisiana Infantry, wrote that Vicksburg had been

> visited with a terrible scourge. Signs wrenched from their fastenings; houses dilapidated and in ruins, rent and torn by shot and shell; the streets barricaded with earth-works. . . . The avenues were almost deserted, save by hunger-pinched, starving, and wounded soldiers, or guards lying on the banquettes, indifferent to the screaming and exploding shells. The stores, the few that were open, looked like the ghost of more prosperous times, with their empty shelves, and scant stock of goods. . . .

Palatial residences were crumbling into ruins, the walks torn up by mortar shells, the flowerbeds, once blooming in all the regal beauty of spring loveliness, trodden down, the shrubbery neglected. . . . Fences were torn down, and houses pulled to pieces for firewood. Even the enclosures around the remains of the revered dead were destroyed, while wagons were parked around the graveyard, horses trampling down the graves, and men using the tombstones as convenient tables for their scanty meals. . . .

Dogs howled through the streets at night; cats screamed forth their hideous cries; an army of rats, seeking food, would scamper around your very feet and across the streets and all over the pavements. Lice and filth covered the bodies of the soldiers. Delicate women and little children, with pale, careworn and hunger-pinched features, peered at the passerby with wistful eyes from the caves in the hillsides.

Add to all these horrors, so faintly portrayed, the deep-toned thunder of mortars and heavy guns, the shrill whistle of rifle-shot, or the duller sound of flying mortar shells; the crash of buildings torn into fragments; the fearful detonation of the explosions shaking heaven and earth; the hurtling masses of iron continually descending, and you may form some conception of the conditions of the city.

Mary Loughborough sat deep in her cave nursing her two-year-old daughter, who was ill with fever and weak from hunger. A soldier brought the child a tiny jaybird to cheer her up. The girl fondled the bird listlessly for a short time but quickly grew so fatigued that she had to put it down. Mary's maid wanted to make soup from the bird; the child needed food for strength more than she needed a toy. Mary consented and the maid returned with a cup of soup and a plate of the cooked white meat of the little bird.

The stench of death hung like a fog over the city. Mules, horses, and cows keeled over from lack of forage and lay for days where they had fallen before workmen carted them to the river and tossed them in.

Often, starving people descended on the carcasses with knives or bayonets to slice off chunks of the rotting flesh for food.

Compounding the stink from dead animals was the overpowering smell of undigested peas. The army diet now included little more than peas, but the soldiers' digestive tracts had been so taxed by malnutrition that the peas tended to pass through the body whole. Mounds of undigested excreted peas lay behind every yard of the eight-mile trench line. The pestilence, hunger, and disease reached into every outpost, cellar, and cave. Erysipelas, a highly contagious skin inflammation, was spreading rapidly, but there was no medicine to treat it. Measles broke out, especially among children and slaves. The only remedy available was strong corn whiskey, which frequently brought on nausea.

To Dora Miller, the entire city seemed like a sick ward. Most houses and buildings had been turned into hospitals and convalescent homes, and the army's giant tent infirmaries were so crowded that there were not enough beds for all the patients. By the closing days of June, nearly six thousand rebel soldiers were in hospitals, many for sickness rather than combat wounds. And many more soldiers—some estimates put the figure at half the rebel strength—were so ill they should have been hospitalized. Some refused to be treated out of a strong sense of duty; others because they were terrified of catching erysipelas, now endemic in the hospitals. They considered themselves safer in the trenches.

All the while the Union shells exploded and the bullets flew, carrying away more men every hour. The Reverend Dr. Lord witnessed the killing of an orderly holding an officer's horse. His son, William, described what happened.

Even as my father watched him, admiring his erect and soldierly bearing, the [cannon] ball struck the orderly's head from his shoulders and left the headless trunk, still holding the reins of the horse and standing as erect and soldier-like as when alive. The noiseless cannon ball had so quietly done its deadly work that the horse took no alarm but stood as still as the corpse that held it.

At dusk on June 28, a letter was slipped into General Pemberton's headquarters. No one saw who put it there. Its contents were dismal and chilling. The letter began by praising Pemberton for his leadership and patriotism during the siege. The anonymous writer also praised the troops for their patient endurance of the dangers and hardships faced so gallantly for forty-two days.

Everybody admits that we have all covered ourselves in glory, but alas! alas! general, a crisis has arrived in the midst of our siege.

Our rations have been cut down to . . . not enough scarcely to keep soul and body together, much less to stand the hardships we are called upon to stand. . . .

Men don't want to starve, and don't intend to, but they call upon you for justice, if the commissary department can give it; if it can't, you must adopt some means to relieve us very soon. The emergency of the case demands prompt and decided action on your part.

If you can't feed us, you had better surrender us, horrible as the idea is, than suffer this noble army to disgrace themselves by desertion. I tell you plainly, men are not going to lie here and perish, if they do love their country dearly. Self-preservation is the first law of nature, and hunger will compel a man to do almost anything.

You had better heed a warning voice, though it is the voice of a private soldier. This army is ripe for mutiny, unless it can be fed.

The letter was signed, simply, "Many Soldiers."

Some of Pemberton's staff officers claimed that no Confederate soldier would have written such a defeatist letter to his commanding general. It must be clever Yankee propaganda. They may have been correct. Admiral Porter had ingeniously floated propaganda messages over Vicksburg using kites. Although Porter never admitted that the letter signed "Many Soldiers" was his idea, the admiral's biographer, Chester Hearn, described it as "characteristic of his wit and looked like his scribbling. . . . The prose is classic Porter."

Whoever wrote it, from whichever side, the sentiment was accurate enough. The rebel troops were starving and most of the men were reaching the limit of their endurance.

The Union soldiers already knew that to be true. They saw clear evidence of it daily in the increasing numbers of deserters who came across from the other side. Charles Dana observed,

Every new party of deserters which reached us agreed that the provisions [in Vicksburg] were near the point of total exhaustion, that rations had been reduced lower than ever, that extreme dissatisfaction existed among the garrison, and it was generally expected (indeed, there was a sort of conviction) on the part of all hands that the city would be surrendered on Saturday, July 4th, if, indeed, it could hold out so long as that.

Brig. Gen. William Orme of the Ninety-fourth Illinois Regiment agreed with Dana. In a letter to his wife, Nannie, written on June 29, he said that he was "inclined to think that Vicksburg cannot hold out many days longer. They are now reduced to short rations, and in a few days longer, say a week or two, they must surrender, unless our information is very incorrect. . . . I should like very much to have them surrender before the 4th of July so that we could have a grand military celebration on that day."

Increasingly, soldiers on both sides sensed, or hoped, that the end would come as soon as July 4. This realization led to a degree of caution among the men in the trenches. If Vicksburg was about to fall anyway because of starvation, why should Union soldiers take undue chances? No one wanted to be killed or maimed to no purpose, when the sacrifice would not affect a fate already decreed. As a consequence of this attitude, the fighting, as the month of June came to an end, was noticeably less aggressive.

This newfound prudence was evident on July 1 when Union troops detonated another mine underneath a Confederate fort. The explosion destroyed the fort, opening a twenty-foot crater, but the Union troops did not advance. "No attempt to charge was made this time," General Grant wrote, "the experience of the 25th [with the previous mine] admonishing us."

Grant apparently recognized the mood of his men and knew that if he had ordered a charge, they would have done so only halfheartedly. He laid on a massive bombardment to follow the explosion but did nothing more to take advantage of the breach in the rebel line. On the other side, Major Lockett, Pemberton's chief engineer, called the action "the last stirring incident of the siege."

The Confederates paid a terrible price even though the Union forces did not advance. Sgt. Willie Tunnard saw the wounded and dying being rushed to the hospitals after this last great explosion.

> The spectacle was horrible in the extreme. Some writhing in the agonies of death, others bruised, torn, mangled, and lacerated by shell and shot, while others were blackened and burned from the effects of the explosives. . . .
>
> Surgeons with sleeves rolled up to their elbows, hands, arms, and shirts red with human gore, hastened hither and thither, or were using their keen-edged instruments in amputating some shattered limb, extracting balls and fragments of shells from the lacerated bodies, or probing some ghastly wound of the sufferers. Men, fearfully mangled in body and limbs, groaning with agony . . . others with crushed, bruised bodies lingering in speechless torment! Such were the scenes of war on this hot afternoon.

The will to fight may have languished, the end may have been inexorable, but still men died.

—•▧◍◌▧•—

BACK EAST, IN Maryland, George Meade wrote to his wife on June 29, resolutely announcing his intentions. "We are marching as fast as we can to relieve Harrisburg but have to keep a sharp lookout that the rebels don't turn around and get at Washington and Baltimore in our rear. . . . I am going straight at them and will settle this thing one way or the other. The men are in good spirits . . . and with God's blessing I hope to be successful."

Meade was assembling his scattered army and moving northward, but he still did not know where the rebels were heading. He explained his quandary in a telegram to General Halleck. "If Lee is moving for Baltimore, I expect to get between his main army and that place." He told Halleck that he thought the Confederates had passed through Hagerstown and were on their way to Chambersburg. Meade's information was partially accurate. Lee had, indeed, been through Hagerstown but his advance units had reached Chambersburg two weeks before, and much of the army was well beyond Chambersburg by June 29.

Meade attempted to assure Halleck that he was pursuing Lee aggressively, "my main point being to find and fight the enemy." But he could not fight them until he found them, and, by the following day, he was still looking. He established new headquarters in Taneytown, just south of the Pennsylvania border, and told his corps commanders to be prepared to march against the enemy at any moment. His army was spread out along a twenty-mile line with its right wing toward Hanover and its left toward Gettysburg, which Meade now believed was Lee's objective.

Meade told his commanders that "the enemy are advancing, probably in strong force, on Gettysburg. It is the intention to hold this army pretty nearly in the position it now occupies, until the plans of the enemy have been more fully developed." Thus, Meade was waiting to see what Lee did next before he made a move.

Meanwhile, Meade had to be in readiness either to attack or to defend his position, so he ordered his chief engineer and artillery commander to survey the countryside for a strong natural defensive line between Lee's probable location and the city of Baltimore. If Baltimore was Lee's objective, then he would have to fight his way through the entrenched Army of the Potomac to reach it. The defense line they selected meandered west to east along Pipe Creek about four miles south of Taneytown. Four of Meade's corps were north of the line, but he kept three corps behind it, ready to move into place on the line if necessary.

The line along Pipe Creek was intended as a defensive position to which Union forces could withdraw, should the rebels attack. Meade then decided to challenge Lee first by moving two corps farther north toward Gettysburg. Meade also issued a message to the troops intended to be inspirational. The commanders were to tell the men about

> the immense issues involved in the struggle. The enemy are on our soil; the whole country now looks anxiously to this army to deliver it from the presence of the foe. Our failure to do so will leave us no such welcome as the swelling of millions of hearts with pride and joy at our success would give to every soldier of this army. Homes, fire-sides, and domestic altars are involved. The army has fought well heretofore; it is believed that it will fight more desperately and bravely than ever, if it is addressed in fitting terms.

If those terms were not sufficiently inspiring to the troops, if the men were still not fully motivated to fight, Meade closed on a sterner note: "Corps and other commanders are authorized to order the instant death of any soldier who fails in his duty at this hour."

❖▰◗❖

DURING THOSE LAST two days of June, Meade's army appeared to weave northward slowly and erratically. The weather was hot and humid. By noon each day most of the troops were marching in their underwear with bandannas tied around their necks to stop the sweat. Some removed their socks and shoes, but that did little to cool them.

Hundreds of soldiers fell by the roadside, victims of sunstroke, and lines of stragglers trailed the columns for miles. Few units reached their assigned destination on June 29; many did not arrive until the morning of June 30, or later.

The men of the First Minnesota Volunteers marched thirty-three miles. Whenever their officers called a brief halt, the men dropped to the ground exhausted. They rarely had the energy to boil water for coffee. Sgt. Henry Taylor, survivor of many a long march, fell out just a mile and a half from camp at Uniontown, near the Pennsylvania border.

Those who did reach camp got a special treat. The townswomen provided cakes, pies, bread, and milk, delicacies rarely seen. Most of the ladies refused payment for the food. When Sergeant Taylor heard what he had missed, he made the rounds of the local farms. He was welcomed and given all the food he could eat. He told his family, "A good Union lady gives me a quart of apple butter. We live on the 'top shelf' today." The next morning, the Union troops crossed over into Pennsylvania and found the residents almost indifferent to their presence. No one offered any food, not even for money.

But then they came across a small group of women at the roadside who hailed them and said how pleased they were to see Union soldiers pass by. Sgt. John Plummer recalled hearing the men cry out, "God bless you!" to the women.

"Just that little expression," Plummer wrote to his brother, "and the way it was expressed, seemed to put new life into all of us, and we resolved, if possible, to give them yet more pleasure by driving the invaders from their soil."

⊷⊶◉⊷⊶

THERE WAS NO pleasure to be had in Washington, D.C., at the War Department's telegraph office during the harrowing last two days of June. Jeb Stuart captured a Union army wagon train at Rockville, fewer than fifteen miles from the White House. Lee may not have known where Stuart was, but the people in Rockville, especially the Union soldiers captured there, surely did.

The telegraph line linking Washington to Meade's headquarters had been cut. On the night of June 29, Halleck telegraphed Gen. Darius Couch in Philadelphia, commander of the Department of the Susquehanna, with the news that he had had no communication with Meade. There was nothing Couch could do about that, nor could he supply any reliable information. He did not know where Meade or Lee or Stuart were either. But he did spread the alarming news that Washington had lost all contact with its Army of the Potomac.

Edgar Cowan, a Pennsylvania congressman, telegraphed the information to Governor Curtin of his state. "Stanton can hear nothing from the Army of the Potomac, and we all fear that it has met with some disaster." That same night, Secretary of State Seward cabled Thurlow Weed, the Republican political leader in New York, to warn him that the federal government was in extreme danger.

The residents of the northeastern states now feared for their lives and the survival of the nation. Baltimore officials declared martial law. The edict directed that no arms or ammunition could be sold without a permit from the commanding general. No one was allowed to leave without a pass signed by the provost marshal, or to enter the city between the hours of 10 P.M. and 4 A.M. Tight restrictions were placed on all businesses. Resorts and clubs—places where people sympathetic to the South might congregate—were closed immediately and could not reopen without permission of the army.

The directive also included the following:

all bars, coffee-houses, drinking-saloons, and other places of like resort shall be closed between the hours of 8 P.M. and 8 A.M. Any liquor dealer or keeper of a drinking-saloon, or other person selling intoxicating drinks, who violates this order, shall be put under arrest, his premises seized, and the liquors confiscated for the benefit of the hospitals.

Baltimore had become an armed camp, full of anxious citizens who expected to find the Confederates in the streets at any moment—and the Union force not large enough to stop an attack.

Lincoln was deluged with telegrams, alerting him to the urgency of the situation, as if he were not already aware. Hundreds of people wrote to warn him that the nation was headed for destruction. They did not hesitate to offer advice about what must be done to save it.

At eleven o'clock on the morning of June 29, two railway officials in Philadelphia contacted the president to say they had reliable information that the rebel army was, in their words,

> marching on Philadelphia, and also on points on the Philadelphia, Wilmington, & Baltimore Railroad. Philadelphia once taken, they think they will be able to dictate terms to the Government. There should be 50 pieces of artillery and 20,000 veteran forces on the railroad and at Philadelphia as soon as possible; 10,000 to move at once.

At 5:55 that evening, Lincoln received a wire from the governor of New Jersey. "The people of New Jersey are apprehensive that the invasion of the enemy may extend to her soil. We think that the enemy should be driven from Pennsylvania." The governor recommended reinstating George McClellan, even though he had already proven several times he would not aggressively pursue Robert E. Lee. Nevertheless, McClellan remained a popular figure. With McClellan in charge, declared New Jersey's governor, the people would rise as one and defeat the rebels once and for all.

At 8:40 that same night, Lincoln received a message from Simon Cameron, the influential Pennsylvania senator and former secretary of war. Cameron claimed to have entirely reliable information that Lee had assembled nearly 100,000 troops in the area between Chambersburg and Gettysburg, and that he would shortly cross the Susquehanna River to capture Harrisburg. Cameron added,

> Let me impress on you the absolute necessity of action by Meade
> tomorrow, even if attended by great risk, because if Lee gets his army
> across the Susquehanna . . . you will readily comprehend the disas-
> trous results that must follow to the country.

But it was not only officials in Pennsylvania who were alarmed. The
following day, June 30, Secretary of War Stanton sent a message to
Halleck, general in chief of all the Union armies, expressing concern
that the capital city was not adequately defended. He urged Halleck to
position artillery batteries on the roads leading into town and at strategic points throughout Washington.

> I beg to direct your attention to the subject, and to ask that you will
> see that every possible means of security is adopted against any sud-
> den raid or incursion of the enemy, by day or by night season, and
> also that you will report as soon as convenient whether all available
> military means have been employed for that purpose.

Halleck replied at once to try to mollify Stanton's concerns. The secretary of war may not have been relieved to learn from Halleck that
there were not enough artillery units available to cover all the access
roads, but Halleck did assure him that artillery batteries could be transported quickly to any point that came under attack. "I know of no
available military means which have not already been employed to prevent a rebel raid on this city," Halleck said. Fine words of encouragement, but both men knew that if Lee outflanked Meade's army and
marched on Washington, the city was his for the taking.

◦→═◉═→◦

ROBERT E. LEE'S mood on the morning of June 29 matched the
gloomy, rainy weather at his headquarters outside Chambersburg. He
was still tormented by the uncertainties that had plagued him for
days—not knowing about Meade or Stuart. As he made ready to leave

camp, he spied a former member of Stonewall Jackson's staff who had just arrived from Virginia to rejoin the army. Here was someone fresh from home who might be able to tell Lee where Stuart had gone. But the news only made Lee feel worse.

The officer reported that some cavalrymen had told him they had seen Stuart two days ago in Prince William County in Virginia. Lee was astonished. Why was Stuart still in Virginia as recently as June 27? As Lee rode eastward, he kept inquiring for news of his cavalry, but nobody had anything to tell him.

By the time he set up headquarters at Greenwood, ten miles west of Gettysburg, he was tense and restless. He paced nervously, occasionally clutching his head. This was uncharacteristic behavior for Lee, who tried not to betray his apprehension publicly because he knew the effect it could have on morale. He made an effort to calm himself when John Bell Hood came by. Lee greeted him with a smile. "Ah, general," Lee said, "the enemy is a long time finding us; if he does not succeed soon, we must go in search of him."

He strode vigorously along the road beside the camp in an effort to ease his anxiety. When he briefed his staff later that afternoon, he seemed as composed as anyone recalled seeing him. "Tomorrow, gentlemen," he announced, "we will not move to Harrisburg, as we expected, but will go over to Gettysburg and see what General Meade is after."

One man asked what he thought of the new Union commander. Lee replied that the Union cause might benefit from Meade's promotion, but that Meade would find it difficult assuming command in the middle of a campaign. He added, "General Meade will commit no blunder in my front, and if I make one he will make haste to take advantage of it."

On June 30, Lee continued moving his army east toward Gettysburg. As far as he knew, based on information provided by men who had come from Virginia to rejoin the army, Meade's troops were at Middletown, Maryland, some twenty-five miles south of the Pennsylvania border and forty miles southwest of Gettysburg. That put them at a safe distance and meant that the roads to Philadelphia and Baltimore were clear of Union troops.

Lee was wrong. The information was inaccurate. By the time the sun set over the lush Pennsylvania farmland on June 30, Meade had a brigade of cavalry, three thousand strong, only a mile and a half northwest of Gettysburg, plus two corps, totaling twenty-two thousand men, spread out between four and eight miles southwest of town. In addition, most of the rest of the Union army was within a day's march of Gettysburg. And Jeb Stuart, who was supposed to keep Lee informed of Meade's troop movements—the man on whom Lee depended more than any other at that moment—was at Hanover, thirteen miles away. Stuart did not know where Meade was; he couldn't even find Lee.

⟶⊙⟜

STUART'S EXPLOITS WERE motivated by vanity. Indeed, vanity, ego, wounded pride, and public humiliation were forces that had often driven him, especially over the past several weeks. The cavalry leader's relationship with Robert E. Lee dated from Stuart's days as a West Point cadet when Lee was superintendent of the military academy. After receiving his commission in 1854, Stuart served out west with the cavalry. The following year he married the daughter of an army colonel, a man who later chose to serve on the Union side. Stuart met Lee again in 1859, when he accompanied him on the mission against John Brown's uprising at Harper's Ferry.

After Fort Sumter, Captain Stuart was commissioned a colonel in the new Confederate army. His rise was rapid. Following Bull Run he was promoted to brigadier general. During McClellan's ill-fated Peninsular campaign in 1862, Stuart rode to glory, leading his cavalrymen on a three-day encirclement of the Union's Army of the Potomac, capturing prisoners, horses, and equipment. He returned to Richmond a hero.

The thirty-year-old general constantly craved excitement and adventure. An aide described him as having an "immensely strong physique, and unfailing animal spirits—[he] loved song, laughter, jesting, rough practical jokes, and all the virile divertissements of camp." Some called him vain and frivolous, but none denied his courage, zest for life, and dashing style of leadership. Those qualities, combined with his cavalier manner and distinctive style of dress—an ostrich plume in his hat, a bright yellow sash, a crimson-lined cape—made him a figure of adulation throughout the South.

After the Peninsular campaign Stuart was promoted to major general and given command of all the cavalry in Lee's Army of Northern Virginia. Stuart led them at Second Bull Run, Antietam, and Fredericksburg, and succeeded in riding around McClellan's army a second time. Jeb Stuart could do no wrong, until the moment in early June of 1863 at Brandy Station, Virginia, when his luck changed. It happened the day after a grand review and ball.

"Stuart was in all his glory," Robert E. Lee wrote to his wife describing the review. The cavalry leader's horse was bedecked with a wreath of flowers, a gift from Stuart's many female admirers. When Lee saw the wreath around the horse's neck, he teased Stuart. "Take care, General. That is the way [Union] General Pope's horse was adorned when he went to the battle of Manassas." Pope had suffered a humiliating defeat there, as Stuart was about to do the day after the ball.

Stuart was taken by surprise by a Union cavalry raid led by his former classmate, the dapper Maj. Gen. Alfred Pleasonton. Stuart suffered more than five hundred casualties, including the handsome, courageous, twenty-eight-year-old William Farley, one of Stuart's favorite scouts. Smiling through his pain, the wounded Captain Farley was placed gently on a stretcher. He pointed to his leg, which was lying nearby, neatly sliced off by a Union shell.

"Bring it to me, please. It's an old friend, gentlemen," he said as he clutched the bloody stump to his chest, "and I do not wish to part with it."

Fellow South Carolinians placed Captain Farley in a waiting ambulance.

"Goodbye, and forever. I know my condition. I won't meet you again. Let me thank you for your kindness. It is a pleasure to me that I fell into the hands of Carolinians at my last moment."

Stuart was devastated by the death of Farley and so many others. He had never known defeat before and he felt humiliated, disgraced, and embarrassed. The Richmond newspapers, which heretofore had trumpeted his accomplishments, charged that his security had been lax and that he had been caught off guard. Stuart, the papers said, had been outfoxed and outfought because at the ball the night before, he and his officers had been seen "rollicking, frolicking and running after girls."

Stuart was enraged by the newspaper attacks and the whispers and innuendos that spread around Richmond society. He vowed to erase the shame of Brandy Station by undertaking a more glorious and daring accomplishment than ever before. And his chance came when Lee announced his plans to invade the North.

Stuart proposed to lead his cavalry around the Union army, as he had done in 1862, and meet Ewell's advance guard at York. Lee approved the plan with the obvious expectation that Stuart would observe the movement of the Army of the Potomac, harass and impede its attempts to cross the river, and keep Lee informed of its whereabouts. Lee added a caveat to his orders: Stuart was *not* to attempt to ride around the Union army unless he could do so without jeopardizing the overall invasion plan.

⊷⇒◉⇐⊶

IT ALL WENT terribly wrong from the beginning, from the time Stuart broke camp at one o'clock on the morning of June 25, the same day Lee crossed the Potomac River. The Union army, still under Hooker's command, was not where Stuart expected it to be. Hooker, reluctantly, had begun his march north toward the Potomac. A portion of his force was directly in the path Stuart planned to take. Stuart fired his six cannon at a passing column and turned to the south instead of north.

The next day he set off on a long detour east to avoid further contact with a major Yankee force, but they were long gone. He did not see a Union soldier all day. The detour had been an unnecessary and costly delay, leading Stuart's cavalry to spend fifty hours to cover only forty miles. Historian Bruce Catton wrote that by making the detour south and east, Stuart "rode his cavalry right out of the campaign."

Stuart brought his men across the Potomac River during the night of June 27, three days behind schedule. The men and horses had begun to tire and the long column was forced to stop frequently for rest and forage. Once on the north side of the river, he had no choice about his route: west was the Union army, east were the defenses of Washington.

He headed north, passing near enough to Washington to create a scare. At noon on June 28 he descended on Rockville, Maryland, within fifteen miles of the capital city. Rockville was on the National Road, a major highway linking Washington to points west, which served as the major supply route for the Union army. Shortly after Stuart arrived in Rockville he learned that a large Union wagon train was due. To Stuart, desperate for glory, this was too big a trophy to pass up. He would capture the supplies and present them to Lee as a gift.

The rebels bore down on the train, chasing after it as the drivers tried to pull their horses around and escape. Stuart took his prize, 125 of the 150 wagons. One of his officers wrote, "The wagons were brand new, the mules fat and sleek and the harness in use for the first time. Such a train we had never seen before and did not see again." The wagons were loaded with oats and corn for the horses, along with bread, crackers, bacon, sugar, hams, and a large supply of whiskey. By the time the goods were delivered to Lee, the whiskey had disappeared, but most of the food remained.

Lee did not need the wagonloads of food. He needed information and Stuart was not there to deliver it. Even if Stuart had located the Union army by then, he did not know where Lee was. And even if Stuart had known where to find Lee *and* the Yankees, he could not have reached Lee in time for his information to be of use—because he was encumbered by 125 slow-moving wagons.

Some four hundred Union soldiers had been captured along with the wagon train. Stuart's men were required to spend many hours handwriting their individual paroles. The cavalry rode only twenty miles that night, wagons in tow. The next morning they overran the small Union garrison at Cooksville, tore up some railroad tracks, and burned a bridge. These actions all wasted valuable time.

Sometime during June 29, in the town of Sykesville, Stuart read in a Union newspaper that Confederate troops had been spotted at York and Carlisle. This information reassured Stuart that he could carry out his plan to catch up with Ewell at York. But the news was out-of-date. Lee had recalled his troops from York and Carlisle the day before.

Stuart's column moved fifteen miles north to Westminster, arriving at about five in the afternoon. They were met with a spirited attack by a small Union cavalry force but managed to drive it off. The following day, the sixth day since he had last made contact with the rest of the Confederate army, Stuart led his men to Hanover, arriving before ten in the morning.

A Yankee cavalry outfit advanced on them. The Confederates made a bold charge and chased the enemy into the center of town. The Union troopers countercharged, forcing Stuart's men to retreat. Stuart came close to being captured, escaping only by urging his horse to leap some twenty-five feet over a gully. An officer wrote, "I shall never forget the glimpse I then saw of this beautiful animal away up in midair over the chasm and Stuart's fine figure sitting erect and firm in the saddle."

Stuart did not attempt to return to Hanover. The long column, trailing his trophy wagon train, slipped around the town and commenced another exhausting night march. "Whole regiments slept in the saddle," Stuart recalled, "their faithful animals keeping the road unguided." They pushed on toward York, seventeen miles away, while Lee waited on the far side of Gettysburg, thirteen miles due west of Hanover. If only Stuart had known.

ROBERT E. LEE faced another problem that night before the battle. Like the absence of Stuart, it promised to seriously affect the outcome. This additional uncertainty facing Lee was the inexperience of his commanders.

In May, Lee had written in a letter to John Bell Hood that Confederate soldiers were capable of performing outstandingly provided they were properly led. "There is the difficulty," he lamented, "proper commanders. Where can they be obtained?" So many men of promise had been killed or maimed. Some, like Stonewall Jackson, were irreplaceable. But the war would not wait; new leaders had to be found.

Lee had chosen them and now they were to be tested. Three of his nine division commanders were new to their jobs, along with seven newly promoted brigadier generals. Six infantry brigades would fight for the first time under their senior colonels, and one-third of Lee's cavalry units were commanded by men who had just joined the Army of Northern Virginia.

Lee's greatest concern was replacing Jackson, who, with Longstreet, had commanded the two corps. Lee and Jackson worked together perfectly, each with a full and immediate grasp of what the other wanted. Lee never needed to give Jackson detailed orders. Lee made suggestions in a general way and Jackson would proceed, as he proved at Chancellorsville, to do precisely as Lee expected.

Lee divided Jackson's old outfit into two, making a total of three corps. Longstreet would continue in command of First Corps, Richard Ewell would lead Second Corps, and A. P. Hill would have Third Corps. Ewell and Hill were unproven as corps commanders.

Ambrose Powell Hill was a thirty-eight-year-old West Point graduate who had served in the Seminole Indian Wars in Florida. As a young man he lost the woman he wanted to marry to a fellow West Point graduate turned railroad president named George McClellan. Hill later wed the sister of John Hunt Morgan. She was so devoted that Lee often had to order her to leave the front when a battle was imminent.

Hill was high-strung, impetuous, and quick to anger at perceived slights. He once challenged Longstreet to a duel after Longstreet had placed him under arrest. Longstreet accepted the challenge. Their seconds were making the arrangements when Lee learned about it and transferred Hill to Jackson's corps. It did not take long for Hill to feud with Jackson. Angry words were exchanged and Jackson called Hill a liar, but nothing more came of it. Hill fought well for his commanders, even when at odds with them. The Southern cause was more important to him than personal antagonisms.

Hill led his men aggressively at Cedar Mountain, Second Bull Run, Antietam, and Fredericksburg. He went into battle dressed conspicuously in a bright red deer-hunter's shirt. His men knew something was brewing whenever they saw him put on his battle shirt. When Jackson was hit at Chancellorsville, Hill took over until he, too, was wounded. Lee knew he was a daring fighter and an excellent division commander, but could Hill deal with the complexities of leading the three divisions that made up his corps?

The questions about forty-six-year-old Richard Ewell's competence as a corps commander were even more crucial. His Second Corps would spearhead the invasion and set the pace for the rest of the army. "Old Bald Head" had graduated from West Point in 1840 with few demerits and a respectable standing, thirteenth in a class of forty-two. His closest friend at the academy was William T. Sherman. Ewell served out west with the cavalry for several years. He boasted that in his years on the plains fighting Indians he had learned everything there was to know about commanding fifty dragoons—but forgotten everything else he had been taught at West Point.

When he fought in the Mexican War he met a young captain named Lee, who impressed him greatly. At the battle of Churubusco, Ewell several times had his horse shot from under him. He also saved the life of Capt. Philip Kearny. When the war was over, he returned to the States, his health temporarily impaired.

Additional service fighting Apaches followed, but by 1855 his rank was still captain. He had become an excellent leader and tactician, noted for his bravery as one of the army's finest Indian fighters. He loved being a soldier chasing after Indians but hated the boredom of peacetime garrison life.

In April 1861, Captain Ewell became a lieutenant colonel in the new Confederate army. By June, he wore the single star of a brigadier general, and a mere seven months later was a major general serving under Stonewall Jackson.

A nervous and forgetful man, Ewell tended to lisp when he was tired or pressured. He referred to himself in the third person, and he was so edgy that he seldom slept. With his bald head and beaklike nose, he was said to resemble a woodcock, an impression reinforced by his habit of cocking his head to one side when he spoke. He was frequently ill with malaria, dyspepsia, and other mysterious maladies that he believed could be controlled only by eating wheat prepared in a special way.

He professed to dislike command and once startled a subordinate by asking the man why he thought Jefferson Davis ever chose Ewell to be a major general. Ewell obviously preferred fighting to commanding; in fact, he often turned over responsibility for his unit to a subordinate so he could go up to the front line to take potshots at the Yankees, hoping Stonewall Jackson would not catch him.

Ewell greatly admired Jackson and was one of his most aggressive generals, but he sincerely believed Jackson was crazy, especially after Jackson announced that he never put pepper on his food because it made his left leg weak. Ewell did refer to Jackson as inspired. He said that he "admired [Jackson's] genius, but was certain of his lunacy." Nevertheless, Ewell stopped eating pepper himself. Ewell's men idolized him and were prepared to follow him anywhere, despite his Jacksonlike tendency to lead them on long forced marches toward the enemy.

At Second Bull Run in August 1862, Ewell lost his leg. He found religion and a wife by the time he returned to the army nine months later. Both influences curbed his profanity, at which he had been a master, and smoothed his rougher edges. He had also become wealthy, thanks to his wife, a beautiful widowed cousin who had rejected him years before to marry a man named Brown. In the joy and excitement of his newly married state Ewell sometimes introduced her as "My wife, Mrs. Brown." Ewell adored her. An aide commented that "Old Ewell is worse in love than any eighteen-year-old that you ever saw."

Would Ewell live up to Lee's expectations? Men who had served closely with Ewell, had they been asked, might have told Lee about a characteristic of Ewell's that would not serve him well as corps commander: Ewell lacked self-confidence in his own ideas. He rarely acted on a plan of his own without first soliciting the opinions of others. In addition, Ewell, like any good subordinate of Stonewall Jackson, had learned to follow orders to the letter and not to exercise any personal judgment or discretion. Therefore, he could not be trusted to operate merely on suggestions from Lee, the way Jackson had. This was bound to cause problems for Lee, who preferred to offer only guidelines to his key subordinates, leaving them to implement his ideas.

Thus, both of Lee's new choices for corps commander were questionable. Lee's biographer, Douglas Southall Freeman, noted, "Gettysburg was to show the results of A. P. Hill's inexperience and of Ewell's indecision in the face of discretionary orders."

⊷≍◉≍⊶

GETTYSBURG WAS ALSO about to show the results of James "Pete" Longstreet's failure to communicate. The forty-two-year-old Longstreet had always wanted to be a soldier, ever since he was a boy in Georgia reading books about Julius Caesar, Napoleon, and George Washington. When Pete was nine, he and his father decided on a West Point education, and the boy never wavered from it.

Wanting to be a soldier and studying to be one were entirely different matters. Cadet Longstreet did not do well at the military academy. Always in the bottom third of his class academically, he also accumulated large numbers of demerits for such offenses as being absent from roll call, having a dirty room, needing a haircut, and disobeying orders.

If not exactly a model cadet, he was certainly a popular one. Fun loving and carefree, with a quick sense of humor, he relished the outdoor life of a cadet: the swordplay, horsemanship, football, and other vigorous games. He showed a disregard for the rules, a quality that appealed to others of similar bent. He was voted the handsomest cadet but graduated fifty-fourth in a class of fifty-six. His closest friend at West Point was his opposite, the quiet, serious Sam Grant. They would remain lifelong friends.

Longstreet liked the soldier's life. He married into the army, choosing as his bride Louise Garland, daughter of the regimental commander at his first post, Jefferson Barracks, Missouri. But before the wedding, Longstreet went to war in Mexico and learned that he was good at it. After the attack on Mexico City, his first time in battle, he was promoted to the brevet rank of captain for his bravery under fire in leading a charge against a heavily fortified position.

Five days later, he led a charge against the strongly fortified Mexican Military Academy at Chapultepec. He was out in front of his men carrying the regimental flag when he was hit in the leg. Before he fell, he handed the colors to Lt. George Pickett. Longstreet's war was over. His wound took a long time to heal, but six months later he was able to walk well enough to marry Miss Garland in Lynchburg, Virginia. That summer, the Longstreets traveled to Missouri for Sam Grant's wedding to Julia Dent.

The Longstreets had ten children. Pete thought they could be ordered about just like soldiers in the army. When he realized, early on, that they resisted his role as commanding officer and would not always obey orders, he delegated the duties of parenthood to his wife and concentrated on his career.

He served in Texas, Kansas, and New Mexico and had reached the rank of major when the Civil War began. There was no question of his sympathies; he was a Southerner, after all. But like so many others, he found it sad to part with old friends and to leave familiar posts.

He became a brigadier general for the new Confederacy and fought with the Army of Northern Virginia in almost every battle it faced. By October 1861, with the war only six months old, he was promoted to major general. A year later Longstreet wore the three stars of a lieutenant general, becoming one of the highest-ranking Southern officers.

His personal life, however, was tragic. Two children had died, and suddenly, within one week, he and Louise lost three more in a scarlet fever epidemic that swept through Richmond. A grieving Longstreet returned to the army as quickly as he decently could. His religious passion grew from his despair, and he vowed to give up gambling, his favorite pastime.

When Lee took over the army after Joe Johnston was wounded, he and Longstreet became friends. Only four days after their first meeting, Lee wrote to Jefferson Davis that "Longstreet is a Capital soldier. His recommendations hitherto have been good, and I have confidence in him." As their relationship deepened, Lee referred to Longstreet as "the staff in my right hand" and "my old war-horse." The British officer Lt. Col. Fremantle observed that the two men were almost always together. He described their relationship as "quite touching."

Longstreet stood six feet two inches tall and weighed 190 pounds. He had dark hair and a full thick beard, a large fleshy nose, and dark eyes. He was a rough, blunt, tough old soldier of forty-two, likable to those who knew him well, though he could be gruff and aloof to others. Usually, however, he was as personable as he had been as a cadet. He liked his whiskey and kept an ample supply for visitors. Even men who were perpetually irritable, like Jubal Early, livened up in Longstreet's congenial presence. His staff and his soldiers worshipped him, and he brought many a junior officer into his circle. He particularly liked George Pickett and Jeb Stuart. Longstreet had always wanted to be a soldier and had become an outstanding one; but in June 1863, he was facing his most difficult test.

⊶⊷⊷◉⊷⊷

LONGSTREET HAD MISSED the battle of Chancellorsville in May. He had been temporarily detached from Lee's army and assigned an independent command in the Department of Virginia and North Carolina, to protect Richmond from a threatened attack and to gather forage and food for Lee's army. By the time he returned, Lee was preparing his invasion of the North.

Longstreet had a different idea. He wanted to send his corps west in an effort to save Vicksburg. He wrote, "Vicksburg was doomed unless we could offer relief by strategic move." But Lee would not be persuaded. "I found his mind made up not to allow any of his troops to go west," Longstreet wrote. Having lost the argument about Vicksburg, Longstreet then protested Lee's plan to invade the North, but Lee was determined to proceed.

Longstreet tried to persuade Lee to adopt a defensive strategy by forcing the Union army to attack first, once the Confederates were strongly entrenched, instead of moving against the numerically superior Union forces. Longstreet reminded Lee of Second Bull Run and of Fredericksburg, where the Union army had suffered grievous losses by attacking Lee's well-defended troops.

He also recalled that Stonewall Jackson had remarked that while the Confederates were sometimes unsuccessful when charging a strongly held enemy position, the Federals had *never* succeeded in dislodging Lee's army when it was entrenched. To bolster his point Longstreet added Napoleon's admonition that the head of an invading army should carefully select his ground and make the enemy attack him. Longstreet proposed that Lee choose a strong position somewhere in Pennsylvania and let the Union army destroy itself by assaulting the Confederate line, just as it had at Fredericksburg.

Lee listened to Longstreet's impassioned arguments with patience and courtesy, which he extended to all his subordinates, but made no comment or objection—he did not reject the proposal directly. Longstreet apparently, and mistakenly, judged Lee's lack of response as a tacit agreement. "Longstreet mistook courtesy for consent and believed that Lee had pledged himself to defensive tactics."

Thus, both commanders faced battle the following day with false assumptions about the other's ideas. Lee assumed that his good right hand, his war-horse, accepted his intention to attack the enemy, while Longstreet assumed he had persuaded Lee to adopt a defensive approach. Lee did not realize that Longstreet was going into battle expecting to fight in a manner Lee was unwilling to consider.

And so Robert E. Lee at Gettysburg had two inexperienced corps commanders, a third committed to a contradictory strategy, a missing cavalry leader, and no awareness of how near the enemy was.

❖━◉━❖

YANKEE SOLDIERS CAME to town a little before noon on June 30, and the people of Gettysburg turned out to see the sight. The force included two brigades of cavalry, three thousand troopers strong, led by John Buford, a thirty-seven-year-old Indian fighter from Kentucky. He had been trying to find the rebel army and thought maybe he was getting close.

Buford, although a good-natured man to his intimates, appeared at first glance to be hard, even sinister. His dark mustache, close-cropped hair, and general demeanor were indicative of someone who would be an unforgiving and unrelenting enemy. He drove his men mercilessly, sparing no one, including himself, and as a result was destined to die of exhaustion in only six months' time. He dressed plainly in a well-worn hunting shirt, the pockets bulging with tobacco and a pipe, and old corduroy pants tucked into ordinary boots. "He don't put on so much style as most officers," said one of his men with obvious approval.

"I had never seen so many soldiers at one time," young Tillie Pierce of Gettysburg wrote of Buford's troops. "They were Union soldiers and that was enough for me, for I then knew we had protection and I felt they were our dearest friends." She joined other girls on a street corner to watch the cavalry pass by, singing "Our Union Forever." They repeated the chorus over and over because none of them knew the rest of the words.

It took more than an hour for the column to pass through Gettysburg and make camp just beyond the city limits. A captain in Buford's command wrote,

> Men, women and children crowded the sidewalk and vied with each other in demonstrations of joyous welcome. Hands were reached up eagerly to clasp the hands of our bronzed and dusty troopers. Cake, milk, water and beer were passed up to the moving column. . . . Doors, windows and balconies were filled with ladies waving handkerchiefs. Altogether, it was one of the most touching, spontaneous and heartfelt demonstrations my eyes ever witnessed. . . . It inspired us to heroic deeds.

Boys ran alongside the troopers, whooping and yelling as they followed them out to their camp. They stayed the rest of the day helping out with chores. As a reward, some were lifted up high to sit in a cavalry saddle. That evening, many of Buford's men were invited to private homes for dinner and given the best meals they had eaten in a long time.

But one thing Buford's troopers could not find in town was something to drink. Buford suspected that the rebel army was not far away, and he was not about to have his men drunk the night before what could be a major battle. He asked a newspaper owner to print placards that he posted all over town forbidding the sale of liquor to soldiers. He threatened to punish anyone caught violating the order by selling or distributing whiskey. The troopers, however, had prepared for such an emergency by filling their canteens with applejack confiscated when they passed through Maryland. Some shared the brew with the locals. After all, the placards did not say anything about soldiers supplying liquor to civilians.

⋆⊶⊙⊷⋆

BUFORD WAS CORRECT about rebel troops being nearby, but they were even closer than he thought. Maj. Gen. Henry Heth's division, part of A. P. Hill's corps, had been encamped in Cashtown, eight miles northwest of Gettysburg, since the previous day. Sometime on June 29, one of Heth's aides was reading a copy of the *Gettysburg Compiler* and spotted an ad for R. F. McIlheny's dry-goods store.

> 1863 Spring styles, splendid assortment of boots and shoes, compris-
> ing men's fine calf boots, men's balmorals, men's congress gaiters, all
> of which will be sold as cheap as the cheapest. Let all who wish to
> supply themselves with good and substantial work call and examine
> our stock.

If there was anything the division needed it was shoes. The aide brought the ad to General Heth, who promptly ordered Brig. Gen. James Johnston Pettigrew to take a brigade of infantry into Gettysburg to do some shopping. Late on the morning of June 30, Pettigrew reached a hill on the outskirts of Gettysburg in time to see a trail of dust leading from the south into the town. It was John Buford and his two brigades of cavalry.

Pettigrew was under orders not to get involved in a fight, because Lee did not want the battle to commence until all of his army had assembled. Reluctantly, Pettigrew returned to Cashtown and reported to General Heth about the Yankees. Heth was disappointed—his men really needed shoes—and he assumed the Union force was only a small militia or home guard unit that could easily have been whipped.

Heth took Pettigrew with him to report to General Hill, who had arrived at Cashtown that morning. When Hill heard about Pettigrew's sighting of a Federal force in Gettysburg, he said it was nothing more than a small scouting party operating on its own, far from the Army of the Potomac.

"I am just from General Lee," Hill said confidently, "and the information he has from his scouts corroborates what I have received from mine; that is, the enemy are still [in Maryland] and have not struck their tents."

"If there is no objection," Heth said, "I will take my Division tomorrow and go to Gettysburg and get those shoes."

"None in the world," Hill said.

MOST OF GETTYSBURG'S residents slept peacefully, confident they were safe from the rebels with what looked to them to be a large army encamped just outside town. Dan Skelly observed that "the people settled down in their homes with a sense of security . . . and with little thought of what tomorrow had in store for them." Albertus McCreary noted that no one "even dreamed that a great battle would be fought near us."

Ten-year-old Charles McCurdy remembered the complacency among most people, including his parents, who placed no restrictions on his activities. He believed that if they had any idea that a battle was imminent, they would have told him to stay at home. Most folks felt safe for the first time in days.

But not all felt peace of mind. Sallie Broadhead had seen Pettigrew's men on the hill that morning and had been apprehensive all day. She recorded her thoughts in her diary: "It begins to look as though we will have a battle soon, and we are in great fear."

JOHN BUFORD WAS sure the rebels would return to Gettysburg the next day. When one of his officers tried to reassure him that the Union forces could easily fend off a rebel attack, Buford shook his head.

"No, you won't. They will attack you in the morning and they will come booming—skirmishers three deep. You will have to fight like the devil to hold your own until supports arrive."

He was right.

CHAPTER 8

WE NEED HELP NOW

July 1, 1863

CPL. ALPHONSE HODGES, Company F, Ninth New York Cavalry, saw them first. He and three other men of Buford's cavalry were walking a lonely picket outpost near the Chambersburg Pike, a mile and a half west of Gettysburg. They were near the end of their two-hour tour and expected to be relieved soon to return to their company for a breakfast of hardtack, bacon, and strong black coffee.

It was 5:20 in the morning of what promised to be another hot, steamy day. The sunrise provided enough light to reveal the features of the landscape, a welcome sight after staring into near-total darkness. Hodges spotted movement about a mile away on the far side of Willoughby Run. He was sure of it. There were men heading toward his picket post.

He hoped they were farmers out doing chores at dawn before the sun rose too high, but he could not wait to find out. He had orders to report any activity. He sent two men off to notify the adjacent picket posts to their right and left and told the third man of his detachment to report to Colonel Sackett, brigade officer of the day.

Hodges moved warily along the Chambersburg Pike traveling west toward Willoughby Run. When he got near enough to distinguish the figures as rebel soldiers, not farmers, he turned back on the double. The Confederates opened fire. Hodges got off a few rounds and dashed to the cover of the skirmish line that Colonel Sackett was hurriedly forming in response to the shots.

The rebel soldiers who fired at Hodges were the advance guard of General Heth's division, heading for Gettysburg to seize the shoes Pettigrew had failed to obtain the previous day. Heth's men were preceded by a triple line of skirmishers, just as Buford had predicted. Heth heard the gunfire ahead of him but was not concerned. He believed he was facing only a few militia or home guard units. General Hill had insisted that the Army of the Potomac was miles away and therefore no threat to the Confederates.

So Heth pushed his men on with two brigades in the lead supported by a six-gun battery of artillery. To their surprise, they kept meeting stiff opposition. Those home guard troops were better than most and Heth was not making the rapid progress he expected.

⊷═◉═⊷

JOHN BUFORD CLIMBED the steps to the cupola of the Lutheran Seminary and trained his binoculars on the fields to the west. His signal officer recalled that Buford seemed unusually anxious, and he certainly had good reason. Buford's force was outnumbered by more than two to one, and he realized there was a limit to how long he could hold out without help. But until other army units could reach him, he was determined to make the enemy pay for every yard they advanced.

Buford had two things in his favor: weapons and terrain. His troops were equipped with seven-shot repeating rifles that gave them an impressive level of firepower. Each man could get off seven rounds before the enemy could fire and reload once. Of course, this also meant that the troops used up their limited ammunition supply at a faster rate.

The topography of the land west of town was ideal for defense. Its series of ridges were not unlike the waves of the sea. To approach from the west, Heth's troops had to fight their way across each ridge in the face of Buford's repeating rifles. Buford's men would then fall back to the next ridge. The longest ridge, the one nearest to Gettysburg, was called Seminary Ridge, where the Lutheran Seminary stood. This was where Buford planned to make his last stand.

Buford had trained his men to fight as dismounted infantry rather than cavalry, with every fourth man behind the line holding the horses. That reduced his effective fighting strength to no more than 2,200, but their discipline, their position on high ground, and their high rate of fire persuaded Heth that he was facing regular infantry rather than a militia outfit. As a result, Heth made one of those fateful decisions on which battles turn.

Had he continued to forge ahead aggressively, his superior numbers and artillery would have forced Buford's men to fall back. Instead, Heth paused to form a battle line that was two brigades wide for a massive frontal assault. It was a formidable sight to Buford's troopers on the ridge, but it bought them time for reinforcements to arrive. Heth spent nearly an hour assembling his troops, ordering an artillery bombardment, and bringing other units forward. It was past nine o'clock by the time he was ready to advance.

By then, Buford had a new problem. Reports reached him from scouting patrols that sizable rebel units were approaching Gettysburg from the north, part of Ewell's Second Corps from Carlisle. Buford would have to pull out before the new Southerners got too close. Otherwise, he might be caught between two enemy forces. He knew he did not have enough men to contend with that situation.

Buford rode along his line encouraging his men, checking for weak points, and hoping the rest of the Union army would soon reach Gettysburg. He estimated he could hold out about an hour. If reinforcements did not arrive, he would have to abandon the town.

⋄⊷⫸◉⫷⊶⋄

BUFORD HAD SENT a courier to find Maj. Gen. John Reynolds, commander of Meade's First Corps. Considered the Army of the Potomac's most beloved and respected general, Reynolds was the man Meade thought best qualified to lead when Meade himself was selected instead. Reynolds's corps had been camped overnight along Marsh Creek, about six miles south of Gettysburg. When Reynolds received the urgent message from Buford, he broke camp and sent his men north. He rode on ahead with his staff when he heard the sounds of battle. It was about 8:30 when they arrived in town. He found Buford climbing down from another stint in the observation post at the Lutheran Seminary.

"What's the matter, John?" Reynolds asked.

"The devil's to pay," Buford said.

Reynolds insisted on seeing the situation for himself. Buford led him forward, near the fighting, while explaining the disposition of his troops and how they were slowly being pushed back toward town. Reynolds agreed with Buford's defensive plan and asked whether he could hold out another hour or so until his own troops arrived.

Buford thought he could. An officer galloped up with the news that his skirmish line was in danger of collapse. Reynolds immediately dispatched a message to his corps, and to Oliver Howard's Eleventh Corps, also nearby, urging them to push on to Gettysburg with all possible speed.

He summoned his slimmest aide and ordered him to ride hard for General Meade at Taneytown, to ride his horse to the death if need be. The aide bore an oral message for Meade, so he would be carrying nothing in writing if he were captured. He was to tell Meade that

The enemy are advancing in strong force. I [Reynolds] fear they will get to the heights beyond the town before I can. I will fight them inch by inch, and if driven into the town, I will barricade the streets and hold them back as long as possible.

ROBERT E. LEE started the day in a good mood. The weather was clear and bright with no sign of rain. The roads would stay dry, which meant that his army could move even faster. Mud slowed both men and wagons. He stood outside his tent for a moment watching Longstreet's First Corps march past heading east.

Presently Longstreet came along, astride Hero. Lee, riding Traveller, joined him. Lee's mood remained jovial while they ascended the western slope of South Mountain. As they neared the top, they thought they heard thunder from the east. But then, as the two old soldiers climbed higher, they recognized the distant bark of artillery. Somewhere ahead, a battle was in progress.

Lee told Longstreet to stay with his men and hurry them forward. He would ride to Cashtown to find out what was going on. There he found A. P. Hill sick in bed, unable to tell him anything except that Heth had gone to Gettysburg. Hill had passed on to Heth Lee's order not to get involved in battle until the entire army had assembled. But it certainly sounded as if the fighting had already begun.

Lee summoned Gen. Richard Anderson, one of Hill's division commanders. When Anderson reported around ten o'clock, he thought Lee seemed dispirited, glumly listening to the sound of the guns. Lee never said why he wanted to see Anderson. He did not ask about his troops or give him any orders. Anderson recalled that Lee spoke about his dilemma, his uncertainty, seeming to talk more to himself than to Anderson. Lee said,

I cannot think what has become of Stuart; I ought to have heard from him long before now. He may have met with disaster, but I hope not. In the absence of reports from him I am in ignorance as to what we have in front of us here. It may be the whole Federal army, or it may be only a detachment. If it is the whole Federal force, we must fight a battle here.

There was only one way to find out. Lee would have to go to Gettysburg. He mounted his horse and headed east. The historian Douglas Southall Freeman wrote that "Lee galloped toward Gettysburg like a blinded giant. . . . Never had he been so dangerously in the dark."

⊷≡◎═⊷

SALLIE BROADHEAD AWOKE early to get her baking done. She was certain there was going to be a battle and so was not surprised when she heard cannon booming west of town, out on the Chambersburg Pike. She recalled: "People were running here and there, screaming that the town would be shelled. No one knew where to go or what to do."

Tillie Pierce heard the cannon and saw Union soldiers and wagons pass her house heading toward the firing. She noticed some wagons filled with stretchers. "I remember hearing some of the soldiers remarking that there was no telling how soon some of them would be brought back . . . on the stretchers. I hardly knew what it meant, but I learned afterward, even before the day had passed."

Sallie Myers hauled out buckets of water and tin cups to provide drinks for the passing soldiers. She and her sisters "handed the water to the soldiers as they double-quicked through the town. They drank without ever stopping and threw the cups back to us. Besides giving them water, we handed them cake, bread and butter, and anything at all we could find in the house that was good to eat." It was exciting for awhile as the troops of Reynolds's division arrived, but it changed for Sallie Myers a short time later.

At ten o'clock that morning I saw the first blood. A horse was led past our house covered with blood. The sight sickened me. Then three men came up the street. The middle one could barely walk. His head had been hastily bandaged and blood was visible. I grew faint with horror. I had never been able to stand the sight of blood. But I was destined to become accustomed to it.

The young boys of Gettysburg, and quite a few of the men, could not resist this opportunity to witness a battle. Albertus McCreary and several other boys perched on a fence watching the Union troops head toward the front. He told a friend that "there were enough soldiers here to whip all the Rebs in the South."

Union soldiers climbing to the cupola of the Lutheran Seminary disrupted Professor Michael Jacobs's morning class. They made too much noise for him to continue teaching. By then, most of the students and faculty much preferred to see the combat. Many crowded into the cupola. Others joined the townspeople on Seminary Ridge. Robert McClean's attention to the battle was cut short when an errant shell whizzed overhead. He ran home as fast as he could, noting that the near miss led him to "a quickly increased interest in a copy of the New Testament."

One man in his seventies was not content merely to watch the battle; he expected to join it. John Burns, a veteran of the War of 1812, grabbed musket and powder horn and tagged along after a Wisconsin regiment. Sgt. George Eustice of the Seventh Wisconsin remembered Burns dressed in a "swallow-tailed coat with smooth brass buttons. He had a rifle on his shoulder. We boys began to poke fun at him as soon as he came amongst us, as we thought no civilian in his senses would show himself in such a place."

When the men asked Burns what he was doing out there, the old man said that the rebels had stolen some of his cows and milked the others dry. He just wanted to get even with them.

The Wisconsin boys thought Burns would run when the first shot was fired, but he stayed and fought bravely. Sergeant Eustice called him "true blue and grit to the backbone." Burns was wounded four times and captured by the Confederates, but he lived to tell the tale.

The war came early to those who lived on farms west of town where the fighting began. Amelia Harmon lived with her aunt out by Willoughby Run. Yankee soldiers took over the house and told the women to stay in the cellar. They huddled together while rebel troops attacked their now fortified home. When the Yankees were forced to retreat, the Confederates set the house afire, forcing the women out into the fields amid the chaos of rifle and cannon fire. They ran toward the rear of the rebel lines, where they were stopped and given food. Harmon wrote, "We were doubtless the only persons on the Union side who were fed from General Lee's commissary during the battle of Gettysburg."

Elizabeth Plank also lived near Willoughby Run, on a farm some three miles west of town. She recalled the roar of cannon and the softer sounds of rifle fire.

> Not long after this, an [enemy] ambulance arrived at the farmhouse and without any ceremony forced open the front door and carried in a wounded officer and placed him in the guest's room and the best bed in the house. . . . Now it was not long before all beds were filled with wounded, and the floor covered with straw carried from the barn all over the floors in the halls, on the porches, in the out-building, on the barn floor and every place were wounded—hauled there in ambulances, on wagons, gun machines, and every way possible. . . . Many limbs and arms were amputated and their wounds dressed, while the battle raged.

The horrible sights, smells, and sounds overwhelmed Elizabeth and her family. They grabbed some clothing and fled their home, making their way south to friends in Maryland, joining the many other refugees desperate to get out of harm's way.

⟶≡◉═⟵

GENERAL REYNOLDS HURRIEDLY directed every new brigade of troops out to the ridges west of Gettysburg. Each side rushed fresh units to the front as the fighting grew more intense. Shortly after ten o'clock in the morning Reynolds spotted rebel soldiers in an apple orchard left of Chambersburg Pike. They had to be stopped. He twisted in his saddle and shouted to the infantry behind him.

"Forward! For God's sake, forward."

At that instant a rebel bullet struck Reynolds in the neck, toppling him from his horse. His orderly cradled the general in his arms and carried him to a clump of trees. Gently he placed Reynolds on the ground but there was nothing to be done. Reynolds smiled once and within fifteen minutes was dead. One of his division commanders, Abner Doubleday, now the ranking man left, assumed command.

Just then, Confederate general Heth launched a major assault. He sent two brigades forward, one on each side of Chambersburg Pike, with orders to smash through the Yankee defenses. One brigade of Alabamians was led by Gen. James Archer, a Maryland-born, Princeton-educated veteran of the Mexican War who had survived every battle Lee had fought. The other brigade, from Mississippi, was led by Gen. Joe Davis, a cousin of Confederate president Jefferson Davis.

Archer's men got into trouble right away when they had to scale a high fence west of Willoughby Run. That action threw their line into disarray. Just as they were starting to straighten out, a heavy volley of musket fire slammed them back. They had run into the famous and feared Iron Brigade of Reynolds's First Corps, one of the most disciplined and toughest outfits in all the Union armies.

The rebels of Archer's brigade staggered back toward the fence. Immediately they were attacked on their flank by a Michigan regiment. Most of the rebels climbed over the fence to safety, but about seventy-five were captured—including Archer, the first of Lee's generals to be taken prisoner.

Archer was furious. He was handled roughly by the enlisted man who captured him, and a Yankee officer refused to accept his sword. The young captain told the general to keep it—after all, he had one already—and to move off to the rear. Another officer grabbed the sword from Archer a short time later. Then came the embarrassment of being greeted by his old friend, Abner Doubleday.

"Archer!" Doubleday said. "I'm glad to see you."

Doubleday held out his hand, but Archer refused to shake it and replied, "Well, I'm not glad to see you by a damn sight."

Joe Davis fared little better. His assault started well until the rebel troops got caught in a railroad bed. They became trapped in a ditch so deep they could not reach over the top to fire. Doubleday sized up the situation and sent two regiments forward. The Union troops quickly ringed the ditch and aimed their rifles down at the rebels.

More than 250 Confederate soldiers dropped their weapons and surrendered. Joe Davis and the rest beat a hasty, costly retreat out in the open under a hail of fire. More than half of Davis's men were lost; the rest, all inexperienced troops in their first battle, were so demoralized as to be useless.

In the meantime, the Union troops had to deal with a new Confederate threat from the north—the advance units of Ewell's corps—while holding back Hill's men from the west. It was up to John Buford and his cavalry. Buford sent one brigade to Oak Hill, less than two miles northwest of Gettysburg, where the troopers took up strong defensive positions. They forced Ewell's lead division, led by Maj. Gen. Robert Rodes, to halt. This action made it more difficult for Ewell and Hill to coordinate their two-pronged approach to town.

So far the Southern advance had been checked, due to the terrain, the leadership of Buford and Reynolds, and the timely arrival of Union reinforcements. However, Buford was worried. The Confederates vastly outnumbered the Union defenders. He believed it was only a matter of time before they broke through. Stronger leadership was needed if Gettysburg were to be held.

Buford summoned an aide and wrote a brief note to be delivered to his superior, Maj. Gen. Alfred Pleasonton, the cavalry commander for the Army of the Potomac. Pleasonton was at Taneytown. Meade was still headquartered there and no doubt Pleasanton would show him Buford's dispatch.

> A tremendous battle has been raging since nine and one-half A.M. with varying success. At the present moment the battle is raging on the road to Cashtown, and in short cannon range of [Gettysburg]; the enemy's line is a semicircle on the height from north to west. General Reynolds was killed early this morning. In my opinion there seems to be no directing person. We need help now.

Not long after Buford sent his aide south with his plea for help, it arrived, coincidentally, in the form of additional troops and yet another new commander, the third since the battle began. The Eleventh Corps, led by Maj. Gen. Oliver Howard, showed up around eleven o'clock. Howard took over command from Doubleday of all Union forces in Gettysburg. Between Reynolds's First Corps and Howard's Eleventh Corps, more than 22,000 Union troops were now in the area. At the same time, more Confederate troops from Hill's and Ewell's corps were converging on the scene.

The size of the battle grew steadily in a location where no one had planned or wanted a confrontation. As historian Richard Moe wrote,

> Neither Lee nor Meade had planned to fight here, but once the fighting started, the town became a giant magnet, pulling both sides irresistibly toward it. Thus the largest battle ever fought on the North American continent, and the most important engagement of the Civil War, began—almost as an accident.

⋯⟫◉⟪⋯

GEORGE MEADE DID not know a battle was underway until 11:20 that morning, several hours after Corporal Hodges on picket duty saw the first rebel soldiers. Reynolds's aide had arrived with the news that the general would fight the enemy inch by inch. Meade asked the aide to repeat the message, then said, "Good! That is just like Reynolds. He will hold on to the bitter end."

Meade knew that of all his senior commanders, he could depend on Reynolds. During the first days of his command of the Army of the Potomac, he had come to trust Reynolds's judgment. If a battle got underway in Meade's absence, he could not have asked for a better commander on the scene.

However, Meade's first reaction to news of the onset of hostilities was certainly impractical. He wired Gen. Darius Couch, now in Harrisburg, asking if he could harass Ewell's corps from the rear. Couch commanded an ill-trained collection of newly formed home guard and militia units. They would be no match for Ewell's tested veterans. Also, Couch's men were nearly forty miles from Gettysburg.

Meade took no further action, confident that Reynolds could contain the situation with his corps plus Howard's Eleventh and Maj. Gen. Henry Slocum's Twelfth. But around one o'clock that afternoon, Meade received word that Reynolds had been killed.

The courier bearing the message recalled "sorrow and shock reflected in Meade's drawn face. As the word spread, men exclaimed in astonishment, 'Reynolds dead? Reynolds!' . . . It was hard to believe and harder to bear."

An hour later Meade received a dispatch from General Howard confirming Reynolds's fate. Howard also informed Meade that he had ordered Slocum's corps, as well as Maj. Gen. Dan Sickles's Third Corps, to proceed to Gettysburg with all speed. Suddenly more than half of Meade's army was either at Gettysburg or on its way. Not long after, Meade was handed Buford's message complaining that no one seemed to be in control of the battle. Buford had pleaded, "We need help now." It was time for Meade to act.

⊹▬◑═⊱⊹

Ulysses S. Grant

Henry Halleck

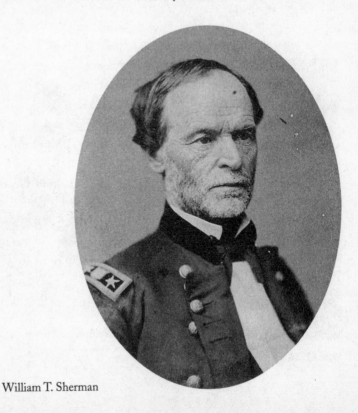

William T. Sherman

John A. Rawlins with wife and child at his quarters at City Point, Virginia, following the surrender of Vicksburg

David Porter

John Pemberton

Joseph Johnston

Drawing of cave life during the bombardment of Vicksburg showing a southern woman praying in her makeshift cave home

Wood engraving from *Harpers Weekly* magazine depicting the surrender of Vicksburg

George Meade

Joshua Chamberlain

Winfield Scott Hancock

Joseph Hooker

John Burns, the old hero of Gettysburg, with gun and crutches

Robert E. Lee

Lee's headquarters at Gettysburg on the
Chambersburg Pike

Field relief wagons of the U.S. Sanitary Commission

John Buford

James (Pete) Longstreet after the war

Dan Sickles at the Washington, D.C., arsenal

A dead Confederate soldier in Devil's Den, Gettysburg

Confederate prisoners at Gettysburg

FORTUNE SMILED UPON Meade with the timely arrival in Taney-town of the Second Corps, led by the man the newspapers called "Hancock the Superb." The thirty-nine-year-old Maj. Gen. Winfield Scott Hancock had graduated from West Point in 1844. He fought courageously in the Mexican War, storming the fortress at Churubusco alongside Pete Longstreet.

Hancock rose quickly in rank in the Civil War, participating in almost every battle fought by the Army of the Potomac. His men wor-shiped him and his superiors had confidence in him. It was McClellan, not often generous with his praise, who had first referred to him as "superb." Lt. Frank Haskell, a thirty-five-year-old Dartmouth graduate and an aide to General Gibbon, described Hancock as

> the most magnificent looking General in the whole Army of the Potomac at that time. With a large, well shaped person, always dressed with elegance even upon that field of confusion, he would look as if he was "monarch of all he surveyed," and few of his subjects would dare to question his right to command, or do ought else but obey.

Hancock was just the person Meade needed to replace Reynolds. He told Hancock to turn over command of his corps to a subordinate, handed him a map, and ordered him to Gettysburg to take charge. Hancock was to decide whether to continue the battle or withdraw Union forces south to the Pipe Creek defensive line Meade had pre-pared.

Meade would stay in Taneytown and continue work on the defen-sive line until Hancock had evaluated the situation and made his report. This placed a heavy responsibility on Hancock. He alone would decide where the decisive battle would be fought.

Hancock left for Gettysburg accompanied by three members of his staff. At first he rode in an ambulance so he could study the map

Meade had provided. Although Hancock had spent his childhood fewer than one hundred miles away, he had never visited Gettysburg and knew nothing of the terrain.

When they got close enough to hear the sounds of battle, Hancock mounted his horse and rode on to Cemetery Hill, overlooking the two armies, arriving at about four o'clock in the afternoon. He was not pleased. One of his staff officers described the scene. "Wreck, disaster, disorder, almost the panic that precedes disorganization, defeat and retreat were everywhere." The Union army was losing the fight.

◆—⇒◎⇐—◆

AT THE SAME hour, no more than a mile distant, Robert E. Lee stood atop Seminary Ridge watching a major Confederate victory unfold. He had reached Willoughby Run approximately two hours before and had been disturbed by what he saw. Union troops appeared to be well entrenched on Seminary Ridge with more easily defended high ground behind them, another ridge to which they could fall back if necessary. The battle was a stalemate.

As Lee swept the hills and fields with his binoculars, Henry Heth rode up and asked if he should launch an attack.

"No," Lee said, sounding uncertain. "I am not prepared to bring on a general engagement today. Longstreet is not up."

Lee did not know whether the Union troops forcing the standstill were the entire Army of the Potomac or only a portion. Without Longstreet's men, the strongest of Lee's three corps, he was reluctant to commit anything more to the battle. Longstreet's troops were strung out ten miles along the Chambersburg Pike, and it could be two hours or more before they would be in position to attack or defend against a Yankee onslaught.

As Lee watched and considered his options, the Union line began to break under pressure from Ewell's men, attacking from the north. Ewell's battle-hardened soldiers hit Howard's Eleventh Corps on their right flank in a repeat of the events at Chancellorsville. The men of

Howard's outfit responded the same way as they had done in May. "They broke and ran. First by ones and two, then by squads and platoons, and finally by companies and regiments . . . they took off rearward in headlong flight."

As soon as Lee saw that, he took advantage of the opportunity. He ordered Hill to send in two divisions, which broke the western line the way Ewell had broken the northern line. Hill succeeded, but casualties on both sides were horrendous.

The Iron Brigade, which had defended the ridges much of the morning, fell back in orderly fashion, having lost two-thirds of its strength—twelve hundred of its original eighteen hundred men. A Michigan outfit pulled back with only ninety-seven left of its five hundred officers and men. Pettigrew's Twenty-sixth North Carolina suffered more grievous losses. One company began with eighty-three men; by four o'clock, two remained standing. Another rebel company had ninety-one men that morning. By day's end, all were wounded or dead.

The Confederates pushed the Federals back from one ridge to the next until, finally, they took the remaining ridge west of town, the one named for the Lutheran seminary. When Lee rode to the top of Seminary Ridge and scanned the view east, choked with men in blue running and dodging to escape their gray-clad pursuers, he knew he had the chance he had hoped for. If he acted immediately, he could beat the Union forces before dark.

⋆⇒◉⇐⋆

AS LEE SCANNED the hills, he also recognized that the Yankees would have the advantage of high ground if they reorganized and dug in before his troops attacked. The terrain favored the defenders—if they were given time to take advantage of it. Lee's men traced an arc around the town, with Ewell's divisions on the northern rim and Hill's troops to the west.

Confronting the Confederate forces was what historians describe as a formidable defensive position shaped like a fishhook or an inverted letter J. Almost directly across from Seminary Ridge, nearly a mile east, was another ridge. A cemetery on a hill at the northern end, only a half mile south of the center of Gettysburg, gave the two-mile bluff its name. A sign at the entrance warned that anyone using firearms on the grounds would be prosecuted.

East of Cemetery Hill was Culp's Hill, with an unnamed hill south of that. Together they formed the semicircle at the top of the fishhook. To the south, at the bottom of the semicircle, stood Big Round Top, so called because it towered one hundred feet above the other hill, Little Round Top. Both were laced with boulders, and stretching in front of them, on their western side facing Lee, was a broad field of boulders known as Devil's Den. The line from Culp's Hill in the north to Big Round Top in the south was four miles long.

As Lee scanned the four miles of terrain from his vantage point on Seminary Ridge, he knew that the Yankees had to be attacked at once, while they were still disorganized.

<hr />

THE UNION RETREAT from Seminary Ridge and from Ewell's foray north turned into a rout. Panicky Yankee soldiers poured into streets, alleys, and buildings trying to escape the rebels, who often were no more than a block or two behind them. Scores of men were shot down in the streets, more than fifteen hundred captured in town, and hundreds more hidden in woodpiles, sheds, and the homes of Gettysburg's residents. The townspeople were no longer spectators. Now they were caught in the middle of the battle.

Fannie Buehler saw Union officers riding furiously in the streets, shouting warnings for people to go to their cellars and stay there. The Confederates were about to shell the town. General Doubleday led his First Corps through town, its retreat more orderly than Howard's Eleventh Corps. Terrified women screamed at him from sidewalks and open windows, pleading with him not to abandon them to the rebels. But there was nothing Doubleday or any Union commander could do for the civilians. The soldiers had to save themselves first, though many had already given up hope.

Albertus McCreary and his parents stood on their front porch watching the fleeing Union soldiers. He recalled them "running and pushing each other, sweaty and black from powder and dirt." Some of the men begged for water. The McCrearys ignored their own peril to run out and give them some. An officer rode up and told them, "All you good people go down into your cellar or you will be killed." Just before they went inside, Albertus glanced down Baltimore Street and saw Northern and Southern troops in hand-to-hand combat a mere half block away.

Most people took shelter in their basements, safe for the moment, but they could hear the gunfire and the screams of the wounded. Sallie Myers recalled,

> Those two hours I can never forget. Our cellar was a very good one and furnished a refuge for many besides our own family. The noise above our heads, the rattling of musketry, the screeching of shells and the unearthly yells, added to the cries and terror of the children, were enough to shake the stoutest heart.

Some of the cellars had small windows, and the people who dared peek outside witnessed scenes so horrible they would never be forgotten. Henry Jacobs looked out onto Washington Street. He saw an exhausted Union soldier stagger down the street with a group of rebels a few steps behind. The soldier carried his rifle but made no effort to use it or to run away. He could easily have been taken prisoner, but someone yelled, "shoot him, shoot him!" A shot rang out and the man fell dead in the street.

Through the window in their cellar the McCreary family watched in fascination as shadows of the men rushing past were thrown up on the opposite wall. They heard footsteps running across their porch and a Southern voice crying, "Shoot!" Albertus McCreary remembered that "a shot banged loudly right by a window. In silent horror [we] imagined the fate of the poor boy seeking to escape over the backyard fence."

Many retreating Union soldiers made their way into homes seeking places to hide. Residents took them in, offering sanctuary in closets and attics, anyplace that seemed safe. The Bayly family bravely answered a knock at their door and found a youngster in a Confederate uniform. The boy said he was tired of war and begged to be hidden from his own outfit. The family took him in and cared for him for three days.

⊷═◉═⊷

THE CIVILIANS BARELY had time to save themselves and hide the fleeing troops when they were called on to help save the wounded. Dwellings soon became hospitals; the women became nurses. Mary McAllister crossed the street from her house to enter Christ Lutheran Church. She had watched as the stretchers were being carried in.

> Every pew was full; some sitting, some lying, some leaning on others. They cut off the legs and arms and threw them out of the windows. . . . The church was full and then there was a shell struck the roof and they got scared, and I was scared. I wanted to go home.

She walked out front and found the church steps filled with more wounded men awaiting help. The street was full of injured soldiers, supported or carried by their comrades, all trying to get out of town. Mary shoved through the crowds to her house and found the front door standing open. The steps were covered with blood. Casualties filled the hallway and dining room and more were being brought in.

There was little she could offer for medical treatment but she helped in other ways. A colonel asked her to keep his diary safe from rebel hands; she stuffed it inside her dress. A soldier handed her Confederate general Archer's sword to hide. She pushed it under a pile of firewood.

Other men begged her to write down their names and addresses to notify their families of their condition. She offered her husband's coat to a Union officer so he could pass himself off as a civilian when the Confederates came, but he refused to put it on.

Other women worked alongside the surgeons performing operations, washing and dressing wounds, and easing many a man's final minutes. Twelve-year-old Mary Elizabeth Montford accompanied her mother to a warehouse full of wounded troops. Shortly after they arrived, Mary spied her father, a Union soldier, with a serious wound in his side. He had been hit by a shell fragment within sight of his home. She recalled, "Father looked at me and said, 'Mary Elizabeth,' then he closed his eyes." Mrs. Montford sent her home to stay with her grandmother and younger sister. The girl had surely seen enough for one day.

Tillie Pierce thought she was lucky that she had gotten out of town just before both armies poured in. She was staying at the home of a neighbor's father near the hill called Big Round Top. She and the neighbor had no sooner reached it than Union artillery units passed by, drawing enemy fire. A shell hit one of the caissons. The concussion sent the body of a soldier flying through the air. Other men picked him up and brought him into the house where Tillie had just arrived.

As they pass by I see his eyes are blown out and his whole person seems to be one black mass. The first words I hear him say is "Oh dear! I forgot to read my Bible today! What will my poor wife and children say?"

The man was wrapped in cotton and taken upstairs. Soon other wounded soldiers followed. Tillie saw that one had a damaged thumb. She thought that was dreadful.

"Oh," the man said, "this is nothing; you'll see worse than this before long."

"Oh! I hope not," she replied.

But she did. Tillie went out to the barn, which was overflowing with wounded and dying soldiers. There were "the groaning and the crying, the struggling and dying, crowded side by side, while attendants sought to aid and relieve them as best they could." It was all too much for the fifteen-year-old girl. She ran back to the house in tears.

⋅⊷⊜⊙⊶⋅

WHEN THE FIGHTING in town stopped and the majority of Union troops had fled, Confederates began a house-to-house search for those who had gone into hiding. Mary McAllister heard a pounding on her front door. The Union colonel who had refused her husband's coat urged her to answer.

"You must open the door," he insisted. "They know we are in here and they will break it."

Mary opened the door and the rebels burst in. The first Yankee soldier they spied was the colonel. They demanded his sword, which he turned over to them, then they moved on to examine the other soldiers in the house. They herded away the ambulatory and said they would parole the wounded. After they left, Mary hoisted a red shawl on a broomstick from a front window. Someone had told her this would protect the house because the rebels would consider it a hospital and leave it alone.

As she was hanging the shawl, she saw a half dozen rebel soldiers on horseback charge up the street, yelling and firing their pistols in the air. They stopped in front of the Lutheran church and exchanged words with the wounded men resting on the church steps. One of the Confederates fired and a Union soldier fell to the ground. Another cried out in protest that the dead man had been a chaplain. "He was going to shoot," the rebel soldier replied. "He was not armed," a Yankee said. They argued back and forth until the rebels grew tired of it. They rode off again, menacing passersby and firing in the air.

Fannie Buehler, whose house was now full of wounded men, answered the sharp ringing of her doorbell to find rebels on the lookout for Yankee soldiers. "Madam," one said, "you have Union soldiers concealed in your house, and I have come to search for them." Fannie boldly replied, "You are mistaken, sir. There are Union soldiers in my house, but none of them are concealed. They are all lying around on the first floor of my house. Step in and see them."

The Confederates stepped inside and instantly soldiers from both sides recognized one another. They had met often on picket duty, when Northerners and Southerners had developed the habit of gathering at night to talk about the war and about their families, and to trade coffee for tobacco. To Fannie's amazement, the men spent a peaceful half hour reliving old times, but then the rebels recalled their duty and insisted on conducting a thorough search of the house. They looked under beds and inside closets from the attic to the cellar but found no one else. They promised to return with paroles for the Union wounded. Fannie and her houseguests were not bothered again.

The McCreary family hid in their basement, expecting the worst. The cellar's outer door was flung open and five rebel soldiers came in to look for Yankee soldiers. Mr. McCreary said there was no one else in the house, but the Confederates nosed around and found thirteen men hiding in various places. This put the McCrearys in an awkward position. Protests that they did not know Union soldiers had been hiding upstairs would not have been believed. Thinking quickly, Mr. McCreary invited everybody, rebel and Yankee, to join them for supper.

And so they gathered around the dining room table in an amicable atmosphere. Young Albertus McCreary recorded the names and addresses of the Union soldiers and said he would write to their families about their capture. When the meal was finished, the Confederates thanked their hosts graciously and marched their prisoners down the street.

Sallie Broadhead had been hiding in the cellar of a friend's house while the fighting raged in the streets. No soldiers, from either side, had invaded the house, but she was worried about her husband, who had stayed at home. When the firing stopped, she made her way outside.

How changed the town looked when we came to the light. The street was strewn over with clothes, blankets, knapsacks, cartridge-boxes, dead horses, and the bodies of a few men, but not as many of the last as I expected to see.

Sallie stopped some rebel soldiers to ask if it was safe for her to walk home. They assured her that she would be fine. To her relief, she found her husband and home untouched. "As I write all is quiet, but O! how I dread tomorrow."

⊷═◁▶═⊶

ALL WAS NOT so safe or quiet a half mile away on Cemetery Hill, where General Hancock was trying to establish a defensive line. He had surveyed the terrain when he arrived, approvingly calling it "the strongest position by nature that I ever saw."

Now he had to fortify it, and that meant bringing order out of the chaos of the retreat. The two corps that had been in the fighting had lost more than ten thousand men killed, wounded, captured, or missing, more than half their strength. Many other soldiers in the retreat had kept on running out of town, leaving Hancock with no more than seven thousand effectives, which might not be enough to repulse an attack. Hancock needed additional troops, so he sent orders to Sickles and Slocum to speed up their march to Gettysburg.

Hancock rode along the hilltop visiting his men, calming them, bolstering morale, and re-forming them into companies, regiments, and brigades. His presence, bearing, and reputation instilled in the troops the confidence and spirit that had been lost in the rout. They began to believe they were an army again, united to survive and fight.

As he organized the men into effective units, Hancock positioned them behind the stout stone wall that faced the town from Cemetery Hill. He was certain the rebels would attack at that point and he wanted a highly visible presence. Once that point was secured, he strung the rest of the men along Cemetery Ridge. He also ordered Doubleday to secure Culp's Hill.

Hancock sent a courier south with a message for Meade. He told Meade he thought he would be able to hold his position until dark and that it was an excellent spot from which to mount a major battle with Lee's army.

⋆⇒◉⇐⋆

LEE WATCHED THE Union preparations with growing concern from his vantage point on Seminary Ridge. The rebel attack had stalled once Union troops had retreated to Cemetery Ridge. Many Confederates believed they had scored a major victory by defeating two Yankee corps, and in their haste to celebrate, their units lost all cohesion. The men scattered in Gettysburg's streets and alleyways to savor the fruits of their success and to round up the Union soldiers who had gone into hiding.

But Lee knew there was a greater victory to be won, and it lay only a mile away, where the beaten Yankees were trying to regroup. Four hours of daylight remained. If Lee struck now, he would have ample time to drive the Union army off the high ground they were just beginning to fortify. If he waited, they would become entrenched and reinforced; then the position would be much more costly to take.

General Hill also watched the Yankee movements and agreed with Lee that it was imperative to launch a fresh assault immediately. But when Lee suggested that Hill's Third Corps make the attack, Hill declined, arguing that his men were still exhausted from the last battle and were low on ammunition. He had a fresh division, but it was miles away. If there was to be another attack, it would have to be by Ewell's corps.

Lee called for Col. Walter Taylor, his chief of staff, and told him to take an oral message to General Ewell. Taylor was to tell Ewell that the enemy had been beaten and its troops were confused and disorganized.

Ewell should seize the opportunity and attack at once. As Taylor recalled the message, Lee said, "it was only necessary to press 'those people' in order to secure possession of the heights, and, if possible, he wished General Ewell to do this."

Thus, Lee did not directly order Ewell to attack. Instead, as Lee had been able to do with Jackson, he suggested that Ewell attack "if possible." Lee also repeated his admonition to avoid bringing on a general engagement until the rest of the Confederate army arrived.

Taylor delivered the message and reported back to Lee. They focused their binoculars on the ridge and waited for the attack to begin. Colonel Taylor later wrote that there was no reason to suspect that Ewell would not follow Lee's wishes and prepare an assault.

> General Ewell did not express any objection, or indicate the existence of any impediment, to the execution of the order conveyed to him, but left the impression upon my mind that it would be executed.

But Ewell did not order an attack. Instead, he rode calmly into Gettysburg through the milling crowds of soldiers and was shot in his wooden leg. The few Yankees still in town had opened fire on the general and his staff. An alarmed aide asked if he was hurt.

"No, no, I'm not hurt," Ewell said, joking about his near miss. "But suppose that ball had struck you. We would have had the trouble of carrying you off the field, sir. You see how much better fixed for a fight I am than you are. It don't hurt a bit to be shot in a wooden leg."

He sustained his good mood, pleased with his success in forcing the Yankees all the way back to Cemetery Ridge. But he seemed in no hurry to renew the assault as Lee desired. His subordinates, particularly those who had served with Stonewall Jackson, became increasingly impatient and frustrated. If Ewell did not attack soon, the opportunity would be lost.

"Oh, for the presence and inspiration of 'Old Jack' [Jackson] for just one hour!" said one.

"It was a moment of critical importance," wrote another staff officer. "Some of us who had served on Jackson's staff sat in a group in our saddles, and one said sadly, 'Jackson is not here.'"

Gen. Isaac Trimble was the most impatient and angry. He minced no words with Ewell.

"Well, General," he demanded, "we have had a grand success. Are you going to follow it up and push our advantage?"

Ewell said his orders were not to start a large-scale engagement until the entire army had arrived. Trimble persisted, arguing that Lee's orders did not apply to this unique situation in which battle had already been joined and it required only a quick final push to finish the job. Trimble pointed to Culp's Hill and noted that it commanded the town. Since the Federals had not yet occupied the heights, the Confederates should take it right away. But Ewell would not budge. Furious, Trimble stalked away, muttering that he would refuse to serve under Ewell again.

More time slipped away. Ewell's only action was to send for Jubal Early and Robert Rodes, two of his division commanders. He planned to consult with them before deciding to issue orders. While he waited, more and more Union troops dug in on Cemetery Hill and Cemetery Ridge. Daylight ebbed, his subordinates chafed, and Lee listened in vain for the sounds of firing that would signal the onset of the attack.

In town, the sporadic shooting continued. Ewell's staff persuaded him to move to a house on the outskirts of Gettysburg. That was where Early and Rodes tracked him down. They urged him to renew the offensive and to take the high ground from the Yankees, but only if Lee would send Hill's men to provide support on their right flank. They wanted Hill to attack the Yankees from the west while they struck from the north.

Early and Rodes believed they needed assistance because their own forces were small and disorganized. Rodes had lost twenty-five hundred men that afternoon. His troops were exhausted and spread out all over town. Early had sustained five hundred casualties but had only three of four brigades ready for an attack. In addition, the Confederates were encumbered with four thousand Yankee prisoners to guard, which drained away manpower.

Edward Johnson's division was at least an hour's march away. Therefore, given what they saw as their limited resources, Rodes and Early believed they could succeed only with support on their right flank, to prevent the Union troops on Cemetery Ridge from striking them there. Also, if Hill attacked from the west, drawing fire, then Ewell's men would have fewer Union troops to face.

Ewell dispatched a message to Lee requesting support, only to be told that it was not possible. In his reply, Lee urged Ewell to attack with his Second Corps alone, but once again Lee added those fateful words, "if possible." He reminded Ewell about avoiding a general engagement until the whole army was up and announced that he would visit Ewell in person. Stonewall Jackson would have taken the hill by now, but Jackson was gone. And so was the opportunity for a sweeping one-day victory.

⋆⇒◉⇐⋆

AT FIVE O'CLOCK that afternoon, Longstreet joined Lee on Seminary Ridge and spent ten minutes carefully studying the Union position. Longstreet's biographer noted, "He did not like what he saw. The ground on which the Federals were regrouping appeared naturally strong." The situation was exactly what Longstreet had hoped to avoid, a battle in which Confederate troops had to assault an entrenched and fortified position. Surely Lee was not planning to attack the enemy there, dug in as they were, not when he had agreed, at least in Longstreet's mind, to fight a defensive campaign by forcing the Yankees to attack first?

Longstreet told Lee that the Federals were in a perfect position for the Confederate defensive plan. All the Confederates had to do, he explained to Lee, was to shift around the enemy's left flank, move south, and take up a strong position between the Union army and the capital city of Washington, D.C. Then the Yankees would be forced to move out and come for them.

Lee was adamant. Shaking his fist, he told Longstreet, "The enemy is there, and I am going to attack him there."

"If he is there," Longstreet argued, "it will be because he is anxious that we should attack him: a good reason, in my judgment, for not doing so."

"No," Lee insisted. "They are there in position, and I am going to whip them or they are going to whip me."

Longstreet was silent for several moments. He swept the area with his binoculars again. He said he could see the Yankees strengthening their position by the minute. He was still opposed to attacking when the enemy held the high ground, but if Lee was determined to do so, then it should be done now.

When Lee asked Longstreet where his corps was, his reply was vague and noncommittal. It was strung out between Gettysburg and Cashtown, he said, at least six miles away. Lee said that he dared not launch a general assault until Longstreet's men were in position to support it. Longstreet apparently made no reply and left a short time later.

Around six o'clock that evening, Lee received news from two of Jeb Stuart's troopers. They reported that Stuart's cavalry division was headed toward Carlisle, where they expected to link up with Ewell's Second Corps. Lee was relieved to learn that Stuart was alive and that his unit was intact not far away. He issued orders for the troopers to head for Carlisle at once and to tell Stuart to get to Gettysburg as quickly as possible. Finally, though it would not be until the following day, Lee would have his cavalry back. He would no longer be blind about the enemy's position.

At seven o'clock, with little more than an hour of daylight remaining, Lee rode to Gettysburg to meet Ewell. He found him with Rodes seated in an arbor behind a house. Jubal Early joined them. Lee asked about the condition of the troops and from the gloomy answers he received, it was clear that Ewell had no intention of attacking the Northern forces that evening. Lee talked about his plans.

"Can't you with your corps attack on this flank tomorrow?" Lee asked.

Ewell did not answer, but Early more than made up for his commanding officer's reticence. Early was known for speaking plainly and that evening was no exception. He said he was much opposed to attacking the Union position. He believed it would be extremely costly and would ultimately fail.

The terrain in front of the Second Corps, Early argued, was steeper and more rugged than at any other point along the line. The Federal position was considerably stronger there than it was elsewhere. It seemed more sensible to Early to attack farther south along Cemetery Ridge, the area fronting Hill's Third Corps.

Ewell and Rodes agreed with Early, apparently relieved to have someone else carry the brunt of the assault. Lee did not try to dissuade them, nor did he order the attack. Perhaps he accepted their reluctance and knew that insisting on a fight most likely would not result in victory. But surely he was disappointed by their timid behavior. If Jackson were there, he would already have led his corps to glory. But Ewell, Lee could now plainly see, was no Jackson.

Some years later, shortly before his death, Robert E. Lee confided in a cousin: "If I had had Stonewall Jackson with me . . . I should have won the battle of Gettysburg." When Ewell later reflected on the battle, he said to a fellow officer that "it took a dozen blunders to lose Gettysburg," and Ewell knew he had committed many of them.

Lee had no choice but to assign the attack to another corps. Longstreet would make the assault against the Union left flank. Ewell would make a diversionary feint in his sector on the right flank and mount a full-scale assault if the situation looked promising. But again, these were discretionary orders. Whether Ewell made a determined attack on the Yankees was entirely up to him.

And so as July 1 ended, Lee faced the coming battle having placed the major responsibility on Pete Longstreet, who had made it clear that he disapproved of taking the offensive in this campaign.

⋅→═◦═←⋅

JULY 1 WAS also a disappointing day for John Pemberton, in command at Vicksburg. It was one of the darkest days of Pemberton's life, for he finally had to accept his situation. He had no chance to save Vicksburg. Joe Johnston was not coming to his relief. With sadness, Pemberton composed a letter to his division commanders, inquiring about the condition of their troops. He wrote:

> Unless the siege of Vicksburg is raised or supplies are thrown in, it will be necessary very shortly to evacuate the place. I see no prospect of the former, and there are very great, if not insuperable, obstacles in the way of the latter. You are, therefore, requested to inform me, with as little delay as possible, as to the condition of your troops, and their ability to make the marches and undergo the fatigues necessary to accomplish a successful evacuation.

Pemberton was already aware of the condition of the soldiers. He knew they were too weak and malnourished to attempt to fight their way through the Yankee cordon. However, he believed it would lessen the blame that would be placed upon him for surrendering if he had in writing from his four subordinate commanders their corroboration that the men were in no condition to attempt an evacuation.

Meanwhile, Ulysses S. Grant was restless and impatient. He had seen no signs of imminent surrender of the Southern forces and he knew his troops were now too cautious to carry on the war aggressively. Trenches were being dug too lazily. The fighting had slowed too much. A new assault was needed to invigorate the men.

Grant ordered that another mine be dug under a Confederate strongpoint, to be filled with twenty-two hundred pounds of gunpowder. This time he would direct an attack to coincide with the mine's explosion. Grant was determined that this assault break through the enemy lines. He scheduled the attack for July 6, only five days away.

Joe Johnston was also making plans. He commanded a force of thirty-two thousand men, and as June turned to July, he set them moving south. He hoped to create enough of a diversion to force Grant to shift some of the Union army away from Vicksburg. Perhaps then Pemberton would be able to fight his way out of town. Johnston planned to attack Grant in six days, on July 7.

⋯⟼◉⟻⋯

WEARY SOLDIERS ON both sides of the line at Gettysburg tried to get some rest. Others were still on the move, hoping to reach Gettysburg before daybreak. The First Minnesota Volunteers had been marching all day in the hot sun. Late in the afternoon they heard artillery fire up ahead and saw large numbers of deserters heading toward them. The men wore the badge of the Eleventh Corps, the one that broke at Chancellorsville. The Minnesotans jeered and taunted them as they passed.

That was when they learned their destination. "At Taneytown we hear there has been fighting at Gettysburg today," Isaac Taylor wrote in his diary. At 8:45 that night, the men stopped to set up camp a few miles from Gettysburg. They were worn out. Over the past two weeks they had averaged more than fourteen miles a day, a demanding march, even for seasoned veterans.

Their officers were nervous and kept countermanding orders almost as soon as they were issued. "Three times we got permission to have fires and twice they were put out," recalled twenty-two-year-old

Matthew Marvin. Four times the men were told they could boil coffee, but three times they had to dump it out and fall in line again.

Isaac Taylor and his brother Henry tried to sleep but found themselves too anxious to rest. "We talked a few moments of the great battle we expected in the morn," Henry wrote. He told Isaac that "we could whip Lee if our forces were well handled and our troops would fight." Although they were sure of themselves, they were less confident in the other units. The Eleventh Corps was not the only outfit to have behaved disgracefully in the past.

The Twentieth Maine, led by Col. Joshua Chamberlain, formerly a professor at Bowdoin College, was also on the road, coming from Hanover in the east. They, too, heard the artillery and learned of the desperate battle at Gettysburg and the death of the beloved General Reynolds. They knew they would be called on the next day and they pushed themselves harder on a march the survivors would not soon forget.

When darkness fell and the full moon rose, the bands struck up and the colors were unfurled again. Farmers and townspeople came out of the houses and to the roadside, hailing their deliverers and bringing water and food. Young women, all made to seem beautiful by the soft light, sang, waved handkerchiefs, and flirted with young staff officers, who lingered to talk in low, hurried tones and sometimes, perhaps, bent down from their horses to steal a kiss. A group of girls at the wayside began singing "The Star Spangled Banner," and [brigade commander] Strong Vincent, inspired by the almost magical mood, looked at his country's flag. Baring his head, he declared to those riding with him: "What death more glorious could any man desire than to die on the soil of old Pennsylvania fighting for that flag? . . . Now boys, we will give 'em hell tomorrow."

Joshua Chamberlain, who had come to love the life of a warrior, recalled how everything along their route seemed to be magnified in intensity and mystery. When a rumor spread through his regiment that the ghost of George Washington had been seen near Gettysburg, he came close to believing it himself.

After midnight the men halted. They slumped to the ground and slept where they fell. They were still three miles from Gettysburg. Every man knew they would be there in plenty of time for the coming day's battle.

◦═◉═◦

FEW OF GETTYSBURG'S residents got much sleep that night. Except for the southern portion adjacent to Cemetery Hill, the town was now occupied by rebel troops. "At night all was quiet," Alice Powers wrote, "but the tramp of the guards reminded the town that its citizens were prisoners."

Dead soldiers littered streets, yards, and alleyways. Casualties filled public buildings and many private homes. As the wounded groaned and cried in pain, others quietly slipped into death. Surrounding the town, as far as the eye could see, campfires pricked the darkness like hundreds of fireflies. Everyone knew that, come morning, the men now huddled around those fires would be killing one another.

John Crawford and his family had some unwelcome guests. General Ewell and his staff had set up headquarters in a barn next door. Late that night, Ewell and several officers crossed to the Crawford house to ask for a cup of tea. The women were tending wounded Union soldiers and made it clear that the Confederates were unwelcome. But they did provide tea for them and later admitted that the Southerners had been polite. A few were even called charming and handsome.

Ewell asked if they might return for tea in the morning. Crawford agreed. In gratitude, Ewell placed a guard at the door to bar any intruders from among his own troops. He also promised to do his best to keep them supplied with food. However, when one woman started to cry while describing the death of a soldier in the house, Ewell replied coldly, "Madam, we become hardened to such things in war."

GENERAL MEADE ARRIVED at Cemetery Hill just before midnight. He had left his Taneytown headquarters at ten o'clock after receiving several messages from Hancock assuring Meade that Hancock's position at Gettysburg was a good one from which to do battle. Meade ordered the remainder of the army to converge on Gettysburg as rapidly as possible.

Meade rode slowly past the tombstones and monuments at Cemetery Hill and entered the small gatekeeper's house. When his commanders arrived, he requested their assessment of the situation. Was this the place to fight the decisive battle? All agreed that it was.

"I am confident we can hold this position," General Howard said, speaking for all of them.

"I am glad to hear you say so, gentlemen," Meade replied. "I have already ordered the other corps to concentrate here and it is too late to change."

CHAPTER 9

THE BLOOD STOOD IN PUDDLES

July 2, 1863

GEORGE MEADE AWOKE early. He was out inspecting the defenses on Cemetery Hill and Culp's Hill before the sun rose. He approved of the sturdy barricades the men had fashioned out of trees and cords of wood. He studied the long spine of Cemetery Ridge down to Big Round Top and Little Round Top, the hills that marked the ridge's southern end. He seemed pleased with what he saw.

A soldier overheard Meade say, "We may fight it out here just as well as anywhere else." And the word spread that the general thought this was a good place to fight. This report was reassuring to the men watching the terrain to the east toward Seminary Ridge, and to the north toward town, both places packed with troops in gray calmly boiling their ground-acorn coffee.

Meade saw the Southern forces and was sure his army outnumbered them. At least he hoped so, although he had no precise information about the size of the army that he was preparing to fight. His army of effectives was about eighty thousand strong; Lee's force numbered about fifty thousand on the line.

But it was the lay of the land that gave Meade the real advantage.

His men were deployed over less than three miles of defensive line, while Lee, with fewer men, had to occupy a five-mile line. This meant that Meade could position some twenty-seven thousand men to the mile, whereas Lee had to cover his front with approximately ten thousand troops to the mile. The Northerners also outnumbered the Confederates in artillery, with 354 cannon to 272.

Thus, Meade had several reasons to feel confident about the outcome, and those who saw him that morning thought he seemed optimistic. An officer who rode with him on his predawn inspection described him as "quick, bold, cheerful, and hopeful, and he so impressed others." Another recalled his "self-possession and absolute coolness, strong and pronounced."

As Meade rode along the length of the ridge, his troops did not rise to cheer him, as they would have done for McClellan. This morning they were too busy preparing for the fight. Also, Meade was still unknown to most of the men and not the most charismatic of generals. Yet, the fact of his presence seemed to bolster their spirits. They had been let down by so many commanders in the past. Perhaps with this one they would win.

⊷═◉═⊷

LEE WAS ALSO up before daybreak. After a quick breakfast in the dark, he made his way to the crest of Seminary Ridge as the sky began to lighten, to take another look at the enemy line. He needed to know how many Yankee reinforcements had arrived during the night.

He scanned the Union position and could hardly believe what his eyes told him must be true. Cemetery Hill remained heavily occupied, more so than the previous evening, but the southern end of the ridge appeared to be empty. There were no Yankee troops in sight, which could only mean that no reinforcements had arrived overnight. Lee concluded that the only Union troops he would face were the remnants of the two corps his men had defeated yesterday. If he attacked now, he could expect to finish the battle before noon.

Lee had sent one of his engineers, Capt. Samuel Johnson, to reconnoiter the southern end of Cemetery Ridge and the two Round Tops to see if they were, in fact, as empty of defenders as his own observation now revealed. If Johnson's report confirmed what Lee saw through his binoculars, then Longstreet's attack, planned the previous evening, should succeed easily.

But where were Longstreet's men? They should already have been in position. Lee expected to see them assembling, ready to move off from Seminary Ridge, but they were nowhere in sight. Lee had known since last night that Longstreet's nearest divisions were only six miles away. He scanned the terrain behind him, looking for columns approaching from the west, but there were none.

Longstreet arrived unaccompanied by his troops. He informed Lee that the lead elements of his corps were not so far behind but the rest were strung out along the Chambersburg Pike. Longstreet did not seem to be in any hurry, but he was clearly bothered. He again argued against a frontal assault and reiterated his plan to outflank the Union position and establish a defensive line that the Yankees would then have to attack.

It was a repeat of the discussion Longstreet and Lee had engaged in the day before. Lee interrupted and insisted that he would attack the Federals where they were. Longstreet said no more.

He walked away to speak to one of his division commanders, John Bell Hood, and remarked, "General [Lee] was a little nervous this morning; he wishes me to attack; I do not wish to do so without Pickett [whose division was farthest from Gettysburg]. I never like to go into battle with one boot off."

Longstreet was not alone in noticing that Lee seemed nervous. Others observed that he appeared impatient and restless, that he lacked the "quiet self-possessed calmness" he had had at Chancellorsville. He was "not at his ease," another subordinate said, and looked careworn, "more anxious and ruffled than I had ever seen him before."

Lee may have had good reason for his unease. Little seemed to be going well for the Confederates since Ewell had been unable, or unwilling, to attack the routed and weakened enemy on the previous day. And now here was Longstreet urging a defensive campaign after Lee had made it clear that he wished to press the attack.

Worse, Longstreet showed no urgency about moving his corps into position to assault the Yankees, who were still at a disadvantage with much of Cemetery Ridge apparently undefended. An aide observed, "Lee seemed very much disappointed and worried that the attack had not opened earlier, and very anxious for Longstreet to attack at the very earliest possible moment."

Sometime before eight o'clock that morning Captain Johnson returned from his reconnaissance around the southern end of Cemetery Ridge. He brought good news. There were no Union troops on the entire southern portion of the ridge or on the two Round Tops. Lee asked specifically if Johnson had seen this for himself. Johnson replied that indeed he had.

Johnson may well have explored the area in person, but he was wrong about the absence of Union troops. Hundreds of soldiers from Dan Sickles's Third Corps were camped by Little Round Top at the time Captain Johnson said he was in the area. If he had not seen these troops, who may have been hidden by the morning ground mist, he should at least have heard them breaking camp. The men were under no orders to be quiet. For whatever reason, Johnson claimed he did not see them and Lee had no reason to doubt his report.

Based on Johnson's information, Lee fashioned his plan of attack, which was little different from the one he had announced the previous night. Longstreet would take the southern end of Cemetery Ridge, then turn northward to attack Cemetery Hill from the rear. At the same time, Ewell would assault Cemetery Hill from the north.

It was close to 9 A.M. when another of Longstreet's division commanders, Lafayette McLaws, arrived on Seminary Ridge. He reported that his division was a mile and a half away and ready for battle. While Longstreet listened, Lee told McLaws where to place his division and where to attack. When McLaws said he wanted to take a small party to reconnoiter the terrain, Longstreet, his immediate superior, ordered him not to leave his troops and told him where to place his division. Lee contradicted him.

"No, General," Lee said. "I wish it placed just opposite."

Prior to this, no one had ever known Lee to bypass the chain of command to correct one of his senior generals in public. McLaws noticed that Longstreet was upset. When McLaws again requested permission to survey the terrain before attacking—a reasonable, even routine, request—Longstreet refused. Visibly annoyed, Longstreet made no attempt to hide his feelings. Lee remained silent. Perhaps he should have spoken out or taken Longstreet aside and chastised him for seeming reluctant to attack the enemy. But as historian Douglas Southall Freeman observed,

> Had he been Jackson, he would of course have relieved Longstreet of command without further ado and would himself have directed the operations of the First Corps. But that was not Lee's method of dealing with his lieutenants. Never in his whole career did he order a general officer under arrest. . . . In this instance, if he felt any resentment, he did not show it. Instead, he assumed that Longstreet would do his duty. He simply ignored the insubordination.

Lee left his observation post on Seminary Ridge and rode to Ewell's headquarters north of Cemetery Hill. Isaac Trimble met him and led him to the cupola of the poorhouse from which they had an excellent and sobering view of Cemetery Hill and Culp's Hill. Both were bristling with Union troops and artillery. Since the previous day, when Ewell refused to move against them, the Yankees had converted both positions into impregnable strongholds.

"The enemy have the advantage of us," Lee told Ewell. "We did not or could not pursue our advantage of yesterday and now the enemy are in good position."

Although Lee was disappointed, he saw no reason to alter his battle plan. If anything, he realized with even greater urgency the importance of a timely attack. "The attack must be made *at once*," he repeated, "*at once*." Ewell dissuaded Lee, insisting that his corps should not attack until after Longstreet had moved. Lee agreed, reluctantly, but emphasized that Ewell must advance as soon as he heard Longstreet's artillery open fire.

Throughout the time he spent with Ewell, Lee kept expecting to hear the reassuring sounds of Longstreet's guns. But there was nothing, and Lee was growing increasingly puzzled by the delay.

By eleven o'clock, when Lee returned to his observation post on Seminary Ridge, Longstreet's troops still had not begun their attack. An aide described Lee as suffering "more impatience than I ever saw him exhibit upon any other occasion." For Lee had discovered that Hood's and McLaws's divisions of Longstreet's corps, intended to spearhead the attack, had not budged.

Worse, while Longstreet's men remained in the same place, the Yankees were on the move. As Lee peered at Cemetery Ridge, he saw more blue uniforms occupying it. The Confederates had waited too long and now faced a sizable force that had not existed just two hours before. Although the advantage had been lost, Lee was still optimistic. He said,

> Ah, well, that was to be expected. But General Meade might as well saved himself the trouble, for we'll have [Cemetery Ridge] in our possession before tonight.

The attack would proceed as planned, just as Lee had explained it to Longstreet more than two hours before. For what may have been the first time in the war, Lee went beyond merely suggesting troop movements to a subordinate. He issued a direct order to Longstreet to attack the Union forces on Cemetery Ridge.

Longstreet would obey. He was a soldier. There was no question of his refusing to carry out a direct order from Robert E. Lee. But he would do it reluctantly, resentfully, and in his own good time. The order to attack, given shortly after eleven, would not be carried out until almost five hours later.

⊷≡◉≡⊷

LEE MAY NOT have known until eleven o'clock that morning that so many Union troops occupied Cemetery Ridge, but young Tillie Pierce knew hours earlier. She had sought shelter with a friend's family at their farm near Big Round Top and was finding out that it was no refuge at all.

Early on the morning of July 2, Tillie saw large numbers of Union troops, artillery, and ammunition trains pass by the house. A little later she noticed a pile of long, crudely constructed boxes beside the road near the garden fence. They were coffins. The passing soldiers joked about them. One said, "There was no telling how soon [I] would be put in one of them." Another added, "I will consider myself very lucky if I *get* one."

Tillie saw an officer hitting a soldier with the flat of his sword. The man was crawling on hands and knees, a victim of sunstroke, but the officer struck him several times. When the officer moved on, the soldier's buddies carried him into the house, hoping to save his life.

"We will mark that officer for this," one of them told Tillie. When she wrote about the incident twenty-five years later, she commented that it was "a pretty well established fact that many a brutal officer fell in battle, from being shot other than by the enemy."

Some officers invited her to come up to the roof, which they were using as an observation post. They asked if she wanted to see what was happening. She recalled,

> The sight I then beheld was wonderful and sublime. The country for miles around seemed to be filled with [Union] troops; artillery moving here and there as fast as they could go; long lines of infantry forming into position; officers on horseback galloping hither and

thither! It was a grand and awful spectacle, and impressed me as being some great review.

The situation looked considerably less grand for the civilians back in Gettysburg, particularly those at the southern end of town near Cemetery Hill. The rebels had commandeered most of the homes for use by snipers to take potshots at the Yankees up on the hill. Confederate sharpshooters fired from windows and doorways and in turn became targets when the Union troops fired back.

Families trapped by the crossfire huddled in their cellars, risking their lives whenever they ventured upstairs. Billy McClean, curious to see the action, went up to a second-floor room in his house and opened the shutters to take a look. He was lucky. He turned away from the window just before a Yankee bullet tore through, "in direct line with where my breast had been a few seconds before."

Albertus McCreary and his family were also trapped in their home, not daring to peek outside or run the short distance to the barn. A rebel soldier firing from a second-floor window was killed. The McCrearys later cleaned up the blood, wrapped the soldier in a blanket, and buried him.

The Hollinger family, living close by Culp's Hill, spent most of the day in the basement hearing bullets strike the brick walls of their home. Jacob Hollinger tried to get to the barn; chickens and cows had to be fed, war or no war. With every step he took, rifle shots followed him, some coming perilously close. He confronted a Confederate officer to ask why the Union troops seemed to be deliberately shooting at him.

"Why, man, take off that gray suit," the officer said. "They think you are a reb." Hollinger changed clothes and survived the day.

GETTYSBURG WAS BECOMING a battlefield. All over town the Confederates erected barricades in streets and alleys, anticipating a

Union attack. A wall that had run the length of a street for as long as anyone could remember was dismantled so that the stones could be used for the barricade. Fences enclosing private yards were torn down so troops could move freely from one yard to the next. Some houses were torn down and the materials used to construct fortifications.

The gashouse was closed, leaving people with no source of light other than candles and lanterns. Finding food became a major concern. Too many people, townsfolk and soldiers, were competing for the limited supply. One woman watched hungry Confederate soldiers ransack a store and "knock the tops from the kegs of salt mackerel, snatch the fish from the brine and eat them, heads, tails, and all."

Some people hid their cows and chickens in the parlor, cellar, or attic to keep them out of rebel hands. Mary McAllister's family was low on food. "About all I lived on was strong tea and crackers . . . which I had hid in the attic." She stashed some bacon under a pile of grain sacks on the dirt cellar floor but was not able to conceal a barrel of molasses. She managed to save one bucketful for her family, but the Confederates took the rest, filling every container imaginable, no matter how filthy. "If you were as hungry as we are," a soldier told her, "you would not care."

Many civilians risked their lives to hunt for food. Sallie Broadhead recalled that her husband

> went to the garden and picked a mess of beans, though stray firing was going on all the time, and bullets from sharpshooters or others whizzed about his head in a way I would not have liked. He persevered until he picked them all, for he declared the rebels should not have one. I baked a pan of shortcake, and some neighbors coming in joined us, and we had the first quiet meal since the contest began. I enjoyed it very much.

Harriet Bayly was more daring than most. She lived on a farm outside of town where there was no fighting or rebel troops. She could have remained there in safety but chose instead to pack a basket with bread, butter, wine, and bandages and go to town to offer help. She soon came upon a group of wounded Union soldiers who had been abandoned in the scorching sun for more than twenty-four hours without food, water, or first aid. Confederate soldiers nearby had ignored their cries for water.

Harriet fed them and dressed their wounds. Then she accosted a rebel officer and berated him for failing to provide water for the men. "Soon we had plenty of water," she said. No doubt her actions saved some lives that day.

Sallie Myers also tried to help. Just the day before she had not been able to stand the sight of blood. On the morning of July 2, she steeled herself to help with the wounded at St. Francis Xavier Catholic Church, a few doors from her home.

When she arrived, still uncertain about her nerve, she found the church full.

> Some of the wounded lay in the pews, and some lay on the floor with knapsacks under their heads, and there were very few persons to do anything for the poor fellows. Everywhere was blood, and on all sides we heard groans and cries and prayers.

Sallie stepped inside and knelt next to the first man she saw, Sgt. Alexander Stewart, who had been shot in the lungs and spine. His wounds were mortal; there was no hope of recovery.

"What can I do for you?" she asked. "He looked up at me," she remembered, "with mournful, fearless eyes, and said, 'Nothing. I am going to die.'"

Overcome by her emotions, Sallie ran outside sobbing and collapsed on the church steps. But she pulled herself together and went back inside the church, determined to stay and do whatever she could. She went to Sergeant Stewart and began to talk to him. He told her about his parents, wife, and brother, who was back home on the family farm in western Pennsylvania recuperating from a war wound. He asked her to read to him from the Bible, the fourteenth chapter of John. This was the passage his family had read together the day the two brothers went off to war.

"'Peace I leave with you,'" Sallie read. "'My peace I give to you. . . . Do not let your hearts be troubled or afraid.'"

⋯═◎═⋯

THAT AFTERNOON, JEB Stuart finally returned to the Army of Northern Virginia. He had been out of touch with Lee since June 25. The flamboyant cavalry leader was in high spirits, expecting to be hailed as a hero. He had led his unit through miles of Yankee territory, ridden close to Washington, D.C., and captured the wagon train to present to Lee. The reality of the reunion was quite different from Stuart's expectations. Witnesses recalled, "It was painful beyond description."

Lee's face reddened dangerously when he saw Stuart and he actually raised his arm as if to strike him.

"I have not heard from you for days," Lee said, "and you the eyes and ears of my army."

Stuart seemed to wilt at the tone of Lee's rebuke.

"I have brought you 125 wagons and their teams, General," Stuart explained.

"Yes, General," Lee said, "but they are an impediment to me now."

Suddenly Lee's manner changed from the tough father reproaching his wayward son to the tenderness of an older brother.

"Let me ask your help now," Lee said. "We will not discuss this matter longer. Help me fight these people."

Many Southern generals as well as members of Lee's staff faulted Lee for being so forgiving of Stuart's escapade. They talked among themselves of court martial, demotion, and other forms of punishment. One aide proposed that Stuart be shot. But none of them said anything to Lee, and he never spoke of the matter again.

Stuart was told to take his division two and a half miles out the York

Pike northeast of Gettysburg, there establishing a defensive position to protect Ewell's left flank from a surprise attack. Stuart was also to reconnoiter the rear of the Union position and attack if he believed there was an opportunity to do so. His cavalry would stay there on the periphery of the battle until it ended—so Stuart would have no more of a role to play in the major engagement than he had in its preparation.

About an hour after Stuart arrived, George Pickett, in command of the only infantry division not yet in Gettysburg, reported to his superior, Longstreet. Pickett's outfit of fifty-eight hundred Virginians had stayed at Chambersburg with orders to destroy all public property and all businesses that manufactured goods that could be useful to the enemy.

At one o'clock in the morning, Pickett's men had begun the twenty-three-mile trek over South Mountain to Gettysburg. They marched under the broiling sun until two that afternoon, setting up camp a few miles outside town on the Chambersburg Pike. Pickett had ridden ahead to report to Longstreet; he sent an aide to report to Lee.

Pickett chatted amiably with his commander while they waited for his aide to arrive with a communication from Lee: "Tell General Pickett I shall not want him this evening, to let his men rest, and I will send him word when I want them."

When Pickett returned to his division he instructed his men to be prepared for an early start in the morning. The soldiers, weary from their forced march in the heat, welcomed the chance to rest. Some wondered whether the occasional artillery fire they were hearing in the distance might be over before they got to town, denying them the chance to be a part of a major battle.

Others feared the fighting certain to take place the next day. Lt. Tom Dooley felt an uncharacteristic dread come upon him that even invaded his sleep.

An intangible, gut-churning fear lingered over him throughout the night, punctuated by the recurring visions of horribly mutilated corpses and horrific suffering which intensified as the hours passed. With each conscious thought of what lay ahead the images of gore became more diverse and more vivid.

⊶━◉⊂━⊷

NOON CAME AND WENT. Lee waited for Longstreet's attack to begin. An hour later he was still waiting, but at least Longstreet had begun to move his troops out. Longstreet had sent two aides on a reconnaissance mission around eleven o'clock to make sure that the extreme southern edge of Cemetery Ridge was still free of the enemy. No Yankee soldiers were seen. Longstreet ordered two of his divisions to advance, those of McLaws and Hood, to take up positions opposite Little Round Top.

Their march was a fiasco from the outset. The distance to cover was supposed to be three miles but it proved to be twice that far. Some units marched even farther. The purpose of a roundabout march was to bring the troops into place for the attack without being seen by the small Union signal post on Little Round Top. Meade had positioned only a few soldiers there. Although they could not have stopped an attack, their vantage point gave them widespread views of the country-side. Had they spotted two divisions of Confederate troops on the march, they would immediately have signaled headquarters. Meade would have rushed units to the south end of the ridge to repel Longstreet's attack.

McLaws's division led the one-and-a-half-mile-long column. After marching some distance, they discovered that they would become visible to the observers on Little Round Top if they continued on the same heading. Their only option was to turn around and countermarch a mile or so and try another route. When McLaws learned he had to backtrack, he let loose a burst of profanity. A soldier recalled that the general said things that "I would not like to teach my grandson."

Turning an entire division is difficult and time-consuming. Additional time was lost when Hood's column ran into the rear of McLaws's troops. Around three o'clock, the head of the column reached the western side of Seminary Ridge, hidden from the Union signal post. Longstreet caught up with McLaws just as the men reached the top of the ridge.

"How are you going in?" he asked McLaws.

"That will be determined when I can see what is in my front," McLaws said.

"There is nothing in your front," Longstreet said. "You will be entirely on the flank of the enemy."

That was the reason for taking the southern end of Cemetery Ridge: it was empty of Union troops. And that was why the Confederates had taken such care to reach their position without being seen by the enemy. There were not supposed to be any Yankee soldiers on the ridge opposite. Or, if there were, it would only be a small force easily overrun.

Satisfied that his men were in place and that the assault would begin shortly, Longstreet turned and rode away. Many who saw him remembered that his expression was gloomy. He remained solidly opposed to making the attack. A soldier who watched him ride by recalled Longstreet's "eyes cast to the ground as if in deep study, his mind disturbed."

Lafayette McLaws rode to the top of Seminary Ridge and peered over to the other side. "The view presented astonished me," he recalled. Cemetery Ridge was full of men in blue, from near Little Round Top to the point opposite a peach orchard, precisely where McLaws's division was set to attack. What looked like an entire Yankee corps, at least ten thousand men, were marching toward the orchard to extend the Union line forward.

When John Bell Hood brought his men into position on McLaws's right flank, he was confronted by the same staggering sight, thousands of Union troops—who were not supposed to be there—waiting for the Confederates to launch their attack. Dismayed by the prospect of a futile frontal assault, Hood sent scouts around the southern end of Big Round Top. They reported back that there was no Union presence guarding the end of the line.

John Buford's cavalry division was supposed to take its place on that end of the line to prevent any flanking maneuver by the rebels. However, Meade had told Buford to take his men out of the line because they desperately needed a rest. The cavalry division Meade had ordered to replace Buford's had gotten into a skirmish with Jeb Stuart's men and were then several miles from where Meade expected them to be. Meade's left flank stood totally unprotected. Hood could swing his division around Big Round Top and meet no opposition. He would then be in the enemy's rear, capable of creating a disaster for the Union army.

Hood sent an aide to Longstreet to explain the situation and advise him of the amazing opportunity that had become available to the Confederates. He asked permission to swing around the enemy's left flank. Longstreet insisted on adhering to the original plan.

"General Lee's orders are to attack up the Emmitsburg Road," Longstreet said.

Hood sent a second officer to Longstreet saying that nothing could be accomplished by making the frontal assault as planned against such a well-defended position. He repeated his request to slip around the Union flank. The reply was the same.

On his third try, Hood's idea was rejected again with the identical message from Longstreet about attacking up the Emmitsburg Road. And as if three times were insufficient, Longstreet sent a staff officer, a colonel, to repeat the same order. Hood sent no more messages and moved his troops into position.

When Longstreet himself rode up, Hood tried to persuade him in person, making an emotional appeal. To charge the enemy would be costly and futile. To outflank and surprise them in their rear could mean a Union rout. Longstreet's answer was simple.

"We must obey the orders of General Lee."

⚬

ALL THROUGHOUT THE morning, George Meade had been expecting an attack against Cemetery Hill. Fully half of his army, eight corps,
was concentrated there to repel any assault by Ewell's force. Of Meade's
eight remaining corps, three were in reserve and five were stretched
along the eastern slope of Cemetery Ridge where the enemy could not
see them. Meade waited throughout the morning and into the afternoon, much as Lee was waiting. The anticipated attack did not come.

Halfway through the morning, his impatience growing, Meade considered attacking the Confederates in front of Culp's Hill before they
could launch their own assault. He sent the commander of the Twelfth
Corps, Maj. Gen. Henry Slocum, to reconnoiter the ground to see if it
favored an attack. After examining the area, Slocum recommended
against an attack in that sector.

Meade tried to prepare for every contingency. He even asked his
chief of staff, Maj. Gen. Dan Butterfield, to work out a plan for retreat,
should it come to that. Butterfield mapped out the plan in the cramped
attic of Meade's headquarters.[1] In the meantime, all Meade could do
was wait for Lee to act. Meade suspected that Lee had his entire army
at Gettysburg, or marching hard toward it, but as yet only Ewell's and
Hill's men were visible to the north.

Around noon Meade received news from the signal station on Little
Round Top. Observers there began reporting sightings of troop movements behind Seminary Ridge. Despite their marching and counter-
marching, some of Longstreet's men had been spotted. Additional
reports to Meade confirmed more Confederate troops on the move,
heading toward the south end of Seminary Ridge, opposite the point
where the Round Tops met Cemetery Ridge. That settled Meade's
uncertainty about the whereabouts of the rest of Lee's army.

---

[1] General Butterfield's permanent legacy to the U.S. Army is "Taps," a bugle call he
composed.

Meade sent some of his troops to fortify the length of the ridge. The Round Tops were protected by Buford's cavalry, so far as he knew, so there was no chance for the rebels to outflank the position and surprise them in the rear. At three o'clock Meade summoned his corps commanders to headquarters for a war council. He composed a telegram to General Halleck in Washington to announce that he was awaiting an attack.

He also told Halleck that he would not attack first but that he was prepared to fall back if necessary to a stronger position. By the time his message was received in the War Department's telegraph office at 10:30 the next morning, there was no more talk of falling back.

Meade's war council never got underway. By the time the officers gathered at headquarters, sporadic gunfire was being heard from a portion of the line. The last general to arrive was Dan Sickles; the firing came from his sector. Meade met him at the door and ordered him to return to his men. Meade mounted his horse, Old Baldy, and rode after him.

⊷═◉═⊶

DAN SICKLES ALWAYS chose to go his own way at his own fast pace regardless of the consequences. One historian wrote, "Whether he was drinking, fighting, wenching or plotting, he was always operating with the throttle wide open." A major general at the age of thirty-eight, Sickles had been a Tammany Hall politician who had become a wealthy lawyer, a secretary of the legation in London, a New York state senator, a United States congressman, and the most notorious man in America.

His goal was to become president of the United States—and he might have succeeded had he not murdered the most handsome man in Washington society, Francis Scott Key's son, who was having an affair with Sickles's wife. Sickles shot young Key in broad daylight across the street from the White House. The trial became a media circus. His attorney, Edwin Stanton, now secretary of war, argued that Sickles was not guilty because of temporary insanity, the first time such a plea had been invoked.

It worked. Sickles was found not guilty and hailed as a hero for a wholly justifiable crime of passion. Sickles had gotten away with murder. His political star once again was on the rise. Then he committed a truly unpardonable sin. He publicly forgave his wife for her adultery. That was too much. Killing her lover was one thing, but condoning the behavior of a disgraced woman was quite another. In the strict social code of the day, that was unacceptable.

Sickles was ostracized socially and politically. A New York newspaper wrote that "His political aspirations, his career in life, once so full of encouraging brightness, and his business prospects, have all been blasted by this act." He was unwelcome in the best homes. Former friends and acquaintances refused to acknowledge him on the street. In Congress, no one would sit near him. Mary Boykin Chesnut, a senator's wife, wrote of seeing Sickles "sitting alone on the benches of the Congress. . . . He was as left to himself as if he had smallpox. There he sat, unfriended, melancholy, slow, solitary, sad of visage." His wife suffered a similar fate. She became "an infinitely lonely little woman in a huge house that no one would enter."

The war saved Dan Sickles, as it had Grant and Meade, and gave him the opportunity to overcome his past. He raised a volunteer brigade in New York and led it through the Peninsular campaign of 1862. The following year he was promoted to major general and given command of the Third Corps, the command he now led to the south end of Cemetery Ridge on the afternoon of July 2. But when Sickles got there, he was displeased. The ridge in his sector gradually got lower, dwindling almost to ground level before the rise of Little Round Top.

Sickles found the terrain unsatisfactory. Looking ahead of the slight ridge, some two thousand feet west, he saw somewhat higher ground along the Emmitsburg Pike parallel to his present location. Atop that ground was a peach orchard. It appeared to Sickles that if the rebels occupied it with artillery, they could drive him out. He wanted to get there first.

He sent a note to Meade explaining the situation and asking if he could exercise his own judgment in the placement of his corps.

"Certainly," Meade replied, "within the limits of the general instructions I have given to you."

That was enough for the impetuous Sickles. When he heard that rebel troops had been spotted on the other side of Emmitsburg Pike, he was convinced they were heading for the peach orchard's high ground. He ordered his men to advance.

Off they marched, bands playing, flags flying, as if in a grand review, altogether an impressive spectacle to thousands of onlookers. Among the spectators was Lt. Frank Haskell, an aide to General Gibbon.

It was magnificent to see those ten or twelve thousand men—they were good men—with their batteries, and some squadrons of cavalry upon the left flank, all in battle order, in several lines, with flags streaming, sweep steadily down the slope, across the valley, and up the ascent.

Everyone agreed it was quite a sight, but many, including some of Sickles's officers, thought it was foolhardy and dangerous, a move toward disaster. The corps now formed a vulnerable salient bulging far out from the main Union line, a pocket that could be attacked from three sides. And the peach orchard, which turned out to be only a dozen feet higher than Sickles's original position, provided few natural defenses and little cover.

In addition, Sickles's advance had left a half-mile gap between his right flank and the left flank of the Second Corps on Cemetery Ridge. Finally, his original line, which had been a little over a mile long, was now almost twice that length, which meant it could not be defended in depth.

When Meade caught up with Sickles in the peach orchard he was angry. He pointed out the vulnerability of Sickles's new position.

"General, I am afraid you are too far out," Meade said.

Sickles tried to defend the move by saying that he now occupied higher ground.

"General Sickles," Meade said, "this is in some respects higher ground than that to the rear, but there is still higher in front of you, and if you keep on advancing, you will find constantly higher ground all the way to the mountains."

Sickles relented. There was a limit to how far even he would try Meade's patience. He offered to withdraw to his original position.

Before Meade could reply, the rebels opened fire with artillery. A cannonball landed just behind Meade's horse.

"I wish to God you could [withdraw]," Meade shouted, trying to make himself heard over the explosions, "but those people will not permit it."

The Confederate attack had begun.

⋯⟶◉⟵⋯

REBEL ARTILLERY POURED forth a massive bombardment as regimental bands played polkas and waltzes. Longstreet's assault began with Hood's soldiers attacking first. They headed toward the extreme south end of Cemetery Ridge and the Round Tops.

Union artillery returned fire as Hood's sixty-nine hundred men advanced, raked mercilessly by Yankee shells that cut them down by rows. Within twenty minutes of the onset of the attack a shell struck Hood's arm, knocking him out of action. Evander Law assumed command and continued to drive the men on into the hail of artillery and musket fire.

The assault led the Confederates directly into the difficult terrain of Devil's Den at the base of Little Round Top. A warren of ravines, mossy boulders, and thick tangled vines, Devil's Den was eerily dark;

the sun never penetrated. Yankee sharpshooters hid in crevices and behind rocks that measured up to fifteen feet high. The Northerners took a bloody toll of Law's men.

There was no chance to maintain military formation once the men rushed into that deadly ground. Regiments, companies, and even platoons could not stay and attack together the way they had been trained. The men were forced to fight as individuals or in small groups, yard by bloody yard, and chase the sharpshooters up some two hundred feet over Big Round Top's steep craggy slope.

The man leading the mission was twenty-seven-year-old Col. William Oates, an Alabama lawyer. Before the battle, Oates had ordered a detail of two men from each of the eleven companies of his regiment to take all the canteens one hundred yards to the rear to fill them at a spring. That kind of consideration for the soldiers' welfare had made him a popular commander.

The order to advance was issued before the water detail returned with the full canteens. The water carriers tried to catch up with the regiment but they got lost in the woods and were captured by Union troops. Oates's men would suffer dearly from the lack of water.

But they started out well, pushing the sharpshooters up the hillside. Colonel Oates recalled,

In places the men had to climb up, catching to the rocks and bushes and crawling over the boulders in the face of the fire of the enemy, who kept retreating, taking shelter and firing down on us from behind the rocks and crags which covered the side of the mountain thicker than gravestones in a city cemetery.

When his Alabamians reached the top, many of them collapsed from exhaustion, heat, and thirst. Only minutes later a message came from Evander Law to abandon their hard-won prize, which overlooked the entire Union position and the town of Gettysburg to the north.

The new orders were to move on to capture Little Round Top, closer to the Union line on Cemetery Ridge.

Oates protested, arguing that Big Round Top's greater height now gave the Confederates the commanding view of the battlefield. His protest was overruled and he ordered his weary men to their feet and started down the north slope. Oates saw one consolation: Little Round Top was undefended except for a handful of Yankee signalmen waving their flags. At least, Oates thought, his troops would not have to claw their way up that hill.

⊹⊱═◉═⊰⊹

OATES WAS NOT the only person to notice that Little Round Top was devoid of fighting troops. At about five o'clock in the afternoon, Meade's chief engineering officer, thirty-three-year-old Maj. Gen. Gouverneur K. Warren, rode up to the signal station to get a clear view of the battle. He saw rebel soldiers approaching the hill and rode off to find Meade, who passed the word to send troops to reinforce the hill immediately.

The nearest unit was a brigade commanded by Col. Strong Vincent, who took his four regiments up the slope and arranged them in a defense line. At the left he placed the 350 men of the Twentieth Maine, led by Col. Joshua Chamberlain. Vincent told Chamberlain that his men would shortly come under attack and that he had only one order to issue: "Hold that ground at all hazards."

Colonel Vincent walked the length of the line, shouting and encouraging his men. "Don't yield one inch!" he told them. Those were his last words. As the Confederates charged up the hill, a rebel bullet cut Vincent down. The Southerners hit the entire line, most viciously at the left end, where Chamberlain's men found themselves up against William Oates and his Alabamians.

The troops on both sides fought as if each man knew this was the most crucial of all battles, that if the rebels reached the hilltop, the

Union army would face defeat. The Alabamians made charge after charge, only to be repelled each time. But as the minutes passed, then one hour, and two, Oates's men drew ever closer, concealing themselves behind rocks and trees.

One of Chamberlain's men recalled,

Again and again was this mad rush repeated, each time beaten off by the ever-thinning line that desperately clung to its ledge of rock, refusing to yield. Continually, the gray lines crept up by squads and the firing became at closer and closer range. . . . The dead and the wounded clogged the footsteps of the living.

Oates's men were suffering from their lack of water. As they ripped apart cartridges with their teeth, the acrid gunpowder acted like a sponge, soaking up what little moisture was left in their mouths. They ached from thirst and needed water not only for themselves but also for their weapons. They had no way to clean out the residue of black powder that built up inside the rifle barrels. Each man could fire no more than a dozen rounds before the buildup caked the barrels so thickly that he could no longer ram down the charges. The soldiers resorted to searching for rifles among the dead and wounded.

Chamberlain's men had water but were running low on ammunition. As they fired the last of the sixty cartridges each man had carried up the hill, they foraged among the bodies to find more. The Twentieth Maine lost half its men. On the rebel side, Oates saw his brother hit eight times and others drop all around him. "The blood stood in puddles on the rocks," he wrote. And still he pushed his men forward.

And then the battle changed. Chamberlain sensed that the rebels had pulled back a bit—in anticipation, he assumed, of another charge. He knew his men could no longer resist. Within a few minutes, they would lose the hill. "My thought was running deep," he wrote.

Actually, Oates had given the order to withdraw, believing that additional assaults on the Union force would be suicidal. Given the high number of casualties, Oates assumed that the remainder of his unit would be unable to take the hill. But as soon as the word to withdraw began to filter from man to man, Chamberlain's Yankees rose up with fixed bayonets and charged down the hill toward the Alabamians.

Chamberlain had ordered "fix bayonets." According to Chamberlain's most recent biographer, the men charged spontaneously as soon as they heard the call to fix bayonets. Chamberlain may have intended to order a charge with his next breath—and perhaps he did, although he would not have been heard over the din—but no one who participated in the action testified to having heard the order.

Nevertheless, the charge began and succeeded. The sight of nearly two hundred Yankees pounding down the hill with outstretched bayonets shattered the Confederate will. Many soldiers froze, dropped their weapons, and raised their hands in surrender. Others ran or were cut down.

Oates later admitted, "We ran like a herd of wild cattle." Union soldiers swarmed over the Southerners' position. Oates saw one of his men hit in the face, another from the side, a third from the rear. "As we ran," Oates recalled, "a man named Keils, of Company H, from Henry County, who was to my right and rear had his throat cut by a bullet, and he ran past me breathing at his throat and the blood splattering."

The fight for Little Round Top was over.

⊶═◉═⊷

AT 5:30, THE rest of Longstreet's attack got underway. LaFayette McLaws ordered his division forward against Sickles's corps, which was standing on its own in the salient at the peach orchard, bulging out from the rest of the Union line. Longstreet accompanied McLaws for a while, then doffed his hat and waved the troops on. Longstreet then rode on to Brig. Gen. William Barksdale's Mississippi Brigade and watched them move out.

He joined a brigade of Georgians and rode with them for a time. The men greeted Longstreet with cheers. He called to them, "Cheer less, men, and fight more!" He stayed with them as far as the edge of the peach orchard before turning back.

The Confederate troops swept over Sickles's position like a whirlwind, wiping out whole regiments at a time. With no natural barriers for protection, open to attack from three sides, the Yankees were easily swept away. The Third Corps, which had marched out so proudly with flags and banners flying, had become rabble running frantically from the rebels.

Sickles sustained a hit and fell from his horse, his right leg shattered and hanging in shreds. He remained calm, ordering one of his men to take a saddle strap and wrap it above the wound as a tourniquet. He selected one of his division commanders to take over his corps, then allowed himself to be placed on a stretcher and carried off the field. His biographer, W. A. Swanberg, wrote,

> Despite his pain and shock, Sickles was not one to allow this moment to pass without making full use of its dramatic value. Being informed that a rumor had gone around that he was mortally wounded, he requested a stretcher bearer to remove a cigar from a case in an inside pocket and light it for him. He was carried away with the Havana projecting jauntily from his mouth.

He was carried to the rear and given a large amount of brandy for the shock before physicians cut off his leg far above his knee. The leg, carefully wrapped in cloth, was saved for the general's disposition instead of tossed on the pile of hundreds of other severed limbs.[2]

The peach orchard was a killing ground, first for Sickles's men as they were routed by the Confederates, and then for the Southerners who chased them back to Cemetery Ridge. Forty Federal cannon on the crest of the ridge and down the slope blasted endless rounds of

---

[2] The bones of Dan Sickles's severed leg can be seen at the National Museum of Health and Medicine in Washington, D.C.

solid shot and cannister directly into the lines of charging rebels. The gunfire frequently struck Yankee as well as Confederate troops, so close were pursued and pursuer. But it was the only way to stop the massive, hard-hitting attack. Wave after wave of Confederates charged the line, but Meade always had fresh troops to meet them and push them back.

"Great God!" Longstreet exclaimed. "Have we got the universe to whip?"

Meade moved up and down the line, masterfully pulling troops from one sector and sending them to plug holes in another. At one point he found himself with only his four aides, facing a line of Southerners six hundred yards away. Reinforcements had been ordered up, but they had not yet arrived. There was no one else to stop the enemy.

His aides looked at the advancing rebel line and then at Meade, who appeared not at all disturbed. Meade straightened in his saddle and drew his sword. His aides drew theirs, worried that the general was going to lead them in a charge. At the last possible moment, fresh troops arrived to hold off the rebels. An officer rode up to Meade and offered him a drink from his flask. Meade took a swig, seeming not to notice when a rebel shell exploded and showered him with dirt.

The new troops cheered at Meade's calmness under fire. He galloped ahead, took off his hat, and rallied the men. "Come on, gentlemen," he cried, preparing to lead the charge. A lieutenant who followed Meade toward the rebel line recalled, "this act of pluck and daring helped inspire the men with confidence."

⋆⟞◉⟝⋆

THE CONFEDERATES SPOTTED another gap in the Union line and headed for it just as General Hancock ordered up two divisions to close it. But when Hancock looked back at the advancing rebel troops, a brigade of sixteen hundred Alabamians, he realized they would reach the gap at least five minutes before his men. Once the rebels passed through the gap and moved behind the ridge, the entire Union line might bolt and run.

A small Union regiment of 262 men came riding over the crest of the ridge. Hancock saw a chance, a slim chance, to buy the precious five minutes he needed. The regimental commander, Col. William Colville of the First Minnesota, reported. Hancock pointed to the advancing Confederate brigade, eight times the size of the First Minnesota, and ordered, "Charge those lines."

Every man of the Minnesota regiment knew that the orders meant their doom. They were being sacrificed to gain time to save the rest of the Union line. It was their bad luck that they happened on the scene at that moment. Colville stepped out in front of his regiment and asked if the men would follow him. Not a man refused.

With bayonets fixed, the Minnesotans charged down the slope of Cemetery Ridge and hit the center of the Confederate line. The rebels stopped briefly, regrouped, and enveloped the Union troops. Colville and most of the regiment's officers and 215 of the men were overwhelmed, killed or wounded. Only three officers escaped. "We had no time to weep," one man wrote. "Great heavens, how fast our men fell. . . . It seemed as if every step was over some fallen comrade. Yet no man wavered."

When it was over, when Hancock's two fresh divisions had plugged the gap in the line, a captain led the few dozen survivors of the Minnesota regiment back to Cemetery Ridge. Their appalling losses earned them the dubious honor of having sustained the highest casualty rate, eighty-two percent, of any Union regiment in the war. Without their sacrifice, the Union could easily have lost the battle for Gettysburg that afternoon.

Longstreet watched his corps continue to smash itself against the Union line. By dusk he concluded that although his men were fighting magnificently, they were not going to breach the enemy defenses. No matter where they struck, Meade had fresh troops to meet them. Longstreet wrote,

We felt at every step the heavy stroke of fresh troops, the sturdy regular blow that tells a soldier instantly that he has encountered reserves or reinforcements. We received no support at all. . . . To urge my men forward under these circumstances would have been madness, and I withdrew them in good order to the peach orchard.

The fighting in Longstreet's sector had begun at four o'clock in the afternoon, but Ewell did not send his infantry forward until nearly three hours later. By then the daylight had faded and Longstreet's assault was played out. Ewell's attack seemed doomed even though his force outnumbered the Union defenders on Cemetery Hill and Culp's Hill.

Ewell's men fought bravely until well after dark. Casualties on both sides were high but when the last shots were fired late that night, the Yankees retained their hold on the high ground. In the judgment of Nancy Scott Anderson and Dwight Anderson, authors of a dual biography of Lee and Grant, Ewell's advance was "ill-timed, ill-coordinated, ill-advised, and very brutal." Ewell had failed again.

Under Meade's energetic and capable leadership, the Union force on Cemetery Ridge remained intact, despite the danger brought on when Sickles moved his corps too far forward. Throughout the day Meade had vigorously directed the action and often exposed himself to danger. A rebel bullet had struck his saddle flap and wounded his horse, missing Meade by inches. One officer commented, "Now Sickles' blunder is repaired." And Meade himself, when he overheard someone say how close the Union army had come to disaster, said with justifiable pride, "Yes, but it is all right now. It is all right now."

⋆⇒◉⇐⋆

THE BATTLE WAS over; the death and desolation remained. Lt. Frank Haskell of the Union army described the aftermath that night.

Now all is silent; not a gunshot sound is heard, and the silence comes distinctively, almost painfully, to the senses. [The fields] are desolate now, trampled by the countless feet of the combatants, plowed and

scored by the shot and shell, the orchards splintered, the fences pros-
trate, the harvest trodden in the mud.

More dreadful to Haskell was the sight of the debris strewn across
the fields.

The knapsacks cast aside in the stress of the fight, or after the fatal
lead had struck; haversacks, yawning with the rations the owner will
never call for; blankets and trousers, and coats and caps, and some
are blue and some are gray; muskets and ramrods, and bayonets, and
swords, and scabbards and belts, some bent and cut by the shot or
shell; broken wheels, exploded caissons, and limber-boxes, and dismantled guns, and all these are sprinkled with blood; horses, some
dead, a mangled heap of carnage, some alive with a leg shot clear off,
or other frightful wounds, appealing to you with almost more than
brute gaze as you pass.

And then there were the men, the thousands of men.

There was no rebellion here now. The men of South Carolina were
quiet by the side of those of Massachusetts, some composed, with
upturned faces, sleeping the last sleep, some mutilated and frightful,
some wretched, fallen, bathed in blood, survivors still and unwilling
witnesses of the rage of Gettysburg.

Walking over the fields, the survivors searched for lost friends.
Henry Taylor of the First Minnesota wandered in the darkness searching for his brother, Isaac. They had been through the war together, side
by side. Now Isaac was among the missing.

Taylor found among the wounded the regiment's Colonel Colville
and brought him to a hospital tent. Taylor wrote, "I help our colonel off
the field but fail to find my brother who, I suppose, is killed. I rejoin
the regiment and lie down in the moonlight, rather sorrowful."

⋆══◗══⋆

THE CIVILIANS OF Gettysburg sustained no deaths during the long battle of the afternoon and evening but suffered nonetheless. Fannie Buehler recalled that

> the dreadful slaughter of human life, the roar of the artillery and musketry, with the groans of the wounded and dying, baffled all description. At one time it was all so near to us that we closed our ears [and] crouched into a corner, not knowing how to endure it. The ground trembled, on which our house stood.

Sallie Broadhead and her husband fled to a neighbor's cellar. A Union shell struck the house. It did not explode but stuck in the wall, a grim reminder of how close they had come to sudden death.

Errant shells and minié balls struck many houses in town. Henry Jacobs and his father, Michael, ventured out in the yard, the better to hear the cannon fire. Before long they also heard bullets whistling dangerously close and they scurried back indoors. A rebel soldier perched on their sloping cellar door was hit by a stray bullet. "He suddenly groaned and we heard his body fall over and gently slide downward," young Jacobs said.

George Little, his wife, and eight neighbors took shelter in a back room of the Littles' brick house. Two shells blew up in the backyard. When a third exploded even closer to the house, everyone rushed for the cellar. A fourth shell destroyed the room in which they had been hiding.

Mary McAllister braved the artillery fire to dash to Buehler's drugstore to buy whiskey for the wounded Union officers she was housing. They had begged her for something strong to dull their pain. While Buehler was filling her canteen, a shell struck the doorway but did not explode. She made it home safely with her purchase.

Sallie Myers was caring for the dying Sgt. Alexander Stewart. He had asked to be moved from the hospital to her home since nothing could be done to save his life. He lay on a bed in the ground-floor front room. When the shelling started, Stewart urged Sallie to go to the cellar, but she refused to leave him.

He said he did not want her to risk her life when he was going to die anyway. The shelling and the rifle fire increased. The air inside the house became hot and fetid; doors and shutters had been closed in the hope of keeping out stray bullets. Sallie was determined to stay. "While fanning him," she recalled, "being in an uncomfortable position, I changed it and a moment later a ball struck the floor where I had been sitting, scattering over us the plaster which it had displaced."

Albertus McCreary ventured outside to the street behind his house to talk to a unit of Confederate soldiers waiting in reserve. He said,

> Most of them were ragged and dirty and they had very little to eat. I saw one man with a loaf of moldy bread and a canteen of molasses. He would break off a piece of bread, pour molasses over it, and eat it with what seemed great relish. I asked him if that was all he had to eat. He answered, "Yes, and glad to get it, too."

Tillie Pierce was still at the house near Big Round Top. Throughout the battle shells flew overhead constantly, some exploding quite near. "It seemed as though the heavens were sending forth peal upon peal of terrible thunder, directly over our heads; while at the same time, the very earth beneath our feet trembled." Soon the house, barn, and yard were crammed with wounded soldiers in need of medical treatment.

John Wertz, an eighty-seven-year-old farmer, lived at the edge of the peach orchard, the site of the day's worst fighting. The commander of a rebel artillery battery, who was ordered to set up his cannon in Wertz's yard, turned out to be Wertz's son. The young man had journeyed south twenty-four years before and had never returned. He told his father to go to the cellar and stay there. Both men survived the day.

When darkness fell and the firing halted, the townspeople emerged from their shelters desperate for news. Which side had won? Would the Confederates remain in town? Would there be more fighting tomorrow? Michael and Henry Jacobs lingered on the street, listening to the conversations of the rebel soldiers. "The Yankees have a good position," said one, "and we must drive them out of it tomorrow." Others talked about how discouraged they were by the way the fighting had gone so far. That all sounded like good news to the residents.

Sallie Broadhead was told by the rebels that all civilians would have to leave Gettysburg the next day because it was going to be shelled. That night she wrote in her diary,

> I cannot sleep. It is out of the question for me either to eat or sleep under such terrible excitement and such painful suspense. We know not what the morrow will bring forth, and cannot even tell the issue of today. We can gain no information from the Rebels.

⊷⟾⟾⊶

FOR THE PEOPLE of Vicksburg, July 2 was also a horrible day. General Pemberton's division commanders had put Pemberton's question about the condition of the troops to their senior subordinates. Their answers confirmed what Pemberton must have realized before he ever asked the question. His men were no longer capable of attempting a breakout from Vicksburg.

Brigadier General Barton wrote,

> The command suffers greatly from intermittent fever and is generally debilitated from the long exposure and inaction of the trenches. Of those now reported for duty, fully one-half are undergoing treatment. These I think are unfit for the field.

Brigadier General Cummings added, "From shortness of rations, and greatly more from a confinement of forty-five days to the trenches, under the summer sun of a debilitating climate, few, if any, of [my] men are in their ordinary health and vigor." He added his judgment that fully fifty percent were "unfit to encounter the fatigues incident to the life of a soldier in the field."

Colonel Reynolds noted, "my men are much reduced in strength, and in many instances, entirely prostrated. . . . I regret to say that two-thirds are unable to endure a march of ten miles." Maj. Gen. John Forney agreed with the unanimous judgment of his brigade and regimental commanders "that the physical condition and health of our men are not sufficiently good to enable them to accomplish successfully the evacuation."

These reports ended any indecision Pemberton may have had. The men could not fight their way out. Joe Johnston was unable or unwilling to fight his way in to relieve them. Supplies of food, medicine, water, and ammunition were almost depleted, and the hardships of soldiers and civilians trapped in the city could only become more severe.

That night Pemberton called his senior officers to a council of war. He related the responses he had received from all of them concerning the condition of their men. The total effective fighting force was no more than eleven thousand. The rest of the troops were too weak or too ill to be counted on. Pemberton also said he had abandoned all hope of being relieved by General Johnston.

He was left with two bleak alternatives, "either to surrender while we still had ammunition enough left to give us the right to demand terms, or to sell our lives as dearly as possible in . . . a hopeless effort to cut our way through the Federal lines." He asked his officers to vote on surrender. All but two of the dozen or more present voted to do so. The two dissenters, when questioned, could offer no reasons for their vote or any workable alternative.

Pemberton then sided with the majority. He said,

I have heard your vote and I agree with your almost unanimous decision, though my own preference would be to put myself at the head of my troops and make a desperate effort to cut our way through the enemy. That is my only hope of saving myself from shame and disgrace. Far better would it be for me to die at the head of my army . . . than to surrender it and live and meet the obloquy which I know will be heaped upon me. But my duty is to sacrifice myself to save the army, which has so nobly done its duty to defend Vicksburg.

He told them he would propose to General Grant that the army surrender on July 4. Some officers objected to capitulating on that hallowed holiday for the Union. The dissenters did not want to give the Yankees the satisfaction of such an important victory on their Independence Day. Pemberton said he deliberately chose that date. "I am a Northern man," he told them. "I know my people; I know their peculiar weaknesses and their national vanity; I know we can get better terms from them on the 4th of July than on any other day of the year. We must sacrifice our pride to these considerations."

Gen. John Bowen spoke up in support of Pemberton. It was time to end the useless suffering. More deaths would accomplish nothing. Bowen, who was a friend of Grant's, would be the one selected to deal with him. First, however, Pemberton would have to draft a letter to the Union commander requesting an armistice during which surrender terms would be discussed. It would not be an easy letter to write.

While Pemberton and his officers were making their difficult decision, Vicksburg residents were rejoicing over a story in that day's *Daily Citizen* newspaper. It may have been printed on the reverse side of wallpaper, but it gave desperate people reason to hope for a quick Southern victory back east. Such a welcome event could end the war, or at least relieve the siege of Vicksburg.

The story was about Robert E. Lee's invasion of the North. As usual, it was more wishful thinking and propaganda than hard news. Excited Southerners read about Lee's brilliant victories threatening Washington City, and within a few miles of Baltimore, onward and upward their war cry, our brave men under Lee are striking terror to the hearts of all Yankeedom. . . .

Today the mongrel administration of Lincoln . . . are in search of a father, for their old Abe has departed to parts unknown. Terror reigns in their halls, Lee is to the left of them, the right of them, in front of them, and all around them; and daily do we expect to hear of his being down on them. . . . Today Maryland is ours, tomorrow Pennsylvania will be, and the next day Ohio. . . . Success and glory to our arms! God and right are with us.

No wonder people thought salvation was at hand! It was nothing less than a miracle. Surely Lee's startling victories in the east would force Grant to divert his army there to defend Washington and other Northern cities. Vicksburg's siege would be lifted. But Pemberton knew better. Even if the news reports were true, it was too late to help them.

⌐=◉=⌐

IN GETTYSBURG THAT night, Lee evaluated the day's battle reports and concluded that his army had come close to winning a great victory. He told his staff that tomorrow they would drive the Yankees from their positions. The morale of his army was high, whole divisions were still unused, and the troops of Stuart's and Pickett's commands had arrived.

Other officers were less confident of victory. Even Lee's devoted aide, Maj. Walter Taylor, criticized the general, after the war, when he described the battle of July 2 as disjointed. Unlike Meade, who had taken such an active, aggressive role in the unfolding events, Lee had spent the day at his command post on Seminary Ridge.

He had not issued a single order. Despite being able to observe the action in the field, Lee, according to historian Shelby Foote, "made no attempt to control or even influence the action once the opening attack had been launched." Lee had no conversations with his three corps commanders once the battle began. He did not visit them, nor did they come to him.

That evening Lee experienced a debilitating attack of diarrhea. Several men near headquarters saw him make repeated trips to the latrine, bent double in pain. Some speculated later that the discomfort and weakness, particularly for someone his age, may have diminished his mental capacities.

He did not meet with his commanders that night, either, when he was drawing up his plans for the following day. He sent a message to Ewell suggesting that he launch his attack on Cemetery Hill at daybreak, and to A. P. Hill to detach two brigades to assist in that attack. He sent no dispatches to Longstreet, whose corps was once again responsible for the major assault. Nor did he communicate with Pickett, who was slated to play a major role in the attack. On one of the most crucial days of the war, Lee was strangely silent.

→→≡◑≡←←

GEORGE MEADE, WHO had been in constant touch with his senior commanders throughout the day, met with them again that night. They gathered at his headquarters, a small house a hundred yards behind Cemetery Ridge, half a mile south of Cemetery Hill. The purpose of the war council was to solicit opinions about the next day's actions.

Meade put several questions to his commanders. Should they hold their present positions? Should they attack Lee in the morning or wait to see if he would strike first? If they chose to wait for a rebel attack, how long should they wait before taking action themselves? A consensus was reached quickly. The majority felt they should stay where they were and wait for Lee to move.

"Such then is the decision," Meade announced after counting the vote.

As the commanders filed out, Meade detained thirty-six-year-old Brig. Gen. John Gibbon, who led the second division of Hancock's

Second Corps, and spoke to him briefly.[3] Gibbon's men held a sector near the center of Cemetery Ridge close to Meade's headquarters.

"If Lee attacks me tomorrow," Meade told Gibbon, "it will be in *your* front."

"Well, General," Gibbon replied, "I hope he does, and if he does, we shall whip him."

[3] Gibbon was considered a traitor by his three brothers, who all served in the Confederate army.

CHAPTER 10

THE SLAUGHTER WILL
BE TERRIBLE

July 3, 1863

ROBERT E. LEE arose at three o'clock in the morning. Daybreak was only an hour away. That was when Ewell was scheduled to launch his attack on the Union right flank at Cemetery Hill and Culp's Hill, while Longstreet sent his corps against the Union center. But for some reason—no one knows why—Lee did not inform Longstreet or Pickett of his plans. Pickett was camped almost three miles way, far enough to delay any attack for at least two hours. Now Ewell would have to be told that the attack could not take place at dawn.

Lee sent an aide racing to Ewell's headquarters with a message to postpone the assault. Lee mounted his horse, Traveller, and rode up the western slope of Seminary Ridge to find Longstreet. When he reached the top, he was startled to hear the bark of artillery fire from Ewell's front to the north. Maybe Lee's courier had not reached Ewell in time, and for once Ewell was showing the aggressive spirit Lee had desperately wanted from him. Or perhaps Meade had launched a surprise attack and Ewell was on the defensive.

Lee found Longstreet at the south end of Seminary Ridge at a point opposite Big Round Top. The Georgian was in a good mood, expansive and exuberant, and Lee soon found out why. Longstreet still had hopes of changing Lee's mind about the plan of attack.

"General," Longstreet exclaimed heartily to Lee, "I have had my scouts out all night, and I find that you still have an excellent opportunity to move around to the right of Meade's army and maneuver him into attacking us."

Longstreet again insisted that his defensive style of battle was preferable to attempting another frontal assault against an entrenched position. Lee was annoyed. He gestured impatiently toward the Union line on Cemetery Ridge and repeated what he had told Longstreet twenty-four hours before, when Longstreet proposed his flanking maneuver. "The enemy is there," Lee said, "and I am going to strike him."

Lee said that Longstreet should attack with all three divisions—those of Pickett, Hood, and McLaws. But Longstreet objected to using the troops of Hood and McLaws. They were in close proximity to the Union line, holding positions from yesterday's attack. If Longstreet pulled them out to launch an assault on the Union center, the Yankees would move in to the vacated terrain and threaten Longstreet's right flank and rear. Lee relented, agreeing that those two divisions could remain where they were. In their place, Lee would give him units from Hill's corps, including Henry Heth's division and two brigades of Pender's division to join Pickett in the attack.

Longstreet was angry that his defensive strategy was being overruled again. He had no confidence in the success of a frontal assault with a force of that size, and he told Lee so in no uncertain terms.

That will give me fifteen thousand men. I have been a soldier, I may say, from the ranks up to the position I now hold. I have been in pretty much all kinds of skirmishes, from those of two or three soldiers up to those of an army corps, and I think I can safely say there never was a body of fifteen thousand men who could make that attack successfully.

Longstreet told his commanding officer clearly that his plan of attack could not work. That insubordination was reason enough for outright dismissal. But, as Longstreet wrote later, "General [Lee] seemed a little impatient at my remarks, so I said nothing more." Lee did not censure or chastise Longstreet or relieve him of his command. He could not do so, no matter how angry or disappointed he may have been, because there was no one else as capable as Longstreet available to lead a corps. Some writers have suggested that Lee might have placed Hill in charge of the assault force since two-thirds of the troops would come from his corps. But Lee knew that Hill was not capable of directing a crucial battle. One historian wrote that Lee "preferred Longstreet, recalcitrant, to Hill cooperative."

And so the attack would proceed with Longstreet in command for an assault he was convinced he could not win. Lee ordered him to send for Pickett's division and to place it and Hill's units on the western slope of Seminary Ridge. An intense artillery barrage was to precede the attack. Lee pointed to a clump of trees atop Cemetery Ridge, less than a mile away. That was the objective, Lee said, the point Longstreet's men were to take. "Nothing was left but to proceed," Longstreet wrote.

⋅≫◉◎≪⋅

GEORGE MEADE WAS up even earlier than Lee that morning. He was awakened well before daybreak by a courier from Maj. Gen. Henry Slocum, commanding the Twelfth Corps on Culp's Hill. During the night, rebel soldiers of Gen. Edward Johnson's division of Ewell's Second Corps had infiltrated a portion of the hill's lower spur. From there they were in position to launch a surprise attack on the hill, which, if successful, could lead to a breakthrough in the rear of Meade's line. Meade ordered Slocum to attack at daybreak.

At 3:45 A.M., Slocum's artillery began firing, the sounds Lee heard when he climbed Seminary Ridge to find Longstreet. The bombardment lasted an hour, but before the Union troops could launch their attack, Johnson's men charged. Bitter, savage fighting raged on the hillside for more than six hours. The rebels made repeated charges up the steep slope but the Yankees were too well entrenched to be dislodged.

The terrain was thickly wooded—in peacetime it had been a favorite picnic spot—but it was cut to pieces by the rapid fire of cannon and muskets. The forest "was shot to death that morning," one writer noted, "some trees having close to two hundred musket balls imbedded in their trunks." The remaining trees "crumpled into dust in a few years and for half a century at least that particular 'plateau of death' remained a hillside of desolation."

One of the Confederate casualties of that battle had grown up in Gettysburg but moved to the South as a young man. The previous night he had visited his sister in town and stayed for dinner and conversation about the old days. His sister begged him to stay the night. "No, Annie, I can't," he said, "but I'll come back in the morning." He never did. John Wesley Culp was killed around eight o'clock on the hill that bore his family name, the piece of ground owned by his cousin, on which he had often played as a child.

The Confederate soldiers, like the trees through which they charged, were slaughtered. Dead and dying lay in tangled heaps. "Human beings, mangled and torn, in every manner, from a single shot through the body or head to bodies torn to pieces by exploding shells, were everywhere."

It all could have been avoided if Lee's order to Ewell to cancel the dawn attack had arrived thirty minutes earlier. By the time Ewell received the message, it was too late. His troops were already committed and could not be withdrawn in an orderly fashion without opening up the rebel front to a Union breakthrough. The battle had to be fought to its brutal, deadly end.

And this time there was a civilian casualty. Not far from Cemetery Hill, in a brick house at the south end of Baltimore Street, twenty-year-old Jennie Wade was kneading dough. Jennie and her mother had moved into her sister's house to help care for her sister's five-day-old infant. When the firing started Jennie remarked to her mother, "If there is anyone in this house that is to be killed today, I hope it is me, as Georgia has that little baby."

A few houses in the neighborhood, as well as an orchard, were occupied by Union snipers, who had been exchanging shots with rebel sharpshooters located on a rise. Jennie and the family felt safe inside the sturdy brick house even though bullets had been striking the outside walls since daybreak.

While Jennie stood in the kitchen, wiping her hands on her apron, her mother turned toward the fireplace; Jennie's sister was playing with the baby in the next room. The sister's husband was off with the Union army. Jennie's fiancé, Jack Skelly, a local boy, had also enlisted. She carried a daguerreotype of him in the pocket of her dress. She did not know that Jack had been wounded and captured in Winchester, Virginia, on June 15, and was in a Confederate hospital. He would die nine days later.

Bullets kept thudding against the walls until one, apparently from the Confederate side, sliced through two wooden doors and struck Jennie in the back, killing her instantly. Her mother turned around in time to see Jennie fall to the floor. Dazed, she walked into the parlor and announced, "Georgia, your sister is dead."

‹•➡═◉═‹•

AT THE OTHER end of Cemetery Ridge, about two miles from the house where Jennie Wade was killed, Henry Taylor of the First Minnesota had learned the fate of his brother, Isaac. At about 8:30, a friend reported that he thought he had seen Isaac's body and offered to take him to the spot.

I find my dear brother dead! A shell struck him on the top of his head and passed out through his back, cutting his belt in two. The poor fellow did not know what hit him. I secured his pocketbook, watch, diary, knife, etc. and . . . buried him at ten o'clock a.m. by a stone wall where he fell. . . . I placed a board at his head on which I inscribed:

> *No useless coffin enclosed his breast,*
> *Nor in sheet nor in shroud we bound him,*
> *But he lay like a warrior taking his rest,*
> *With his shelter tent around him.*

Taylor was so despondent that it would be three days before he could write to his parents with the news.

Tillie Pierce returned to the farmhouse near Big Round Top to keep her promise to visit a wounded soldier. "I hastened down to the little basement room, and as I entered, the soldier lay there, dead. . . . I had kept my promise, but he was not there to greet me."

Sallie Myers's wounded soldier, Sgt. Alexander Stewart, continued to cling to life, but there was no hope for survival. "He seems better," she wrote, "but the poor fellow will not get well." She sometimes left to tend the wounded at the churches, but hurried back because her presence was so comforting to him. "Mr. Stewart cannot bear to have me away from him."

Anna Gerlach's family remained in the cellar, frightened by the fighting around Culp's Hill. Someone burst through the front door. Furious, Anna's mother rushed upstairs in time to see a Confederate soldier climbing the stairs for the second floor. She grabbed him by his jacket and demanded to know what he wanted. He told her that sharpshooters were about to take over the house so they could fire on the Yankees from her second-story windows.

"You can't go up there," she insisted. "You will draw fire on this house full of defenseless women and children." She ordered him to leave at once, and to her surprise, he obeyed. He paused in the doorway to fire a shot and zigzagged across the street to another house, dodging bullets as he went.

Sallie Broadhead was awakened at 3:45 in the morning when the shelling began. Shortly thereafter, rebel soldiers pounded on the door and warned her to leave right away because the neighborhood would soon come under fire from the Yankees. Mr. Broadhead declared that he would not leave his home "while one brick remained upon another." They repaired to the cellar, fearful and hungry, for there had been no time for breakfast.

Albertus McCreary had gathered up eight rifles on the first day of the battle and hidden them under a pile of leaves in a shed. That morning a squad of rebel soldiers went door-to-door searching for guns. The boy denied having any but they did not believe him. One grabbed Albertus by the shoulder. "Now 'Johnny,'" he said, "I know you have a lot of guns. Show me where they are."

Albertus again denied having guns, but as the soldiers neared the shed, he began to quake, fearing that if they uncovered the rifles, they would send him South as a prisoner. "The fellow pushed open the door and kicked among the leaves. 'Oh, oh!' he exclaimed, and looked hard at me. My face must have betrayed my fears, for he burst out laughing and patted me on the back, saying in a kind tone, 'Too bad, too bad.'"

Albertus recalled another incident when he was watching wounded rebel soldiers file past his house after the fighting at Culp's Hill. He saw one man with an injured foot, limping and clinging to his horse. When the soldier stopped to rest on the front steps of the McCreary house, the boy ran inside, sawed off a broom handle, and nailed a piece of wood across one end to make a passable crutch. The soldier thanked him and walked on.

Two surgeons from the Union army were billeted at Catherine Foster's house. Although they had been taken prisoner by the Confederates, they were permitted outside to care for the wounded. At six o'clock that morning, they came downstairs, joined the Fosters for a quick breakfast, and left for the makeshift hospitals. Within a few seconds a Union shell demolished their bedroom. A second shell exploded in the breakfast room minutes later, shattering the table and chairs. The family had taken shelter in the cellar so they were unhurt, but Catherine recalled that they were quite apprehensive about what would happen next.

Several blocks away, a stray Union shell smashed into the second floor of Moses McLean's house. It crashed through a wall fifteen inches thick, shattered a roof joist, and clattered down the stairs, coming to rest several feet from where Mrs. McLean was standing. The shell failed to explode. The family kept it as a memento of the day the war came to Gettysburg.

✦⊱═◉═⊰✦

AT NINE O'CLOCK the men of Maj. Gen. George Pickett's division took up their position on the western slope of Seminary Ridge. General Lee, astride Traveller, watched them gravely. According to Lt. John Dooley, "Uncle Robert," as many of the men called Lee, looked anxious. "I must confess that the General's face does not look as bright as though he were certain of success."

Lee rode on to observe another unit slated to join the attack on Cemetery Ridge, that led by Brig. Gen. James Johnston Pettigrew. Pettigrew had taken over Heth's command when Heth was wounded the day before. The division had lost more than twenty-seven hundred men in less than twenty-five minutes.

When Lee saw the remnants of the division, he was shocked. He told an aide that many of the men did not appear fit for duty and should have been sent to the rear. But in reality, he could not afford to lose even these ragged soldiers, though many were bandaged and lame. They came to attention as he passed. Lee noted with sadness how many familiar faces were missing from the ranks. He muttered more to himself than to his companions, "The attack must succeed."

He rode slowly back to Pickett's division. The men assembled in formation and watched him, but they did not cheer. They had been warned to remain quiet so as not to alert the Yankees to their presence.

But every man removed his cap in a gesture of respect and affection. Lee seemed to stare at each man; for some, it would be the last time that he would see them. Slowly he removed his hat in a silent salute to them all.

After Lee moved on, John Dooley's men launched a mock battle of their own, pelting one another with green crab apples from the nearby trees. It was a way to break the tension, and for a while it was fun. Then the heat and the realization of the situation they were facing sobered and quieted them. They dropped to the ground to rest, their mood pensive.

Sgt. Junius Kimble—known to everyone as June—of the Fourteenth Tennessee walked to the crest of the ridge and gazed eastward toward the Union line on Cemetery Ridge. He was a veteran of many a battle and nothing much fazed him, but he felt a stab of fear at what he saw.

"June Kimble," he asked himself, "are you going to do your duty today?" He paused for a moment, then answered himself aloud. "I'll do it, so help me God." As soon as the words were out, feelings of calm and peace overtook him.

Across the way on Cemetery Ridge, Cpl. Wesley Sturtevant of the Fourteenth Vermont spent the morning visiting his cousin in another regiment. Sturtevant was also a veteran, in the thick of the previous day's fighting. He didn't remember being scared at all.

But that night, so he told his cousin, he had dreamed that today's battle would be his last. He would never again see his home. He asked his cousin to tell his family that he loved them and to arrange for his burial back in his hometown. Sturtevant felt no fear, only resignation and acceptance. He handed his cousin all the letters he had saved, to be given to his parents, and said good-bye for what he knew was the last time. His premonition turned out to be correct.

The men of the Third Virginia, like most of the troops on both sides, were subdued and reflective. Col. Joseph Mayo, commander of the Third, walked over to the camp of the Seventh Virginia to see Col.

Waller Tazewell Patton, of the illustrious family that has contributed its sons to virtually every war in American history. Mayo commented that the pending attack "has brought about an awful seriousness with our fellows, Taz."

"Yes," Patton replied, "and well they may be serious if they really know what is in store for them."

⊶═◉═⊷

GEORGE PICKETT WAS the only man who seemed genuinely pleased, even exuberant, about the forthcoming battle. He was in high spirits when he greeted a friend he had known in the Mexican War. This charge, Pickett told him, would be "just like the good old days when [we] stormed Chapultepec together." Pickett rallied General Lee's nephew, Fitzhugh Lee, calling, "Come on, Fitz, and go with us; we shall have lots of fun there presently."

This could be Pickett's chance for the fame and glory that had eluded him since the grand time in Mexico sixteen years ago. He had missed the major battles at First and Second Bull Run, Antietam, Chancellorsville, and the first two days at Gettysburg. Because of a wound at Gaines Mill early on and other ill-timed circumstances, he had had no opportunity to become a hero to a grateful nation, no chance to become an idol to his teenage sweetheart. But he was certain that today's charge would make his name go down in history.

As usual, the thirty-eight-year-old Pickett cut a memorable figure with his dandified appearance: a little blue cap, bright blue cuffs and gauntlets on an immaculately tailored uniform, an elegant riding crop, boots polished to a mirror shine, and sparkling gold spurs. But it was his hair that dazzled people the most. It hung almost to his shoulders in corkscrew ringlets to which he applied liberal doses of perfume. He also scented his beard and long, drooping mustache.

But Pickett had a darker side that showed itself to perceptive observers. A Yankee prisoner who saw him that morning at Gettysburg recalled:

The archetype of a Virginia slave-baron strutted briskly, proud in bearing, head lifted in arrogance. On horseback he looked like the ruler of a continent. Obviously he took pains with his appearance—riding boots aglitter, near-shoulder length hair tonsorially styled—but the color of his nose and upper cheeks betrayed that he pandered the inner man. Pleasures of the bottle left indelible tracks. Indeed, the coarse plebeian features in no way matched the efforts at aristocratic airs.

Others remarked on Pickett's arrogance, quick temper, and weakness for liquor—pointing to his swollen face and fleshiness, and the deep rings under his eyes, as evidence of dissipation. Some questioned his fitness for promotion to major general, insisting he had done nothing to warrant the rank and that it resulted only from Longstreet's fondness for him.

Longstreet's aide, Lt. Col. Moxley Sorrel, wrote that "taking Longstreet's orders in emergencies, I could always see how he looked after Pickett and made us give him [orders] very fully; indeed, sometimes stay with him to make sure he did not get astray."

Pickett had even been accused of cowardice. Col. Eppa Hunton of the Eighth Virginia claimed to have once seen Pickett ride out of the line of fire with his head pressed against his horse's neck, hardly an example of the courageous leadership expected of a general officer in the Army of the Confederacy. Pickett had a lot to prove that day at Gettysburg, to the men who would fight alongside him and to himself as well.

⋆⇒◉⇐⋆

THERE HAD BEEN times when the parents of young George Pickett wondered what would become of him, whether he would ever amount to anything. He was charming enough, good at dancing, singing, and hunting, but he was spoiled, boisterous, disobedient, and lacking self-control and perseverance. His mother called him indolent.

His childhood years were spent on the family's thousand-acre plantation twelve miles from Richmond. His neighbors and boyhood friends included the most powerful and well-connected families in Virginia. The Picketts were among the chosen few. Regardless of George's material and social advantages, however, the question remained of what he would make of himself. His mother fretted about the flaws in his character, particularly "his lack of self-reliance and discipline, direction and ambition. She wondered if he would ever mature into a respectable gentleman."

Sending him away to private school did not change his behavior. George performed poorly in his classes. He defied his teachers, disobeyed rules, and enjoyed raising hell. Only the military training at school interested him; he was inspired by tales of his ancestors' exploits in the Revolutionary War and the War of 1812.

He fared little better when his parents sent him to study law with his uncle, a successful attorney in Illinois. George did not appear to like the idea of serious study or work of any kind. His parents then decided that West Point was the answer.

Pickett entered the military academy in 1842, and he quickly became popular with his fellow students. Although all agreed that he was fun to be around, he was one of the worst cadets of that or any other year. He tested the limits of the established order, seeing how far he could go in breaking the rules. He seemed to know instinctively when to stop, always just short of expulsion. For the first time in his life, he showed some self-discipline and self-control.

That said, his behavior as a cadet was outrageous. From the outset he violated almost every one of the academy's large body of regulations. He was often late for roll call, drill, reveille, chapel, the posting of the guard, and evening retreat. He was even late for meals. He smoked, styled his hair, marched out of step, wore soft rather than the prescribed stiff linen collars, and allowed his musket to rust. His academic performance was also poor—Pickett studied just enough to avoid being expelled for low grades.

He frequented the notorious Benny Havens's, a tavern off-limits to all cadets at all times. Once he got so drunk he passed out in the snow on his way home. Luckily for him, a classmate was on guard duty and smuggled him inside before he was discovered by a senior cadet—or froze to death. A biographer, Edward Longacre, observed that Pickett's

aptitude as a class clown proved another barrier to high standing. In a blatant bid for attention, he repeatedly appeared at drill in nonmilitary clothing. While marching he would swing his arms exaggeratedly as though to poke fun at the rigid bearing of his peers. Once he tried to start a food fight in the mess hall; on another occasion he was caught urinating on Academy property. Perhaps his most notable prank was an attempt, while marching in formation, to trip a file of fellow cadets, presumably to watch them collide and fall like so many tenpins.

By the end of his senior year, Pickett had accumulated a record of demerits that took four legal-size pages to list, a total of 195; 200 meant expulsion. But again he seemed to know the limits and stopped just short of disaster. He graduated in 1846, ranking fifty-ninth in his class—a class of fifty-nine.

He finished West Point in time for war, where he quickly demonstrated that although he may have been a terrible cadet, he was a fine, brave young officer. He proved his worth during the U.S. assault on the fortress at Churubusco, where he led his company forward against the Mexican earthworks. His troops fought right behind those of Lt. Pete Longstreet.

Pickett was wounded slightly but remained on his feet, pushing on with a pistol in one hand and a sword in the other. He was mentioned in dispatches and recommended for promotion to brevet first lieutenant for "gallant and meritorious conduct." He had learned that he was good in combat—but also that he liked it. He later distinguished himself in the attack on Chapultepec. This time his outfit attacked the fortress following the unit commanded by Lt. Lewis A. Armistead, who would be with him at Gettysburg.

Pickett was the first of his company to scale the ladders tilted precariously against the walls of the Mexican fort. As he reached the top, the officer waving the regimental flag—Pete Longstreet—fell with a bullet in his leg. Longstreet handed the colors to Pickett and told him to place them atop the Mexican stronghold. Pickett fought his way to the top parapet, tore down the enemy flag, and raised the regimental colors.

Promoted to the brevet rank of captain, Pickett became a national hero. He received congratulations from his men and also from the enemy. Shortly after the battle, a Catholic priest presented Pickett with a crucifix as a token of admiration for his bravery. Though not Catholic, Pickett wore it around his neck from then on.

But when the excitement, glory, and accolades ended with the close of the war, Pickett endured seven years of boring, routine duty at small posts in Texas. In 1850 he married Sally Minge, from a wealthy Virginia family, and took her out to Texas, to the brutal, primitive life on the plains. There she died in childbirth, along with their baby, a son. Grief changed Pickett. He became melancholy and depressed, emotions he had never shown before but which would return periodically to mark his life.

Pickett's fortunes changed again on a visit to the beach near Fortress Monroe, Virginia, just before Christmas of 1852. He sat in the sand under an umbrella, brooding and trying to read a book. Soon he noticed that a quiet, lonely four-year-old girl named LaSalle Corbell was staring at him. Young Sallie, suffering from whooping cough, had been isolated from family and friends. She intently watched the handsome twenty-seven-year-old officer with the long flowing hair and wondered why he looked so unhappy.

Years later, recalling that moment, she wrote that she could imagine "but one reason for his desolation and in pity for him, I crept under his umbrella to ask him if he, too, had the whooping cough."

When Pickett told her that his wife and child had died, she solemnly promised to be his child now and his wife when she grew up. Moved by this sweet declaration, Pickett gave her the ring he wore on a chain around his neck and a golden heart inscribed with the name of his late wife, Sally. Sallie Corbell knew at that instant, so she wrote later, that one day she would marry the man she always called "my soldier."

After Pickett returned to duty in Texas, he received letters from her, which Sallie dictated to her mother to write. He found them comforting and always replied, keeping up a correspondence that lasted for years. Her childish remarks could often dispel his recurring depression. Three years later, while he was stationed at Fortress Monroe, Sallie often came to watch her soldier drill his troops.

In 1855, Pickett was posted to Fort Vancouver on the Columbia River in Washington Territory, where he found someone else to assuage his loneliness—Morning Mist, a young Indian woman, allegedly a princess. He lived with her for a year and a half. She gave birth to their son, named James Tilton Pickett, but died shortly thereafter.

Pickett sent the boy to live with a white family in the territory and rarely saw him, although he did leave him a Bible inscribed with his name. When the Civil War began and Pickett was reassigned, he gave a friend one hundred dollars with instructions to use it for the child's welfare. He never saw the boy again.

For reasons not made clear, Pickett did not begin his journey east until July 24, 1861, some three months after the war began. When he arrived in Virginia in September, he came under heavy criticism for taking so long to join the cause. He wrote, "So bitter is the feeling here, that my being unavoidably delayed so long in avowing my allegiance to my state has been most cruelly and severely criticized by friends—yes, and even relations, too." He was given a commission in the Confederate army, but only as a captain, the rank he had already held for six years.

His relationship with Sallie Corbell continued to blossom. She was now thirteen and very attractive; he found her quite charming. They saw each other only rarely because she was attending a school for young ladies in Lynchburg, Virginia, more than eighty miles from Richmond. They corresponded regularly, and he kept her apprised of his career.

Pickett was promoted to colonel two weeks after his initial appointment as a captain, but he was given a backwater command with a force based largely on paper: his regiment was nonexistent, and the military district he commanded was merely a hodgepodge collection of counties. Longstreet pushed for Pickett's promotion to brigadier general, which was granted in December, and gave him command of a brigade in his division.

Pickett fought in the Seven Days' battles of the Peninsular campaign. He was wounded in the shoulder and recuperated at his sister's home in Richmond, nursed by Sallie, who left school to rush to his bedside. She changed his dressings, read to him, and sang his favorite songs. They talked a great deal about their future. She also kept visitors at bay to make sure he got sufficient rest, though she did allow President Jefferson Davis in to see her soldier.

While he rested to regain his strength, the war was passing him by. He was determined to rejoin the army, over Sallie's protests. He caught up with Longstreet in the Shenandoah Valley, pleased to learn that his old friend now commanded a corps. Longstreet promoted Pickett to major general and gave him command of a division.

Longstreet's corps was sent south, headquartered at Petersburg, to guard Richmond and gather forage and supplies for the Army of Northern Virginia. Again Pickett found himself in the rear echelon. By the time the troops returned to Lee's army, they had missed Chancellorsville, one of the outstanding victories of the war.

Sallie Corbell dropped out of school and boarded at her aunt's house, only fifteen miles from Pickett's headquarters. He made the round trip almost every night, regardless of whether he had obtained official permission. Longstreet had become increasingly reluctant to approve his daily requests for leave. Some of Pickett's staff officers complained that his absences interfered with the functioning of the division.

Pickett tried to outwit Longstreet by dealing with Moxley Sorrell, the chief of staff, but Sorrel told him that only Longstreet could approve the leaves. "But he is tired of it, and will refuse," Pickett pleaded, "and I must go, I must see her. I swear, Sorrel, I'll be back before anything can happen in the morning." Sorrel refused permission, and Pickett went anyway. Sorrel was unhappy about it. "I don't think his division benefitted by such carpet-knight doings in the field," Sorrell said. Longstreet knew about the unauthorized absences, of course, but never chastised Pickett for them.

In early May, when Lee ordered Longstreet's corps to rejoin the army, Pickett and his beloved Sallie became officially engaged. They agreed to put off the wedding until summer, after she finished school. But before that date there would be Gettysburg, a hot day in July, and George Pickett's chance to recapture the glory days of the Mexican campaign.

⋆═◦═⋆

By ELEVEN O'CLOCK on the morning of July 3, the sounds of the battle at Culp's Hill, which had started at 3:45, stopped. A stunning silence descended over Gettysburg.

One hour before that, the guns fell silent in Vicksburg. For the first time in forty-seven days, the firing ceased. Soldiers on the line and civilians sheltered in their caves were startled. Families ventured outside; men climbed out of their trenches. Was this another truce called so each side could bury their dead? Was it a period of calm before more fighting, or could it be the prelude to surrender, the widespread hope that so many dared not voice?

White flags appeared along a segment of the rebel line. Two Confederate officers, one carrying a large white flag, emerged from their trench and walked slowly toward the Union side. The standard-bearer was Col. Louis Montgomery, an aide to General Pemberton. With him was Gen. John Bowen, a Georgia-born West Point graduate who had become a successful architect in St. Louis, the city where Grant had failed so miserably in business. Bowen had befriended the penniless Grant during those years. Now he carried Pemberton's letter proposing a truce to discuss surrender terms.

When he reached the Union line, Bowen asked to see Grant, but the general refused to meet with him. Bowen handed the letter to Gen. A. J. Smith, who passed it on to Grant. Pemberton had written,

> I have the honor to propose an armistice with the view to arranging terms for the capitulation of Vicksburg. To this end, if agreeable to you, I will appoint three commissioners, to meet a like number to be named by yourself, at such place and hour today as you may find convenient. I make this proposition to save the further effusion of blood, which must otherwise be shed to a frightful extent, feeling myself fully able to maintain my position for a yet indefinite period.

Grant was in no mood to consider surrender terms or to have the matter discussed by commissioners from both sides. As far as he was concerned, there could be no terms save the one for which he was already famous: unconditional surrender. And no one else to accept a surrender but Grant himself.

Bowen, fearing such an impasse, then suggested through General Smith that Grant meet directly with Pemberton. He agreed to do so at three o'clock that afternoon. Grant penned a message for Bowen to take back to Vicksburg's commander.

> Your note of this date is just received proposing an armistice for several hours, for the purpose of arranging terms of capitulation through commissioners, to be appointed, etc. The useless effusion of blood you propose stopping by this course can be ended at any time

you may choose by the unconditional surrender of the city and garrison. Men who have shown so much endurance and courage as those now in Vicksburg will always challenge the respect of an adversary, and I can assure you that you will be treated with all the respect due to prisoners of war. I do not favor the proposition of appointing commissioners to arrange the terms of capitulation, because I have no terms other than those indicated above.

If Pemberton still harbored any thought of negotiating for better terms, he should have been disabused of the notion by Grant's letter. Yet when Bowen said that Grant was willing to meet him in person at three o'clock, Pemberton took that as an indication that Grant remained receptive to additional negotiations. Pemberton, mindful of his place in history, hoped for a chance to salvage some honor.

⊷≡◦⊂≡⊷

BY NOONTIME IN Gettysburg the temperature had risen to its peak. The men sweltered, sweated, and soaked in their itchy wool uniforms. Soldiers who clustered in groves of trees found even those conditions insufferable because the foliage cut off what little breeze there was. The troops out in the open had no shelter from the brutal sun. Water was scarce. Unit commanders were reluctant to let men leave the line to go to the rear for water, fearing that a sudden order to attack would catch them understrength. There was nothing for it but to lie low and conserve energy, for surely the eerie silence that forced them to whisper could not last much longer.

And so they waited, and the longer the silence dragged on with nothing but their thoughts to dwell on, the more morbid and frightened many soldiers became. Cpl. Charles Loehr of the First Virginia left his position to find a well to fill his canteen. He located one near an artillery battery, one of many that stretched over two miles, the length of the rebel front. He talked to the gunners about the Yankees across the way on Cemetery Ridge. He remembered being sobered by the sight. When Loehr returned to his outfit, he told a friend, "I would not give twenty-five cents for my life if the charge is made."

Many of the men wrote their last letters home, telling their families not to grieve because they surely died bravely for a good cause. Others withdrew into themselves, trying to summon the courage not to fail their fellow soldiers or disgrace themselves in front of the others. The more battle-hardened men slept easily, confident they would survive to see yet another sunrise. Not so Tazewell Patton. He told a friend he expected to die.

Lee, Longstreet, and Pickett sat in the shade of an apple tree talking about the battle plan. Longstreet repeated his objection: the troops could not take such a strongly fortified position as the enemy held on Cemetery Ridge. Pickett disagreed, promising Lee that his division would drive the enemy off the ridge and carry the day.

Some officers nearby, eavesdropping on the conversation, heard Lee pressure Longstreet to ask his men if they believed they could dislodge the enemy. Longstreet ordered Maj. James Risque Hutter of the Eleventh Virginia to lead a couple of companies up to the crest of the ridge so they could see the Union line for themselves. Hutter, accompanied by Capt. Thomas Horton, also of the Eleventh,

watched their men's reaction when they heard what was intended for them. With typical fatalism, the veterans turned to each other and shook hands as if they were embarking on distant journeys. Hutter heard one of them say, "Boys, many a one of us will bite the dust here today, but we will say to General Lee if he wants them driven out, we will do it."

But two brigadier generals who studied the Yankee line on Cemetery Ridge were considerably less sanguine about their prospects. Dick Garnett said, "This is a desperate thing to attempt," and Lewis Armistead replied, "The slaughter will be terrible."

❖━◉━❖

AT 11:45, TWENTY-EIGHT-YEAR-OLD Col. Porter Alexander, Longstreet's artillery chief, received a disturbing and disagreeable note from him. Alexander, in West Point's class of 1857, was among the elite graduates chosen to serve as an engineer. Immediately after receiving his commission he was assigned to teach at the academy, another acknowledgment of his distinction. Before the war, he had developed the wigwag method of signaling, using semaphores to transmit messages over distances up to several miles.

Alexander had been up since before dawn, spotting his artillery batteries, a total of eighty guns, along a one-mile front. An additional sixty-three guns from the Third Corps, under his command for this operation, extended the line of artillery to 143 guns over a distance of two miles. This was the largest concentration of cannon ever assembled, and the intention was that a prolonged bombardment of such magnitude would pulverize the Union line. Longstreet's infantry would advance over the remnants of the crushed Yankee position. Longstreet had ordered Alexander to observe closely the effects of the artillery fire on the enemy. When he judged that it had inflicted sufficient damage to demoralize the Yankees, Alexander was to give the order for Pickett's outfit to charge.

Thus Longstreet ceded to Alexander the responsibility for ordering the start of the assault. Longstreet remained firmly opposed to the attack. He was so convinced that it would fail that he was unable to order his men forward. Later he wrote,

> Never was I so depressed as upon that day. I felt that my men were to be sacrificed, and that I should have to order them to make a hopeless charge. I had instructed Alexander, being unwilling to trust myself with the entire responsibility, to carefully observe the effect of the fire upon the enemy, and when it began to tell, to notify Pickett to begin the assault.

Longstreet, evading both his orders and his responsibility as corps commander by shifting the decision to a subordinate, then compounded the dilemma: Longstreet now attempted to force Alexander to decide whether it should be launched at all.

This was the disturbing message Alexander received at 11:45. He referred to it as a "sudden shock." Longstreet later explained, in war chronicles published in 1879, that he sent it because he "was so much impressed with the hopelessness of the charge."

> Colonel [Alexander]: If the artillery fire does not have the effect to drive off the enemy or greatly demoralize him, so as to make our efforts pretty certain, I would prefer that you should not advise General Pickett to make the charge. I shall rely a great deal on your good judgment to determine the matter and shall expect you to let Pickett know when the moment offers.

Alexander understood immediately that Longstreet was holding him responsible for the entire attack, a burden he was unwilling to accept. An operation of this scale, a decision of such importance, should not be expected of a colonel. Alexander also knew that Longstreet doubted the success of the charge and may have been trying to create a face-saving way to call it off. That thought made Alexander himself question the wisdom of the planned assault.

He showed Longstreet's note to a friend, Brig. Gen. Ambrose Wright, and told him of his misgivings. On Wright's urging, Alexander sent a reply to Longstreet, who was taking a nap when it arrived.

> General [Longstreet]: I will only be able to judge the effect of our fire on the enemy by his return fire, for his infantry is but little exposed to view, and the smoke will obscure the whole field. If, as I infer from your note, there is any alternative to this attack, it should be carefully considered before opening our fire, for it will take all the

artillery ammunition we have left to test this one thoroughly, and if the result is unfavorable we will have none left for another effort. And even if this is entirely successful it can only be so at a very bloody cost.

Longstreet later remarked that he acted out of a desire to save his men. He "felt that if the artillery did not produce the desired effect, [he] would be justified in holding Pickett off." Thus he indicated that there might be legitimate grounds for canceling the attack. But again Longstreet appeared unwilling to make the final determination on the effectiveness of the bombardment. He dispatched yet another note to Alexander.

Colonel [Alexander]: The intention is to advance the infantry, if the artillery has the desired effect of driving the enemy off, or having other effect such as to warrant us in making the attack. When the moment arrives advise General Pickett, and of course advance such artillery as you can use in aiding the attack.

Alexander showed the message to General Wright. "He has put the responsibility back upon you," Wright said.

"Tell me exactly what you think of this attack," Alexander asked.

"Well, Alexander, it is mostly a question of supports. It is not as hard to get [to Cemetery Ridge] as it looks. I was there yesterday with my brigade. The real difficulty is to stay there after you get there, for the whole infernal Yankee army is up there in a bunch."

Alexander mulled over his situation and concluded that it had become impossible for him to avoid making the crucial decisions. Longstreet had left him no choice. Alexander reminded himself that the plan for the assault had come directly from Robert E. Lee. Camp rumor had it that Lee planned to send every available man in support. Therefore, it must surely have been well thought out. That being the case, Alexander noted, who was he to decide to call it off?

As a final check, Alexander went to see Pickett. He found him in high spirits, optimistic about the outcome. That settled the matter. Alexander wrote, "I felt that I could not make any delay or let the attack suffer by any indecision on my part."

At 12:30, Alexander informed Longstreet that "When our artillery fire is at its best, I shall order Pickett to charge." Now if there was to be any order rescinding the decision to charge, it would not come from Colonel Alexander.

⋅═◈═⋅

ON THE UNION side, two generals and their staffs were enjoying a pleasant lunch courtesy of General Gibbon. The general's cook had organized a feast, preparing a huge pan of stewed chicken, along with potatoes, toast, bread and butter, and coffee. Gibbon's division occupied the portion of the line that included the clump of trees Lee had selected as the aiming point for Pickett's charge.

But in the noonday sun, enjoying that welcome repast, the war was far from anyone's mind. Gibbon and his guest, General Hancock, were perched on the only stools available. Their food was set atop a mess chest, which they used as a table. Their staff officers sat cross-legged on the ground, balancing their plates on their laps.

General Meade rode by, accompanied by his son and aide, George, who had disappointed his father by accumulating enough demerits at West Point for expulsion. He was now a captain. Of course the commander of the Army of the Potomac and his son had to be invited to join the meal. Meade was given an empty cracker box for a chair; his son joined the other aides on the grass.

Meade was upset about an incident that occurred that morning. A local resident had slipped past Meade's staff and confronted him directly, complaining that Union troops were using his house as a hospital, burying soldiers in his garden, and littering his lawn with amputated arms and legs. The irate man demanded that Meade provide compensation. Historian Bruce Catton described Meade's response as follows.

> Short-tempered Meade blew up at him, told him that if this battle were lost he would have no government to apply to and no property that was worth anything, and hustled him out of there with the warning that if he heard any more from him he would give him a musket and put him in the ranks to fight.

The man wisely retreated. Meade calmed himself and wrote a note to his wife assuring her that all was well. "We had a great fight yesterday . . . today at it again. [The] army is in fine spirits and everyone determined to do or die. George and myself well."

The men enjoyed after-lunch cigars while Meade described the battle plan. Lee had concentrated 160 guns in the center of his line and would open fire on the center of the Union line. That meant Gibbon's position, Meade said. Their artillery would immediately return fire, commencing what he described as a grand artillery duel. When it ended, the rebels would attack in force. Meade reminded them that they would need every available man. Even the provost guards should be sent to the front, instead of remaining in the rear to stop stragglers and deserters.

General Gibbon summoned Captain Farrell of the First Minnesota, in command of the provost guard for his division, and told him to rejoin his regiment. Farrell and his men had missed the First Minnesota's deadly charge the day before but would now return to supplement their weakened ranks. Gibbon's aide, Lt. Frank Haskell, watched Farrell salute and turn away. "He was a quiet, excellent gentleman and thorough soldier," Haskell said. "I knew him well and esteemed him. I never saw him again."

General Meade departed at 12:30. Haskell recalled:

We dozed in the heat and lolled upon the ground, with half-open eyes. Our horses were hitched to the trees munching some oats. A great lull rested upon the field. Time was heavy, and for want of something better to do, I yawned and looked at my watch. It was five minutes before one o'clock. I returned my watch to my pocket, and thought possibly that I might go to sleep.

CHAPTER 11

FOR GOD'S SAKE, COME QUICK!

"LET THE BATTERIES open." Longstreet issued the order at 1:07 in the afternoon. The signal for the commencement of the Confederate bombardment was two cannon shots, one right after the other. When the first cannon roared, all gunners along the line stood ready to shoot as soon as the second gun fired. But there was only a prolonged strained silence. The second gun in the signal battery had misfired. Quickly, the battery commander ordered his number three gun to fire. No sooner had it roared than the entire two-mile line exploded in a long sheet of flame and smoke. Historian Bruce Catton described it:

> Then every gun in the line was fired in one titanic, rolling crash—the loudest noise, probably, that had ever been heard on the American continent up to that moment—and a hurricane of exploding shells came sweeping over Cemetery Ridge and the air was all smoke and stabbing flame and unendurable noise and deadly flying iron.

Union soldiers on Cemetery Ridge dove for cover, scrambled, dug, and clawed the earth, ran behind trees, rocks, and walls, trembling as 160 shells exploded overhead and on the ground around them. The shells sent thousands of pieces of jagged red-hot shrapnel slicing the air, along with thousands more missiles of shattered stone and wood and timber, parts of muskets and bits of human flesh. In the seconds following, more shells struck and exploded, and then still more. General Gibbon's camp, peaceful and serene a moment before, was suddenly a roaring inferno.

Gibbon leaped to his feet, grabbed his sword, and called for his orderly to bring his horse. When the man did not appear, the general started on foot toward the front line to see how his men were bearing up under the assault. Lt. Frank Haskell, Gibbon's aide, ran for the horse. "I found him tied to a tree nearby, eating oats, with an air of the greatest composure, which under the circumstances even then struck me as exceedingly cool. I am not sure but that I learned a lesson then from a horse."

The camp was in chaos. Horses, mules, and wagons were shattered and scattered in an instant. General Gibbon's groom took his horse and rode off after the general, with Gibbon's horse in tow. A shell tore into his chest, knocking him to the ground in a bloody heap. The horses galloped off.

Meade's headquarters camp became a killing ground within the first minute of the battle. A visiting reporter counted sixteen dead horses in a row, their halters still tied to the fence post. A wagon careened wildly with one horse blown to bits in its traces and the other pulling madly on three legs. At the house serving as Meade's headquarters, a Confederate shell crashed into the steps, others destroyed the pillars supporting the porch roof, and more penetrated the roof and the walls. One cannonball smashed the legs of a table at which two officers were consulting a map.

Meade stepped outside and felt the wind of a shell that whizzed past him. The officers quickly evacuated the house; there had been no casualties. They huddled behind the house, as if its fragile wooden frame could protect them from the rebel artillery. Meade paced calmly up and down, amused by the sight of his staff bunched together. He decided to lighten their mood with a little story, later recounted in his memoirs:

> Gentlemen, are you trying to find a safe place? You remind me of the man who drove the ox-team that took ammunition for the heavy guns on to the field of Palo Alto [during the Mexican War]. Finding himself within range, he tilted up his cart and got behind it. Just then General [Zachary] Taylor came along, and seeing this attempt at shelter, shouted, "You damned fool, don't you know you are no safer there than anywhere else?" The driver replied, "I don't suppose I am, general, but it kind o' feels so."

No one laughed. As Meade finished telling the story, a cannonball tore through the house and exploded, wounding a visiting staff officer. It was time to move on. Meade led them several hundred yards away to a barn near the Taneytown Road.

⊰═◉═⊱

THE SHELLS FELL and men died. At first the rebel fire was extremely accurate, blanketing the Yankee infantry on the western slope of Cemetery Ridge. But before many minutes had elapsed, smoke obscured the ridge. The rebel gunners, now blind, kept firing at what they presumed were the targets they had aimed at initially—the infantry on the slope of the ridge. However, the recoil action after each shot caused the trail end of the cannon to dig a little deeper into the ground, raising the muzzles slightly. Shells began to creep up to the crest of the ridge, where most of the Union artillery was located, and to the valley on the far side.

In the valley, panic erupted among the rear echelon units—the reserves, ammunition trains, supply wagons, ambulances, quartermaster units, and the dregs of an army that congregate in the rear, the skulkers and shirkers. Suddenly they came under a constant rain of shells, and many men fled east and south, clogging the roads and preventing additional supplies and combat units from moving forward.

By contrast, once the ridge was shrouded in smoke, the Union infantry troops on the western side were relatively safe. "This soon became monotonous," one soldier said. Although some shells still fell short, the intense heat of the day soon seemed like a greater threat than the enemy bombardment.

The men crowded together, not daring to stand, and the smoke added to their discomfort. Most canteens were nearly empty and the closest water supply was several hundred yards behind the lines where the shells were bursting. One man, desperate with thirst, gathered up some canteens from his friends and made a run for it. He returned unscathed but recounted close calls along the way. "The water is cold enough, boys," he said, "but it's devilish hot around the spring."

Lieutenant Haskell and General Gibbon settled in close to the crest to watch the action. All around them, men were being hit, particularly the gunners manning the artillery pieces. "We see the poor fellows hobbling back from the crest," Haskell recalled, "or unable to do so, pale and weak, lying on the ground with the mangled stump of an arm or leg, dripping their life-blood away."

Haskell watched a man shouldering several canteens make his way to the ridge, carrying water to his buddies. A shell struck his knapsack and tore it from his back, leaving his body untouched. "The soldier stopped and turned about in puzzled surprise, put up one hand to his back to assure himself that the knapsack was not there, and then walked slowly on again unharmed, with not even his coat torn."

Another soldier lay flat on the ground with his head six inches from a large rock that he hoped would protect him. A shell pulverized the rock but left the soldier with not so much as a scratch.

The First Minnesota once again found itself in the wrong place at the wrong time. Its strength was up to 150 men with the return of the companies that had served as General Gibbon's provost guard and on other special duty. The men were spread partway down the west side of Cemetery Ridge. About four hundred feet to the left was the clump of trees Lee had chosen as the aiming point for the attack. If the rebels were able to cross the valley between the two ridges, the Minnesota troops would be among those bearing the full force of the attack.

The soldiers hugged the ground as the bombardment continued hunkering down behind low barriers constructed of fence rails, stones, sticks, and dirt into which they had stuffed blankets and knapsacks. No one on the line was hit by the rebel shelling, but the wounded from yesterday's battle who believed they were safe in the hospital behind the ridge did not fare so well. Matthew Marvin saw a man blown up by a shell only ten feet from where he was lying. Another shell demolished the upper branches of the apple tree under which he and a few others had taken shelter.

On the front line the Minnesotans knew that as terrible as the shelling was now, worse was to come when the shelling stopped. Henry Taylor wrote, "As we lay there, we were talking of what was yet to come, for we knew that the infantry would be sent forward as soon as shelling slackened, and then the men must fall."

-◦≡◦〇◖≡◦-

WHILE THE UNION infantry remained relatively safe on the west-ern slope of Cemetery Ridge, the artillery on the crest was taking repeated hits. The gunners had begun to return fire within minutes of the initial bombardment. Most of the rebel shells fell on and around their positions. The limber chests holding the ammunition for each gun rapidly exploded, sending thick acrid black smoke high in the air and spraying shrapnel for yards around.

Cannon shattered, their jagged pieces becoming deadly missiles to bring down more men. Iron wheels were sliced in two, caissons broken, horses maimed. Hundreds of gunners became casualties. Unlike the men of the infantry who could cling to the ground and hide behind rocks, artillerymen were exposed, out in the open to load, aim, and fire. A Minnesota man observed that nothing taller than four feet was likely to survive.

The center of the Union line bore the greatest devastation, close to the trees that were the focus of Lee's attack. That was the location of Battery A, Fourth U.S. Artillery, commanded by Lt. Alonzo Cushing, a twenty-two-year-old West Point graduate. Early on, two of his four guns were damaged beyond use, most of the horses were dead, and the caissons and limbers had been ruined. Cushing had barely enough men to fire the two remaining pieces.

The wounded lay where they fell because no soldiers could be spared to carry them to the rear. This made them vulnerable to additional attacks. One gunner, horribly mutilated from his wounds, went berserk as more shells exploded around him. He managed to clutch his revolver, squeeze the trigger, and shoot himself in the head.

Another of Cushing's guns was hit, disabling the wheels. The impact so frightened a veteran sergeant that he panicked and began to run away. Cushing pulled out his revolver and ordered the sergeant back to his post. The man returned to his duty. Cushing shouted for all the gunners to hear, "The first man who leaves his post again I'll blow his brains out!" Cushing himself was hit three times in the groin. Relying on a sergeant to support him, he continued to follow the battle and issue orders.

South of the central clump of trees, Battery B, First Rhode Island Light Artillery, commanded by Lt. Charles Brown, took a worse pummeling. Sgt. Albert Straight's gun received a direct hit on the axle, but he and his men kept up their fire. Pvt. William Jones pushed the sponge down the barrel, tapped the muzzle twice, and took his assigned position between the wheel and the muzzle. At the same moment Pvt. Alfred Gardner picked up the next shell to be fired, turned to his left, and hoisted it to the end of the barrel, ready to insert. Everything ran smoothly, exactly as planned, just the way that they had practiced the drill hundreds of times.

But this time a rebel shell struck the muzzle of the gun and exploded. Jones's head disintegrated instantly. Gardner's left arm was shattered, the stump attached to his shoulder only by a thread of flesh. A third man died and a fourth was wounded severely. Sergeant Straight tried to load the gun but the barrel was so badly deformed that he could not ram the ball down. While he tried to hammer it down with an ax, another shell hit the gun, demolishing the weapon but leaving Straight and another man untouched.

Private Gardner, lying in a pool of his own blood, asked Straight to send his Bible to his wife and to tell her that he died a happy man. Sinking into delirium he shouted, "Glory to God! I am happy! Hallelujah!"

⋅◈═◎═◈⋅

THE UNION ARTILLERY was causing its own terrible destruction among the Confederate infantry. Rebel soldiers lay helpless on the reverse slope of Seminary Ridge, waiting for the order to attack. But until the artillery duel came to a close, they could do nothing to retaliate.

Lt. John Dooley of Pickett's division flattened himself to the ground, aware that men all around him were being hit. One soldier raised his head a mere six inches and a shell struck him in the face, tearing off his head. Dooley tried to tune out the moans of the wounded and concentrate on the distinct sounds of the different types of shells. "They screech, sing, scream, whistle, roar, whirr, buzz, bang, and whiz."

Col. Joseph Mayo of the Third Virginia and his friend, Col. Waller Tazewell Patton of the Seventh Virginia, watched the shells tear into the ranks of their regiments. Patton raced to the site of the first impact and found two men dead and three severely wounded. More shells flew and more screams followed. Colonel Mayo knelt beside one of his officers whose legs had been shattered. He saw two brothers, one dead, the other mortally wounded. Several others were badly hurt and obviously would not survive. They could not move the men to safer ground. They had to wait, prepared to attack as soon as the word was given.

Pvt. Randolph Shotwell of the Eighth Virginia was watching a wounded horse struggling to regain its footing when a shell whizzed overhead and exploded not far behind him. He glanced around to see what had happened.

> The heavy missile had descended six feet behind me and ploughed through the bodies of Morris and Jackson of my own company. Poor fellows! They were devoted friends and lay side by side on their blankets; and side by side were ushered into eternity.

Lt. John Lewis of the Ninth Virginia remembered the oppressive heat, even though the smoke from the artillery duel obscured the sky like giant thunderclouds. Lewis had other recollections of that day:

> Man seldom sees or hears the likes of this but once in a lifetime; and those that saw and heard this infernal crash, and witnessed the havoc made by the shrieking, howling missiles of death as they plowed the earth and tore the trees will never forget it. It seemed that death was in every foot of space and safety was only in flight; but none of the men did that.

Confederate losses were high among the infantry waiting to attack. Some brigades lost up to fifteen percent of their force; companies reported losing as many as ten out of thirty men. Casualty estimates, killed and wounded, in Pickett's division ranged from three hundred to five hundred. It was difficult to obtain an accurate count; this was no time for a roll call.

Major Hutter of the Eleventh Virginia was sprawled on the ground talking to a friend who lay beside him. The friend said something Hutter could not hear, so he asked the man to repeat it. When he got no reply, Hutter turned and saw that his friend was dead. Sgt. Maj. D. E.

Johnston of the Seventh Virginia, Colonel Patton's outfit, crouched beneath an apple tree. When he raised his head for a quick breath of air, his commanding officer warned him to get down or he'd likely get his head knocked off. "A man had about as well die that way as to suffocate for want of air," Johnston said. No sooner had he spoken than a shell sheared the heads off two men, from the ears up.

Farther down the line, the University Grays, a regiment comprising students from the University of Mississippi, were also under fire. One shell exploded in midair, catching Sgt. Jeremiah Gage. Most of his left shoulder was destroyed by the shrapnel. Another piece tore through his pelvis, damaging the bladder, intestines, spleen, and a rib. Friends bore his mangled body to the nearest field hospital.

"Doctor," he said, "they have got Jere Gage at last. I thought I would get through safely, but they got me." While the surgeon examined his wounds, Gage asked how long he had to live. Only a few hours, he was told. "Doctor," Gage said, "I am in great agony. Let me die easy, dear doctor; I would do the same for you."

The surgeon asked his assistant for his two-ounce bottle of black drop, a deadly amount of concentrated opium. He poured the drug into a cup of water and asked Gage if he had any final messages.

"My mother," Gage cried. "O, my darling mother! How could I have forgotten you?"

The doctor helped Gage sit up and scrawl a farewell letter home. He told his mother he was dying like a man for his country and regretted that he would no longer be able to help his sisters. He added, "My dying release to Miss Mary (you know who)." He pressed the reverse side of the paper to his wound. "This letter is stained with my blood."

⋅→═◦═←⋅

COLONEL ALEXANDER, LONGSTREET'S artillery officer, could see nothing through the smoke that covered the Union line on Cemetery Ridge. That was what he feared would happen when Longstreet left the decision to him about when to order the infantry forward.

Alexander had no way of knowing how effective his bombardment had been in reducing the enemy defenses. But he could tell by the steady rate of return cannon fire that the Yankee artillery remained strong. He would not order Pickett across the valley in the face of such intense fire. He would have to keep up the bombardment until he sensed that the Union artillery had been damaged sufficiently to give Pickett's outfit a chance.

And so the barrage continued steadily for fifteen minutes, half an hour, an hour, the shells roaring and whizzing and exploding until it seemed no man could stand another moment. The generals on both sides sensed that the limit of human endurance was near. It was time to set an example, to show the men that they could survive this level of hell.

None of the Union soldiers who witnessed the sight and lived to tell of it ever forgot the presence of Gen. Winfield Scott Hancock, commander of the Second Corps. Amid the smoke and flames and explosions, bold as brass, Hancock rode the full length of his line along the crest of the ridge. The newspapers called him Hancock the Superb. And that was how he looked to his men that day.

Dressed as though for a formal review with immaculate white shirtfront and cuffs, Hancock rode a coal-black horse, with his full staff in attendance behind him. By his side rode an orderly carrying the corps flag. Hancock kept a slow pace, never ducking or flinching when shells flew too close. He appeared as serene as if he were conducting a routine inspection. His horse seemed to sense the danger, however, and became so unmanageable that Hancock had to change mounts.

Up and down the line, men cheered as he passed. They were cautious though, none of them standing upright to salute Hancock. A man could get killed doing that. But they shouted their approval and watched until he was lost in the smoke. Hancock did what generals are supposed to do, inspire their men to bear the burden of combat a little longer, to hang on and do what needs to be done. A brigadier general reminded him that a corps commander should not risk his life like that. "There are times," Hancock said, "when a corps commander's life does not count."

General Gibbon also put himself at risk, walking nonchalantly before the men of his division. He paced slowly along the line between them and the rebel bombardment, drawing hearty cheers. One of Gibbon's officers thought it was dangerous and foolhardy. Although admittedly the general's presence did boost morale, the officer wondered what would happen to that morale if Gibbon were cut down in full view. But the men obviously appreciated the gesture. Henry Taylor of the First Minnesota saw Gibbon walk "along the line in front of us, seeming to say, 'Boys, this is the way to face danger.'"

⋯⊷⫸◉⫷⊶⋯

ON THE CONFEDERATE side, General Longstreet rode unaccompanied along the length of his line. A soldier recalled that the general looked "as quiet as an old farmer riding over his plantation on a Sunday morning." One of his officers, Gen. James Kemper, hailed him.

"General," he said, "this is a terrible place."

"What!" Longstreet said. "Is your command suffering?"

"Yes. A man is cut to pieces here every second while we are talking. Sometimes a dozen men are killed at one shot."

"Is it possible?" Longstreet said. "Can't you find any safer position for your men?"

"No. We are exactly behind the line of this crest. [It is] the very safest place around here."

"I am greatly distressed at this," Longstreet said, "greatly distressed at this; but let us hold our ground a while longer. We are hurting the enemy badly, and we'll charge him presently."

Longstreet said no more. He moved on to the next portion of the line. The troops watched in admiration, their spirits heightened. But the mood turned when a burst of shells fell nearby. Some men became angry. What if they lost Pete Longstreet? What would happen to them? Who could replace him? They began to yell at him, urging him to go to the rear where he belonged. "You'll get your fool head knocked off," one shouted. "We'll fight without you leading us."

⋆⇒◉⇐⋆

LONGSTREET'S MEN WERE ready, eager to get the job done, to march across the valley toward the Yankees on the other side. They also knew fear, but by then any kind of action would be preferable to lying about helplessly, to dying without a chance to fight back.

The plan of attack was simple and had been explained to everyone, from division commanders to the privates in the ranks. They knew the objective, the nature of the enemy they would face, the distance across the valley, and the units that would protect their flanks. More important, each man understood that success in today's battle could mean a Confederate victory and an end to the war. Cross the valley—some three-quarters of a mile—and take the ridge. That was all.

Eleven brigades would make the attack, up to fifteen thousand men. That was the rebel strength before the artillery duel. No one knew how many were left when the barrage ended, but estimates put the number around twelve thousand, though it was probably higher.

While those brigades attacked the center of the Union line, Ewell's Second Corps would threaten the area around Cemetery Hill and Culp's Hill so that Meade would be unable to draw troops from that sector to meet the main assault. The rest of Hill's corps (part of it had been assigned to Longstreet for the attack) would provide support for Longstreet's left flank. The divisions of Hood and McLaws on Longstreet's right flank would stay in place to prevent Union troops from attacking the assault force from that direction.

The attacking units, with Pickett's men in the center, would advance in two waves following the skirmishers. To Pickett's right would be the units of Cadmus Wilcox, James Lane, and Alfred Scales, all part of

Hill's corps. Henry Heth's division would be on Pickett's other side. When Heth had been wounded, command passed to James Johnston Pettigrew, the officer who had gone into Gettysburg searching for shoes for his men. That morning seemed a lifetime ago.

Pettigrew, who would be thirty-five if he lived another day, was a North Carolina native of considerable intellectual accomplishment. He had earned the highest grades in the history of the University of North Carolina and was skilled in boxing and fencing. A noted scholar in Hebrew and classical Greek, he was also fluent in most modern European languages. He had written about his extensive European travels and undertaken a brilliant career in law. There were those who predicted that Pettigrew would become president, or at least chief justice of the Supreme Court. But then came war, and Pettigrew became as good a soldier as he had been a lawyer.

Pickett's division, "the flower of Lee's army," as it was called, started the day with a complement of 4,761 officers and men. Two brigades in the first line of attack would advance side by side, with the third brigade in the second line. James Kemper and Dick Garnett commanded the first two brigades; Lewis Armistead had the third.

Kemper was a thirty-nine-year-old Virginia lawyer and politician who had proven himself a leader in battle since First Bull Run. Garnett, a handsome forty-five-year-old West Point graduate, had won rapid promotion early in the war, but his reputation was tarnished at Kernstown, Virginia, in March 1862, when he directed his men to withdraw, to avoid annihilation or capture. Stonewall Jackson had placed him under arrest for ordering a retreat without permission, tantamount to charges of cowardice and desertion. The court-martial was interrupted by the demands of war. The army moved on, months passed, and the trial never resumed. Garnett remained in disgrace. Finally, Lee intervened and transferred him to Longstreet's corps, where the matter of his behavior at Kernstown was not an issue to anyone else.

Garnett still seethed at what he believed to be a great injustice. He needed an act of valor to clear his name. Unfortunately, he was not physically fit for duty and should not have been on the line. He had been kicked in the knee by a horse, which left him limping and in great pain. He was also fighting chills and a high fever. Although clearly in no condition for battle, Garnett was determined to grasp this chance for redemption. Some accounts describe him buttoned to the neck in his old blue overcoat, despite the July heat, whereas other descriptions have him wearing a new gray uniform. Nevertheless, he was eager to lead his men toward the enemy.

Lewis A. Armistead was a forty-six-year-old career soldier who had failed his first-year courses at West Point three years in a row. He left the military academy because of a disciplinary infraction that allegedly involved hitting Jubal Early over the head with a plate in the mess hall. Despite this unpromising start to his military career, Armistead received a direct commission as a second lieutenant in 1839. (The fact that his father was a general probably had something to do with the appointment.)

Armistead fought in the Seminole Indian Wars in Florida and in other Indian campaigns out west. Once the Civil War broke out, he was in almost every battle in which the Army of Northern Virginia participated. He was a widower and such an ardent admirer of the ladies that close friends nicknamed him Lo, short for Lothario. He was also the subject of one of the most famous and poignant tales of the war.

He had been stationed at a small army post in California when word of the events at Fort Sumter came. Old friends at the post were parting, some going to fight for the Union and others, like Lo Armistead, for the Confederacy. On the last night most of them would ever spend together, they attended a farewell party at the home of Capt. Winfield Scott Hancock. The mood was sad, full of grieving for a lost way of life and broken friendships. "Hearts were filled with sadness over the sundering of life-long ties," wrote Hancock's wife, Allie. Mrs. Albert

Sidney Johnston sat at the piano and sang "Kathleen Mavourneen," a sad ballad of farewell.[1]

> Mavourneen, mavourneen, my sad tears are falling
> To think that from Erin and thee I must part.
> It may be for years, and it may be forever;
> Oh, why art thou silent, thou voice of my heart?

Armistead had tears in his eyes as he placed his hands on Hancock's shoulders. "Hancock, good-bye. You can never know what this has cost me." Now Hancock was waiting for Armistead on the other side of the valley.

⋯⊙⋯

ALTHOUGH COLONEL ALEXANDER claimed that the artillery barrage from both sides lasted not much more than half an hour, everyone else agreed that the shelling continued unabated for nearly two hours, until a little before three o'clock that afternoon.

Brig. Gen. Henry Hunt, Meade's artillery chief, watched the exchange with immense satisfaction from his observation post atop Cemetery Hill. He was pleased to see that the rebel bombardment had not dislodged his guns or caused any noticeable reduction in their rate of fire. As gratified as he was with the conduct of his gunners, however, one thing began to trouble him. If his artillery was too successful, then the enemy might postpone any assault against a position perceived to be so strongly fortified—an unfortunate outcome, Hunt thought, because he was certain the rebels would fail in such an attack.

Hunt shared his concern with Maj. Thomas Osborn, chief of artillery for the Eleventh Corps. Osborn asked whether Meade considered an attack by the rebels desirable. "General Meade expressed the

---

[1] My thanks to Kim Kennedy for providing this version of "Kathleen Mavourneen," as written by Anne Crawford and Frederick W. Nicolls Crouch.

hope that the enemy would attack," Hunt said, "and he had no fear of the result." "If this is so," Osborn said, "why not let them out while we are all in good condition? I would cease firing at once, and the enemy could reach but one conclusion, that of our being driven from the hill."

Hunt agreed and ordered his men to cease firing. As the word spread southward from Cemetery Hill, the Union guns fell silent one by one. Hunt rode down the line to inspect his batteries. He found those posted around the central clump of trees to be in terrible shape, with ammunition low, many weapons destroyed, and scarcely enough men standing to operate the guns.

He ordered Lt. Alonzo Cushing's battery of the Fourth U.S. Artillery to the rear. Cushing, so weak from his groin wound that he could not stand unaided, refused to relinquish command of his battery. Hunt permitted him to stay with his men so he could die at his post.

Hunt moved on to the First Rhode Island Light Artillery, commanded by Lt. Charles Brown, stationed just south of the clump of trees. They had fared even worse from the bombardment. Hunt ordered these men to the rear. Off they went, dragging three heavy guns by hand.

On Seminary Ridge, Col. Porter Alexander watched them leave the line and, through the smoke, spotted three cannon being dragged to the rear. Hunt's ruse, to let the rebels believe they had savaged his artillery, was about to work.

Alexander had been increasingly worried that his ammunition supply would run out before he destroyed enough of the Yankee guns to order Pickett's men to advance. Pickett had already dispatched two messages asking when he could launch the assault.

Thus Alexander faced a dilemma. He could not maintain his own bombardment much longer because he had to save ammunition to support Pickett, if his assault was ordered. That decision was still Alexander's to make. But if the Union batteries kept up the same rate of fire, any assault against them would be, in Alexander's words, "madness." No troops could attack in the face of such a barrage. His situation had become desperate. He received yet another message from Pickett inquiring about the time for the assault. Alexander could delay no longer. He worded his reply carefully to pass responsibility for the decision to Pickett.

> If you are coming at all you must come at once, or I cannot give you proper support, but the enemy's fire has not slackened at all. At least eighteen guns are still firing from [the area around the clump of trees].

No sooner had Alexander sent the note to Pickett than he heard the enemy fire slacken. Brown's Rhode Island artillery pieces were the only ones sent to the rear, but in his excitement or confusion, or perhaps wishful thinking, Alexander insisted that he saw many more guns pulling back from the ridge. He later wrote, "At first I thought it only crippled guns; but soon, with my large glass, I discovered entire batteries limbering up and leaving their positions."

He watched through his telescope, expecting to see replacement batteries set up on the ridge, but none arrived. "If they don't put fresh batteries there in five minutes, this will be our fight," he said. But no new guns appeared. The Union rate of fire slowed and then stopped altogether. Alexander ordered his guns to cease firing to conserve ammunition for the charge. Silence descended over the battlefield.

Alexander waited another ten minutes and checked again for the presence of new Yankee guns to replace all those he believed he had seen retreating. Then he wrote a final note to Pickett.

"For God's sake, come quick. The eighteen guns are gone. Come quick or I can't support you."

⋆⇒◉⇐⋆

PICKETT SHOWED THE note to Longstreet, who read it in silence.

"General, shall I advance?" Pickett asked.

Longstreet did not answer.

"My feelings had so overcome me," Longstreet recalled, "that I would not speak, for fear of betraying my want of confidence to him." Later he commented, "I was convinced that he would be leading his troops to needless slaughter, and did not speak."

Finally, Longstreet nodded his head in affirmation.

"Sir," Pickett said, "I shall lead my division forward."

Pickett saluted and strode away. According to Sallie Corbell, writing as Mrs. Pickett years later, Pickett then walked back to Longstreet and handed him a letter addressed to her. On the envelope he had scrawled, "If Old Peter's nod means death, goodbye, and God bless you, little one."

Longstreet rode up to Colonel Alexander, who reassured him that the Yankees had withdrawn their artillery from the point of attack, the central clump of trees. But Alexander added that he was concerned about whether his ammunition supply was sufficient to support the charge. For an instant that information seemed just what Longstreet desired, a legitimate reason to delay the charge.

"Go," he ordered Alexander. "Halt Pickett right where he is and replenish your ammunition."

"General, we can't do that. We nearly emptied the [supply] train last night. Even if we had it, it would take an hour or two, and meanwhile the enemy would recover from the pressure he is now under. Our only chance is to follow it up now, to strike while the iron is hot."

"I don't want to make this attack," Longstreet said. "I believe it will fail. I do not see how it can succeed. I would not make it even now but that General Lee has ordered and expects it."

Alexander later recorded his impression that Longstreet was on the verge of calling off the charge and was looking to Alexander for support and encouragement. But Alexander said nothing.

"I then saw that there was no help for it," Longstreet wrote, "and that Pickett must advance under his orders."

⊹⟜◉⟝⊹

PICKETT RODE TO the front of each brigade and passed the orders for the men to form up and prepare to move out.

"Charge the enemy and remember old Virginia," he shouted.

As the men stood, they were stunned to see how many did not. Lt. Tom Dooley noted,

> We rise to our feet, but not all. There is a line of men still on the ground with their faces turned, men affected in four different ways. There are the gallant dead who will never charge again; the helpless wounded, many of whom desire to share the fortunes of the charge; the men who have charged on many a battlefield but who are now helpless from the heat of the sun; and the men in whom there is not sufficient courage to enable them to rise.

All along the line, the men who acted as file-closers (those who kept troops from fleeing a fight) watched the known shirkers and malingerers and made sure they were up and ready. One file-closer, Sgt. D. B. Easley of the Fourteenth Virginia, was told by his company commander to kill any men who refused to fight: his soldiers would either make the charge or die by Easley's hand; the commander did not care which.

Most of the men needed no prodding from a file-closer. They were proud to serve the Confederacy. They exchanged farewells with their friends, sang hymns, and bowed their heads when the chaplains made the rounds offering prayers.

Armistead rode out in front of his brigade, calling to his troops. "Remember, men, what you are fighting for. Remember your homes and your firesides, your mothers and wives and sisters and your sweethearts."

He turned to the color bearer for the Fifty-third Virginia.

"Sergeant, are you going to plant those colors on the enemy's works over yonder?"

"Yes, General, if mortal man can do it, I will."

Other commanders offered their own words of encouragement. General Pettigrew called to one of his brigade commanders, "Now, Colonel. For the honor of the good old North State, forward."

The soldiers listened to the fine words, and some were heartened, but all knew that many men would be wounded or killed within the next half hour. Col. Eppa Hunton of the Eighth Virginia remembered that

All appreciated the danger and felt it was probably the last charge to most of them. All seemed willing to die to achieve a victory there, which it was believed would be the crowning victory and the end of the war.

Lt. John Lewis of the Fourteenth Virginia also remembered:

If I live for a hundred years I shall never forget that moment or the command as given by General Lewis A. Armistead on that day. He was an old army officer, and was possessed of a very loud voice, which could be heard by the whole brigade. [He] gave the command, in words, as follows: "Attention, second battalion! Battalion of direction forward; guides center; march!" . . . He turned, placed himself about twenty paces in front of his brigade, and took the lead. His place was in the rear, properly. After moving, he placed his hat on the point of his sword, and held it above his head in front of him.

⟶═◉═⟵

THE UNION SOLDIERS atop Cemetery Ridge awaited the rebel advance. They never forgot the sight, especially the moment when twelve thousand rebel soldiers, spread out in lines a mile and a half long, first came into view. Bruce Catton described the reaction of the Union troops:

They were old soldiers and had been in many battles, but what they saw then took their breath away, and whether they had ten minutes or seventy-five years yet to live, they remembered it until they died. There it was, for the last time in this war, perhaps for the last time anywhere, the grand pageantry and color of war in the old style, beautiful and majestic and terrible: fighting men lined up for a mile and a half from flank to flank, slashed red flags overhead, soldiers marching forward elbow to elbow, officers with drawn swords, sunlight gleaming from thousands of musket barrels, lines dressed as if for parade.

A line of skirmishers came first, each man six feet from the next. A hundred yards behind them marched a second line of skirmishers and a hundred yards farther back the main assault force had assembled. Six brigades lined up at the northern end, marching under red flags, and to the south were two lines of five brigades, all under blue pennants. Everything was executed precisely, absolutely by the book, the men evenly spaced, the regiments and brigades the same distance apart.

They moved as one in stately, deliberate formation. Each man marched at 110 steps per minute, taking the same thirty-inch stride. Every minute they advanced nearly one hundred yards. They carried their weapons at right shoulder arms, their gleaming bayonets sparkling in the sunlight like so many thousands of tiny mirrors. One Yankee soldier described the sight as a river of silver flowing inexorably. Behind the main line, following each regiment and brigade, came the officers and their staffs with their regimental flags limp in the torpid air.

Behind the advancing units, regimental bands played jaunty martial airs. The steady, relentless, rhythmic beat of the drums and the cadence of many thousands of footfalls beating on the hard ground was mesmerizing. It was magnificent. It was frightening. It seemed that nothing could stop such a force.

To the Union troops clustered around the clump of trees in the middle of the Union line, the march was particularly awesome. The focus of the Confederate advance seemed to be on their sector. The 150 men of the First Minnesota were there, four hundred feet to the left of the trees. Sgt. James Wright described the Confederates as "A rising tide of armed men rolling toward us in steel crested billows. It was an intensely interesting sight, especially to us who must face it, brest it, break it, or be broken by it."

Lt. Frank Haskell, General Gibbon's aide, watched in fascinated horror as this "ocean of armed men" swept toward him. Later he described how "the dull gray masses deploy, man touching man, their horsemen gallop up and down . . . barrel and bayonet gleam in the sun, a sloping forest of flashing steel, magnificent, grim, irresistible."

The Union troops watched, prayed, and hunkered down behind whatever shelter they could improvise. Gibbon's portion of the line, the center where Meade had correctly predicted the Confederates would attack, had 5,750 men. They would be outnumbered by more than two to one. The stone walls of the Union line were only two to three feet high, not tall enough to keep cows in, so the local farmers had built rail fences over them. The soldiers heaped up rocks, bushes, tree limbs, even their own equipment to raise the barriers, hoping they would provide some protection from rebel bullets.

At one point a rail fence angled sharply to the east for a distance of 239 feet, then turned north again when it met another stone wall. Behind that angle sat the two guns of Lt. Alonzo Cushing's battery of the Fourth U.S. Artillery. Clutching his hands to his blood-soaked groin to keep his intestines from spilling out, he remained at his post, waiting with his men for the enemy to get close enough to kill.

All up and down the Union line, the scene was the same. As Lt. Frank Haskell described it,

The click of the lock as each man raised the hammer to feel with his fingers that the cap was on the nipple; the sharp jar as a musket touched a stone upon the wall when thrust in aiming over it, and the clicking of the iron axles as the guns were rolled up by hand a little further to the front, were quite all the sounds that could be heard. Cap-boxes were slid around to the front of the body; cartridge boxes opened, officers opened their pistol-holsters.

It would not be long now.

CHAPTER 12

THEY'VE BROKE ALL TO HELL!

THE LONG LINE OF rebel troops marched forward, keeping pace at a hundred yards a minute. They stopped to scale a five-foot rail fence then realigned their formation. The Union artillery chose that moment to open fire. Cannon from Cemetery Hill and Little Round Top, from the center and the flanks of the Union forces, spewed shells all along the Confederate line. The slaughter had begun, but the rebels relentlessly pushed on.

But at what cost! The bursting shells tore huge gaps in the formation. Every time a man fell, the rest automatically closed ranks. Projectiles exploded and solid shot tore through the lines of skirmishers, the front ranks, the second line of attack, and the file-closers bringing up the rear of the assault force. A single shell brought down fourteen men in one company.

Still they dressed ranks and moved on. A Union captain watching from the heights wrote in awe, "No one who saw them could help admiring the steadiness with which they came on, like the shadow of a cloud seen from a distance as it sweeps across a sunny field." No one stopped to aid the wounded. They stayed where they fell, to help themselves as best they could. Many were hit again where they lay.

One officer did halt when he saw a young soldier go down. Col. Eppa Hunton was there when Capt. Michael Spessard of the Twenty-eighth Virginia stopped to kneel and cradle a dying soldier's head. "Look at my poor boy, Colonel," Spessard said to Hunton. Spessard kissed his dead son and laid him gently on the ground. Then he drew his sword and raced toward the enemy. "Forward, boys!" he shouted.

The bombardment had become so intense by then that not all rebel soldiers were advancing so bravely. At first only a few men turned tail. The file-closers caught them and sent them back but the trickle quickly became a flood. Soon whole squads were running away. Officers blocked their paths, screaming at them and threatening to shoot—and surely some did.

But the majority of the soldiers acted honorably and followed orders. When they crossed half the distance to the Union line, which had taken eight minutes, they reached a swale that hid them from the Yankees' view. There Pickett halted and re-formed his troops so that when they marched out of the swale, they were once again at parade-ground perfection, although their lines were considerably shorter than when they started.

General Kemper rode back to Armistead, whose brigade marched behind his.

"Armistead," he shouted, "I am going to charge those heights and carry them and I want you to support me!"

"I'll do it," Armistead said. "Look at my line. It never looked better on dress parade."

⊷⧫⊶

THE LEAD ELEMENTS of the Confederate advance were almost 250 yards from the Union fortifications, within musket range. Given the command to fire, every man in Gibbon's division shot at the solid wall of rebel soldiers. Half the flags fell immediately as color bearers were cut down. Others retrieved the fallen colors but all formation vanished. There was no more grand review. Now the men rushed forward individually or in small groups, a ragged line full of holes.

"Their front line went down like grass before the scythe," wrote a sergeant in the First Minnesota. "Again and again we gave it to them."

"Close up!" Lt. Tom Dooley shouted. He later described what the advance was like.

Close up the ranks when a friend falls, while his life blood bespatters your cheek or throws a film over your eyes! Dress to left or right, while the bravest of the brave are sinking to rise no more! Still we press on. Oh, how long it seems before we reach those blazing guns. Our men are falling faster now, for the deadly musket is at work. Volley after volley of crashing musket balls sweeps through the line and mows us down.

Below the southernmost end of the rebel force, where Kemper's brigade was positioned on Pickett's right flank, was a nine-hundred-man unit from Vermont. Led by Brig. Gen. George J. Stannard, a former dry-goods merchant, the Second Vermont Brigade was composed of nine-months' men, whose enlistments were nearly up. They had spent most of their service on guard duty in Washington, D.C., and this was their last chance to show their fighting spirit before going home.

The Vermonters' portion of the line extended one hundred yards out in front of the other Union outfits, which allowed Stannard to see that Kemper's brigade was vulnerable to an attack on its open flank. Stannard ordered two of his three regiments to move forward, swing right, and open fire on Kemper's exposed flank. The results were devastating. Kemper's troops, fired on from the front and the side, fell by the hundreds.

"Glory to God! Glory to God!" shouted Gen. Abner Doubleday as he saw the rebels go down. "See the Vermonters go it!"

Hancock also witnessed Stannard's advance. As he watched, a rebel bullet passed through the pommel of his saddle and embedded itself in his groin, along with wood splinters and a ten-penny nail from the pommel. Hancock pulled out the nail, held it aloft, and allowed as how the rebels must be pretty hard up if they were shooting things like that at him. Aides applied pressure to stop the bleeding but Hancock refused to be taken to the hospital.

Gen. John Gibbon was wounded in the left shoulder. Bleeding heavily, he soon became so weakened that he had to be transported to the rear for treatment.

At almost the same time that Stannard's Vermonters dealt the Confederate right flank such a staggering blow, the Eighth Ohio attacked the left. It was a classic example of double envelopment, in which an attacking force is struck simultaneously on both flanks. As the Ohio troops opened up with blistering musket and cannon fire, Pettigrew's division on the Confederate left flank seemed to dissolve in smoke.

The carnage was so extensive that witnesses recalled seeing human limbs, parts of guns, even knapsacks blown high in the air by the force of the explosions. "A moan went up from the field, distinctly to be heard amid the roar of battle." It was the eerie sound of the wounded and dying. Pettigrew's division pressed on, but as they neared the Union line, artillerymen in front of them fired canisters loaded with buckshot. Other gunners on Cemetery Hill hit them with solid case and explosive shells until even the most battle-hardened veteran could take no more. Shattered, Pettigrew's troops ran.

Moxley Sorrel, Longstreet's aide, described it as a "sight never before witnessed—part of the Army of Northern Virginia in full, breathless flight." The stream became a torrent of retreating men. A few officers brandished weapons and regimental colors, trying to threaten or shame the men back into line, but there was no way to stop the rout. Half of

Pettigrew's men—nearly one-quarter of the total assault force—were in flight. As if the panic were contagious, nearby units also joined the retreat. Pettigrew's line of advance, which had extended more than three thousand feet, suddenly had shrunk to no more than eight hundred feet.

Kemper's troops at the other end of the rebel line, on Pickett's right flank, which had been hit so hard by the Vermonters, also started to break apart. Kemper tried to rally the men after the Union attack. He had risen in his stirrups, pointed his sword at the stone wall ahead of them, and shouted, "There are the guns, boys. Go for them!" But his call to glory was ignored. The men turned and ran in the opposite direction, back to Seminary Ridge where they had started.

It was only a handful of soldiers at first, but that was all it took to demoralize the men, considering how many friends they had already lost and how hopeless the fight appeared. The rebels were caught between solid walls of shot and shell from front and right. The unit drifted leftward, away from Stannard's troops. Soon they were no longer moving toward Cemetery Ridge but parallel to it. That put them under fire from the rear, from Stannard's men, and from the side by the main Union line. When Kemper went down, badly wounded, their confusion and terror mounted. Thus, for the Confederate line as a whole, the right flank could no longer be counted on to press the attack.

With both flanks unprotected, Pickett's division at the center was not large enough to carry the fight by itself. Reinforcements would be needed.

⚬

CAPT. ROBERT BRIGHT pushed his way to the rear, looking scornfully on the hundreds of men he considered cowards and skulkers. He tried to stop a few but they paid him no heed. He caught the attention of one enlisted man and asked why he was running away. The man stared at him, confused, and said, "Why, good gracious, Captain, aren't you runnin' yourself?"

Bright suddenly realized that his rapid ride toward the rear made him seem like a common deserter. He hurried on toward Seminary Ridge to find General Longstreet. Bright was carrying a message from General Pickett.

He found Longstreet sitting atop a fence rail staring into the distance. Retreating soldiers swept by on all sides, some wounded, many not. Bright saluted and passed on Pickett's message: Pickett was confident he could capture the Union position, but he would not be able to hold it unless Longstreet sent reinforcements. Longstreet asked Bright what had happened to the troops on Pickett's flanks.

"Look over your shoulder and you will see them," Bright said.

Lt. Col. Arthur Fremantle rode up. Despite his senior rank in the Coldstream Guards and his time visiting armies in North and South, he had never witnessed combat. He was quite excited about the battle.

"I wouldn't have missed this for anything," he said to Longstreet.

"The devil you wouldn't!" Longstreet said with a brief laugh. "I would like to have missed it very much. We've attacked and been repulsed. Look there!" He pointed to the ranks of Confederate soldiers retreating from the direction of Cemetery Ridge. "The charge is over."

Longstreet turned to Pickett's aide.

"Captain Bright, ride to General Pickett and tell him what you have heard me say to Colonel Fremantle."

⁂

IT HAS BEEN described as the "valley of death, covered with clover as soft as a Turkish carpet." Despite Longstreet's assertion that the charge was over, the Virginians of Pickett's division plodded forward, heads down, bodies slanted as though breasting a strong wind. About thirty yards from the Yankee line, they loosed their rebel yell, fired their muskets, and ran toward the enemy.

Union gunners opened up as Pickett's men came within canister range, firing as rapidly as they could reload those large tin cans filled with inch-thick steel balls that sprayed a wide pattern like oversize shotguns. Some gunners loaded their pieces with double canister, firing two cans at a time. The results were deadly. Few could withstand such an onslaught.

The Confederate charge also took its toll. Lieutenant Cushing of the Fourth U.S. Artillery, despite grievous wounds to his groin, managed to fire canister shot. In obvious pain, he raised his field glasses to his eyes. A bullet struck him in the mouth and spun him to his right. Sgt. Frederick Fuger caught him and gently laid him on the ground. Cushing was dead.

Another officer moved to take Cushing's place. He, too, was hit. A third man ran to the gun. A bullet passed through his chest, killing him instantly. Brig. Gen. Alexander Webb, commander of Gibbon's Second Brigade, ordered Sergeant Fuger to salvage what was left of the battery. The horses had long since been killed, so the men pulled the serviceable guns by hand through the rebel musket fire. The Fourth U.S. Artillery was out of action.

Pickett's men crept forward into the hail of fire, nearing the stone walls. Young Tom Dooley was hit.

Shot through both thighs, I fall about thirty yards from the guns. By my side lies Lieutenant Kehoe, shot through the knees. Here we lie, he in excessive pain, I fearing to bleed to death, the dead and dying all around. Oh, how I long to know the result, the end of this fearful charge. What can our poor remnant of a shattered division do?

The survivors of the rebel advance no longer formed a wide front. The men massed together in a rough, irregular wedge, running, yelling, firing, converging on the clump of trees at the center of the Union line, a short distance behind the low stone wall.

Waiting for them were the men of the Seventy-first and Sixty-ninth

Pennsylvania Volunteers. The troops of the Seventy-first were at the Angle, the point where the wall bent straight back to the east before turning north again. The outfit was inexperienced, lacking discipline and cohesion as a unit, and overwhelmed by the fury of the rebels bearing down. The scared, green troops believed they were outnumbered— that no matter how many rebels they cut down, there would be more behind them. The Seventy-first could not kill them fast enough and now the rebels were almost at the wall.

And so the Seventy-first Pennsylvania turned and ran, the color-bearers and officers as well. Only a few men stayed at their post, only to be captured or killed on the spot. The Confederates were almost gleeful as they scaled the stone wall. They had breached the Yankee line. And if they could force one Union regiment to panic and run, then they could do the same to others.

The Yankee regiment to the right, next in line, was the Sixty-ninth Pennsylvania. But when the rebels looked ahead, following the fleeing enemy, they saw a solid line of Union infantry two hundred feet beyond the wall preparing to open fire. A quick glance to the rear showed that no rebel units were behind them. There were no reinforcements, no fresh troops to support their advance. And so the Confederates slipped back over the wall, hunkered down behind it, and returned the Yankee fire, wondering what had happened to their commander, General Garnett.

Garnett was dead, shot through the brain and toppled from his horse, Red Eye, which stampeded across the field bleeding from a massive shoulder wound. Garnett's aide knelt beside him but found no signs of life. He took Garnett's watch, to return to his family, and left the general's sword by his side.

General Webb, commander of the Second Brigade, found himself ranking Union officer on the field where the rebels had chased the Seventy-first Pennsylvania from the wall. He rode over to the Seventy-second Pennsylvania, which had been held in reserve. This was the outfit that fired on the rebels when they jumped the stone wall. Webb urged them to charge the Confederates and dislodge them from their position beyond the wall, but the Pennsylvanians would not budge.

They maintained a steady fire on the rebels and continued to take casualties in return, but they refused Webb's order to move out. The issue for the Seventy-second was not bravery—they had not run when the Seventy-first broke—but the fact that the soldiers did not know who Webb was. He had been in command only six days; many of the men had never seen him before. Under these conditions, they were not about to obey a total stranger.

Webb shouted his orders again but could not be heard over the noise of battle. He brandished his sword overhead and pointed toward the rebels, but the Seventy-second did not move. Now desperate and angry, Webb grabbed the regimental flagstaff from Color Sergeant William Finnessey, thinking that if he advanced with the regimental colors in hand, surely the men would follow. But Finnessey refused to relinquish the flag. Color-bearer was a high honor. Men selected to carry the flag had vowed to hold on to the colors to the death.

So there they stood, the general and the color sergeant, while bullets whizzed all around them, engaging in a tug-of-war for the flag. Finally, in disgust, General Webb released the staff and stalked off to the next regiment along the stone wall, the Sixty-ninth Pennsylvania. When he reached their position he ordered the three companies nearest the break in the line to fall back and form a new line at a right angle to the wall.

Now if the rebels climbed the wall again, they would be boxed in by Union troops at their front and their right flank, with the stone wall at the Angle on their left. But if the Pennsylvanians could not hold them there, the way would be open for the Confederates clear to the rear of Cemetery Ridge. Webb knew that the battle could be lost at the Angle.

→─◉─←

ANOTHER GENERAL ALSO saw the opportunity afforded by the undefended stretch at the Angle that had been abandoned by the Yankees. Lewis Armistead—his sword supporting his old black hat, though it had slipped down to the hilt—led his brigade toward the sector held by the Sixty-ninth Pennsylvania. He noticed to his left that Confederate soldiers were already at the wall. He turned in that direction. Col. Rawley Martin of the Fifty-third Virginia was at his side. They reached the wall and found Garnett's brigade behind it, firing at the Yankees. Armistead turned to Martin.

"We can't stop here," he shouted. "We must go over that wall."

"Then we'll go forward," Martin said. "Forward the colors!" he yelled to his men.

Martin was hit immediately in the leg and fell back. Armistead pushed his battered hat to the tip of his sword, and stepped over the wall.

"Come on, boys," he called, "we must give them the cold steel. Who will follow me?"

Approximately one hundred men—though some put the number as high as three hundred—followed Armistead over the wall and up the slope toward the Seventy-second Pennsylvania. That outfit and the three companies of the Sixty-ninth positioned by General Webb poured on devastating fire.

One of the many cut down was Col. Tazewell Patton, who had predicted he would die that day. He and another officer had joined hands and were stepping atop the wall together. "It's our turn next, Tazewell!" the other man shouted. A musket ball tore away most of Patton's lower jaw. One of his men leaned over him to ask how badly he was hurt. Patton could not speak; his tongue had been torn away and blood gushed from his mouth. Although he did not die that day, soon his wound would prove fatal.

Twelve days after being wounded, Tazewell Patton wrote to his mother:

It has now been nearly two weeks since I have been stretched out on this bed of suffering. You will doubtless have heard before this reaches you that I was badly wounded and left in the hands of the enemy. My sufferings and hardships during about two weeks that I was kept out in the field hospital were very great. As soon as I am able to travel, I will hurry homeward.

He died six days later.[1]

⊷═◯═⊶

ARMISTEAD AND HIS rapidly dwindling band of followers struggled up the slope of Cemetery Ridge toward one of the guns Alonzo Cushing had left behind. Sgt. Drewry Easley, the file-closer, was with them. A fresh volley from Union guns slammed into the small rebel band. Armistead doubled over, dropped his sword, and clutched at his stomach with his left hand. His right hand closed over his blood-splattered left arm to steady himself.

He stayed on his feet and staggered toward Cushing's number three cannon. Reaching out blindly with both hands, Armistead groped the air until he touched the gun's barrel. He held on for a moment, dropped to his knees, and fell on the ground beneath the muzzle of the gun.

That was the moment historians have called the Confederacy's high-water mark, when "the road lay open to Washington." The rebels who had crossed the wall had in fact breached the Union line. Had there been sufficient numbers of them, and more advancing behind them, they could have carried the day and perhaps the war. But Armistead's charge was as far as Pickett's troops would go and as close to victory as the Confederates would ever come.

When Armistead went down, the rebel advance collapsed. Discipline deteriorated; it was every man for himself. Pvt. Milton Harding of the Ninth Virginia tried to aid Armistead. He gave the general a sip

---

[1] Tazewell Patton's loyal servant carried a strip of the colonel's bloodstained under-shirt back to the family in Virginia. It became a treasured keepsake for his grandson, George.

of brandy from his canteen and offered to take him back to Confederate lines. Armistead refused, ordering Harding to save himself.

Sergeant Easley remained with Armistead, returning the Yankee fire. It soon became too dangerous for him to stay. Bullets struck the ground so close that Easley was stung by gravel flung up by the Union fire. A Yankee musket ball snapped his ramrod, preventing him from reloading. Easley, Harding, and a few others were able to return to the Angle at the wall, but most of the men did not.

Easley grabbed a weapon from a wounded soldier, but when he tried to load it, the ball went only halfway down the barrel. The soldier on the ground rolled over and told him the rifle was already loaded. Easley looked the man over and saw that he was only pretending to be wounded. He was a shirker, refusing to do his duty. Easley was furious. Enraged, he raised the musket over his head and smashed the butt against the man's head.

It looked as if the rebels were all about to die there, hugging the ground on the western side of the wall. No one was coming to help them. The only men in gray they could see were racing back toward Seminary Ridge.

The ending to Pickett's charge at the Angle—the Bloody Angle—was savage. Frenzied Union soldiers closed in for the kill. The First Minnesota was once again in the thick of the fighting. Lt. William Harmon wrote,

If men ever became devils, that was one of the times. We were crazy with the excitement of the fight. We just rushed in like wild beasts. Men swore and cursed and struggled and fought, grappled in hand-to-hand fight, threw stones, clubbed their muskets, kicked, yelled and hurrahed. But it was over in no time.

It was about four o'clock in the afternoon, and most of the rebels at the Angle flung up their hands in surrender. Looking down on the scene from Cemetery Hill, Capt. James Stewart shouted, "By God, boys, we've got 'em now. They've broke all to hell!"

And out beyond the Bloody Angle, hundreds of bodies of Confederate dead and wounded lay in the scorching sun. Among them, Lt. Thomas Dooley, in pain and immobile from his wounds, heard the yells coming from the victorious Union forces:

There—listen—we hear a new shout, and cheer after cheer rends the air. Are those fresh troops advancing to our support? No, no! That huzzah never broke from southern lips. Oh God! Virginia's bravest, noblest sons have perished here today and perished all in vain!

⊷═◉═⊷

NO MORE THAN six thousand of those who marched so smartly and proudly across the valley to meet the enemy made their way back. The rest had been killed or captured. Many of those who returned were wounded. "We gained nothing but glory," one Confederate officer said, "and lost our bravest men."

Everywhere one looked, in every direction, lay death and destruction. The place of greatest devastation was where it ended, the Bloody Angle. Henry Taylor of the First Minnesota gazed at the dead rebels there and in the valley beyond and felt he had avenged the death of his brother. Another soldier, one of General Stannard's Vermonters, described the scene:

If there was any one spot on that great field of battle that approximated more nearly than any other the maelstrom of destruction, this was the place. They lay one upon the other clutched in death, side by side. The dead, dying, and horribly wounded, some had on the blue, but nearly all wore the gray. . . . This was indeed the great slaughter pen on the field of Gettysburg.

Now there were the living to deal with, the hundreds of Confederate troops to be rounded up. The Minnesotans alone took five hundred prisoners that afternoon, and most came along peacefully, though Lt.

William Harmon had a close call: "[A Confederate soldier] drew a bead on me and was about to shoot when I covered him with my revolver and told him to drop his gun. He did, too, and it was all I could do to keep the boys from killing him."

There is no record of rebel soldiers being killed while surrendering to Union troops. Most of the prisoners were too dazed and spent to cause trouble. They dropped their muskets and ambled along wherever they were ordered to go. A few Union officers grew concerned that the number of Confederate prisoners was far larger than the number of Union troops herding them to the rear. What if the rebels decided to reclaim the discarded muskets and pistols and turn on their captors?

But the Southern troops were too weary and dispirited to rally. After a while, the Yankee soldiers realized that the prisoners presented no threat. Out of pity, they began to share food and drink from their own limited supplies. Some Union soldiers removed their caps as the prisoners filed by, a mark of respect for brave opponents.

When the Confederate officers surrendered, each handed his sword to a Union officer of equal or higher rank, by custom. Many Yankee officers soon found themselves burdened with more swords than they could carry, and they passed them on to others for souvenirs. The Confederates expressed surprise at how few Union troops were guarding them. One colonel looked around at the handful of Union soldiers and asked where all the troops were that they had fought. When told that these soldiers had fought unaided at the Angle, the colonel was amazed.

"If we only had had another line, we could have whipped you," he said. Then he looked around again and shook his head. "By God, we could have whipped you as it was!"

Some rebel soldiers took a bit of persuading before they would surrender, and a few others refused to give up at all. Sgt. Drewry Easley was loading a new rifle, having used his old one to bash the head of a shirker, when he found three bayonets pointed at him. He surrendered quietly.

Maj. John Timberlake of the Fifty-sixth Virginia ordered his men to cease firing when Union troops closed to within twenty feet. Some refused until the last moment, when the Yankees threatened to run them through with their bayonets.

Timberlake was dressing a soldier's wound when a Union officer demanded that he surrender. At least a dozen men surrounded him, leveling their rifles. He said he would not surrender until he finished aiding the wounded man. The Yankees waited, and when Timberlake finally rose and handed his sword to the Union officer, the man accepted it with a remark Timberlake never forgot. "You are a damned brave set of fellows," he said.

Maj. John Richardson of the Fifty-second North Carolina had been badly wounded. His captors realized that nothing could be done except to give him opium to dull the pain and ease his death. As the drug took effect, Richardson spotted an American flag nearby. "After all, after all," he whispered, "that is the glorious old flag." He died moments later.

Badly wounded rebel soldiers expecting to die often wrote last letters home, hoping that a kindhearted Yankee would post them. A man from Alabama wrote to his mother,

I am here a prisoner-of-war and mortally wounded. I can live but a few hours more at the farthest. I was shot fifty yards [from] the enemy's lines. They have been exceedingly kind to me. Do not mourn my loss. I had hoped to have been spared, but a righteous God has ordered it otherwise and I feel prepared to trust my care in His hands. Farewell to you all. Pray that God may receive my soul. Your unfortunate son, John.

Sgt. June Kimble resigned himself to surrender. He lay down his rifle and unbuckled his cartridge belt, then changed his mind. He raced back toward Seminary Ridge. Abruptly he turned and walked backward for awhile, horrified at the thought that he might be found shot in the back. He did not want to die and also be thought a coward.

Capt. Michael Spessard, who had lost his son on the march to Cemetery Ridge, rose up from behind the stone wall to confront three Union soldiers. Determined not to be taken prisoner, Spessard grabbed some rocks from atop the wall, threw them at the soldiers, and fled in the resulting confusion.

Most of those who ran for safety reached Confederate lines, despite the distance and the absence of cover. Union fire at the fleeing troops was sparse. The commander of the Thirteenth Vermont had ordered his men not to shoot at the rebels. And many a Yankee soldier thought there had already been enough killing for one day.

One man who had no chance to get away was Lewis Armistead. Nor did he have much chance to live very long. He had remained conscious and alert enough to recognize a familiar face, Sgt. Frederick Fuger, of the Fourth U.S. Artillery. Fuger had served under Armistead out west in the old army before the war. Armistead called out Fuger's name.

"I thought it was you, Sergeant," Armistead said, "and if I had known that you were in command of that battery, I never should have led the charge against you."

Without a word, Fuger abruptly turned away and left the badly wounded man on the ground. A Union captain passing by stopped beside Armistead. When the general identified himself as a Mason, the captain, who was also a Mason, offered to help. He rounded up two soldiers who placed Armistead on a stretcher and carried him to a surgeon at the rear. When the surgeon examined him, he confirmed what Armistead probably already knew. Nothing could be done to save him.

An aide to General Hancock happened by, noticed the braid on Armistead's uniform, and volunteered to see that any valuables the general wished for his family to have would be conveyed to them. When Armistead learned that the young man was Hancock's aide, he said he was an old friend and asked the aide to pass on a message to

Hancock. There are at least two versions of Armistead's words at that moment. They became highly controversial, even incendiary, in the South, because they give the impression that on his deathbed, Armistead renounced the Confederate cause.

"Say to General Hancock for me that I have done him, and you all, a grievous injury, which I shall always regret." The other version reads, "Tell General Hancock that I know I did my country a great wrong when I took up arms against her, for which I am sorry, but for which I cannot live to atone."

Armistead told the aide to take his watch, spurs, and other personal items to Hancock. General Hancock, who was standing only a few hundred yards away at the time, never saw his old friend again.

⸻◉⸻

SHORTLY AFTER THE end of the battle at the Bloody Angle, while the prisoners were being rounded up, Gen. George Meade appeared over the crest of the hill. The first person he saw was Gibbon's aide, Lt. Frank Haskell.

"How is it going here?" Meade asked.

"I believe, General, that the enemy's attack is repulsed."

Incredulous, Meade stared at the lieutenant.

"What! Is the assault already repulsed?"

"It is, sir."

"Thank God."

Meade lifted his right hand as if to raise his hat in a cheer but could not bring himself to complete the gesture. Instead, he gave a feeble wave of his hand and in an unemotional tone of voice uttered, "Hurrah." His son, considerably less restrained than his father, snatched off his hat, waved it wildly in the air, and shouted "Hurrah! Hurrah! Hurrah!"

General Meade sat quietly astride his horse for several more minutes, looking over the battlefield. Then, knowing that both Gibbon and Hancock had been wounded, told Lieutenant Haskell to pass his orders to whomever had assumed command in their sector. He wanted the troops back on the line as soon as possible in case the rebels launched another attack. He informed Haskell that he would arrange for reinforcements to be sent up. "If the enemy does attack," Meade said, "charge him in the flanks and sweep him from the field."

Meade said nothing about a counterattack, about assaulting the Confederates while they were on the run in temporary disarray. But others were urging Meade to do just that. Not far from the Angle, General Hancock lay on a stretcher penning a note to Meade. His aide brought him Lo Armistead's personal effects and spoke his old friend's final words. There is no record of Hancock's reaction.

Hancock urged Meade to use the Fifth and Sixth Corps to counterattack and destroy the rebels. He added, "The enemy must be short of ammunition, as I was shot with a tenpenny nail. I did not leave the field until the victory was entirely secured and the enemy no longer in sight."

Other corps commanders, notably Doubleday and Howard, also urged an immediate attack against the Confederate forces. But the officer who urged an offensive more aggressively than anyone else, at least according to his own account, was Meade's cavalry commander, Maj. Gen. Alfred Pleasonton. And he made his plea in person, not in writing. He spurred his horse, rode up to Meade, and congratulated him on his splendid victory.

"General, I will give you half an hour to show yourself a great general. Order the army to advance, while I will take the cavalry and get in Lee's rear, and we will finish the campaign in a week."

Meade was not persuaded. He suggested to Pleasonton that they had done quite well enough, and there was still the question whether Robert E. Lee might try to launch another assault. Pleasonton pressed his case, arguing that Lee had lost too many men over the past three days to continue the campaign so soon. Also, the rebels had to be low on artillery ammunition and were far from their base of supplies.

Meade did not answer. He had made his decision and had nothing more to say about the issue. As far as he was concerned, this was not the time to attack the rebels. His army was not up to it. Almost one-fourth of the Union troops were dead or wounded, the rest exhausted from three days of fighting. He felt that their own supply of artillery ammunition was inadequate. And even if the men were in condition to attack, they would be charging the enemy over an open field against a strongly fortified position. That was precisely what Lee had just done and suffered a major defeat. No, to Meade, a counterattack was out of the question.

As he rode along the front line, his men cheered loudly and lustily. Somewhere in the background a regimental band played "Hail to the Chief." A newspaper reporter edged his way close to Meade.

"Ah! General Meade," he said, "you're in very great danger of being President of the United States."

Meade thought that was quite enough victory, enough triumph, for one day.

⊷⊶

THERE WERE NO cheers on the Confederate side; the triumphant yells of the Yankees could be heard from across the way. George Pickett was in tears as he slowly rode back to Seminary Ridge.

"Don't stop any of my men," he told the officer commanding the picket line. "Tell them to come to the camp we occupied last night."

He spied Col. Walter Taylor, Lee's chief of staff.

"Taylor," Pickett sobbed, "we've lost all our friends."

He rode on until he reached Longstreet.

"General," Pickett said, "I am ruined, my division is gone. It is destroyed."

Longstreet tried to console him, to assure him that all would be well, given time. But Longstreet was wrong. Pickett had lost his bid for fame and would never have such a chance again. He could not know how history would eventually record the events of Gettysburg, that long after his death he would be accorded glory. All he knew at the moment was that his reputation had been shattered, his good name destroyed.[2]

There were those who believed Pickett got what he deserved. Some thought his behavior had been disgraceful, even cowardly. He had begun the advance as a division commander should, riding behind his brigades in a position from which he could see and direct their movements. As his troops neared Cemetery Ridge, Pickett and his staff withdrew behind a barn, one of the few structures in the valley, where he had an unobstructed view of the entire operation. Again, this was a logical position from which to exercise command of such a sizable force spread out over a great expanse.

But once it could be seen that Pickett's men faced defeat all along the Yankee line, particularly at the Angle, Pickett became, according to historian George Stewart, "only an agonized spectator of the disaster":

He had become wholly useless. At this point, honor and military procedure both demanded that he should gallop forward, join his own troops, and either inspire them to an advance, or give them orders suitable to the emergency.

A 1998 biographer, Lesley Gordon, issued a harsher judgment. Instead of rushing forward to his men,

---

[2] After Gettysburg, Pickett married young Sallie; but his military career ended abruptly when he lost most of his division at Five Forks, Virginia. His men were attacked by Union troops while he was some distance away enjoying himself at a shad bake. At Appomattox, Lee relieved Pickett of command the day before the surrender. Broken in spirit and facing financial ruin, Pickett first failed at farming and then took a job selling insurance policies. After his death in 1875, however, he was proclaimed a hero of epic proportions throughout the South. For decades Sallie promoted his reputation in lectures, magazines, and books, embellishing the legend with elaborate distortions of the truth.

Pickett stood transfixed in horror and disbelief as his Virginian division crumbled before his tear-filled eyes. In his self-absorbed despair, he failed to answer to the needs of his battered troops, and he again exhibited a loss of control.

When his men were beaten back to the western side of the stone wall and the Yankees were closing in, all of which Pickett could clearly see, he spurred his horse around and rode to the rear.

After Pickett declared to Longstreet that he was ruined, he met up with Robert E. Lee, who told him to place his division nearby and prepare to repel an enemy attack.

"General Lee," Pickett said bitterly, "I have no division now."

"Come, General Pickett," Lee said, "this has been my fight and upon my shoulders rests the blame."

And those were the words Lee used to greet every man who returned that afternoon, each soldier of every rank from private to general. The defeat had been his fault, he repeated to the survivors. He was the one who lost the fight. All would be well in the end, but now they must rally and be prepared for the inevitable Union attack.

At no time that afternoon or for the rest of his days did Lee ever attempt to shift the blame for the Confederate defeat onto anyone else. Then, as later, he would say only, "All this has been my fault. It is I that have lost this fight."

To the British observer, Colonel Fremantle, Lee admitted, "This has been a sad day for us, Colonel, a sad day, but we can't expect always to gain victories."

Among the returning troops were a few Union soldiers who had been captured. When one wounded man saw Lee, he called out, "Hurrah for the Union." Everyone stopped, wondering how the great general would react. Lee dismounted and walked over to the soldier, who later said he expected to be killed on the spot. Instead, Lee extended his hand. "My son," he said, "I hope you will soon be well."

FOR THE RESIDENTS of Gettysburg, the afternoon had been long and terrifying. Most people, like Sallie Broadhead and her husband, huddled in their cellars during the two-hour bombardment and the battle that followed. Sallie recorded her thoughts about the suffering going on around them:

> We knew that with every explosion and the scream of each shell, human beings were hurried, through excruciating pain, into another world, and that many more were torn, and mangled, and lying in torment worse than death.

She also dreaded the possibility that the rebels might win, but there was no way to get any news. "We shall see tomorrow," she wrote in her diary. "It will be the 4th of July, and the Rebels have promised us a glorious day. If it only ends the battle and drives them off it will be glorious, and I will rejoice."

All afternoon townspeople waited in the shelter of their homes, wondering about the outcome, and praying that a stray shell would not harm them. But by the third day of the fighting, people were restless. It was increasingly hard to keep the children indoors. The mind-numbing heat made everyone miserable, and the stench of decay was overpowering.

> The combination of overburdened privies, the decomposition of the bodies of men and horses lying unburied in the town, thousands of unwashed bodies, and the decaying of amputated flesh deposited outside the hospitals, were beginning to make the air in Gettysburg putrid.

Sallie Myers spent her time in the churches that had been converted to hospitals. She described the conditions as horrendous:

Along with the stench of unwashed bodies and infected wounds was the sight of blood everywhere, on walls and floors, covering pews, doorways and even the altars themselves. Amputated limbs quickly accumulated in piles, hastily carried or even thrown out doors and windows, part of a grisly, grotesque assembly line of heart-rending proportions.

Young Albertus McCreary and his friends soon got used to the shelling, the explosions, and the deep rumbling vibrations that shook the foundations of their houses. Full of adolescent curiosity, they climbed to the rooftops for a better view. Albertus watched a man on a neighboring roof peer around his chimney. A bullet chipped a piece of brick just above the man's head. Two bullets struck the roof of the McCreary house, within inches of Albertus and his brother. They scurried down to wait inside until the cannon fire ceased.

Many others watched from upper-story windows but were disappointed because they could see little through the dense smoke. Professor Michael Jacobs used his telescope and witnessed a stunning sight from his vantage point on Seminary Ridge. "There, as though I was almost upon them, I beheld Pickett's Division swinging into position." Jacobs called to his son to take a look. "Quick! Come! Come! You can see now what in your life you will never see again."

Conditions were difficult for fifteen-year-old Tillie Pierce, staying at a friend's house near Big Round Top on the Union side of the line. That morning the women had been sent away in case the farmhouse came under shellfire. They came back in the evening after the firing stopped.

"The whole country seemed filled with desolation," Tillie wrote. Fences had been smashed and the debris of war littered the ground. Tillie saw knapsacks, canteens, blankets, and other personal gear cast off by the soldiers. The most horrible sights were at the house. Wounded and dying men lay in the yard. People approaching the house had to step carefully around the bodies. Inside, surgeons were operating and amputating in almost every room. Tillie, who just a few days ago had been unable to stand the sight of blood, now capably cared for the wounded.

> To the south of the house and just outside the yard, I noticed a pile of limbs higher than the fence. It was a ghastly sight! Gazing upon these, too often the trophies of the amputating bench, I could have no other feeling than that the whole scene was one of cruel butchery. . . . Twilight now falls; another day has closed; with the soldiers saying that they believed this day the Rebels were whipped, but at an awful sacrifice.

--➤═◉═◄--

AT THREE O'CLOCK that same afternoon in Vicksburg, at the same time the long lines of doomed Confederate soldiers started toward Cemetery Ridge, General Pemberton rode to his meeting with Ulysses S. Grant. Accompanying him were General Bowen, Grant's old friend, and Colonel Montgomery.

As they rode, Pemberton was overheard to say,

> I feel a confidence that I shall stand justified to my Government if not to the Southern people. Should it be otherwise, the consolation of having done the only thing which in my opinion could give security to Vicksburg and to the surrounding country . . . will be reward enough.

Grant and Pemberton met on a hillside only a few hundred feet from Confederate lines. With Grant were Generals A. J. Smith, Edward Ord, James McPherson, and John Logan, as well as members of Grant's staff.

General Grant described the meeting:

> Pemberton and I had served in the same division during part of the Mexican War. I knew him well therefore and greeted him as an old

acquaintance. He soon asked what terms I proposed to give his army if it surrendered. My answer was the same as proposed in my reply to his letter. Pemberton then said, rather snappishly, "The conference might as well end," and turned abruptly as if to leave. I said, "Very well."

General Bowen salvaged the meeting by suggesting that he and General Smith discuss the situation. Grant and Pemberton agreed, and while their subordinates talked, the two commanders moved a short distance away to the shade of a stunted oak tree. Neither man revealed what was said, but their conversation did not break the impasse.

Bowen proposed that Confederate troops be allowed to march out from Vicksburg carrying their small arms and field artillery, with full military honors accorded them by the Union army. Grant "promptly and unceremoniously rejected" this suggestion. The meeting was over. The Confederates assumed that fighting would resume within minutes, no longer than it would take for Pemberton, Bowen, and Montgomery to ride back to their lines.

To Pemberton's surprise, Grant told him that he would send Pemberton a letter no later than ten o'clock that night, giving the final terms Grant would consider as a basis for surrender. Until then, the truce would remain in effect.

Grant returned to his headquarters and summoned his corps and division commanders. He described the morning's events and Pemberton's unwillingness to surrender unconditionally. He asked for their suggestions. This was the closest Grant had ever come to holding a council of war. Waging war by committee and consensus was not Grant's style. He typically made his own decisions and kept his own council about the factors that may have influenced his judgment.

And, characteristically, that was precisely what he did at Vicksburg. His war council was nearly unanimous as to the next step in the Union campaign but Grant acted against it. He wrote to Pemberton offering to parole all Confederate troops instead of taking them prisoner. This was completely contrary to the advice of his officers. But Grant opposed making such a sizable force prisoners of war, which would require the services of too many Union soldiers as well as navy transports to ship thirty thousand rebels to Cairo, Illinois, the nearest transportation hub. Such a venture would easily have taken a month. Grant wanted to end the siege and declare victory on the Fourth of July, and so he offered parole as an inducement for Pemberton to surrender.

That night, he wrote to Pemberton proposing that one Union division march into Vicksburg the following morning to maintain order while the formal surrender took place.

> As soon as rolls can be made out and paroles be signed by officers and men, you will be allowed to march out of our lines, the officers taking with them their sidearms and clothing; and the field, staff, and cavalry officers one horse each. The rank and file will be allowed all their clothing, but no other property. If these conditions are accepted, any amount of rations you may deem necessary can be taken from the stores you now have, and also the necessary cooking utensils for preparing them. Thirty wagons also will be allowed to transport such articles as cannot be carried along.

After Grant sent this letter, containing what he considered to be generous conditions, he told his commanders to instruct their men on guard duty to mention his decision to their counterparts on the rebel side. The Union soldiers were to tell the rebels that Grant had offered to parole them if Pemberton surrendered. If Pemberton rejected Grant's offer, he hoped the rebel soldiers would make their displeasure known.

Pemberton believed that Grant would offer parole for his men even before he received the letter. The Confederate intelligence service had intercepted flag signal messages between Grant and Admiral Porter. Porter had complained that shipping thirty thousand prisoners of war north to prison camps would be an impossible burden for his transport system. That information may have encouraged Pemberton to press Grant for an additional concession, which he stated in his reply:

> In the main, your terms are accepted; but, in justice both to the honor and spirit of my troops, manifested in the defense of Vicksburg, I have to submit the following amendments, which, if acceded to by you, will perfect the agreement between us. At ten o'clock A.M. tomorrow I propose to evacuate the works in and around Vicksburg, and to surrender the city and garrison under my command, by marching out with my colors and arms, stacking them in front of my present lines, after which you will take possession.

Grant received Pemberton's letter after midnight, in the early hours of July 4. If surrender were to occur on that auspicious day, agreement would have to be reached quickly. But Grant could not allow himself to accept Pemberton's proposal that his troops leave the city and continue on their way without waiting for each man to receive a formal parole. If that happened, the Confederates would be neither prisoners nor parolees and so would be free to join Joe Johnston's army and fight the Union again.

Grant insisted that the rebel troops be formally paroled so they could not officially fight again until the cumbersome and time-consuming process of exchange would eventually allow them to return to active duty. Also, Grant knew, as did Pemberton, that many paroled soldiers simply went home and never returned to the army.

Grant replied immediately to Pemberton's request:

> The amendment proposed by you cannot be acceded to in full. It will be necessary to furnish every officer and man with a parole signed by himself, which, with the completion of the roll of prisoners, will necessarily take some time. If you mean by your proposition for each brigade to march to the front of the lines now occupied by it, and stack arms at ten o'clock A.M., and then return to the inside and

there remain as prisoners until properly paroled, I will make no objection to it. Should no notification be received of your acceptance of my terms by nine o'clock A.M., I shall regard them as having been rejected, and shall act accordingly.

Pemberton knew he had no choice. He accepted Grant's proposal and the siege of Vicksburg was over.

⋆⇒◉⇐⋆

VICKSBURG'S SOLDIERS AND civilians did not realize on July 3 that their fate was being decided. To many, the truce was like a holiday. Rebels and Yankees crossed each other's lines, socializing and reveling in the peace. Pvt. Isaac Jackson of the Eighty-third Ohio described the day in a letter to his brother and sister. "All during the day the forts on both sides covered with men, parties met halfway between the forts and had quite a social time indeed. The Rebs were very low in spirits. They could not entirely hide it."

Hosea Road of the Twelfth Wisconsin recalled hearing one of his buddies, Henry Marston, cry out to another soldier:

"Joe, come here with your gun, quick—mine isn't loaded! Look at that Johnny right on top of the works! What does he mean by getting up there in that way! There's another, and another! Why, the whole Rebel army is coming up! What in the name of General Grant is going to happen now!"

Hank's animated remarks brought every man to his feet, and, sure enough, the whole Rebel line was swarming with men in gray who seemed to have nothing to do but gaze towards us.

Suddenly one of the Union soldiers announced that he was going over to shake hands with those rebels, and off he went, running toward the Confederate line. A rebel soldier ventured out to meet him. They shook hands as men on both sides looked on. Then they dropped their guns and tumbled out of their forts and trenches, racing toward each other, many with outstretched arms, "shaking hands as cordially as if they were brethren."

The day was not so happy for the civilians of Vicksburg. Although relieved that the shelling had stopped, most people were apprehensive about the future. "What could it mean?" Mrs. Lord asked. She knew that Pemberton and Bowen had gone to meet with the Yankees. "A sickening dread and anxiety filled our hearts," she recalled. Just before dark, a friend of the Lords, one of General Bowen's staff officers, visited them.

He said he was not certain of the details, "but he greatly feared the meeting was to arrange terms for surrender. At all events there was to be no firing that night, and in the morning we would know it was all right if they resumed firing."

The officer added that General Bowen had requested him to thank Mrs. Lord for embroidering the wreath around the stars on his collar. She replied,

> I told the Major to say to General Bowen, I had felt it an honor to be employed in such a manner for so brave a man, but if he had worn it in an interview with General Grant for the surrender of Vicksburg, I could only wish that I could take out every stitch I had put in.

Lucy McRae, recovered from her injuries when a Yankee shell struck her cave, recorded the events of July 3. On that evening, she wrote,

> All was quiet. People could be seen walking around, concluding that the silence meant dreadful things on the morrow. We were all sitting outside the cave, twilight approaching, when father came in sight. Mother thought father [who had remained at home] had decided to die with his family the next day, for everybody thought that General Grant would make the effort of his life to take the city on the 4th. Father came to mother, looking sad, with tears in his eyes, and said,

"You can all come home for a night's rest. General Pemberton has surrendered, and General Grant will enter the city in the morning." We went home.

⊸≡⊜⊱

IT WAS AFTER midnight—the Fourth of July had begun—when Robert E. Lee returned to his headquarters camp. Brig. Gen. John Imboden, commander of an independent cavalry brigade, was waiting for him, as ordered. Imboden took note of "an expression of sadness that I had never seen upon [Lee's] face." Neither man spoke for a long time. Finally, to break the embarrassing silence, Imboden said, "General, this has been a hard day on you."

"Yes, it has been a sad, sad day to us," Lee replied, lapsing into silence again. After some minutes, he spoke again, his voice trembling with emotion.

"I never saw troops behave more magnificently than Pickett's division of Virginians did today in that grand charge upon the enemy. And if they had been supported as they were to have been—but for some reason not yet fully explained to me, were not—we would have held the position and the day would have been ours."

Imboden recalled, "After a moment's pause, [Lee] added in a loud voice, in a tone of almost agony, 'Too bad! *Too bad!* Oh. Too bad!'"

Lee invited Imboden into his tent, where he grew calmer.

"We must now return to Virginia," he said.

Robert E. Lee was going home.

CHAPTER 13

THE MOST GLORIOUS FOURTH

July 4, 1863

"THIS MORNING, ABOUT six o'clock, I heard a great noise in the street," wrote Sallie Broadhead, "and going to the door I saw a rebel officer on horseback hallooing to some soldiers on foot, to 'Hurry up, the Yankees have possession of the town and all would be captured.' I looked up the street and saw our men in the public square, and it was a joyful sight, for I knew we were now safe."

Mary McAllister was asleep in a chair by the front window of her house when she was awakened by a noise in the street. It was the sound of wagons, and she knew instantly what it meant. She told her sister, "I believe the Confederates are retreating."

"The rebels have left," Sallie Myers noted in her diary, "and we are once again in possession of the town. I never spent a happier Fourth."

It was over. The Confederates were in retreat but the wreckage they left behind in the town was awful. As people cautiously crept out of their homes and cellars, many saw for the first time the terrible devastation.

"All around us were evidences of a great battle," Fannie Buehler remembered.

The wounded, the dead and dying, all heaped together; horses that had fallen beneath their riders, with limbs shattered and torn—dead, wounded and bleeding—broken down artillery wagons, guns and knapsacks, cartridge boxes, capes, coats and shoes; indeed all the belongings of a soldier, and the soldier himself, all lying in the streets, so far as we could see, either up or down. Such was the awful scene spread out before us, as we ventured to the front of our house on the morning of the Fourth of July, 1863.

Many streets were barricaded as high as a man could reach, piled with wagons, furniture, rocks, lumber, fence rails, even kitchen stoves. Many of the houses, especially those near Cemetery Hill, had been scarred and pitted by musket balls and artillery shells that had torn gaping holes in walls and roofs.

The damage was worse inside houses that had sat empty during the three days of battle. Rebel soldiers had looted homes whose owners had fled. Any unoccupied house was an easy target for vandalism. Many small items had been stolen; whereas larger, heavier possessions—such as furniture, pianos, beds, and china—were typically smashed and destroyed. Albertus McCreary wrote,

There were some sorry-looking homes in our neighborhood. [At a friend's house] almost everything had been either cut to pieces or destroyed in some way. Pieces of furniture were burned and broken, a desk had been destroyed, bookcases knocked down, and the books torn and shattered. To add more to the disorder and destruction, the soldiers had taken a half-barrel of flour, mixed it with water to make a thin paste, put into this the feathers from feather-beds and thrown it over everything—walls, furniture and down the stairways.

The aroma over the town carried the stench of bodies—corpses of horses and men—left to decompose in the extreme heat over the past three days. The nauseating odor of rotting flesh would remain until autumn brought some cool weather. Millions of flies, and other insects and vermin, descended on Gettysburg to feast on the decaying flesh, spreading among the populace fears of pestilence and plague.

Before long a new odor threatened to overwhelm the residents. Chloride of lime, a powerful disinfectant, was spread daily over streets and sidewalks to fight the possibility of disease. Albertus McCreary remembered how people toted small bottles of pennyroyal or pepper-mint oil to try to camouflage the putrid smells. Others doused them-selves with cologne. Many ladies kept camphor and smelling salts with them at all times.

But regardless of the destruction and the odors, the citizens rejoiced when they realized their occupiers had fled. People crowded the side-walks to celebrate their freedom when Union troops marched into town. "It was a noisy demonstration," Daniel Skelly said. "The boys in blue marching down the street, fife and drum corps playing, the glori-ous Stars and Stripes fluttering at the head of the lines." What a joyous Fourth of July this would be! Mary McAllister watched a Union band playing and said, "I think I never knew anything sweeter, and I never felt so glad in my life."

⟿▱◖═◗▱⟸

THE JOY DID not last long. With surprising suddenness, the civilians and the Union soldiers marching into town that morning came under fire. Although the rebels had left the town proper, they remained encamped along Seminary Ridge, near enough for sharpshooters to have a clear field of fire down the length of several major streets. The Con-federates fired at any moving target they could get a bead on, and within minutes Union sharpshooters were in position, returning the fire.

Bullets struck the grounds of Sallie Broadhead's house, and she quickly ducked back inside. "We were between two fires and were kept close prisoners all day, not daring either to go out or even to look out of the windows on account of the bullets fired at every moving object."

Henry Jacobs saw a Union horseman shot down as he tried to cross the intersection by the Jacobs' house. Henry's sister Julia saw it too. She resolved to prevent anyone else from being hurt. She waited in the open doorway of the house and shouted a warning whenever Union soldiers approached the crossing. "Look out! Pickets below! They'll fire on you!"

Although Julia's actions saved a number of lives, the rebel sharpshooters quickly saw what she was doing. They took the once-unthinkable step of firing on a woman. As bullets struck the doorframe beside her, Julia retreated a few steps into the hall for safety but continued to call out her warnings.

Just before the shooting started, twelve-year-old Mary Warren left her grandfather's house, where she had taken shelter during the battle, and was walking to her home. Union soldiers were marching past and the band was playing, so it seemed safe for her to venture out. As she approached a corner, a bullet whistled by her ear. She had come within an inch of being killed. Her father, who was watching from across the street, raced to her and pulled her out of the line of fire. They did not reach their house, only a block and a half away, for several hours.

Mary McAllister strolled up to a friend's house when a boarder inside yelled a warning to take care lest she get shot. No sooner had he called to Mary than he cried out, dumbfounded, "Oh, I believe I am shot!" Two other civilians were slightly wounded on Gettysburg's first day of peace.

Other families were forced from their homes by Union sharpshooters who needed upper-story windows as vantage points to fire on the Confederates. Some people who had remained in their dwellings throughout the three days of occupation had to evacuate within an hour of the town's liberation.

A rumor spread that the rebels planned to resume their bombardment of Gettysburg. Some people packed their valuables and prepared to flee. Other voices whispered that the rumor was untrue; people should remain in their cellars. The rebels may have left town, but the war was not yet over for its residents.

—≡◎═—

ROBERT E. LEE had good reason to keep sharpshooters firing at the Union troops moving into Gettysburg. He expected Meade to launch an attack against the Confederate forces on the Fourth of July. The rebels would be in a highly vulnerable position as they began their withdrawal. Lee had to act to persuade Meade that the Confederate army remained strong behind Seminary Ridge.

During the early morning hours of the Fourth, Lee ordered Ewell's corps to pull back to Seminary Ridge from their position in front of Cemetery Hill. It was Ewell's men that the residents of Gettysburg saw leaving town. Once the troops reached the ridge, they constructed visible breastworks and settled in, ready to defend their sector if Meade attacked. The other two corps prepared for the trek back to Virginia.

Lee also wanted to bring back the Southern soldiers captured by the Yankees. Given his staggering losses over the last three days, he needed every man. A prisoner exchange would also relieve him of the burden of transporting his four thousand Union captives. Accordingly, at 6:35 that morning, he dispatched a message through the lines to General Meade.

> General: In order to promote the comfort and convenience of the officers and men captured by the opposing forces in the recent engagements, I respectfully propose that an exchange be made at once.

Meade did not receive Lee's request for nearly two hours, at 8:25 A.M. His answer was immediate and unequivocal: "It is not in my power to accede to this proposed arrangement." Each side would keep its prisoners of war, a situation that worked more to Meade's advantage than to Lee's. Not only did Lee have to take his captives south, but he could not replace the numbers he had lost.

The Confederates had no reserve troops to serve as provost guard for escorting the prisoners. Lee believed he had no choice but to assign his weakest unit to the job. That was George Pickett's division. Pickett was irate; he protested the assignment vigorously. In the event of another battle, Pickett did not want to miss it. He felt that his division was unfairly being "reduced to guard duty instead of being elevated to a post of honor for its valor and losses in the charge of July 3rd."

To assuage Pickett's wounded pride, Lee posted a letter for Pickett's men to read. Lee noted that it was with reluctance and regret that he was compelled to assign them the duty of escorting prisoners. He said that he held them in high esteem and apologized for any disappointment they felt. "I still have the greatest confidence in your division," Lee wrote, "and feel assured that with [Pickett] at its head, it will be able to accomplish any service upon which it may be placed."

But Pickett was not appeased and he never forgave Lee for, as he put it, destroying his division and forcing the survivors to guard Yankee prisoners. To Pickett, Lee's decision was a gross insult heaped upon a grievous injury.

Pickett conveyed his frustration in a letter to Sallie, written on the Fourth of July.

Well, it is all over now. The battle is lost, and many of us are prisoners and many are dead, many wounded, bleeding and dying. Your soldier lives and mourns and but for you, my darling, he would rather, a million times rather, be back there with his dead, to sleep for all time in an unknown grave. The sacrifice of life on the blood-soaked field on the fatal Third was too awful for the heralding of victory, even for our victorious foe, who, I think, believe as we do that it decided the fate of our cause.

In a statement made two days later, Pickett reiterated his belief that the war had been lost at Gettysburg.

The prisoners have been far more cheerful than we have been, for they have not only had strong hope of being retaken by their own arms within a few days but their army has gained a great victory, and though dearly bought, it has, I fear, decided the fate of our newborn nation.

Probably the only Confederate general in a good mood on that morning of July 4 was Pete Longstreet. He was highly amused by a message he had received from the Union lines brought over under a flag of truce. The note announced that General Longstreet had been wounded and captured; he was now a prisoner and being well cared for. Longstreet replied that "he was extremely grateful, but that being neither wounded nor a prisoner, he was quite able to take care of himself."

⋅→▪◎◄▪←⋅

ALTHOUGH GEORGE MEADE was uncertain about Lee's plans, he did know, as soon as it became light enough to see, that the rebel troops in front of Cemetery Hill and Culp's Hill had been withdrawn to Seminary Ridge. But was this troop withdrawal from the right end of Meade's line merely a feint? Would the Confederates attack elsewhere along the line? Did Lee intend to return to Virginia or to shift his troops somewhere else? Would he move on Washington, D.C.? Meade knew that Lee's army had sustained a considerable number of casualties over the three days of battle, but he had no idea of its present strength.

At seven o'clock that morning, Meade sent a message to General Halleck at the War Department, noting his unease with the current situation.

This morning the enemy has withdrawn his pickets from the positions of yesterday. My own pickets are moving out to ascertain the nature and extent of the enemy's movement. My information is not sufficient for me to decide its character yet, whether a retreat or maneuver for other purposes.

While Meade waited, he wrote his General Orders Number 68, a tribute to the men of his army.

> The commanding general, in behalf of the country, thanks the Army of the Potomac for the glorious result of the recent operations.
>
> An enemy superior in numbers [an assertion that was untrue], and flushed with the pride of a successful invasion, attempted to overcome and destroy this Army. Utterly baffled and defeated, he has now withdrawn from the contest [a more decisive statement than Meade had made to Halleck]. The privations and fatigue the Army has endured, and the heroic courage and gallantry it has displayed, will be matters of history to be remembered.
>
> Our task is not yet accomplished, and the commanding general looks to the Army for greater efforts to drive from our soil every vestige of the presence of the invader.

It was Meade's last phrase, about driving the enemy from our soil, that would arouse the ire of Abraham Lincoln. But that was later. Now, on the morning of the Fourth of July, Meade cautiously ordered out patrols and scouting missions to determine Lee's intent. Until he received sufficient information, Meade was determined to wait.

The last option Meade would consider at that moment would be to launch an attack on the rebel army. His orders, when given command of the Army of the Potomac, were to defend Washington, D.C., and Baltimore. He believed that for the present he had no choice but to remain behind a strongly fortified position, to deny Lee the chance to march on these cities.

The morning passed with no movement. At noon, five hours after his last message to Halleck, Meade dispatched another, saying that he would require some delay before his army was ready to take the offensive. "I shall require some time to get up supplies, ammunition, etc., [and to] rest the army, worn out by long marches and three days' hard fighting." Meade's lack of any sense of urgency was a preview of what lay ahead.

‒‒◉‒‒

WHILE LEE PREPARED for his withdrawal and Meade waited to see what Lee would do, Union soldiers and civilians began to explore the killing ground. "Such a sight I never want to see again," wrote a soldier from New Hampshire. "The men had turned black, their eyes had swelled out of their head and they were twice the natural size, and the stench of the field was awful and dead men were thick." A New Yorker remembered that "the look of the bloated, blackened corpses was a thing to murder sleep."

Capt. Francis Donaldson of the 118th Pennsylvania wrote,

> there was scarcely room to move without treading upon the dead body of an enemy. As far as the eye could see the dead lay in all manner of shapes, some upon their faces, others upon their backs. . . . There were others who had clutched the leaves and grass in their death struggle, whilst their mouths were filled with the soil as they had literally bitten the dust.

Col. Charles Wainwright walked around the base of Culp's Hill, which the rebels had tried so hard to take. He recalled that

> All the trees on the northeast side of the hill were full of bullets way up to their tops, big branches actually cut off by them; it was very apparent how wild the firing had been. It had not all been thrown away, however, for I passed several hundred of the rebel dead lying around among the rocks and boulders.

From Culp's Hill, Wainwright ambled due south along the base of Cemetery Ridge until he came to the Bloody Angle.

Outside the wall the enemy really lay in heaps. There was about an acre or so of ground here where you could not walk without stepping over the bodies, and I saw perhaps a dozen cases where they were *heaped* one on top of the other.

Albertus McCreary explored the battlefield that day and remembered the grisly, terrible sights. He saw a mass of forty dead horses, bodies bloated and swollen to bursting, stiff legs sticking up in the air.

Dead soldiers were everywhere. Near a small house lay the bodies of two Confederate soldiers, and on looking into the house I saw two others, one on a bed and the other on the floor. I went in to see if the one on the bed might not be alive. He was dead.

Tillie Pierce climbed to the peak of Little Round Top. She wrote,

surrounded by the wrecks of battle, we gazed upon the valley of death beneath. The view there spread out before us was terrible to contemplate! It was an awful spectacle! Dead soldiers, bloated horses, shattered cannon and caissons, thousands of small arms. In fact everything belonging to army equipments was there in one confused and indescribable mass.

From the debris on the battlefield, the Union army would retrieve some twenty-seven thousand muzzle-loading muskets in working order. Fully twenty-four thousand of these were loaded. At first, it appeared that their owners might have been shot down before they had a chance to fire, but when the muskets were examined more closely, something startling was discovered. Half of the muskets had been loaded twice; some had been loaded up to ten times. The soldiers kept cramming balls down the long barrels again and again without firing. Ordnance experts concluded that in the frenzy of battle, "many soldiers lost their heads, loaded, forgot to fire, and then forgot their muskets were loaded. . . . each soldier in battle fired away about his own weight in lead before he killed one of the opposition." Panic, confusion, and terror had governed the fighting.

Among the more gruesome tasks for the Union army on the Fourth of July was to bury the dead. It had to be undertaken as soon as possible to prevent the spread of disease. There were some seven thousand bodies to be disposed of and few shovels and pickaxes with which to dig graves. Most of the tools were in the supply wagons far behind the lines. The soldiers had to improvise with tools borrowed or stolen from civilians to complete this monumental job.

Throughout the day, in the boiling heat and rising humidity, the men hacked graves out of the earth. At first, some tried to do the work properly, digging deep rectangular beds and respectfully laying the remains to rest, at least for the Union dead. But as a sense of urgency overtook them, they began hewing out shallower graves, and then soon it was simply long trenches into which bodies could be crammed. Sometimes corpses were piled one atop the other and covered with only a few inches of dirt. The trenches were dug as near as possible to clusters of bodies so they would not have to be dragged so far.

The men had long before grown indifferent to death. Still, their callousness could be shocking. Pockets were turned inside out. Rings, money, and anything of value was taken. The dead had no need of such things, and the living could always find a use for them. An officer yelled at one burial party when he saw a soldier break a corpse's stiff outstretched arm so that it would fit in the trench. The soldier shouted back that since the man was dead, a broken arm wouldn't bother him. Another group of grave-diggers found a wounded Confederate soldier among the dead, but they dug a grave big enough to include him anyway because they expected him to die at any moment.

The field of battle was a vast cemetery. Bodies were buried in farmers' fields, in yards and gardens, in the woods and alongside roadways and paths. Hundreds of troughs and ditches were scraped out of the earth and filled with twenty, or fifty, or even seventy-five bodies. Inevitably, many corpses were overlooked, hidden where the soldiers had fallen, in deep undergrowth, between boulders, or concealed in trees. It would take weeks to locate them all and by then the pigs, buzzards, and worms had done their work.

Some of the deceased, like Henry Taylor's brother Isaac, of the First Minnesota, were given a proper burial by soldiers from their units. The dead of Joshua Chamberlain's Twentieth Maine were laid out neatly side by side in a sunny nook on the east side of Little Round Top. Chamberlain and the other survivors of the outfit interred them in a single grave. They dismantled ammunition boxes to make crude markers from the slabs of wood. They carefully carved out each man's name and set the marker in place where he lay.

The men of the Twentieth Massachusetts attempted to bury Luther White. His ear had been torn off, his jaw shattered, and his throat ripped open by enemy bullets. As they transported his body and two others on a stretcher to the burial trench, one of the men slipped and dropped his end of the stretcher. White tumbled to the ground. He raised his head and looked around.

"Boys, what are you doing?" he whispered.

"We came to bury you, Whitey," said a very surprised soldier.

"I don't see it, boys. Give me a drink of water and carry me back."

White survived that day but eventually succumbed to his wounds in a hospital outside of Philadelphia.

And even as Gettysburg was scarred by graves, scores of funeral pyres blazed to dispose of dead horses and mules. One estimate put the number of dead animals at five thousand. Using ropes and chains, teams of horses dragged carcasses to mounds that were set afire.

⊷≈⊜⇐⊶

THAT MORNING IN Vicksburg, deep in the cave where she had lived for so long, Margaret Lord watched her husband walk toward her. His face was deathly pale and bore what she described as a look of agony.

"Maggie," he said, "take the children home directly. The town is sur-rendered, and the Yankee army will enter at ten o'clock."

"I was speechless with grief," she recalled. "No one spoke, even the poor children were silent, [and] all the weary way home I wept inces-santly, meeting first one group of soldiers and then another, many of them with tears streaming down their faces."

Mary Loughborough learned of the surrender at about the same time. "It's all over," her husband told her. "The white flag floats from our forts. Vicksburg has surrendered!"

Lucy McRae had heard the news the night before and had gone back to her house. She wrote,

> The morning of the 4th. How sad was the spectacle that met our gaze; arms stacked in the center of the streets, men with tearful eyes and downcast faces walking here and there; men sitting in groups feeling that they would gladly have given their life-blood on the bat-tlefield rather than hand over the guns and sabers so dear to them!

The majority of the Confederate soldiers did not learn of the surren-der until the morning hours of July 4. They were stunned, saddened, and angry. When Sgt. Willie Tunnard's buddies in the Third Regi-ment, Louisiana Infantry, received the surrender orders, it was the

> signal for a fearful outburst of anger and indignation, seldom wit-nessed. The [men of the Third] expressed their feelings in curses loud and deep. Many broke their trusty rifles against the trees [and] scattered the ammunition over the ground. In many instances, the battle-worn flags were torn into shreds and distributed among the men as a precious and sacred memento.

Of course, for the troops of the Union army, the surrender of Vicksburg was an altogether different experience. Isaac Jackson of the Eighty-third Ohio wrote to his family,

About ten o'clock, from where we were, we could see the Stars and Stripes floating on a Rebel fort. Then on the next [fort], a white flag appeared. We now knew that the forts were ours. And as the white emblem appeared on fort after fort, from left to right, the cheering went up in crowds opposite to the different forts. This was the most Glorious Fourth I ever spent.

"Oh! What a glorious Fourth of July," wrote Gen. William Orme of the Ninety-fourth Illinois to his wife, Nannie. "What a proud day for those of us so fortunate as to have taken part in this siege. This is a proud day, Nannie, and I would not have missed it for anything. Only think of it!"

A few weeks later, he told his wife how he and other Union officers felt about the importance of the army's actions at Vicksburg. "I think the fall of Vicksburg is the turning point of the rebellion and I can almost see my way home to remain there permanently within three or four months."

Sgt. Charles Wilcox of the Thirty-third Illinois noted his thoughts in his diary.

Saturday, July 4th. This day in American history is only second to the one of which today is the eighty-seventh anniversary. The fate of the American Republic has positively been decided this day. All will sing "Hallelujah!"

⊷═◎═⊷

AT TEN O'CLOCK, the Confederate army filed out of its line with colors flying. When the Southerners reached the checkpoints between the lines, they saluted their flags, neatly stacked their arms, and marched back to the city.

The Union troops stood along their trench line watching in silence. There was little cheering, and what could be heard was not in celebration, but rather in salute to a worthy adversary. It was not the time or place for gloating, not when the Yankees saw how weak and thin, how dispirited, the rebels were.

Shortly after the Confederate troops returned to the city, Gen. John Logan marched his division into Vicksburg to formally take possession. His men were parade-ground smart. They had blackened their boots, put on their best uniforms, and added their seldom-worn paper collars and white gloves. The division band played "Hail Columbia" followed by "The Star-Spangled Banner." Many men broke into tears, but they straightened their backs and marched as if those dusty roads under the hot Mississippi sun were the site of a grand review.

Logan's soldiers did not cheer when they reached the center of town. They were too appalled by the physical appearance of the rebels. In sympathy, past animosities melted away. The Confederates were starving; the Yankees were well fed. Within minutes, the Northerners pulled hardtack biscuits from their haversacks and passed them around. An officer in the Quartermaster Corps broke open his wagons and emptied them of bread, real coffee, and sugar—luxuries the Confederates had not seen in many weeks.

The troops mingled easily. The Confederate soldiers wolfed down their food and joked with the men in blue. As General Grant put it, "The men of the two armies fraternized as if they had been fighting for the same cause."

Willie Tunnard, who, an hour earlier, had smashed his rifle against a tree rather than see the Yankees get it, was gratified by the enemy's respectful treatment of the Southerners. He was also thankful for the food they gave away so generously. He noted that nearly every Yankee he saw "brought haversacks filled with provisions, which he would give to some famished Southerner with the remark, 'Here, Reb, I know you are starved nearly to death.'" The comments were offered kindly, with no offense intended and none taken.

Isaac Jackson recalled,

I was talking with one who had been eating mule meat for four days and but one biscuit per day for over a week. This is a fact. It looked hard to see the poor fellows pitch in to our hardtack, which our boys gave them. We had plenty, and they carried them off by the armload. Poor fellows, they needed them.

GENERAL GRANT AND his staff entered the city at eleven o'clock that morning. Their first stop was a call on General Pemberton at his headquarters on the Jackson Road. Grant quickly learned that the open, friendly mingling of the soldiers of both sides did not extend to the Southern commander. Pemberton, habitually aloof and stiff in his dealings with others, was hostile and rude to Grant. Many of his staff followed his example.

Col. John Wilson, who accompanied General Grant, recalled the cold formality of the Confederates.

No one even offered Grant a seat, and when he asked for a glass of water, a member of the Confederate staff merely told him where he could find it. The situation was a trying one, but Pemberton and his officers met it badly. Their behavior was unhandsome and disagreeable in the extreme.

By contrast, three younger staff officers, including Major Lockett, the chief engineer, displayed the gracious manners and courtesy for which Southerners are noted. As a result, Colonel Wilson noted, "their haversacks and canteens were well filled with provisions and whiskey when they bade us goodbye."

If Grant was distressed by Pemberton's behavior, he never gave any indication of it. However, he did not linger long where he was obviously unwelcome.

Grant's next stop was by the river, where he boarded the *Black*

Hawk, Admiral Porter's flagship. After hearty handshakes and congratulations all around, the conviviality was heightened and hastened when the admiral opened his wine locker. Grant, however, did not partake. When he was handed a glass of wine, he simply held it. He seemed quite content to smoke his cigars.

From the dock, Grant and his staff rode back up through the dusty streets, past crowds of cheering slaves and knots of civilians staring at them with curiosity. They rode past the entrances to the caves cut into the hillsides, where the townspeople had taken shelter, and they noted the many damaged homes and buildings. Grant stopped for a moment to gaze at the American flag flying atop Vicksburg's courthouse, then moved on to the house of a wealthy planter, which would be his new headquarters.

Grant had achieved a monumental victory. He had taken thirty-one thousand rebel prisoners at Vicksburg plus six thousand in the campaign leading up to the siege. The Confederates had sustained six thousand casualties in battle, for a total loss of some forty-three thousand troops. In contrast, Grant had lost fewer than ten thousand men in the entire campaign. The North had also taken 172 cannon and sixty thousand rifles, many of which were better weapons than those with which the Union troops were equipped.

That afternoon, Grant received a message from his old friend, General Sherman. The previous day, Grant had told Sherman to prepare to lead his men east, to chase down Joe Johnston as soon as Pemberton surrendered Vicksburg. Sherman dispatched a letter of congratulation, and cautioned Grant not to be taken in by the praise and flattery the press would soon heap upon him. Sherman knew as well as Grant how quickly the newspapers could turn against him. But above all, Sherman added, "This is a day of jubilee, a day of rejoicing to the faithful."

Grant sent a young captain from his staff off to Cairo, the nearest telegraph station, some 375 miles north, with a message to be wired from there to President Lincoln.

The enemy surrendered this morning. The only terms allowed is their parole as prisoners of war. This I regard as a great advantage at this moment. It saves, probably, several days in the capture, and leaves troops and transports ready for immediate service. Sherman, with a large force, moves immediately on Johnston, to drive him from the State.

Admiral Porter had notified Washington earlier that morning; his message arrived in three days' time, before Grant's did. "I have the honor to inform you," Porter wrote, "that Vicksburg has surrendered to the U.S. forces on this 4th of July." When Secretary of the Navy Gideon Welles received the telegram, he rushed to the White House. He found the president studying a map of Vicksburg. Welles told Lincoln the news and the president stood up, grabbed his hat, and declared he would immediately telegraph word to General Meade at Gettysburg.

He smiled broadly and put his arm around Welles's shoulder. "I cannot, in words, tell you my joy over this result. It is great, Mr. Welles, it is great!"

⊷══◉═══⊶

THERE WAS NO joy in Vicksburg that afternoon, at least among the Confederates. Many were bitter about their defeat and they turned on their leader in frustration and resentment. It was said that Pemberton had surrendered the city against the will of its defenders and residents. Had it been up to them, they said—no doubt in an effort to salve their shame—they would have fought to the last bullet. Pemberton, the traitor, had sold them out for who knew how much money.

Southern soldiers swore they would never serve under Pemberton again. If ordered to do so, they pledged to desert. Some even told their Yankee captors how they felt. "The people and the rebel soldiers I have met here are very bitter on General Pemberton," wrote General Orme of the Ninety-fourth Illinois to his wife. "They denounce him as a traitor and as everything else despicable and mean."

The civilians heard the same talk. Willie Lord recalled, "Men felt very bitterly toward General Pemberton because they were so determined that the place should not be taken on the Fourth and never dreamed that a surrender was ever thought of."

These words may have made some people feel better about themselves, but it would have been hard to argue that Vicksburg could have held out much longer without help from Joe Johnston's forces. (No one blamed Johnston, of course, because he was Southern born.) But the signs of devastation had been plain. People had only to see the worn, pinched, diseased faces of their friends, the mounting casualties and widespread destruction, and the Union trenches and sap rollers closing in, to know that it was only due to their own grit and determination—and Pemberton's, too, if they could admit it—that Vicksburg had survived for so long.

"The town is literally knocked to pieces by our shells," General Orme wrote to his wife. "There are vast numbers of rebel sick and wounded soldiers."

Isaac Trimble of the Eighty-third Ohio wrote to his family about his impressions of Vicksburg:

It was a desolate looking place, I tell you. I did not notice a house but that was shot through. Where the mortar shells fell on the ground, it would dig a hole about six feet in diameter and three or four feet deep. I seen one house where a shell went through. It made only a small hole in the gable where it entered but it went into a room about twenty feet square and bursted under the floor, tore the whole floor up and the pieces nearly tore the ceiling all down. It was a horrible looking place. Every house I noticed was struck in some way or other.

When Maggie Lord and her children returned home, she was shocked by the condition of her house.

Such a scene of desolation you can hardly imagine. The dressing room was in ruins; the end where the fireplace had been was blown entirely out. The nursery uninhabitable, a hole deep almost as a cistern in the middle of the floor. Every room in the house injured and scarcely a window left whole. . . . Our poor soldiers soon came in a continuous stream past the house, so pale, so emaciated and so grief-stricken, panting with the heat and Oh!, saddest of all without their colors and arms.

Eventually Joe Johnston did try to save Vicksburg. By July 3 he had marched his army close to Big Black River, no more than sixteen miles from town. While Pemberton was negotiating the details of his surrender to the Union forces, Johnston sent him a message that was never received. Johnston stated that he hoped to attack the Union army on July 7 to create a diversion so that Pemberton's men could attempt to fight their way out.

On the morning of the Fourth of July, as Johnston's army proceeded southward, he noticed that he no longer heard cannon fire from the direction of Vicksburg. Surely on this day the Yankees would be mounting an especially heavy bombardment to celebrate the holiday. But Johnston heard nothing. The weighty silence told him that he was too late.

⊶≡●≡⊷

PRESIDENT LINCOLN SPENT the day of July 3, and much of that night, pacing the floor of the telegraph office. Every incoming message told of heavy fighting and mounting losses at Gettysburg. Whenever he returned to his office, he would sit at his desk, staring morosely at the wall map with colored pins indicating troop movements, victories, and defeats. He had received no news from Vicksburg. As far as the president knew, the Confederates remained defiant, despite General Grant's efforts to wear them down. Robert E. Lee's forces were still at large in Pennsylvania, perhaps by now even heading for Washington, D.C.

Senator Zachariah Chandler of Michigan visited the White House and reminded the president that the nation's fate and future seemed to be hanging in the balance. Lincoln was restless, Chandler noted, "as he paced up and down the room, reading dispatches, soliloquizing, and often stopping to trace positions on the map."

Late on July 3 a stream of messages poured in from Gettysburg telling of a massive assault by as many as fifteen thousand Confederates against the Union line. And the Union troops had held. Lee might not be able to counterattack. Indeed, he might even be contemplating a retreat to Virginia. Did Lincoln dare hope that the end of the war was in sight?

At ten o'clock on the morning of the Fourth of July, the president issued a cautiously optimistic press release to the nation.

> The President announces to the country that news from the Army of the Potomac up to ten P.M. of the Third, is such as to cover that army with the highest honor; to promise a great success to the cause of the Union, and to claim the condolence of all for the many gallant fallen; and that for this he especially desires that on this day, He, whose will, not ours, should ever be done, be everywhere remembered and ever revered with profoundest gratitude.

Many residents of the capital city had been awake all evening noisily commemorating the nation's birthday. Rockets and fireworks lightened the night sky. People roamed the streets, shouting hurrahs and singing patriotic songs. Rumors swept the crowds that Lee was losing in Pennsylvania. Some expressed their opinion that the war would be over in a week.

At ten o'clock in the morning, coinciding with Lincoln's press release, the *Washington Star* newspaper posted a bulletin outside its office on Pennsylvania Avenue announcing a major victory at Gettysburg. Now it was official. People went wild. The city had not seen a celebration of this magnitude in many years. Crowds gathered on the south lawn of the White House, where local political figures and dignitaries hurried to join them. But, curiously, Lincoln did not appear.

Congratulatory speeches were forthcoming and the Declaration of Independence was read aloud. The U.S. Marine Band played the National Anthem, and church bells pealed throughout the day. Margaret Meade, daughter of the general whose victory at Gettysburg was being hailed, later wrote, "I never knew such excitement in Washington as when the news arrived that he had whipped Lee. Several persons have called to know if I could give them a good picture of him." Mathew Brady, the remarkable half-blind photographer, called on Miss Meade to express his fervent wish for a photograph of the general, or even of Mrs. Meade.

In Philadelphia, the mayor and city council, the influential Union League Club, and a brass band gathered outside the Meade house at 2037 Pine Street. Mrs. Meade came to the front door and graciously acknowledged the many fine words of praise for her husband. She went back inside, still hearing "deafening applause for herself and [for] the victor of Gettysburg."

At some time during the glorious Fourth of July, Lincoln's mood darkened when Meade's General Orders Number 68 came over the wire at the telegraph office. James Fry of the adjutant general's office was present:

I saw him read General Meade's congratulatory order to the Army of the Potomac. When he came to the sentence about "driving the invaders from our soil," an expression of disappointment settled upon his face, his hands dropped upon his knees, and in tones of anguish he exclaimed "Drive the *invaders* from our soil! My God! Is that all?"

As far as Lincoln was concerned, the entire country, North and South, was "our" soil. Meade's job, Lincoln fumed, was not merely to stop Lee's invasion and force him back to Virginia, to "his" alleged soil, but to annihilate Lee's army and put an end to this rebellion.

George Meade needed to do more than win this battle. He had to follow up immediately, pursuing the beaten Confederate army until he destroyed it. If he acted at once, the war might truly be over in a week. But it was clear to Lincoln that if Meade did not act—if he permitted Lee to escape to Virginia—then the fighting could drag on for years.

⋆⇒◉⇐⋆

"SHORTLY AFTER NOON on the 4th the very windows of heaven seemed to have opened. The rain fell in blinding sheets; the meadows were soon overflowed, and fences gave way before the raging streams." So wrote Brig. Gen. John Imboden, the man entrusted with the toughest assignment in the Army of Northern Virginia. His task was to transport to Virginia all wounded Confederate soldiers who could be moved. He had counted between ten and twelve thousand men, and they had to be taken across the Potomac as quickly as possible. The army could not treat their wounds until they reached safety. Imboden's wagon train, when finally assembled on the afternoon of July 4, stretched for seventeen miles.

Soldiers with wounds in the lower extremities were allowed to ride in the wagons. Those with injuries to their arms, shoulders, or other nonvital parts had to walk back home. The rain was constant, relentlessly lashing the long, slow-moving column.

Imboden penned a vivid description of their return to Virginia.

During the storm, wagons, ambulances, and artillery carriages by the hundreds—nay, by thousands—were assembling in the fields along the road from Gettysburg to Cashtown, in one confused and apparently inextricable mass. As the afternoon wore on there was no abatement in the storm. Canvas was no protection against its fury, and the wounded men lying upon the naked boards of the wagon-bodies were drenched. Horses and mules were blinded and maddened by the wind and water, and became almost unmanageable. The deafening roar of the mingled sounds of heaven and earth all around us made it almost impossible to communicate orders, and equally difficult to execute them.

At four o'clock the column got underway with small detachments of troops and artillery distributed every quarter mile for defense. Imboden's orders were simple: No stopping, for any reason. If a wagon broke down, push it off the road immediately. Transfer the occupants to other wagons. If there was no room for them, leave them behind. And no stops for food, either, though most of the men had not eaten in thirty-six hours. When canteens ran dry, there would be no time to fill them.

"On! On! We *must* move on," Imboden wrote.

During the journey Imboden rode the length of the column from the rear to the head. It took four hours. Above the noise of the constant storm he heard the groans and cries of the wounded. Bloody clothing and dressings chafed open wounds. The springless wagons bounced over roads left muddy and rutted by the rain. The jolting was agony for many of the men. Imboden remembered their cries.

"Oh God! Why can't I die?"

"Will no one have mercy and kill me?"

"Stop! For God's sake, stop just for one minute. Take me out and leave me to die on the roadside."

"I am dying! I am dying! My poor wife, my dear children, what will become of you?"

Even at night the wagons rolled on, never stopping, their wretched cargo never silent. The rumbling of the wagons and the screams of the wounded awakened farmers along the route. Jacob Snyder, who lived near the town of New Franklin, was awakened around midnight. Within minutes, his yard was filled with walking wounded soldiers begging for food, water, and shelter from the rain. Some huddled on the porch as the wagons moved on. They told Snyder they would rather die or be captured by the Yankees than go on.

At four o'clock in the morning, the Reverend J. C. Smith, who lived outside Greencastle, was awakened by the dull rumbling of the wagons.

He did what he could to help the few men who stopped, but mostly he watched in horror as they passed by. "No one," he wrote, "with any feelings of pity, will ever want to see such a sight even once in a lifetime."

By dawn, the wagon train had wound its way through Greencastle, having covered twenty-five miles since leaving Gettysburg the previous afternoon. In their wake were left "dead horses, broken down and abandoned wagons, cannons, carriages and caissons, new made graves. . . . It was simply a road covered with wrecks."

The Confederates were no more than fifteen miles from the point on the Potomac River where they could cross and go home. Imboden was thankful that so far they had been lucky enough to evade the Yankees.

IN GETTYSBURG, AT his headquarters behind Cemetery Ridge, General Meade was counting his losses and still trying to anticipate General Lee's next move. As the casualty figures accumulated, it became clear that Meade had lost not only twenty-three thousand men but also many experienced officers, from corps commanders to brigade leaders. New leaders would have to be found to fill those vacancies, and the troops needed to be rested and reequipped before they could be expected to fight again.

Meade ordered out additional reconnaissance patrols throughout the day of his victory, but whenever they ventured near Seminary Ridge, they were met with gunfire. From Little Round Top, Meade received word that the signal officers stationed there had seen rebel wagon trains bearing the wounded off to the west. But the remainder of Lee's army appeared to be in place.

Meade received a message from Gen. Francis Barlow, a division commander in the Eleventh Corps who had spent three days in Gettysburg recovering from a wound. He told Meade that Lee's evacuation of the ground around Cemetery Hill, Culp's Hill, and the town of Gettysburg itself was a feint. It was designed to mislead Meade into thinking that the Confederates were retreating. In reality, Barlow said, Lee was maneuvering to entrap Meade if he decided to attack. Meade believed what Barlow told him. He had no reason not to; after all, Barlow had been behind enemy lines for the past three days.

The only good news Meade received that day was that a roving Union cavalry force had reached Williamsport, Maryland, along the Potomac River. They cut loose the boats and pontoons along the northern bank, the transports that the Confederates had used to cross the river and which they would need for their safe return to Virginia. More important, the Union cavalry troops had burned a Confederate bridge. If Lee's forces expected to cross the river at that point, they would be in for a surprise.

CHAPTER 14

A STRANGE AND BLIGHTED LAND

July 5, 1863

THE ARMY OF Northern Virginia was on its way home, but the aftermath of the war was still very much with the people of Gettysburg. It remained in the form of twenty-two thousand wounded and dying soldiers from both sides who needed medical treatment, food, and shelter from the torrential downpours. When the Union army left town the following day, to begin its slow pursuit of Robert E. Lee, the civilians were left to cope on their own. The chaos of the situation led one harassed medical officer to observe that "the period of ten days following the battle of Gettysburg was the occasion of the greatest amount of human suffering known to this nation since its birth."[1]

The town had become one vast hospital, with every church and most houses and public buildings containing their share of wounded. Fannie Buehler's home was full of wounded soldiers, and she divided her time between there and the courthouse. She wrote,

---

[1] A twentieth-century resident of Gettysburg remembered that her grandmother referred to the three-day battle as "the war." "Mother would tell her, 'this is not the war, Mother! It is only one battle,' but she would reply, 'It is all the war I ever want to see.'"

The sights and sounds at the Court House for a week after the battle are too horrible to describe. Limbs were amputated amid the cries and groans of suffering humanity [no anesthetics were available] and often have I stopped my ears that I might not hear the groans of those poor unfortunate men, whom I could not relieve. Loads of arms and legs of those poor soldiers, that were amputated, and— possibly under other circumstances might have been saved—were carted outside of the town and were either burned or buried.

Sallie Broadhead went to the Theological Seminary on the morning of July 5, after the rebel army left, because she had been told the building was full of wounded men who needed comfort. She found the scene so tragic that she never forgot it, but she overcame her emotions and did what she could to help.

Can we endure the spectacle of hundreds of men wounded in every conceivable manner, some in the head and limbs, here an arm off and there a leg, and just inside a poor fellow with both legs shot away? It is dreadful to behold, and, to add to the misery, no food has been served for several days. The little we have will not go far with so many. What can we do? is the only question, and the little we brought was distributed. It is heart-sickening to think of these noble fellows sacrificing everything for us, and saving us, and it out of our power to render any assistance of consequence. I turned away and cried.

Sallie Myers was housing fourteen wounded men, which left no space for her to sleep. But she had little time to rest, anyway, for she was working nearly round the clock. The day the Union army left, she lost Sgt. Alexander Stewart, the mortally wounded soldier to whom she had given such devoted care.

He had been sinking all morning. At nine o'clock he had a hard spell of coughing and until ten he suffered dreadfully. I held him in my arms until nearly eleven when his head sank on the pillow and he died with only a slight struggle. I have never been so much interested in a stranger. I was with him almost constantly, wrote to his wife and friends. They will come for the body.[2]

Many of the Confederate wounded—those considered too ill to travel in Imboden's wagon train—were scattered among some two dozen sites out of town. Some were convalescing in barns, but many had no shelter and even fewer medical supplies and less food than did the soldiers in the town. Some of Pickett's men were taken to the farm of the Schwartz family and, although Union soldiers were given priority, allowed to rest in the house and on the wide front porch.

"Its every room was a chamber of death and the boards of the shambling porch that girdled it were stained with the blood of the men for whom there was no room inside." These were the fortunate ones. Some rebel soldiers were jammed side by side in cattle pens to lie amid the animal waste. Nighttime was worse. "The men, restless, suffering and unable to sleep, tossed and moaned and raved in wild delirium. The weather-beaten barn resounded with a horrid chorus of curses, imprecations and groans that sounded doubly awful at dead of night."

Lt. Tom Dooley, one of Pickett's officers, had lain on the battlefield where he had been hit in both legs. Perhaps because he was an officer, he was taken to a Union hospital a day later but received no treatment. He lay on the ground in the rain, wet and hungry, unable to move, along with hundreds of Union soldiers.

Dooley watched men die whose lives might have been saved had any medical care been available. "This is a horrid night," he wrote, "cold and wet and rainy. Groans and shrieks and maniacal ravings; bitter

[2] When the Stewart family came to Gettysburg to claim the body, Sallie and Henry Stewart, the deceased sergeant's brother, fell in love. They married in 1867 and had a son, but Henry died the following year. Sallie became a schoolteacher; their son became a doctor.

sobs, and heavy sighs, piteous cries; horrid oaths; despair; the death rattle; darkness; death." It was six days before Dooley received medical attention for his maggot-infested wounds. Then he and several hundred others were crowded into freight cars, transported to Baltimore, and imprisoned at Fort McHenry.[3]

The situation in Gettysburg seemed hopeless. The people simply could not cope with the huge numbers of wounded soldiers without additional supplies and medical personnel. Meade had taken the bulk of the supplies, rations, and surgeons with him when the army pulled out. Of the 650 army physicians, only 106 were left to treat twenty-two thousand men in desperate condition. Sufficient bandages, gauze, splints, medicines, even lanterns, were lacking. And there were few tents, blankets, or other coverings to protect the men from the rain. As for food, one Union hospital had two boxes of soda crackers for more than three thousand patients.

It was a nightmare of gigantic proportions. Thousands would die needlessly unless a massive relief effort could be organized. The government could do nothing. The only organization even minimally capable of coping with such a large-scale tragedy was the army, and it was moving farther from Gettysburg by the hour.

Throughout the Northeast, calls went out for doctors and nurses, food, medicines, and other supplies. It was the largest relief effort ever attempted. The appeal was spread in newspaper headlines, from pulpits, and by word of mouth, and soon people were heading toward Gettysburg by train, carriage, wagon, horseback, and on foot. It was a spontaneous, voluntary, selfless, and heroic effort. As historian Gerard Patterson described it,

---

[3] Dooley was then sent to a prison camp at Johnson's Island in Lake Erie; he was paroled in 1865. He returned to Georgetown University intending to become a Jesuit but died at the age of thirty-one, less than a year before he would have been ordained.

From here and there, doctors, nurses, and ministers started for Gettysburg to offer assistance. Wives and mothers came to sit by and care for their loved ones. . . . Those with no special healing skills accumulated supplies of every description that they perceived might be in demand, and consigned their offerings by whatever means possible to this town in Pennsylvania few recognized by name.

⊷═◉═⊶

SHORTLY AFTER DAWN on July 5, Gen. John Imboden's seventeen-mile long wagon train with its thousands of wounded men headed south out of Greencastle. They had gone no more than a mile when an angry crowd of some forty ax-wielding Northerners suddenly set upon them. The men darted for the wagon wheels and chopped at the spokes, causing the wagons to drop flat onto the roadbed. Imboden ordered a squadron of cavalry in pursuit with orders to capture the attackers and treat them as prisoners of war.

"That stopped the trouble there," Imboden recalled, "but the Union cavalry began to swarm down upon us from the fields and crossroads, making their attacks in small bodies, and striking the column where there were few guards." The harassment continued all day until the wagons reached Williamsport. There, Imboden learned that the Yankee cavalry had destroyed the bridge. The torrential rains had raised the Potomac River more than ten feet above fording level. The wagon train was trapped. Unable to move on across the river, Imboden focused his attention on the wounded.

Williamsport was turned into a hospital. Imboden ordered the residents to prepare food for the Confederate wounded. The citizens complied—they knew that if they refused, the Confederates would simply take over the kitchens. Imboden told his surgeons to treat as many patients as they could while the caravan rested. Then, out scouting the area, he located two small flat ferryboats that could hold approximately thirty men each.

He set the boats going back and forth, conveying the ambulatory wounded across if they thought they could walk on to Winchester, a distance of almost thirty miles. Many men were willing to try. Even if they could not make it all the way, at least they would be back in Virginia, safe from marauding Yankee cavalry.

The trip across the swollen Potomac took fifteen minutes each way; on the return trip, the boats carried food and ammunition. With at least ten thousand men to take across, Imboden estimated forty hours to complete the evacuation of troops as well as the wagons, which were virtually all the transportation Lee's army had.

On the morning of July 6, Imboden received word that a force of seven thousand Union cavalry was heading his way. He deployed cannon on the hills outside of town and organized his seven hundred drivers, the wagoners, into companies of one hundred men each. These outfits were led by wounded officers and equipped with guns from wounded soldiers. Overall, with the wagoners and regular troops guarding the wagon train, Imboden had a total of three thousand men and was outnumbered by more than two to one.

The Union attack began with an artillery barrage at 1:30 that afternoon. The rebel cannon kept up such a fast rate of return fire that one battery soon ran out of ammunition. Just in time, two wagonloads of ammunition arrived on one of the ferryboats. The crates were hauled directly to the guns, broken open with axes, and quickly the battery resumed firing.

The Union assault that began so aggressively became more timid. Imboden's men and wagoners fought with ferocity, borne of the knowledge of the consequences of their defeat. Not only would they all be captured, but Lee would lose the wagons. At dusk, a courier brought good news, a message from Fitzhugh Lee that his force of three thousand troops would reach them in no more than a half hour.

Imboden spread the word among his men. A wild, exultant cheer erupted along the length of the line, further dampening the Yankees' fighting spirit. No sooner had the cheering stopped than Imboden heard the sound of firing from behind the Union position. It was Jeb

Stuart's cavalry. The threat was over. Imboden's wagon train and the cargo of wounded soldiers were safe.

—◦➤◦◖◦—

BY JULY 7, the second invasion of Gettysburg had begun. Relief workers and supplies poured in as Northerners responded to Gettysburg's plight. Where the government was helpless, the people responded with massive generosity. Sallie Broadhead saw the first sign of that assistance early in the morning.

> This morning we started out to see the wounded, with as much food as we could scrape together, and some old quilts and pillows. It was very little, but yet better than nothing. We found on reaching the hospital that a wagonload of bread and fifty pounds of butter had arrived, having been sent from the country.

It was the beginning of an avalanche of aid that descended upon the town.

Among the first to arrive were twelve nuns from the Sisters of Charity convent in Emmitsburg, Maryland, eleven miles from Gettysburg. The sisters, draped in black with huge white cornettes—which the soldiers dubbed "angel's wings"—framing their faces, immediately set to work. They cleaned and dressed wounds, assisted in operations and amputations, and tore their own garments into strips to make bandages.

As Sister Mary Selena washed encrusted blood from the face of a badly wounded soldier, she discovered that the victim was her brother, whom she had not seen in years. Devotedly, she nursed him back to health. All the women worked tirelessly for many weeks. In the process, they helped some people overcome their prejudices against Catholics, so prevalent at that time. They also made converts of more than a few of their patients.

The largest national relief organization was the ill-named U.S. Sanitary Commission. Although chartered by Congress to provide relief and sustenance to the army, it was not a government organization but funded and run entirely by volunteers. Led by the Reverend Henry Bellows, a Unitarian minister from New York City, and Frederick Law Olmstead, the designer of Central Park, the organization raised huge sums of money from fund-raising fairs in major cities. Thus, the group was highly influential in the care, treatment, and rehabilitation of wounded soldiers throughout the war years. It also provided everyday items, from books to blankets, in greater quantity and quality than those offered by the government.

The first train to reach Gettysburg after the battle contained two freight cars of supplies from the Sanitary Commission. One car was cooled by a ton of ice and held several tons of eggs, butter, meat, fruits, and milk. The other car carried tents and furnishings for temporary hospitals. Olmstead, who coordinated the relief effort from Baltimore, arranged and paid for forty tons of supplies to be shipped to Gettysburg daily. During the first week alone, the commission spent twenty thousand dollars on the relief effort, a staggering sum. In little more than two weeks, commission members raised seventy-five thousand dollars in contributions for aid to the stricken town. Thousands of lives were saved by their generosity, diligence, and efficiency.

The U.S. Sanitary Commission helped friend and foe alike, only discriminating in that they provided medical attention to the Union wounded first. As the Reverend Bellows observed, "The rebels, as was just, had to wait their turn for having their wounds dressed, or their limbs amputated till the Union men had been cared for. They were treated with equal kindness and attention."

The commission's largest rival in fund-raising was the United States Christian Commission, an outgrowth of the YMCA. While the Sanitary Commission treated the wounded and fed the hungry, the Christian Commission was more concerned with saving souls. They came equipped with Bibles instead of bandages, offered prayers and hymns instead of medical care, and erected tents for religious services instead of makeshift hospitals. But they did distribute useful items such as soap, needles, socks, blankets, towels, mosquito netting, and canned foods. They also provided stationery and postage to enable the soldiers to write to their families.

Many representatives of the Christian Commission were clergymen. The convalescents welcomed those who were sympathetic and compassionate but were less well-disposed toward those considered excessively pious. A rebel soldier from Texas with the unlikely name of Decimus et Ultimas Barziza (named by his parents for what he was, their tenth and last child) described a particular type of preacher the men could have done without:

> New England preachers, indelibly and unmistakably stamped with the hypocritical sanctity of Puritanism, stalked back and forth, with long faces and sanctimonious pretensions; they would occasionally come into a room and after sighing, and wheezing, and sucking their breath, would condescendingly give a poor rebel a tract and a cracker.

A wounded Union captain from Ohio recalled two types of clergymen who came to town with the Christian Commission: "those who depended upon prayer and works, and those who relied exclusively on prayer without works." In the latter category was one minister who always appeared with a Bible and hymnal but never even asked a patient if he would like a glass of water.

⋅→═◉═←⋅

THE ARRIVAL OF so many people to help tend the wounded was a mixed blessing for the women of Gettysburg. The newcomers provided valuable and welcome assistance, but they all needed places to stay. The inns and hotels quickly filled up, and the only facilities left where the visitors could find room and board were private homes. As soon as the wounded soldiers could be transferred out of the houses into the tent hospitals erected by the U.S. Sanitary Commission, the visitors moved in, filling every bed, couch, hallway, and storage closet.

"Many persons have called today wanting lodging," Sallie Broadhead wrote in her diary on July 12, "but we cannot accommodate all. Our house has been constantly full, and every house I know of has been, and is, full. One who called told me that he had set up on a chair in front of a hotel last night and was glad to get even such quarters." The next day she added, "Twenty are with us tonight, filling every bed and covering the floors."

Not all those who came to help were with the U.S. Sanitary Commission or the United States Christian Commission. Many women, some trained as nurses, came on their own, wanting to be part of the relief effort. Cornelia Hancock, a twenty-three-year-old nurse from Salem, New Jersey, started for Gettysburg as soon as she learned of the need for medical personnel, but she was nearly prevented from making the trip because she was considered too pretty.

All the volunteers traveling to Gettysburg by train had to go through the Baltimore terminus. There at the railroad depot stood the legendary Dorothea Dix, the formidable and autocratic superintendent of army nurses. She had the authority to determine the acceptability of the women who expressed interest in tending Gettysburg's wounded soldiers. She believed that no female under the age of thirty who was at all physically attractive was a suitable candidate to tend vulnerable young men. She rejected Cornelia Hancock immediately, but Miss Hancock boarded the train anyway, refused to relinquish her seat, and got away with it by sheer force of will.

She arrived in town on July 6 and was appalled by the conditions. "There was a tiny brook running down from where the surgeons were working, and the blood of the soldiers mingled with the water of the brook until it was all red, and was a veritable river of blood." She set to work at once, first at a church and then at the Second Corps hospital, though it hardly deserved the name. There were no tents yet for the patients, and the surgeons were operating on a crude table set in the woods. For an entire week, the table was red with blood.

"There are no words in the English language to express the sufferings I witnessed today," Miss Hancock wrote to her family. "Four surgeons, none of whom were idle 15 minutes at a time, were busy all day amputating arms and legs. I gave to every man that had a leg or arm off a gill [quarter pint] of wine." Later, when supplies arrived, she was put in charge of eight large tents full of amputees. She described it in a letter home as

> a melancholy sight, but you have no idea how soon one gets used to it. Their screams of agony do not make as much impression on me now as the reading of this letter will on you. You will think it a short time for me to get used to things, but it seems to me as if all my past life was a myth, and as if I had been away from home 17 years.

Cornelia Hancock stayed at Gettysburg for two months and continued as a nurse with the Army of the Potomac for another two years.

Euphemia Goldsborough, a twenty-seven-year-old Southern sympathizer from Baltimore, arrived in Gettysburg on July 12 to help the Confederate wounded. She worked incessantly for nine weeks, enduring occasional taunts and jeers from some Northerners. Among her patients was the mortally wounded Colonel Tazewell Patton. "Miss Effie," as the men called her, developed a special relationship with Sam Watson, a soldier from Texas.

> Samuel Watson, 5th Texas Regiment. Lost his right arm. One of the most attractive boys I ever saw. Very ill. Little hope of his recovery but hope for the best. . . . Better today, decidedly. . . . Much better today. Strong hope of his recovery. . . . Died Sept. 13th at sundown Sunday afternoon, 1863. Buried in grave no. 3. . . . My poor lost darling. Would to God I could have died to save you, but all is over,

worldly sufferings are ended. If tears or love could have availed, I would have not been left to weep by his graveside.

Miss Goldsborough left Gettysburg after Watson's death and returned home to Baltimore—where, at first, her sister and mother did not recognize her. She looked exhausted, disheveled, and careworn. Her sister said, "she was never the same joyous girl again."[4]

+--=o⊂==--+

NOT EVERYONE WHO flocked to Gettysburg came to tend the wounded. Some were searching for loved ones, some were tourists there to gawk at the sights, and others planned to make a profit from the tragedy. The relatives came by the hundreds—mothers and fathers, wives with small children in tow, sisters and brothers—all looking for their soldiers. A few found a marked grave, others found their men recovering, or dying, from their wounds. Many visitors stayed on to care for their own and, later, to nurse some other lonely boy who had no family with him.

And people traveled from the South, making the difficult and dangerous journey through enemy territory. When they finally reached a hospital, they were told they could not enter the facility until they took an oath of allegiance to the United States. Some did, but others could not commit what to them was an act of disloyalty. They turned away, bitter and angry.

The sight-seeing crowds usually arrived on Sundays, dressed in their

----

[4] Euphemia Goldsborough was arrested three months later at her home in Baltimore and charged with treason for her activities at Gettysburg and for smuggling food and other items to Confederate prisoners held at Fort McHenry. Banished to the Confederacy, she was warned that if she returned to Baltimore she would be shot as a spy. Jefferson Davis gave her a job in the treasury department in Richmond, where she was welcomed and entertained by Colonel Patton's family.

finest clothes. Confederate colonel Robert Powell watched them from his hospital bed, later describing the

> vast concourse of sightseers, whole families with the baby. The big show [the battle] was gone, but they seemed content to look over the ground where it had been. A torn and bloody garment would attract a crowd, which would disperse only to concentrate again to look at a hat perforated by bullets.

What struck Colonel Powell was that all those casual visitors were "animated only by idle curiosity, seeming without thought or care for the hundreds of suffering men lying so near them without notice or sympathy." And without offering assistance in any way. The aftermath of battle, like the contest itself, brought out the best and the worst in people.

There are no recorded instances of the townswomen of Gettysburg charging anyone money for all the meals they prepared and the sleeping accommodations they provided. But many of the local farmers expected to profit as much as they could from the battle. It is true that their fields, fences, crops, and barns had sustained serious damage, but many showed no gratitude for the sacrifices the Union soldiers made to turn back the invaders. One Union officer commented that "The patriotism of the neighboring farmers did not shine very brightly."

Many farmers whose barns were filled with wounded soldiers made no effort to help them or to provide water or food, unless they were given payment. The farmers charged for bread, pies, even straw to rest and die on. An irate group of farmers interrupted surgeons performing amputations to demand reimbursement for the straw on which the wounded were lying.

Greedy people on the roads overcharged the wounded soldiers trying to get to town for medical treatment. Others preyed on men who were attempting to reach the railroad station in the hope of being treated sooner by caregivers in nearby towns. Although some compassionate farmers did offer food and drink, others charged up to a dollar for a loaf of bread. Some detached the handles from their wells so that wandering soldiers could not pump water to drink.

Those with wagons charged these desperately maimed and bleeding men exorbitant prices, up to twenty-five dollars for a ride of two miles to the station. One farmer brought a dozen wounded cavalrymen into town in his wagon and demanded payment of twenty dollars from the quartermaster. The officer was so irate over the demand that he requisitioned the man's horses and made him walk home. A woman who had come to town to help wrote, "Few good things can be said of Gettysburg farmers. I can only use Scripture in calling them 'evil beasts.'"

The morticians also came to Gettysburg, to fill a legitimate need and to turn a neat profit while doing so. They set up shop—often just a couple of boards resting on two barrels—close by the hospitals, a handy location for the relatives of the dead and of those likely to die. Many grieving families were so determined to bring their loved one's body home that they were willing to pay almost any price.

The undertakers were also skilled at disinterring and embalming bodies and preparing them for shipping anywhere in the country. Some touted airtight metal coffins, guaranteed to be suitable for placement in the family parlor without fear of odors escaping. Another offered coffins with compartments for ice in the lids, to help preserve the bodies in the summer heat. Almost anyone who could pound a nail and secure lumber could build and sell coffins by the dozen. A Michigan soldier wrote in his diary, "Many are dying, and it is almost impossible to get a coffin for their remains, so great is the demand for them." Three weeks after the battle, it was estimated that as many as seven hundred coffins had been constructed. And there were more men waiting to die.

Souvenir hunters and plunderers swarmed over the battlefield searching for items of value to sell. These scavengers eagerly stole what was officially still government property. They cut leather harnesses off dead artillery horses; toted away blankets, sabers, muskets, and cartridge boxes; and rifled through the pockets of the dead men's clothing. Some even dug up bodies looking for valuables. The provost marshal had only one hundred cavalrymen to police the area, and he admitted to catching no more than one-tenth of the three to five thousand people roaming the battleground every day. Anyone caught stealing government property was assigned to a burial detail or a work gang collecting discarded equipment.

Young boys and girls also went souvenir hunting, collecting relics for their own amusement and to sell to visitors. Albertus McCreary collected lead bullets and sold them for thirteen cents a pound, at eight to a pound. Cannon balls were in great demand and fetched a higher price. The children also searched the trees. Albertus wrote,

We found that a piece of tree with a bullet embedded in it was a great prize and a good seller. Every boy went out with a hatchet to chop pieces from the trees in which bullets had lodged. I found several trees with bullets in them which had met in mid-air and stuck together. These were considered a great find.

Sometimes the boys did some stupid things, such as emptying the contents of unexploded shells. One boy up on Cemetery Hill hefted a shell and smashed it against a rock. He died from his wounds an hour after the explosion. Some boys stuffed powerful loads of powder and shot in musket barrels, stuck the ramrods in the barrels, and fired the guns in the air. The blasts shattered the ramrods but, amazingly, no one was injured.

"Another trick," Albertus said, "was to go to the woods, place five or six large Wentworth shells among dry leaves and sticks, set fire to the pile, and run off to a safe distance and wait for the explosion. It made a racket that put the Fourth of July in the shade."

Tillie Pierce was helping to care for the wounded at the farm behind

Big Round Top and did not return to her family in town until July 7. It was an uncomfortable journey.

> While passing along, the stench arising from the fields of carnage was most sickening. Dead horses, swollen to almost twice their natural size, lay in all directions, stains of blood frequently met our gaze, and all kinds of army accouterments covered the ground. Fences had disappeared, some buildings were gone, others ruined. The whole landscape had been changed, and I felt as though we were in a strange and blighted land.

❖

THE CITIZENS OF Vicksburg, whose landscape had also been devastated, wanted their city restored as quickly as possible. They began immediately to reclaim it, to wipe away the scars of war. They sealed off the entrances to the caves, partly to keep children from wandering into them and getting lost, but also to close off the memories they evoked. They filled shell craters with dirt and hauled away debris from shattered stores and homes. Sounds of hammers and saws replaced the sounds of artillery.

Daily life was not yet normal, of course. Soldiers of both the Confederacy and the Union wandered the streets, many of them drunk and disorderly. Acts of vandalism were not infrequent, and many stores along Washington Street were burglarized. A large group of Yankees and rebels rolled barrels of sugar out into the street, broke them open, and helped themselves to all they could eat.

Homes that were occupied were usually left alone, but soldiers often entered empty houses. The most popular item to steal was a mirror. But when Grant put a stop to the looting, most of Vicksburg's citizens came to agree, albeit reluctantly, that for a conquering army the Yankees behaved decently.

It was hard to keep the men from drinking, however, and their behavior could be boorish as a result. Margaret Lord found ten Yankees ("common men," as she put it)

> amusing themselves turning over my basket of clean clothes. I was so indignant and so angry that day that I had no fear, so went up to them and said, "What do you mean by such liberty? I should think soldiers would have too much feeling in this hour of our distress to intrude even to the privacy of a lady's home."
>
> They turned and in the most insolent manner pointing to the [war-ravaged] rooms, said, "Do you call this a lady's home? You ought to keep it [in] better order."
>
> "It is all you have left to us for a home, and I will tell you now that I have lived for months in the midst of thirty thousand Confederate soldiers and this is the first insult I have ever received."

Mrs. Lord summoned a Union sergeant, who ordered the men away.

The Lords, and most of the other townspeople, were given food by their Yankee occupiers. Most were grateful, but for some, receiving food from the enemy was a blow to their pride. Margaret Lord's family had been officially classified as in destitute circumstances. Indignant, she told General Grant that "I had no objection to that as the U.S. Army had robbed me of far more than their rations could ever repay."

When some Union soldiers rummaged through the office of J. M. Swords, editor of the *Daily Citizen* newspaper, they came across copies of the July 2 edition, printed on the reverse side of wallpaper. They also found the typesetting for that edition. Among the news items of the day were stories about the food shortage. An article told of a dinner at which cat was the main course, though it was called "rabbit" to make it sound more palatable. Another reported that with proper preparation, mule meat could be an especially savory dish.

Another item from July 2 reported a boast allegedly made by Grant that on the Fourth of July he intended to dine in Vicksburg. The story ended with the comment that "Ulysses must get into the city before he dines in it. The way to cook a rabbit is 'first catch the rabbit.'"

The mischievous Yankee soldiers reprinted copies of that edition, using the wallpaper, but made the following addition.

Two days bring about great changes. The banner of the Union floats over Vicksburg. General Grant has "caught the rabbit." He has dined in Vicksburg, and he did bring his dinner with him. The *Citizen* lives to see it. For the last time it appears on wallpaper. No more will it eulogize the luxury of mule meat and fricasseed kitten [and] urge Southern warriors to such diet nevermore. This is the last wallpaper edition, and is, excepting this note, from the types as we found them. It will be valuable hereafter as a curiosity.

But for the most part, Union and rebel troops in Vicksburg maintained good relations, bantering with each other and enjoying themselves. The soldiers toasted each other, shared their meals, and swapped stories of life in the trenches. Major Lockett, Pemberton's chief engineer, was greeted pleasantly by a man who had tried to kill him. Lockett was astride his white pony, the one he had ridden every day of the siege to patrol the lines. A Union soldier hailed him.

"See here, Mister," he called. "You man on the little white horse! Danged if you ain't the hardest feller to hit I ever saw. I've shot at you more'n a hundred times!" Lockett's reply went unrecorded.

The occupation of Vicksburg had a lasting impact on John Rawlins, Grant's chief of staff. Several attractive young women lived in the large house chosen as Grant's headquarters. One of them, Mary Hurlburt, a governess, was Northern born. The Union officers, Grant included, often found opportunities to be in her company. But one of the men went too far with his attentions. He sent Miss Hurlburt lavish bouquets of flowers with no card or any other indication about the sender. She felt embarrassed and uncomfortable by the unwanted flattery.

Rawlins came to her rescue. He investigated the situation and identified the culprit as a married colonel on Grant's staff. That put an end to the unwelcome advances. Five months later, the crusty widower Rawlins married Miss Mary Hurlburt at her home in Connecticut.

⊷⟹⟸⊶

ON JULY 5, Gen. Joe Johnston learned of Vicksburg's surrender. He decided that there was no point in launching an attack on Grant's superior forces. It was too late to save Pemberton's men. Johnston withdrew to Jackson, Mississippi, and dug in. While waiting for Sherman to attack him, Johnston wrote to Jefferson Davis complaining about the problem Pemberton's paroled soldiers would create when they arrived at his camp. What should he do with them? If they remained within the confines of his department, how could he feed them all? And if they tried to go home, how could he be certain they would return to the army when they were exchanged for Union parolees? Johnston would probably have preferred that Grant make prisoners of them all. At least Johnston would not have had to deal with them.

Jefferson Davis had more pressing matters on his mind. He was trying to find out what had happened at Vicksburg; news of the surrender had not yet reached him. The word from Gettysburg was more promising. The *Richmond Sentinel* newspaper reported on July 7 that Lee had beaten Meade and taken forty thousand prisoners. Davis sent a telegram to the governor of Mississippi asking about the siege at Vicksburg, but Governor Pettus had gone into hiding from the Yankees and knew no more than Davis did.

That afternoon, Secretary of War James Seddon told Davis that he had just found out that Vicksburg had capitulated on the Fourth of July. An angry Davis blamed the loss on Joe Johnston for not moving to Pemberton's aid. When told that Vicksburg was doomed to fall anyway because of inadequate provisions, Davis replied tartly, "Yes, from want of provisions inside and a general outside who wouldn't fight."

Seddon tried to relieve Davis's sour mood by passing on the latest rumor—that Lee was chasing the Northern army all the way to Baltimore. But that only made Davis more anxious, because of the lack of any official report from Lee. He knew that if both Lee and Pemberton were defeated, it would mean the end of the Confederacy.

⊷≡◉═⊷

SOME CIVILIANS IN Vicksburg wanted to leave. They had already lost their homes and businesses and saw no future for themselves and their families in the fallen city. They loaded their possessions onto carts and wagons and headed east. Others left by riverboat. Those who had sworn an oath of allegiance went north; the others ventured south to remain in Confederate territory. Mary Loughborough and her young daughter departed by boat. They would stay with the South. "Saturday evening," she wrote. "Vicksburg, with her terraced hills, with her pleasant homes and sad memories, passed from my view in the gathering twilight, passed, but the river flowed on the same."

The Lord family, bound for New Orleans, boarded a boat full of sick and wounded Confederate soldiers. Willie Lord described their departure.[5]

> As we stepped aboard the boat which was to bear us on toward the unknown experiences that awaited us during the death struggles of the Confederacy, a group of our loving friends and my father's devoted parishioners waved us a sad farewell from the wharf-boat; and as we swung free from the shore amid the songs of Negro "roustabouts," now no longer slaves, we became, without realizing all the hardships and bitterness the word implied, refugees adrift upon the hopeless current of a losing cause.

[5] The Lords moved on to Mobile, then Charleston, fleeing the Union forces. After the war they returned to Vicksburg, where Dr. Lord became pastor of a new church.

On July 11, one week after the surrender, Pemberton's men left Vicksburg. It had taken that long for the rebel officers and men to complete their parole paperwork, given under oath and signed in duplicate. Each man swore

> I will not take up arms again against the United States, nor serve in any police or constabulary force in any fort, garrison, or fieldwork held by the Confederate States of America, against the United States of America, nor a guard of prisons, depots or stores, nor discharge any duties usually performed by officers or soldiers, against the United States of America, until duly exchanged by the proper authorities.

At 11:30 in the morning, with General Pemberton riding at the head of the long column, the troops who had defended Vicksburg for so long marched out. Grant's men were lined up in formation on both sides of the Jackson Road. Sgt. Willie Tunnard of the Third Louisiana remembered passing between the two long lines of Yankees. He wrote, "Not a word of exultation or an outburst of any feeling was manifested by the foe. Honoring the heroic garrison for their bravery, they would not add to the humiliation of their surrender, by a single taunt."

Grant watched them go and was struck by the absence of any cheers or taunts by his men. "I believe," he wrote, "there was a feeling of sadness just then in the breasts of most of the Union soldiers at seeing the dejection of their late antagonists."

Strengthened by a week of Yankee food, the Confederates marched fourteen miles to the Big Black River beneath a scorching sun. The next day they made twenty-one miles. On the third day they approached Confederate lines but by then most of the 31,600 parolees had deserted and were heading home. A few days later, Grant reported that Pemberton had fewer than four thousand men left. The rest had gone. Many of those who remained lived east of Jackson and were merely waiting to get closer to home before they deserted, too. They had had enough of war. Grant had been right.

Pemberton became increasingly depressed as the size of his army dwindled. He knew that most of the soldiers blamed him for the loss of Vicksburg, and that many people throughout the South shared their low opinion of him. He wondered whether he would be allowed to continue to serve the cause of the Confederacy, in which he so fervently believed, or would be forced to resign, his name forever associated with failure, even treachery.[6]

As part of Pemberton's own parole, he was required to report to General Johnston, his commanding officer. In mid-July, on a clear moonlit night, the two men met for the first time in many months. Johnston was sitting with his staff officers atop a knoll. He recognized the tall, handsome man climbing the hill toward him. Johnston jumped to his feet and held out his hand.

"Well, Jack, old boy," Johnston said. "I am certainly glad to see you."

There was a long awkward moment as the formal Pemberton snapped to attention and saluted Johnston, ignoring his outstretched hand. Slowly, Johnston raised his hand and returned the salute.

"General Johnston," Pemberton snapped, "according to the terms of the parole prescribed by General Grant, I was directed to report to you, Sir!"

Neither man moved. Neither man spoke another word. After another embarrassing moment, Pemberton saluted again, executed a smart about-face, and marched down the hill. They never saw each other again.[7]

---

[6] Pemberton requested a Military Court of Inquiry to officially clear him of wrongdoing at Vicksburg. It was never convened; the demands of war prevented enough high-ranking officers from participating. Eight months after the fall of Vicksburg, in March 1864, Pemberton resigned his commission as lieutenant general and offered to serve the Confederacy as an enlisted man. Jefferson Davis appointed Pemberton lieutenant colonel in command of the artillery defending Richmond.

[7] Johnston was given command of the Army of the Tennessee but was unable to stop Sherman's advance on Atlanta. He was replaced by John Bell Hood. Johnston surrendered to Sherman at the end of the war and died in 1891 from pneumonia contracted from standing hatless in a cold rain at Sherman's funeral.

In Vicksburg on the night of July 11, the day the rebel troops left, news was received from back east that caused the Union troops to launch a grand celebration. Gen. William Orme described it in a letter to his wife:

> We have received news here of what seems to be a glorious victory achieved by General Meade. I do hope this news is true. If it be true I can begin to see through the difficulties. In this section of the country, the Rebels have been rather thoroughly cleaned out, and a great victory in Virginia or Pennsylvania will demoralize the whole rebel army. General Meade has made himself a great hero if he has whipped Lee; hasn't he? Oh! That all this news may be true and our bleeding country soon have peace and rest again.

⊷⊜⊶

"IT WAS A grand battle," George Meade wrote to his wife on July 5, "and is in my judgment a most decided victory, although I did not annihilate or bag the Confederate Army. This morning they retired in great haste into the mountains, leaving their dead unburied and their wounded on the field."

On July 6, Meade moved his army out in pursuit of Lee. The following day, his troops arrived in Frederick, Maryland, after tough marching through rain and mud. Meade was pleased with their progress after the decisive victory over the rebels. So was President Lincoln. He said, "Now if General Meade can complete his work, so gloriously prosecuted so far, by the literal or substantial destruction of Lee's army, the rebellion will be over." Meade's son and aide, George, was more confident. He told his mother, "Papa will end the war."

Meade was hailed as a savior when he rode into Frederick. Flags lined the streets, crowds cheered as he passed by, and women sung his praises and presented him with wreaths and bouquets. That evening, a gathering of townspeople serenaded him at the United States Hotel, shouting their gratitude for turning back the Confederate invasion of the North. After the celebration, Meade had a hot bath— a luxury for a field commander—and wrote to his wife to express his pleasure at the accolades she had received at home in Philadelphia. He added,

> I see also that the papers are making a great deal too much fuss about me. I claim no extraordinary merit for this last battle. . . . From the time I took command till today, now over ten days, I have not changed my clothes, have not had a regular night's rest, and many nights not a wink of sleep, and for several days did not even wash my face and hands, no regular food, and all the time in a great state of mental anxiety. Indeed, I think I have lived as much in this time as in the last thirty years.

While Meade was being serenaded in Frederick, Union scouts reported that rebels were ferrying troops across the Potomac River. What the scouts had seen were the two flatboats General Imboden was using to take wounded soldiers across into Virginia and, on the return trip, to replenish his supplies. Meade already had that information, but in Washington, D.C., Lincoln and Halleck interpreted the message to mean that Lee's entire army had reached the Potomac and was crossing the river: the Confederates were getting away, and Meade had to get there and stop them immediately.

Halleck, no doubt at Lincoln's request, urged Meade to push his men forward. "There is reliable information that the enemy is crossing at Williamsport. The opportunity to attack his divided forces should not be lost. The President is urgent and anxious that your army should move against [Lee] by forced marches."

Meade was irate when he received the message. Forced marches!

What did they think his men had been doing for the past three days? He fired off a testy reply that same afternoon.

> My information as to the crossing of the enemy does not agree with that just received in your dispatch. [Lee's] whole force is in position between Funkstown and Williamsport. . . .
>
> My army is and has been making forced marches, short of rations and barefooted. One corps marched yesterday and last night 30 miles.
>
> I take occasion to repeat that I will use my utmost effort to push forward this army.

Meade's scouts reported that General Lee had not yet reached the Potomac but was approaching rapidly. Meade was certain that Lee was headed for the river and that it was Meade's job to prevent the Southerners from getting away. To do that, Meade had to act in the way he had just assured Halleck and Lincoln that he was already doing. He had to push his army hard.

But it did not appear that Meade was making much effort to push the army at all. The movement of the Army of the Potomac seemed downright sluggish. Lee's bedraggled, defeated army took two days to march thirty-four miles from Gettysburg to Hagerstown, Maryland, but it took Meade's men eight days to cover the distance, largely because he chose a route that was twice as long. The Union troops had to march seventy miles to reach Hagerstown. Once there, they were fewer than ten miles from Williamsport.

On July 9, Meade received word from General Buford, who had led his cavalry division to the Potomac, that the river was at least five feet above normal and still rising due to heavy rains. Lee would likely be trapped when he reached the river and therefore would have no choice but to stand and fight. Meade notified Halleck that the most decisive battle of the war would be fought there within the next few days.

He also told Halleck that a deserter from Jeb Stuart's cavalry reported that Lee had already laid a pontoon bridge across the Potomac. Furthermore, the man said, the bridge was not being used to take Lee's army to Virginia but to bring up supplies so it could mount a strong defense against Meade's expected attack. The deserter, who might have been sent to feed Meade this false information, also reported that rebel troops were eager for another chance to fight the Army of the Potomac. In addition to the deserter's remarks, Meade read a Hagerstown newspaper article that quoted Lee telling his men they would soon meet the enemy again.

Thus, Meade had reason to believe that rather than fleeing to Virginia, Lee was preparing a strong defensive position along the Potomac River and would wait for Meade to launch an attack. The situation would be a reversal of Gettysburg, where the Confederates had been forced to assault entrenched positions. Of course, Meade also had to consider the possibility that the audacious Lee might spring a surprise attack while the Union army was still spread out for miles along the roads.

And so Meade advanced cautiously, uncertain of what lay ahead for his army. "I have to grope my way in the dark," he wrote to his wife on July 12. The slower Meade moved, the more impatient Lincoln became and the more frantically he paced the floor of the War Department's telegraph room. Up to July 11, Lincoln felt confident that Meade was closing in on Lee.

The president's secretary, John Hay, made this entry in his diary for July 11:

The President seemed in a specially good humor today, as he had pretty good evidence that the enemy were still on the North side of the Potomac and Meade had announced his intention of attacking them in the morning. The President seemed very happy in the prospect of a brilliant success. He had been rather impatient with General Meade's slow movements since Gettysburg, but concluded today that Meade would yet show sufficient activity to inflict the *coup de grace* upon the flying rebels.

If Meade's attack the following day succeeded, thought Lincoln, it could mean the end of the war. But the morning brought more rain and no word from Meade about an attack. The next day, July 12, Meade wired Halleck that he would attack on the day after, "unless something intervenes to prevent it."

Lincoln was, as usual, in the telegraph room when Meade's wire arrived. One of the telegraph operators, Albert Chandler, watched the president fidgeting, wringing his hands in despair as he read it. Suddenly, Lincoln said, "They will be ready to fight a magnificent battle when there is no enemy there to fight."

⊷⊐◉⊏⊷

ROBERT E. LEE was worried. Col. Porter Alexander, the artillery officer, had never seen Lee looking as anxious as he did on July 10. Not all the Confederate wounded and Union prisoners had been ferried across the river, the water was rising, the food supplies were being exhausted, the horses were nearly out of forage, and the Army of the Potomac was closing in.

"Had the river not unexpectedly risen, all would have been well with us," Lee wrote to his wife, "but God, in His all-wise providence, ruled otherwise, and our communications have been interrupted and almost cut off."

But over the next few days, Lee's situation improved. The water began to subside so the engineers could assemble a pontoon bridge at Falling Waters, five miles below Williamsport, where some of the pontoons from the bridge the Yankees destroyed had come to rest. Also, the men had constructed a formidable defensive line. The Confederate troops had been granted time to make these extensive preparations because Meade's pursuit of them had slowed to a crawl.

"Up to now," Porter Alexander observed, "the enemy had pursued us

as a mule goes on the chase of a grizzly bear, as if catching up with us
was the last thing he wanted to do."

By July 10, the Yankees did catch up with them, but Lee's men were
well dug in behind solid defenses and Meade gave no sign of wanting
to attack. Colonel Alexander recalled "how we all did wish that the
enemy would come out in the open and attack us, as we had done them
at Gettysburg, but General Meade showed no disposition to attack us."

By July 12, Lee was so much more sanguine about his situation that
he sent an optimistic letter to Jefferson Davis.

> So far, everything goes well. The army is in good condition, and
> occupies a strong position covering the Potomac from Williamsport
> to Falling Waters. The river has now fallen to four feet, and a bridge,
> which is being constructed, I hope will be passable tomorrow. Should
> the river continue to subside, our communication with the south
> bank will be open by tomorrow. I still trust that a kind Providence
> will cause all things to work together for our good.

⭑⇒◉⇐⭑

BY JULY 13, it was evident in the telegraph office in Washington,
D.C., that things were not working together for the good of the Union.
Meade had not mounted an attack, and Lincoln knew that every hour
Meade hesitated, Lee's chances of taking his army home intact grew
higher. Lee would be allowed to rearm and reequip and fight another
day. The Southern forces would be stronger and better organized. Why
did none of Lincoln's generals understand? Why did none of them possess the strength and perseverance to press the Confederate army until
Lee was worn down?

Lincoln composed another urgent telegram for Halleck to dispatch
to Meade:

> You are strong enough to attack and defeat the enemy before he can
> effect a crossing. Act upon your own judgment and make your gen-

erals execute your orders. Call no council of war. It is proverbial that councils of war never fight. Reinforcements are being pushed on as rapidly as possible. Do not let the enemy escape.

Lincoln was too late. Meade had called a council of war the night before. And, as Lincoln predicted, it had voted not to fight. The corps commanders listened to Meade describe what he knew of the enemy's situation. Meade announced that he was in favor of assaulting the rebel position but would not order the attack if the majority of his corps commanders voted against it.

Later Meade explained why he thought it necessary to put the matter to a vote of his corps commanders instead of taking the responsibility himself for ordering an attack.

> Having been in command of the army not more than twelve or fourteen days, and . . . knowing that if I were defeated the whole question would be reversed, the road to Washington and to the North open, and all the fruits of my victory at Gettysburg dissipated, I did not feel that I should be right in assuming the responsibility of blindly attacking the enemy without any knowledge of his position.

Only two of Meade's twelve corps commanders, Wadsworth and Howard, voted to attack the Confederates. The rest preferred to wait until they could reconnoiter the rebel defense line and determine its strength. That reconnaissance was scheduled for the next day, July 13. But that night, Meade issued orders for the entire Army of the Potomac to advance the next day on a broad front. Despite the vote of his council of war, Meade decided to attack.

July 13 brought more rain, a driving downpour with fog and mist that obscured the rebel lines. No one on the Union side made any visual sightings except General Howard, who thought he saw a column of rebels in motion. A reconnaissance was out of the question in such weather, and, of course, so was an attack. But the rain did not dampen the optimism of the Union troops. They knew that the river would swell and remain too high for Lee to cross. One of Meade's staff officers told a reporter that Lee could not possibly escape. "He has no pontoons; we have him in a tight place." When Meade returned to headquarters from an inspection of the front, he announced with confidence, "We shall pitch in."

The rain and fog of July 13 was precisely what Lee needed to escape, a gift from a kind Providence at an ideal time. The pontoon bridge at Falling Waters was ready for use and the river at Williamsport, while still deeper than normal, was fordable. It was time to go home.

Lee ordered Ewell's corps to ford the river, while the other two corps and the wagons would use the bridge. But first, there was one more argument to be had with Longstreet, who wanted to stay and force the enemy to attack them. Lee refused to consider that option and issued the order for the exodus to begin that afternoon.

Ewell's men made rapid progress fording at Williamsport. The road down the riverbank was a firm surface despite the rain and pounding feet. The water was cold and fast flowing. The men waded across, lifting their rifles and cartridge boxes high overhead as the water rose to their armpits. Taller soldiers carried the shorter ones. By dawn of July 14, most of Ewell's men were safely on the Virginia side with the rest close behind.

The crossing at the bridge was more difficult. A new road had been cut down the steep embankment and the combination of rain, loaded wagons, and thousands of men sinking deeper into the mud brought traffic to a standstill. The wagons settled down, the wheels hub-deep in the muck, and the men had to stand for hours while Lee waited on the Maryland side shouting encouragement. Colonel Alexander wrote about the crossing:

> The whole night had been spent in groping and pulling through the mud, a few feet at a time, and then waiting for the vehicle in front of you to move again. And men would go to sleep on their horses, or

leaning in fence corners, or standing in the mud. At last, not long after sunrise, we came to the pontoon bridge. It had a very bad approach, steep and on a curve, a bad location and several wagons, caissons, etc. had gone into the river during the night.

August Dickert, a soldier in Longstreet's First Corps, recalled advancing only a few feet at a time, then halting for minutes before dragging on through the mud a few steps more. The men kept one hand on the back of the soldier in front of them to keep from wandering off the path, for they could not even see the next man in line. In one hour, they covered a mere hundred paces. By daybreak, they had traveled such a short distance that they could still see their camp from the day before. Finally,

> [they] came in sight of the rude pontoon bridge, lined from one end to the other with hurrying wagons and artillery, the troops at opened ranks on either side. If it had been fatiguing on the troops, what must it have been on the poor horses and mules that had fasted for days and now drawing great trains, with the roads almost bottomless?

By dawn, the last of Lee's wagons were on the bridge, but Longstreet's and Hill's corps had not yet crossed. The sun rose, promising a fair day. To Lee, that meant good weather for a battle. He expected the Yankees to attack at any minute. Could they not see his men spread out in their columns, easy prey for a sweeping assault?

As the morning wore on, Longstreet's men made their way over the bridge. Col. Moxley Sorrel, Longstreet's aide, reported to Lee that Hill's corps was only three-fourths of a mile behind. Suddenly, Lee heard gunfire.

"There!" he said to Sorrel. "I was expecting it. The beginning of the attack!"

A mile or two from the bridge, Union cavalry swept forward. It was John Buford's division, the same outfit that had held off the first attack at Gettysburg back on the morning of July 1. The rebels who had attacked them then had been led by Johnston Pettigrew. Now, Pettigrew commanded the rearguard of Lee's retreating army. They had all come full circle, fighting the first battle of the campaign and here the last.

The skirmish was quick and nasty; it made no difference in the outcome of the campaign, except that more men died. One was Pettigrew, the erudite scholar from North Carolina who had survived Pickett's charge with only a hand wound. During the fight his horse reared, throwing him to the ground, entangled in the reins. Union troopers surrounded him and demanded his surrender. As he reached for his pistol, a Yankee shot him; the wound would claim his life three days later. Yet Pettigrew managed to draw his pistol and kill the man who shot him.

The Confederate rearguard beat off their attackers and reached the bridge. As soon as they crossed, the ropes holding the pontoons were severed and the boats and planks fell into the river and were swept downstream. Lee uttered a sigh of relief. Jeb Stuart offered him some coffee. Lee drank it down and declared that nothing had ever left him feeling so refreshed. He had brought his army home.

PEOPLE WHO SAW the Union army on the morning of July 14, arrayed in the early morning sun, said it was one of the grandest spectacles of the war. The entire Army of the Potomac was advancing over a two-mile front in columns ten lines deep.

> As far as the eye could reach through fields of wheat, corn, and clover that grand line was moving on with its colors proudly floating in the sunlight. The fields were groaning with yellow-ripened grain, and where the army had passed everything bore the appearance of having a tornado pass over it. Hardly a stalk of grain was left standing in the fields.

Although Meade had decided to attack, he did not order the army into motion until 8:30 A.M. The men advanced ponderously, majestically, magnificently across the Maryland countryside. The men seemed to know that no defenses built by mere man could stop such a force. They felt it; they were invincible. They would sweep the rebels before them like the fields of grain yielding to their mass and energy and belief in themselves. Soon, on this very day, the rebellion would be crushed.

The Northern troops were prepared to face death. Many expected to meet it. But they were not prepared for what they finally did see—the sight of the enemy safe and secure on the far side of the river.

Noah Brooks, the newspaper reporter and friend of Lincoln, was with the Northern troops.

> I looked across the swollen and turbid Potomac where I could see the smoke of the rebel camps rising in the thick Virginia woods on the other side. It is impossible now to describe, almost impossible to recall, the feeling of bitterness with which we regarded the sight. Lee's army was gone. In spite of warnings, expostulations, doubts, and fears, it had escaped.

An anonymous soldier expressed these sentiments more directly. "Well," he said, "here goes for two years more."

Brooks made his way back to Washington that afternoon and went to the White House. He described Lincoln's "grief and anger [as] something sorrowful to behold."

"We had them within our grasp," the president said to his secretary, John Hay. "We had only to stretch forth our hands and they were ours. And nothing I could say or do would make the Army move." Later, he told Hay that "Our Army held the war in the hollow of their hand and they would not close it."

Gideon Welles, the secretary of the navy, wrote that he had rarely seen the president so discouraged. He found a dejected Lincoln sprawled on a sofa in Stanton's office, next to the telegraph room.

"There is bad faith somewhere," the president said to Welles. "Meade has been pressed and urged, but only one [sic] of his generals was for an immediate attack, was ready to pounce on Lee; the rest held back. What does it mean, Mr. Welles? Great God! What does it mean?"

Lincoln added, "It is the same old story of this Army of the Potomac. Imbecility, inefficiency, [they] don't want to *do*. Oh, it is terrible, terrible, this weakness, this indifference of our Potomac generals, with such armies of good and brave men."

Later that afternoon, the president's son, Robert, found his father alone in his room, sitting at a table with his head resting on his arms. Lincoln was sobbing. He told Robert that the Union had just lost the chance to end the war.

"If I had gone up there," he said, "I could have whipped them myself."

Lincoln steeled himself to write to General Meade, pouring out his fury and disappointment.

My dear general, I do not believe you appreciate the magnitude of the misfortune involved in Lee's escape. He was within your easy grasp, and to have closed upon him would, in connection with our other late successes, have ended the war. As it is, the war will be prolonged indefinitely. . . . Your golden opportunity is gone, and I am immeasurably distressed because of it.

He reread the letter and put it away in his desk drawer. He would never show it to Meade. There was no point. The most glorious Fourth was over, the time for celebration and hope long past. The war would go on.

⊷≡◉═⊶

This surrender [of Vicksburg] taken in connection with the Gettysburg defeat, was, of course, very discouraging. . . . For myself, I felt that our last hope was gone, and that it was now only a question of time with us.

—JAMES (PETE) LONGSTREET
LIEUTENANT GENERAL
ARMY OF NORTHERN VIRGINIA

CHAPTER NOTES

Complete information for works cited in the chapter notes can be found in the bibliography.

Chapter 1

3 "I come here to escape my persecutors." Sandburg, vol. 4, p. 240.

4 "Well, I guess I have got down to the raisins." Sandburg, vol. 4, p. 141.

5 "If hell is [not] any worse than this" Burlingame, p. 104.

5 "[I was] as nearly inconsolable as I could be and live." Burlingame, p. 104.

5 "My God! Our cause is lost!" Burlingame, p. 105.

6 "I shall never forget that picture of despair." Brooks, *Washington, D.C.*, p. 61.

7 "Our noble army of the Mississippi is being wasted" Sandburg, vol. 4, p. 119.

7 "I am very sorry, for if you could tell me" Sandburg, vol. 4, p. 120.

9 "gloomiest, most painfully careworn looking man I ever saw." Wert, *Custer*, p. 149.

9 "His hair was grizzled." Brooks, *Mr. Lincoln's Washington*, p. 17.

10 "I long ago made up my mind" Brooks, *Washington, D.C.*, p. 44.

11 "Where are you going now, father?" Sandburg, vol. 4, p. 212.

12 "If you can't feed us, you had better surrender us" Carter, p. 290.

13 "It is all well, general" Hoke, p. 355.

14 "The enemy has attacked me about 4 P.M. this day" Meade, *With Meade at Gettysburg*, p. 137.

Chapter 2

17   "'Papa says'... before I heard the last of it" Grant, pp. 22, 23.

17   "But I won't go" Grant, p. 24.

18   "had not the faintest idea of staying in the army" Grant, p. 27.

19   "The joke was a huge one" Grant, p. 31.

19   "Julia was no beauty" McFeely, p. 24.

19   "One of my superstitions had always been" Grant, p. 35.

20   "You can have but little idea of the influence you have" McFeely, p. 27.

20   "I felt sorry that I had enlisted" Grant, p. 58.

20   "would have been won" Grant, p. 62.

21   "My curiosity got the better of my judgment" Grant, p. 68.

22   "I do nothing but set in my room" McFeely, p. 52.

23   "Grant did not leave the army" McFeely, p. 55.

23   "I was now to commence at the age of thirty-two" Grant, p. 125.

23   "A black cloud fell around me" McFeely, p. 60.

26   "[My] heart kept getting higher and higher . . . My heart resumed its place" Grant, p. 149.

26   "Be careful, Ulyss" Foote, vol. 1, p. 197.

27   "military imbecile who might just possibly make a good clerk" Catton, *Army of the Potomac*, vol. 1, p. 196.

28   "Fort Henry is ours" McPherson, p. 397.

28   "Sir: Yours of this date proposing armistice" Grant, pp. 183–84.

29   "I have had no communication with General Grant" McFeely, p. 105.

29   "General Grant has resumed his former bad habits" McFeely, p. 106.

30   "You cannot be relieved from your command" McFeely, p. 110.

31   "Lincoln remained silent for what seemed a very long time" Catton, *Army of the Potomac*, vol. 1, p. 151.

34   "In a few days I shall be thirty years of age" Meade, *Life and Letters*, pp. 40–41.

35   "was in a melancholy tone . . . Although in my ignorance" Meade, *Life and Letters*, p. 45.

35   "pleasant excitement of victory . . . Such is war" Meade, *Life and Letters*, pp. 93–94.

36   "No, soldiering is no play" Meade, *Life and Letters*, p. 94.

38   "War is a game of chance . . . Upon the whole" Meade, *Life and Letters*, p. 265.

38   "Just think, doctor, of my being shot in the back!" Meade, *Life and Letters*, p. 299.

39   "passed through my hat so close" Meade, *Life and Letters*, pp. 337–38.

40   "I . . . have been making myself (or at least trying to do so) . . . At first I was very much tickled" Sandburg, vol. 4, pp. 335–36.

40 "I . . . do not believe there is the slightest probability . . . It remains to be seen" Meade, *Life and Letters*, pp. 373, 388.

Chapter 3

42 "There were weeds in the fallow gardens" Anderson and Anderson, p. 17.

43 "birth defect" Thomas, *Robert E. Lee*, p. 17.

43 "Robert was always good" Freeman, *R. E. Lee*, vol. 1, p. 30.

43 "showed what the flouting of codes of honor" Smith, p. 24.

44 "exemplary pupil in every respect" Freeman, *R. E. Lee*, vol. 1, p. 46.

44 "Always at the top of his class" Smith, p. 25.

46 "as much enamored of Arlington as he was of Mary" Connelly, p. 171.

46 "a brilliantly handsome and prepossessing young man" Smith, p. 28.

48 "went steadily downhill" Smith, p. 32.

48 "I am as happy as a clam at high water" Connelly, p. 166.

48 "You are right in my interest in pretty women" Freeman, *Robert E. Lee*, vol. 1, p. 198.

48 "Oh Markie, Markie" Thomas, *Robert E. Lee*, p. 106.

48 "I am conscious of having lost a great deal" Anderson and Anderson, p. 169.

51 "Yes, colonel. And if we were all like you" Anderson and Anderson, p. 51.

56 "rent by a thousand anxieties" Anderson and Anderson, p. 203.

56 "I wish I could offer him" Connelly, p. 182.

56 "I can anticipate no greater calamity" Smith, p. 80.

57 "I wish for no other flag" Smith, p. 80.

57 "Colonel, do you intend . . . But it may be necessary" Freeman, *R. E. Lee*, vol. 1, p. 425.

57 "Has it come so soon as this?" Smith, p. 82.

58 "Lee, you have made the greatest mistake" Freeman, *R. E. Lee*, vol. 1, p. 437.

59 "At heart Robert E. Lee is against us . . . General Lee will surely be tried for a traitor" Chesnut, pp. 70, 71.

60 "Gen. Lee in the streets here" Jones, p. 58.

61 "The strength and endurance of this fine animal" Freeman, *R. E. Lee*, vol. 1, p. 615.

63 "It is well that war is so terrible" Smith, p. 143.

64 "Old age and sorrow is wearing me away" Lee, p. 413.

65 "He had planned his campaign like a master" Catton, *Army of the Potomac*, vol. 2, p. 210.

Chapter 4

68 "Although next to [Halleck] in rank" Grant, p. 219.

68 "I was little more than an observer" Grant, p. 224.

69 "Sherman, you know that I'm in the way" Lewis, p. 236.

70 "The result is all I could possibly desire." McFeely, p. 117.

70 "I do not know the object of calling Gen. H. to Washington" McFeely, p. 120.

71 "He wanted someone to go to Grant's army" Dana, pp. 20–21.

71 "I think Grant was always glad to have me with his army" Dana, p. 30.

72 "the most honest man [he] ever knew" Dana, p. 61.

73 "The truth was Gen. Grant had an inordinate love for liquors." Cadwallader, p. 116.

73 "may have been an alcoholic in the medical meaning of that term" McPherson, p. 588.

77 "a quiet but determined way of correcting an evil" Walker, p. 41.

78 "Oh! To see and be in it all" Carter, p. 24.

78 "Went early to the hospital" Walker, p. 68.

78 "It was a sad sight" Walker, p. 69.

78 "Mississippians don't know, and refuse to learn" Walker, p. 91.

80 "Pemberton alone said, no, he would walk" Pemberton, p. 14.

81 "heart and views are that the South is right" Pemberton, p. 24.

81 "born Yankees are awfully unlucky . . . commanders" Chesnut, p. 332.

81 "wanting in polish" Foote, vol. 1, p. 776.

82 "[Lieutenant Johnston] laid hold of a small tree with one hand" Snow, p. 274.

83 "fair fame as a soldier and a man" Symonds, p. 128.

83 "a nominal one merely, and useless *Battles and Leaders*, vol. 3, p. 475.

84 "jackass in the original package" Donald, p. 409.

85 "Began to dig on the canal" Wilcox, pp. 457, 458.

86 "a series of experiments to consume time" Grant, p. 264.

88 "The sight was magnificent, but terrible." Grant, p. 274.

89 "The river was illuminated by large fires" Loughborough, pp. 15–16.

89 "'Our men are all dead men'" Wheeler, *Siege of Vicksburg*, p. 111.

90 "I never understood before the full force of those questions" Wheeler, *Siege of Vicksburg*, p. 115.

92 "I knew well that Halleck's caution would lead him to disapprove" Grant, pp. 290–91.

93 "I shall go immediately" Johnston, p. 506.

95 "Ah! Vicksburg, our city of refuge." Loughborough, p. 29.

96 "Oh, will God forsake us now?" Anderson and Anderson, p. 369.

Chapter 5

97   "Where on earth are you going?" Loughborough, p. 43.

98   "I hope never to witness again such a scene" Carter, pp. 205–6.

98   "Wan, hollow-eyed, ragged, footsore, bloody" Carter, p. 206.

99   "From twelve o'clock until late in the night" Carter, p. 210.

101   "I rode in to get a drink" Sherman, p. 323.

101   "After dark, the whole scene was lit up with fires" Sherman, p. 324.

102   "Just thirty years ago I began my military career" *Battles and Leaders*, vol. 3, p. 488.

102   "If Haines' Bluff is untenable, Vicksburg is of no value" Pemberton, pp. 176–77.

103   "I have decided to hold Vicksburg as long as is possible" Pemberton, p. 179.

104   "[Sherman] turned to me, saying that up to this minute" Grant, p. 309.

104   "The ground about Vicksburg is admirable for defense." *Battles and Leaders*, vol. 3, p. 520.

105   "A long line of high, rugged, irregular bluffs" Catton, *Grant Moves South*, p. 450.

106   "My troops reached the top of the parapet" Sherman, p. 325.

106   "Men who had been gloomy, depressed, and distrustful" Carter, p. 216.

107   "sad when talking of these orders . . . my heart is much depressed" Wilcox, pp. 478–79.

107   "I could see every thing." Sherman, p. 326.

108   "It was the hottest place for men to be in" Jackson, p. 97.

108   "We lay there about eight minutes" Wilcox, p. 479.

108   "I don't believe a word of it" Sherman, p. 327.

109   "fearful burst of indignation from Rawlins" Carter, p. 229.

109   "I now determined upon a regular siege" Grant, p. 312.

110   "[Johnston] lives very plainly" Fremantle, p. 93.

110   "I now heard everyone speaking of the fall of Vicksburg" Fremantle, p. 92.

111   "Am I to expect reinforcements?" Pemberton, p. 186.

111   "You may depend on my holding the place" Pemberton, p. 200.

111   "When may I expect you to move" Pemberton, pp. 202, 205.

111   "you may not hear from me for several days" Oates, p. 348.

111   "I have just finished copying" Bates, p. 155.

112   "one of the most brilliant in the world" Oates, p. 349.

112   "I was distressed to hear of a young Federal lieutenant" Loughborough, pp. 101–2.

113   "Now commenced a strange spectacle . . . Flags were displayed along both lines" Tunnard, pp. 240–41.

113 "I thought this would be a good opportunity" *Battles and Leaders*, vol. 3, p. 490.

114 "The great solicitude I feel for the safety of the army" Anderson and Anderson, p. 371.

115 "stupid in speech and staggering in gait" Cadwallader, p. 103.

115 "I then took the general in hand myself" Cadwallader, p. 104.

116 "fresh as a rose" Dana, p. 83.

116 "procured another supply of whiskey" Cadwallader, pp. 105–6.

116 "went at about full speed through camps and corrals" Cadwallader, p. 107.

117 "shrugged his shoulders, pulled down his vest" Cadwallader, p. 109.

117 "with the utmost good humor" Cadwallader, p. 117.

118 "These missiles weigh about a pound" Tunnard, p. 259.

118 "It has been four weeks since we have been here" Jackson, p. 104.

118 "While I am writing you" Orme, p. 277.

119 "A day or two ago I was out to the front" Orme, p. 283.

119 "my dear friend . . . hail and farewell!" Wilcox, pp. 482–85.

120 "a perfect annoyance to the regiment" Tunnard, p. 247.

121 "the attempt was abandoned amid a general disappointment" Tunnard, p. 248.

121 "I have just finished my dinner" Jackson, p. 104.

121 "fresh beef had long since been used up" Tunnard, p. 250.

122 "Yesterday the Themometer [sic] stood 100 degrees Fah." Wilcox, p. 487.

122 "The variety of bugs here would astonish you" Orme, p. 279.

122 "Yank, why don't you all make a general assault" Wilson, p. 220.

123 "Bombshells in the form of huge iron spheres" William Lord, p. 50.

123 "squalling infants, family quarrels, and the noise of general discord" William Lord, p. 46.

124 "In one of the wings, my bed fitted" Loughborough, p. 61.

125 "go over his body first" Walker, p. 176.

126 "a bombshell burst in the very center of that pretty dining room" Walker, p. 167.

126 "The blood was gushing from my nose, eyes, ears, and mouth" Lucy Bell, p. 13.

127 "from a spent shell which passed so near" William Lord, p. 50.

127 "In that very instant a shell exploded" William Lord, p. 47.

128 "ran into her mother's presence, sinking like a wounded dove . . . The screams of the women of Vicksburg" Loughborough, pp. 92, 131.

129 "Our provisions were becoming scarce" Lucy Bell, p. 13.

129 "most of us lived on corn bread and bacon" Loughborough, pp. 60–61.

129 "The undaunted Johnston is at hand" Walker, p. 187.

130 "General Johnston was at Clinton" Walker, p. 250.

130 "I am trying to gather a force" Johnston, p. 189.

130   "I consider saving Vicksburg hopeless. . . . Your telegram grieves and alarms us" Johnston, pp. 511, 200.

131   "the eyes and hopes of the whole Confederacy are upon you" Johnston, pp. 513–14.

131   "I am too weak to save Vicksburg" Johnston, p. 193.

131   "Our men are becoming much fatigued" Johnston, p. 194.

131   "I hope you will advance with the least possible delay" Pemberton, pp. 210–11.

132   "would be an impolitic confession of weakness" Pemberton, p. 213.

132   "the gloomiest forebodings . . . I hear everyone complaining" Fremantle, pp. 164, 174.

133   "June 25th—Horrible day . . . You must get me out" Walker, p. 197; Carter, p. 284.

133   "How very sad this life in Vicksburg" Loughborough, pp. 81–82.

Chapter 6

134   "It is a sad story" Buehler, p. 6.

135   "Everyone is asking, 'Where is our army' " Broadhead, p. 8.

135   "frightful rumors were afloat" Buehler, p. 7.

135   "people did little more but stand along the streets" Salome Myers Stewart, p. 145.

136   "it appears to me he can't help but win" Oates, p. 350.

136   "Hooker may commit the same fault as McClellan" Oates, p. 350.

137   "The city was a bedlam." Coffin, p. 15.

137   "Philadelphia has not responded" *War of the Rebellion*, vol. 27, p. 169.

138   "Jerseymen!" *War of the Rebellion*, vol. 27, p. 190.

138   "A people who want the heart to defend their soil" *War of the Rebellion*, vol. 27, p. 347.

138   "Arise now in your might." Miers and Brown, p. 13.

138   "we were in a condition to believe anything" Buehler, p. 8.

139   "*June 20.* The report of today is that the rebels" Broadhead, p. 6.

141   "throw an overwhelming force on their advance" McPherson, p. 655.

141   "The [Confederate] staff officers spoke of the coming battle as a certainty" Hoke, p. 42.

143   "Ewell ate as much fruit as the next man." Pfanz, pp. 296–97.

143   "I cannot hope that Heaven will prosper our cause" Freeman, *R. E. Lee*, vol. 3, p. 55.

143   "No private property shall be injured" Stackpole, p. 28.

144   "Soldier after soldier wrote home of stunning landscape" Boritt, p. 9.

145   "You, gentlemen, must have seen for yourselves" Hoke, p. 211.

146   "the handsomest man of his age I ever saw" Fremantle, p. 197.

146   "Oh, I wish he was ours." Freeman, *R. E. Lee*, vol. 3, p. 54.

146   "I have been waiting for the arrival of Stuart" Lee, pp. 516, 518, 523.

147   "seven to ten thousand cavalry who should be with us" Miers and Brown, p. 35.

147   "Never have I seen so much emotion" Hoke, p. 205.

148   "Take a worthless vagabond who has enlisted" Catton, *Army of the Potomac*, vol. 2, p. 262.

149   "Since I last wrote we have been doing some 'Tall' marching. . . . It was one of the most heartbreaking marches . . . I came darned near going under" Moe, pp. 248–49.

149   "We have lost a dozen men or more" Donaldson, pp. 281–83.

150   "much shocked to find such great numbers of bodies" Wheeler, *Witness to Gettysburg*, pp. 72–73.

151   "I presume we will meet the enemy" Moe, p. 253.

152   "Sell my men all the goods they want" Hoke, p. 110.

152   "Their dress consisted of nearly every imaginable color" Hoke, p. 208.

152   "we found the people very sullen" Miers and Brown, p. 25.

152   "All its houses were shut up" Fremantle, p. 191.

153   "The people look as sour as vinegar" Pfanz, p. 295.

153   "Take care, madam" Fremantle, p. 191.

154   "Yes, madam, it's very sad" Fremantle, p. 224.

154   "It must be remembered that we make war only upon armed men" Lee, p. 534.

155   "He replied: 'Do you want the autograph of a rebel?'" Hoke, p. 198.

156   "Our army is in good spirits" Freeman, *R. E. Lee*, vol. 3, p. 58.

156   "When [the Union troops] hear where we are, they will make forced marches" Freeman, *R. E. Lee*, vol. 3, p. 58.

156   "Hereabout we shall probably meet the enemy" Freeman, *R. E. Lee*, vol. 3, p. 59.

156   "On the 26th of June they came in considerable force." Buehler, p. 9.

157   "They came with such horrid yells" Broadhead, p. 8.

157   "At last we have seen the rebels" Salome Myers Stewart, p. 161.

157   "I scrambled in, slammed shut the door" Alleman, pp. 21–22.

158   "I never saw a more unsightly set of men" Buehler, p. 10.

159   "The requisitions asked for can not be given" Hoke, p. 171.

159   "In two months our money will be better than yours." Bloom, p. 168.

160   "We had a pleasant talk" Buehler, p. 12.

160   "Well, we haven't as many men left in the South" Buehler, p. 12.

161   "acts like a man without a plan" Stevens, p. 226.

161   "There is a good deal of grumbling" Donaldson, pp. 283, 286.

162   "only salvation [is] to make it appear" Stevens, p. 227.

162   "He will fight well" Stevens, p. 230.

164   "I've been tried and condemned without a hearing" *Battles and Leaders*, vol. 3, p. 243.

164   "He was standing with bowed head and downcast eyes" Coffin, p. 28.

164   "a brave and accomplished officer . . . The country looks to this army" *War of the Rebellion*, vol. 27, pp. 373, 374.

165   "a damned old goggle-eyed, snapping turtle" Cleaves, p. xii.

165   "As a commander, Meade seemed to me to lack the boldness" Dana, pp. 189–90.

165   "most unlooked for by us all" Donaldson, p. 293.

165   "intelligence that 'Fighting Joe' is superseded by Gen. Meade" Moe, p. 253.

166   "I tell you, I think a great deal of that fine fellow Meade." Cleaves, p. 126.

166   "My predecessor, General Hooker" Hoke, pp. 247–48.

166   "Dearest, you know how reluctant we both have been" Cleaves, p. 127.

167   "I do not know what to do." Freeman, *R. E. Lee*, vol. 3, p. 60.

167   "dirt-stained, travel-worn, and very much broken down" Wert, *General James Longstreet*, p. 255.

Chapter 7

169   "Still in this dreary cave" Mrs. William W. Lord, p. 6.

169   "visited with a terrible scourge" Tunnard, pp. 260–61.

171   "Even as my father watched him" William Lord, p. 51.

172   "Everybody admits that we have all covered ourselves in glory" Hoehling, pp. 241–42.

172   "characteristic of his wit" Lucy Bell, p. 235.

173   "Every new party of deserters which reached us" Dana, p. 93.

173   "inclined to think that Vicksburg cannot hold out many days longer" Orme, p. 287.

174   "No attempt to charge was made this time" Grant, p. 325.

174   "the last stirring incident of the siege" *Battles and Leaders*, vol. 3, pp. 491–92.

174   "The spectacle was horrible in the extreme" Tunnard, pp. 266, 267.

174   "We are marching as fast as we can" Cleaves, p. 131.

175   "If Lee is moving for Baltimore" Meade, *Life and Letters*, vol. 2, p. 11.

175   "my main point being to find and fight the enemy." Cleaves, p. 11.

175   "the enemy are advancing" Stackpole, p. 96.

176   "the immense issues involved in the struggle" Hoke, p. 256.

176 "Corps and other commanders are authorized to order the instant death" Hoke, p. 256.

177 "A good Union lady gives me a quart of apple butter." Moe, p. 255.

177 "Just that little expression" Moe, p. 256.

178 "Stanton can hear nothing from the Army of the Potomac" Hoke, p. 249.

178 "all bars, coffee-houses, drinking-saloons, and other places" *War of the Rebellion*, vol. 27, p. 437.

179 "marching on Philadelphia, and also on points" *War of the Rebellion*, vol. 27, p. 409.

179 "The people of New Jersey" *War of the Rebellion*, vol. 27, p. 409.

180 "Let me impress on you" *War of the Rebellion*, vol. 27, p. 409.

180 "I beg to direct your attention to the subject" *War of the Rebellion*, vol. 27, p. 429.

180 "I know of no available military means" *War of the Rebellion*, vol. 27, p. 429.

181 "Ah, general, the enemy is a long time finding us" Freeman, *R. E. Lee*, vol. 3, p. 64.

181 "Tomorrow, gentlemen, we will not move to Harrisburg" Freeman, *R. E. Lee*, vol. 3, p. 64.

181 "General Meade will commit no blunder" Freeman, *R. E. Lee*, vol. 3, p. 64.

182 "immensely strong physique" Miers and Brown, p. 29.

183 "Stuart was in all his glory . . . Take care, General" Burke Davis, p. 305.

183 "Bring it to me, please" Burke Davis, p. 309.

184 "rollicking, frolicking and running after girls" Freeman, *Lee's Lieutenants*, p. 51.

185 "rode his cavalry right out of the campaign." Catton, *Army of the Potomac*, vol. 2, p. 254.

185 "The wagons were brand new" Freeman, *Lee's Lieutenants*, p. 66.

186 "I shall never forget the glimpse I then saw" Thomas, *Bold Dragoon*, p. 244.

186 "Whole regiments slept in the saddle" Freeman, *Lee's Lieutenants*, p. 71.

187 "There is the difficulty" Lee, p. 490.

189 "admired [Jackson's] genius, but was certain of his lunacy" Pfanz, p. 237.

190 "My wife, Mrs. Brown." Foote, vol. 2, p. 439.

190 "Old Ewell is worse in love" Pfanz, p. 331.

190 "Gettysburg was to show the results" Freeman, *R. E. Lee*, vol. 3, p. 12.

192 "Longstreet is a Capital soldier." Wert, *General James Longstreet*, p. 131.

192 "the staff in my right hand"; "my old war-horse" Wert, *General James Longstreet*, pp. 152, 200.

192 "quite touching" Wert, *General James Longstreet*, p. 254.

193 "Vicksburg was doomed . . . I found his mind made up" *Battles and Leaders*, vol. 3, pp. 245, 246.

194   "Longstreet mistook courtesy for consent" Freeman, *Lee's Lieutenants*, p. 46.

194   "He don't put on so much style" Longacre, *General John Buford*, p. 88.

195   "I had never seen so many soldiers" Alleman, p. 28.

195   "Men, women, and children crowded the sidewalk" Bennett, p. 18.

196   "1863 Spring styles" Stevens, p. 236.

197   "I am just from General Lee" Freeman, *Lee's Lieutenants*, p. 78.

197   "the people settled down in their homes . . . even dreamed that a great battle" Bennett, pp. 18–19.

197   "It begins to look as though we will have a battle soon" Broadhead, p. 11.

198   "No, you won't." Longacre, *General John Buford*, p. 188.

Chapter 8

202   "What's the matter, John?" Longacre, *General John Buford*, p. 193.

202   "The enemy are advancing in strong force" Cleaves, p. 135.

203   "I cannot think what has become of Stuart" Hoke, pp. 290–91.

204   "Lee galloped toward Gettysburg" Freeman, *R. E. Lee*, vol. 3, p. 68.

204   "People were running here and there" Broadhead, p. 11.

204   "I remember hearing some of the soldiers" Alleman, p. 34.

204   "handed the water to the soldiers . . . At ten o'clock that morning I saw the first blood." Salome Myers Stewart, p. 148.

205   "there were enough soldiers here . . . a quickly increased interest" Bloom, p. 172.

205   "swallow-tailed coat with smooth brass buttons . . . true blue and grit" *Battles and Leaders*, vol. 3, p. 276.

206   "We were doubtless the only persons on the Union side" Bloom, p. 173.

206   "Not long after this, an [enemy] ambulance" Conklin, p. 15.

207   "Forward! For God's sake, forward." Miers and Brown, p. 61.

208   "Archer! I'm glad to see you." Foote, vol. 2, p. 470.

209   "A tremendous battle has been raging" Stackpole, p. 135.

209   "Neither Lee nor Meade had planned to fight here" Moe, p. 260.

210   "Good! That is just like Reynolds"; "sorrow and shock reflected in Meade's drawn face" Cleaves, p. 135.

211   "the most magnificent looking General" Haskell, p. 15.

212   "Wreck, disaster, disorder" Foote, vol. 2, p. 482.

212   "No, I am not prepared to bring on a general engagement" Freeman, *Lee's Lieutenants*, p. 86.

213   "They broke and ran" Foote, vol. 2, p. 477.

215   "running and pushing each other . . . 'All you good people'" Bennett, p. 31.

215 "Those two hours I can never forget" Conklin, p. 149.

216 "a shot banged loudly right by a window." Bennett, p. 33.

216 "Every pew was full" Slade and Alexander, p. 66.

217 "Father looked at me" Bennett, p. 25.

217 "As they pass by I see his eyes" Alleman, pp. 41–42.

217 "'Oh, this is nothing'... the groaning and the crying" Alleman, pp. 43–44.

218 "You must open the door ... He was going to shoot" Slade and Alexander, p. 67.

219 "Madam, you have Union soldiers concealed" Buehler, pp. 20–21.

220 "How changed the town looked ... As I write all is quiet" Broadhead, pp. 12–13.

220 "the strongest position by nature that I ever saw." Jordan, p. 84.

222 "it was only necessary to press ... General Ewell did not express any objection" Taylor, p. 95.

222 "No, no, I'm not hurt" Freeman, *Lee's Lieutenants*, p. 93.

223 "Oh, for the presence and inspiration"; "It was a moment of critical importance"; "Well, General, we have had a grand success" Freeman, *Lee's Lieutenants*, pp. 93–94.

224 "He did not like what he saw." Wert, *General James Longstreet*, p. 257.

225 "The enemy is there ... They are there in position" *Battles and Leaders*, vol. 3, pp. 339–40.

225 "If he is there" Wert, *General James Longstreet*, p. 257.

226 "Can't you with your corps attack on this flank tomorrow?" Freeman, *R. E. Lee*, vol. 3, p. 79.

226 "If I had had Stonewall Jackson with me" Freeman, *R. E. Lee*, vol. 3, p. 161.

226 "it took a dozen blunders to lose Gettysburg" Pfanz, p. 322.

227 "Unless the siege of Vicksburg is raised" *War of the Rebellion*, vol. 24, p. 347.

228 "At Taneytown we hear there has been fighting"; "Three times we got permission" Moe, p. 256.

229 "We talked a few moments of the great battle" Moe, p. 257.

229 "When darkness fell and the full moon rose" Trulock, pp. 124, 126.

230 "At night all was quiet" Bennett, p. 42.

230 "Madam, we become hardened to such things" Pfanz, p. 313.

231 "I am confident we can hold this position"; "I am glad to hear you say so" Cleaves, p. 140.

Chapter 9

232 "We may fight it out here" Boritt, p. 17.

233 "quick, bold, cheerful ... self-possession and absolute coolness" Cleaves, p. 143.

234 "General [Lee] was a little nervous this morning" Freeman, *R. E. Lee*, vol. 3, p. 89.

234   "quiet self-possessed calmness . . . more anxious and ruffled" Wert, *General James Longstreet*, pp. 261–62.

235   "Lee seemed very much disappointed" Anderson and Anderson, p. 407.

236   "No, General" Freeman, *R. E. Lee*, vol. 3, p. 89.

236   "Had he been Jackson" Freeman, *R. E. Lee*, vol. 3, p. 90.

236   "The enemy have the advantage of us" Anderson and Anderson, p. 407.

237   "The attack must be made *at once*" Hoke, p. 311.

237   "more impatience than I ever saw him exhibit" Foote, vol. 2, p. 491.

237   "Ah, well, that was to be expected." Anderson and Anderson, p. 408.

238   "There was no telling . . . I will consider myself very lucky" Alleman, p. 49.

238   "We will mark that officer for this . . . a pretty well established fact" Alleman, p. 50.

238   "The sight I then beheld was wonderful" Alleman, pp. 51–52.

239   "in direct line with where my breast had been a few seconds before" Bloom, pp. 177–78.

239   "Why, man, take off that gray suit" Bennett, p. 53.

240   "knock the tops from the kegs" Bennett, p. 47.

240   "About all I lived on was strong tea" Conklin, p. 45.

240   "If you were as hungry as we are" Conklin, p. 46.

240   "went to the garden and picked a mess of beans" Broadhead, p. 13.

241   "Soon we had plenty of water" Conklin, p. 61.

241   "Some of the wounded lay in the pews . . . 'What can I do for you?'" Salome Myers Stewart, p. 152.

242   "It was painful beyond description . . . Let me ask your help now" Burke Davis, p. 334.

243   "Tell General Pickett" Wert, *General James Longstreet*, p. 280.

243   "An intangible, gut-churning fear" Priest, p. 7.

244   "I would not like to teach my grandson" Wert, *General James Longstreet*, p. 269.

245   "How are you going in?" Wert, *General James Longstreet*, p. 270.

245   "eyes cast to the ground" Foote, vol. 2, p. 493.

245   "The view presented astonished me" Wert, *General James Longstreet*, p. 271.

246   "General Lee's orders are to attack" Miers and Brown, p. 109.

246   "We must obey the orders of General Lee." Miers and Brown, p. 110.

248   "Whether he was drinking, fighting, wenching or plotting" Catton, *Army of the Potomac*, vol. 2, pp. 150–51.

249   "His political aspirations" Swanberg, p. 72.

249   "sitting alone on the benches of the Congress" Chesnut, p. 379.

249   "an infinitely lonely little woman" Catton, *Army of the Potomac*, vol. 2, p. 152.

250 "Certainly, within the limits of the general instructions" Swanberg, p. 208.

250 "It was magnificent to see those ten or twelve thousand men" Haskell, p. 36.

251 "General, I am afraid you are too far out" Cleaves, p. 148.

252 "In places the men had to climb up" Anderson and Anderson, p. 410.

253 "Hold that ground at all hazards." Trulock, p. 133.

253 "Don't yield one inch!" Hoke, p. 329.

254 "Again and again was this mad rush repeated" Anderson and Anderson, pp. 410–11.

254 "The blood stood in puddles on the rocks . . . My thought was running deep" Trulock, p. 147.

255 "We ran like a herd of wild cattle." Miers and Brown, p. 132.

255 "Cheer less, men, and fight more" Wert, *General James Longstreet*, p. 276.

256 "Despite his pain and shock" Swanberg, p. 217.

257 "Great God! Have we got the universe to whip?" Wert, *General James Longstreet*, p. 278.

257 "Come on, gentlemen"; "this act of pluck" Cleaves, p. 153.

258 "Charge those lines." Moe, p. 268.

258 "We had no time to weep" Moe, pp. 269–70.

258 "We felt at every step the heavy stroke of fresh troops" Wert, *General James Longstreet*, p. 277.

259 "ill-timed, ill-coordinated" Anderson and Anderson, p. 413.

259 "Now Sickles' blunder"; "Yes, but it is all right now" Cleaves, pp. 153, 154.

260 "Now all is silent . . . The knapsacks cast aside . . . There was no rebellion here now." Haskell, pp. 52–54.

260 "I help our colonel off the field" Moe, p. 275.

261 "the dreadful slaughter of human life" Buehler, p. 22.

261 "He suddenly groaned" Bennett, p. 54.

262 "While fanning him" Salome Myers Stewart, p. 153.

262 "Most of them were ragged and dirty" Slade and Alexander, p. 91.

262 "It seemed as though the heavens" Alleman, p. 56.

263 "The Yankees have a good position" Miers and Brown, p. 156.

263 "I cannot sleep" Broadhead, p. 14.

263 "The command suffers greatly from intermittent fever . . . From shortness of rations . . . my men are much reduced in strength" *War of the Rebellion*, vol. 24, pp. 347, 358, 349.

264 "that the physical condition and health of our men" Pemberton, p. 222.

264 "either to surrender while we still had ammunition . . . I have heard your vote . . . I am a Northern man" *Battles and Leaders*, vol. 3, p. 492.

266   "threatening Washington City" Hoehling, appendix, no page.

266   "made no attempt to control" Foote, vol. 2, p. 521.

267   "Such then is the decision"; "we shall whip him." Meade, *Life and Letters*, vol. 2, p. 97.

Chapter 10

270   "General, I have had my scouts out all night" Wert, *General James Longstreet*, p. 283.

270   "The enemy is there" Anderson and Anderson, p. 415.

271   "That will give me fifteen thousand men. . . . General [Lee] seemed a little impatient at my remarks" *Battles and Leaders*, vol. 3, p. 343.

271   "preferred Longstreet, recalcitrant" George Stewart, p. 23.

271   "Nothing was left but to proceed" Wert, *General James Longstreet*, p. 284.

272   "was shot to death that morning" Stackpole, p. 243.

272   "No, Annie, I can't" Small, p. 30.

272   "Human beings, mangled and torn" Hoke, p. 359.

273   "If there is anyone in this house . . . Georgia, your sister is dead." Small, pp. 32, 34.

273   "I find my dear brother dead!" Moe, p. 277.

274   "I hastened down to the little basement room" Alleman, p. 64.

274   "He seems better" Salome Myers Stewart, p. 153.

274   "You can't go up there" Conklin, p. 50.

275   "while one brick remained upon another" Broadhead, p. 15.

275   "Now 'Johnny,' I know you have a lot of guns." Slade and Alexander, p. 117.

276   "I must confess that the General's face" Miers and Brown, p. 177.

276   "The attack must succeed." Anderson and Anderson, p. 417.

277   "June Kimble" Priest, p. 28.

278   "has brought about an awful seriousness" Priest, p. 31.

278   "just like the good old days" Priest, p. 30.

278   "Come on, Fitz" Gordon, p. 111.

279   "The archetype of a Virginia slave-baron" Gordon, p. 109.

279   "taking Longstreet's orders in emergencies" Sorrel, p. 48.

280   "his lack of self-reliance and discipline" Gordon, p. 8.

281   "aptitude as a class clown" Longacre, *Pickett*, p. 11.

281   "gallant and meritorious conduct." Longacre, *Pickett*, p. 24.

282   "but one reason for his desolation" Longacre, *Pickett*, p. 32.

283   "So bitter is the feeling here" Longacre, *Pickett*, p. 54.

285 "But he is tired of it" Sorrel, pp. 146–47.

285 "I don't think his division benefitted" Wert, *General James Longstreet*, p. 237.

286 "I have the honor to propose an armistice" *Battles and Leaders*, vol. 3, p. 530.

286 "Your note of this date is just received" Grant, p. 328.

288 "I would not give twenty-five cents" Georg and Busey, p. 29.

288 "watched their men's reaction when they heard" Priest, p. 46.

288 "This is a desperate thing"; "The slaughter will be terrible" Wert, *General James Longstreet*, p. 287.

289 "Never was I so depressed" Hoke, p. 421.

290 "sudden shock" Alexander, p. 254.

290 "was so much impressed" Hoke, p. 421.

290 "Colonel [Alexander]: If the artillery fire" Alexander, p. 254.

290 "General [Longstreet]: I will only be able to judge" Alexander, pp. 254–55.

291 "felt that if the artillery did not produce" Hoke, p. 422.

291 "Colonel [Alexander]: The intention is to advance" Alexander, p. 255.

291 "He has put the responsibility . . . Yankee army is up there in a bunch" Alexander, p. 255.

292 "I felt that I could not make any delay . . . When our artillery fire" *Battles and Leaders*, vol. 3, p. 363.

293 "Short-tempered Meade blew up at him" Catton, *Army of the Potomac*, vol. 2, pp. 309–10.

293 "We had a great fight yesterday" Cleaves, p. 158.

293 "He was a quiet, excellent gentleman" Haskell, p. 80.

294 "We dozed in the heat" Haskell, p. 81.

Chapter 11

295 "Let the batteries open" Freeman, *Lee's Lieutenants*, p. 153.

295 "Then every gun in the line" Catton, *Army of the Potomac*, vol. 2, p. 310.

296 "I found him tied to a tree" Haskell, p. 82.

297 "Gentlemen, are you trying to find a safe place?" Meade, *Life and Letters*, vol. 2, pp. 106–7.

298 "This soon became monotonous" George Stewart, p. 149.

298 "The water is cold enough" George Stewart, p. 150.

298 "We see the poor fellows" Haskell, p. 86.

298 "The soldier stopped and turned about" Haskell, p. 87.

299 "As we lay there" Moe, p. 284.

300 "The first man who leaves his post again" Priest, p. 67.

301 "Glory to God!" George Stewart, p. 147.

301 "They screech, sing, scream" Dooley, p. 104.

302 "The heavy missile had descended" Georg and Busey, pp. 47–48.

302 "Man seldom sees or hears the likes of this" Georg and Busey, p. 53.

303 "A man had about as well die" George Stewart, p. 140.

303 "Doctor, they have got Jere Gage at last." Priest, p. 72; George Stewart, p. 141.

305 "There are times when a corps commander's life" Gambone, p. 120.

305 "along the line in front of us" Moe, pp. 284–85.

305 "as quiet as an old farmer" Georg and Busey, p. 43.

305 "General, this is a terrible place." Wert, *General James Longstreet*, pp. 289–90.

306 "You'll get your fool head knocked off" Wert, *General James Longstreet*, p. 290.

307 "the flower of Lee's army" Hoke, p. 369.

308 "Hearts were filled with sadness"; "Hancock, good-bye" Jordan, p. 34.

309 "General Meade expressed the hope" George Stewart, pp. 154–55.

311 "If you are coming at all . . . At first I thought it only crippled guns . . . If they don't put fresh batteries there" Alexander, p. 258.

311 "For God's sake, come quick." Alexander, p. 259.

311 "General, shall I advance?" . . . "My feelings had so overcome me" Hoke, p. 422.

312 "I was convinced that he would be leading his troops"; "Sir, I shall lead my division forward" *Battles and Leaders*, vol. 3, p. 345.

312 "If Old Peter's nod means death" George Stewart, p. 164.

312 "Go. Halt Pickett right where he is" Alexander, p. 261.

312 "I then saw that there was no help for it" Hoke, p. 423.

313 "Charge the enemy" George Stewart, p. 190.

313 "We rise to our feet" Dooley, p. 105.

313 "Remember men, what you are fighting for"; "Yes, General" Sublett, p. 27.

314 "Now, Colonel. For the honor" George Stewart, p. 171.

314 "All appreciated the danger" Georg and Busey, p. 36.

314 "If I live for a hundred years" Georg and Busey, pp. 86–87.

315 "They were old soldiers" Catton, *Army of the Potomac*, vol. 2, p. 314.

316 "A rising tide of armed men" Moe, p. 287.

316 "ocean of armed men . . . the dull gray masses" Haskell, pp. 96–97.

316 "The click of the lock" Haskell, pp. 97–98.

Chapter 12

318 "No one who saw them could help" Priest, p. 92.

319 "Look at my poor boy" Priest, p. 102.

319 "Armistead, I am going to charge" Sublett, p. 28.

320 "Their front line went down" Moe, p. 288.

320 "Close up the ranks" Dooley, p. 106.

321 "Glory to God!" Foote, vol. 2, p. 561.

321 "A moan went up from the field" Catton, *Army of the Potomac*, vol. 2, p. 318.

321 "sight never before witnessed" Sorrel, p. 163.

322 "There are the guns, boys." Priest, p. 122.

323 "Why, good gracious, Captain" Priest, p. 103.

323 "Look over your shoulder" Priest, p. 105.

323 "I wouldn't have missed this for anything"; "Captain Bright, ride to General Pickett" Fremantle, p. 212; George Stewart, pp. 195, 197.

323 "valley of death" Georg and Busey, p. 123.

324 "Shot through both thighs" Dooley, p. 107.

327 "We can't stop here" Georg and Busey, p. 139.

327 "Come on, boys" Hoke, p. 402.

327 "It's our turn next"; "It has now been nearly two weeks" Patton, pp. 49, 50.

328 "the road lay open" George Stewart, p. 221.

329 "If men ever became devils" Moe, p. 290.

329 "By God, boys, we've got 'em now." George Stewart, p. 247.

330 "There—listen—we hear a new shout" Dooley, p. 107.

330 "We gained nothing but glory" Wert, *General James Longstreet*, p. 292.

330 "If there was any one spot" Georg and Busey, p. 141.

331 "[A Confederate soldier] drew a bead on me" Moe, p. 292.

331 "If we only had had another line" George Stewart, p. 251.

332 "You are a damned brave set of fellows" Priest, p. 152.

332 "After all, after all" Priest, p. 161.

332 "I am here a prisoner-of-war" Boritt, p. 26.

333 "I thought it was you, Sergeant" Priest, p. 161.

334 "Say to General Hancock for me" Jordan, p. 99.

334 "Tell General Hancock that I know I did my country a great wrong" Haskell, p. 115.

334 "How is it going here?" Haskell, p. 118.

335 "If the enemy does attack" Haskell, p. 119.

335 "The enemy must be short of ammunition" Jordan, p. 99.

335 "General, I will give you half an hour" Hoke, p. 431.

336 "Ah! General Meade" George Stewart, p. 259.

336 "Don't stop any of my men" Hoke, p. 427.

336 "Taylor, we've lost all our friends" Boritt, p. 24.

336   "General, I am ruined" Gordon, p. 116.

337   "only an agonized spectator . . . He had become wholly useless" George Stewart, pp. 246, 230.

338   "Pickett stood transfixed in horror" Gordon, p. 116.

338   "General Lee, I have no division"; "Come, General Pickett" Gordon, p. 116.

338   "All this has been my fault." Freeman, *R. E. Lee*, vol. 3, p. 130.

338   "This has been a sad day" Fremantle, p. 214.

338   "My son, I hope you will soon be well." Freeman, *R. E. Lee*, vol. 3, p. 131.

339   "We knew that with every explosion" Broadhead, p. 15.

339   "We shall see tomorrow" Broadhead, pp. 15–16.

339   "The combination of overburdened privies" Bennett, p. 62.

340   "Along with the stench of unwashed bodies" Salome Myers Stewart, p. 153.

340   "There, as though I was almost upon them" Bennett, p. 64.

340   "The whole country seemed filled with desolation" Alleman, p. 71.

341   "To the south of the house" Alleman, p. 74.

341   "I feel a confidence" Pemberton, p. 228.

341   "Pemberton and I had served" Grant, p. 329.

342   "promptly and unceremoniously rejected" Grant, p. 329.

343   "As soon as rolls can be made out" Grant, p. 330.

344   "In the main, your terms are accepted" *Battles and Leaders*, vol. 3, p. 533.

344   "The amendment proposed by you" Grant, p. 331.

345   "All during the day" Jackson, p. 111.

345   "Joe, come here with your gun, quick" Hoehling, p. 270.

346   "shaking hands as cordially" Hoehling, p. 270.

346   "What could it mean?" "I told the Major to say" Mrs. William W. Lord, pp. 7–8.

346   "All was quiet" Lucy Bell, p. 13.

347   "an expression of sadness"; "Yes, it has been a sad, sad day"; "We must now return to Virginia" *Battles and Leaders*, vol. 3, pp. 321–22.

Chapter 13

348   "This morning, about six o'clock" Broadhead, p. 16.

348   "I believe the Confederates are retreating" Bennett, p. 68.

348   "The rebels have left" Conklin, p. 162.

348   "All around us were evidences" Buehler, pp. 24–25.

349   "There were some sorry-looking homes" Slade and Alexander, p. 138.

350   "It was a noisy demonstration"; "I think I never knew anything sweeter" Bennett, p. 69.

350 "We were between two fires" Broadhead, p. 16.

351 "Look out! Pickets below!" Conklin, p. 164.

351 "Oh, I believe I am shot!" Bennett, p. 72.

352 "General: In order to promote"; "It is not in my power" *War of the Rebellion*, vol. 27, p. 514.

353 "reduced to guard duty" Georg and Busey, p. 190.

353 "I still have the greatest confidence" Georg and Busey, p. 191.

353 "Well, it is all over now" Schildt, pp. 20–21.

354 "The prisoners have been far more cheerful" Schildt, p. 51.

354 "he was extremely grateful" Fremantle, p. 218.

354 "This morning the enemy has withdrawn" Meade, *Life and Letters*, vol. 2, pp. 113–14.

355 "The commanding general, in behalf of the country" *War of the Rebellion*, vol. 27, p. 519.

355 "I shall require some time to get up supplies" Meade, *Life and Letters*, vol. 2, p. 116.

356 "Such a sight"; "the look of the bloated, blackened corpses" Boritt, p. 25.

356 "there was scarcely room to move" Donaldson, p. 310.

356 "All the trees . . . Outside the wall" Wainwright, pp. 251–52.

357 "Dead soldiers were everywhere" Slade and Alexander, p. 137.

357 "surrounded by the wrecks of battle" Alleman, p. 81.

357 "many soldiers lost their heads" Sandburg, vol. 4, p. 342.

359 "Boys, what are you doing?" Gambone, p. 166.

360 "Maggie, take the children home" Mrs. William W. Lord, p. 8.

360 "It's all over" Loughborough, p. 139.

360 "The morning of the 4th" Lucy Bell, p. 13.

360 "signal for a fearful outburst" Tunnard, p. 271.

361 "About ten o'clock, from where we were" Jackson, p. 112.

361 "Oh! What a glorious Fourth" Orme, p. 288.

361 "I think the fall of Vicksburg is the turning point" Orme, p. 306.

361 "*Saturday, July 4th*. This day in American history" Wilcox, p. 495.

362 "The men of the two armies" *Battles and Leaders*, vol. 3, p. 536.

362 "brought haversacks filled with provisions" Tunnard, p. 271.

363 "I was talking with one" Jackson, p. 112.

363 "No one even offered Grant a seat . . . their haversacks and canteens" Wilson, p. 223.

364 "This is a day of jubilee" Catton, *Grant Moves South*, p. 477.

365 "The enemy surrendered this morning." Grant, p. 334.

365 "I have the honor to inform you" Musicant, p. 290.

365 "I cannot, in words" Hearn, p. 236.

365 "The people and the rebel soldiers" Orme, p. 289.

366 "Men felt very bitterly" Lucy Bell, p. 13.

366 "The town is literally knocked to pieces" Orme, p. 290.

366 "It was a desolate looking place" Jackson, pp. 112–13.

367 "Such a scene of desolation" Mrs. William W. Lord, pp. 8–9.

368 "as he paced up and down the room" Sandburg, vol. 4, p. 343.

368 "The President announces to the country" *War of the Rebellion*, vol. 27, p. 515.

369 "I never knew such excitement" Cleaves, p. 171.

369 "deafening applause" Cleaves, p. 170.

369 "I saw him read General Meade's congratulatory order" Sandburg, vol. 4, p. 344.

370 "Shortly after noon on the 4th" *Battles and Leaders*, vol. 3, p. 423.

370 "During the storm" *Battles and Leaders*, vol. 3, p. 423.

371 "On! On! We *must* move on" *Battles and Leaders*, vol. 3, p. 423.

371 "Oh God! Why can't I die?" *Battles and Leaders*, vol. 3, p. 424.

372 "No one with any feelings" Schildt, p. 15.

372 "dead horses, broken down and abandoned wagons" Hoke, p. 502.

Chapter 14

374 "the period of ten days following the battle" Patterson, p. 4.

374n "Mother would tell her, 'this is not the war'" Bloom, pp. 192–93.

375 "The sights and sounds at the Court House" Buehler, p. 26.

375 "Can we endure the spectacle" Broadhead, p. 17.

375 "He had been sinking all morning" Salome Myers Stewart, p. 154.

376 "Its every room was a chamber of death" Georg and Busey, p. 213.

376 "The men, restless, suffering" Georg and Busey, p. 214.

376 "This is a horrid night" Dooley, p. 111.

378 "From here and there" Patterson, p. 4.

378 "That stopped the trouble there" *Battles and Leaders*, vol. 3, p. 425.

380 "This morning we started out to see the wounded" Broadhead, p. 18.

381 "The rebels, as was just" Patterson, pp. 58–59.

382 "New England preachers" Patterson, p. 106.

382 "those who depended upon prayer" Patterson, pp. 106–7.

383 "Many persons have called today" Broadhead, p. 23.

383 "There was a tiny brook" Gambone, p. 165.

384 "There are no words in the English language . . . a melancholy sight" Conklin, p. 228.

384 "Samuel Watson, 5th Texas Regiment." Conklin, p. 353.

385 "she was never the same" Conklin, p. 357.

386 "vast concourse of sightseers . . . animated only by idle curiosity" Patterson, p. 118.

386 "The patriotism of the neighboring farmers" Patterson, pp. 53–54.

387 "Few good things can be said of Gettysburg farmers" Bloom, p. 191.

387 "Many are dying" Patterson, p. 123.

388 "We found that a piece of tree . . . Another trick" Slade and Alexander, p. 166.

389 "While passing along, the stench arising from the fields" Alleman, pp. 82–83.

390 "amusing themselves turning over my basket . . . I had no objection to that" Mrs. William W. Lord, p. 10.

391 "Two days bring about great changes" Jackson, p. 259.

391 "See here, Mister" *Battles and Leaders*, vol. 3, p. 492.

392 "Yes, from want of provisions inside" Symonds, p. 217.

393 "Saturday evening, Vicksburg" Loughborough, pp. 145–46.

393 "As we stepped aboard the boat" William Lord, p. 53.

394 "I will not take up arms" Tunnard, p. 277.

394 "Not a word of exultation" Tunnard, p. 278.

394 "I believe there was a feeling of sadness" Grant, p. 326.

395 "Well, Jack, old boy" Pemberton, p. 241.

396 "We have received news here" Orme, pp. 298–99.

396 "It was a grand battle" Meade, *Life and Letters*, vol. 2, p. 125.

396 "Now if General Meade can complete his work" Sandburg, vol. 4, p. 347.

396 "Papa will end the war" Cleaves, p. 176.

397 "I see also that the papers" Meade, *Life and Letters*, vol. 2, p. 132.

397 "There is reliable information . . . My information as to the crossing" *War of the Rebellion*, vol. 27, pp. 605–6.

399 "I have to grope my way in the dark" Cleaves, p. 179.

399 "The President seemed in a specially good humor" Hay, p. 61.

400 "unless something intervenes"; "They will be ready to fight" Sandburg, vol. 4, p. 250.

400 "Had the river not unexpectedly risen" Freeman, *R. E. Lee*, vol. 3, p. 141.

400 "Up to now, the enemy had pursued us" Alexander, pp. 270–71.

401 "how we all did wish" Alexander, p. 271.

401 "So far, everything goes well." *War of the Rebellion*, vol. 27, pp. 301–2.

401 "You are strong enough to attack" Sandburg, vol. 4, p. 351.

402 "Having been in command of the army" Hoke, p. 474.

403 "He has no pontoons . . . We shall pitch in." Cleaves, p. 182.

403 "The whole night had been spent" Alexander, p. 272.

404 "[they] came in sight of the rude pontoon bridge" Schildt, p. 102.

404 "There! I was expecting it." Freeman, *R. E. Lee*, vol. 3, p. 143.

405 "As far as the eye could reach" Schildt, p. 113.

406 "I looked across the swollen and turbid Potomac" Brooks, *Washington, D.C.*, p. 91.

406 "Well, here goes for two years more." Greene, p. 178.

406 "grief and anger [as] something sorrowful" Oates, p. 352.

406 "We had them within our grasp . . . Our Army held the war" Hay, pp. 62, 65.

407 "There is bad faith somewhere" Sandburg, vol. 4, p. 352.

407 "It is the same old story" Hay, p. 303.

407 "If I had gone up there" Hay, p. 63.

407 "My dear general, I do not believe you appreciate" Sandburg, vol. 4, p. 354; Oates, p. 353.

408 "This surrender [of Vicksburg]" Foote, vol. 2, pp. 641–42.

BIBLIOGRAPHY

Adams, Michael C. C. *Our Masters the Rebels: A Speculation on Union Military Failure in the East, 1861–1865.* Cambridge: Harvard University Press, 1978.

Alexander, Edward Porter. *Fighting for the Confederacy: The Personal Recollections of General Edward Porter Alexander.* Edited by Gary W. Gallagher. Chapel Hill: University of North Carolina Press, 1989.

Alleman, Tillie Pierce. *At Gettysburg: On What a Girl Saw and Heard of the Battle: A True Narrative.* New York: W. Lake Borland, 1889. Reprint, Baltimore: Butternut & Blue, 1994.

Anderson, Nancy Scott, and Dwight Anderson. *The Generals: Ulysses S. Grant and Robert E. Lee.* New York: Vintage Books, 1989.

Bates, David Homer. *Lincoln in the Telegraph Office: Recollections of the United States Military Telegraph Corps during the Civil War.* New York: Century, 1907.

Battles and Leaders of the Civil War. Vol. 3, edited by Robert U. Johnson and Clarence C. Buel. Secaucus, N.J.: Castle, 1989.

Bell, Lucy McRae. "A Girl's Experience in the Siege of Vicksburg." *Harper's Weekly,* June 8, 1912, pp. 12–13.

Bell, Robert T. *Eleventh Virginia Infantry.* Lynchburg, Va.: H. E. Howard, 1985.

Bennett, Gerald R. *Days of "Uncertainty and Dread": The Ordeal Endured by the Citizens of Gettysburg.* Littlestown, Pa.: Gerald L. Bennett, 1997.

Bloom, Robert L. "We Never Expected a Battle: The Civilians at Gettysburg, 1863." *Pennsylvania History,* October 1988.

Boritt, G. S. *The Gettysburg Nobody Knows.* New York: Oxford University Press, 1997.

Broadhead, Sarah M. *The Diary of a Lady of Gettysburg, Pennsylvania, from June 15 to July 15, 1863.* Hershey, Pa.: Gary T. Hawbaker, no date.

Brooks, Noah. *Mr. Lincoln's Washington: Selections from the Writings of Noah Brooks, Civil War Correspondent.* Edited by P. J. Staudenraus. New York: Thomas Yoseloff, 1967.

———. *Washington, D.C. in Lincoln's Time.* Edited by Herbert Mitgang. New York: Rinehart, 1958.

Buehler, Fannie J. *Recollections of the Rebel Invasion and One Woman's Experience during the Battle of Gettysburg.* Hershey, Pa.: Gary T. Hawbaker, no date.

Burlingame, Michael. *The Inner World of Abraham Lincoln.* Urbana: University of Illinois Press, 1994.

Cadwallader, Sylvanus. *Three Years with Grant: As Recalled by War Correspondent Sylvanus Cadwallader.* Edited by Benjamin P. Thomas. New York: Alfred A. Knopf, 1955.

Carter, Samuel, III. *The Final Fortress: The Campaign for Vicksburg, 1862–1863.* New York: St. Martin's Press, 1980.

Catton, Bruce. *The Army of the Potomac.* Vol. 1, *Mr. Lincoln's Army.* Garden City, N.Y.: Doubleday, 1951. Vol. 2, *Glory Road.* Garden City, N.Y.: Doubleday, 1952.

———. *Grant Moves South.* Boston: Little, Brown, 1960.

Chamberlain, Joshua. *Through Blood and Fire: Selected Civil War Papers of Major General Joshua Chamberlain.* Edited by Mark Nesbitt. Mechanicsburg, Pa.: Stackpole Books, 1996.

Chesnut, Mary. *Mary Chesnut's Civil War.* Edited by C. Vann Woodward. New Haven: Yale University Press, 1981.

Cleaves, Freeman. *Meade of Gettysburg.* Norman: University of Oklahoma Press, 1960.

Coffin, Charles. *Eyewitness to Gettysburg: The Story of Gettysburg as Told by the Leading Correspondent of His Day.* Edited by John W. Schildt. Shippensburg, Pa.: Burd Street Press, 1997.

Conklin, E. F. *Women at Gettysburg: 1863.* Gettysburg: Thomas Publications, 1993.

Connelly, Thomas L. *The Marble Man: Robert E. Lee and His Image in American Society.* New York: Alfred A. Knopf. 1977.

Dana, Charles A. *Recollections of the Civil War: With the Leaders at Washington and in the Field in the Sixties.* New York: Appleton, 1898. Reprint, Lincoln: University of Nebraska Press, 1996.

Davis, Burke. *Jeb Stuart: The Last Cavalier.* New York: Holt, Rinehart and Winston, 1957.

Davis, William C. *The Cause Lost: Myths and Realities of the Confederacy.* Lawrence: University Press of Kansas, 1996.

Donald, David Herbert. *Lincoln.* New York: Simon & Schuster, 1995.

Donaldson, Francis Adams. *Inside the Army of the Potomac: The Civil War Experience of Captain Francis Adams Donaldson.* Edited by Gregory J. Acken. Mechanicsburg, Pa.: Stackpole Books, 1998.

Dooley, John. *Confederate Soldier: His War Journal.* Edited by Joseph T. Durkin. Washington, D.C.: Georgetown University Press, 1945.

Dowdey, Clifford. *Death of a Nation: The Story of Lee and His Men at Gettysburg.* Baltimore: Butternut & Blue, 1988.

Foote, Shelby. *The Civil War: A Narrative.* Vol. 1, *Fort Sumter to Perryville.* Vol. 2, *Fredericksburg to Meridian.* New York: Vintage Books, 1986.

Freeman, Douglas Southall. *Lee's Lieutenants: A Study in Command.* New York: Charles Scribner's Sons, 1942–1944.

———. *R. E. Lee: A Biography.* 4 vols. New York: Charles Scribner's Sons, 1934–1936.

Fremantle, James. *The Fremantle Diary: Being the Journal of Lieutenant Colonel James Arthur Lyon Fremantle, Coldstream Guards, on His Three Months in the Southern States.* Edited by Walter Lord. Boston: Little, Brown, 1954.

Fullenkamp, Leonard, Stephen Bowman, and Jay Luvaas. *Guide to the Vicksburg Campaign.* Lawrence: University Press of Kansas, 1999.

Gambone, A. M. *Hancock at Gettysburg.* Baltimore: Butternut & Blue, 1997.

Georg, Kathleen, and John Busey. *Nothing but Glory: Pickett's Division at Gettysburg.* Hightstown, N.Y.: Longstreet House, 1987.

Gordon, Lesley. *General George E. Pickett in Life and Legend.* Chapel Hill: University of North Carolina Press, 1998.

Grant, Ulysses S. *Personal Memoirs of U. S. Grant.* New York: Charles L. Webster, 1885. Reprint, Lincoln: University of Nebraska Press, 1996.

Greene, A. Wilson. "Meade's Pursuit of Lee: From Gettysburg to Falling Waters." In *The Third Day at Gettysburg and Beyond*, edited by Gary W. Gallagher, pp. 161–201. Chapel Hill: University of North Carolina Press, 1994.

Grimsley, Mark, and Brooks Simpson. *Gettysburg: A Battlefield Guide.* Lincoln: University of Nebraska Press, 1999.

Haskell, Frank A. *The Battle of Gettysburg.* New York: Houghton Mifflin, 1958.

Hay, John. *Inside Lincoln's White House: The Complete Civil War Diary of John Hay.* Edited by Michael Burlingame and John R. T. Ettlinger. Carbondale: Southern Illinois University Press, 1997.

Hearn, Chester. *Admiral David Dixon Porter: The Civil War Years.* Annapolis, Md.: Naval Institute Press, 1996.

Hoehling, A. A. *Vicksburg: 47 Days of Siege.* Englewood Cliffs, N.J.: Prentice-Hall, 1969.

Hoke, Jacob. *The Great Invasion*. New York: Thomas Yoseloff, 1959.

Jackson, Isaac. *"Some of the Boys . . .": The Civil War Letters of Isaac Jackson, 1862–1865*. Edited by Joseph O. Jackson. Carbondale: Southern Illinois University Press, 1960.

Johnston, Joseph E. *Narrative of Military Operations Directed during the Late War between the States*. New York: Appleton, 1874.

Jones, John B. *A Rebel War Clerk's Diary*. Edited by Earl Schenck Miers. New York: Sagamore Press, 1958.

Jordan, David M. *Winfield Scott Hancock: A Soldier's Life*. Bloomington: Indiana University Press, 1988.

Krick, Robert K. "The Parallel Lives of Two Virginia Soldiers." In *The Third Day at Gettysburg and Beyond*, edited by Gary W. Gallagher, pp. 93–131. Chapel Hill: University of North Carolina Press, 1994.

Lee, Robert E. *The Wartime Papers of R. E. Lee*. Edited by Clifford Dowdey and Louis H. Manarin. New York: Bramhall House, 1961.

Lewis, Lloyd. *Sherman: Fighting Prophet*. New York: Harcourt, Brace, 1932.

Longacre, Edward G. *General John Buford*. Conshohocken, Pa.: Combined Books, 1995.

———. *Joshua Chamberlain: The Man and the Soldier*. Conshohocken, Pa.: Combined Books, 1999.

———. *Pickett: Leader of the Charge*. Shippensburg, Pa.: White Mane, 1998.

Lord, Mrs. William W. "Journal Kept by Mrs. W. W. Lord during the Siege of Vicksburg by the Forces of General U. S. Grant, May and July, 1863." Springfield, Mass.: Connecticut Valley Historical Society, no date. Manuscript Division, Library of Congress.

Lord, William W., Jr. "A Child at the Siege of Vicksburg." *Harper's Monthly Magazine*, December 1908, pp. 44–53.

Loughborough, Mary. *My Cave Life in Vicksburg: With Letters of Trial and Travel*. Spartanburg, S.C.: The Reprint Company, 1976.

McFeely, William S. *Grant: A Biography*. New York: W. W. Norton, 1981.

McPherson, James M. *Battle Cry of Freedom: The Civil War Era*. New York: Oxford University Press, 1988.

Meade, George G. *The Life and Letters of George Gordon Meade*. New York: Charles Scribner's Sons, 1913.

———. *With Meade at Gettysburg*. Philadelphia: John C. Winston, 1930.

Miers, Earl S., and Richard A. Brown. *Gettysburg*. Armonk, N.Y.: M. E. Sharpe, 1996.

Moe, Richard. *The Last Full Measure: The Life and Death of the First Minnesota Volunteers*. New York: Holt, 1993.

Morris, Roy, Jr. *The Better Angel: Walt Whitman in the Civil War*. New York: Oxford University Press, 2000.

Musicant, Ivan. *Divided Waters: The Naval History of the Civil War*. New York: Harper-Collins, 1995.

Oates, Stephen B. *With Malice toward None: The Life of Abraham Lincoln*. New York: Harper & Row, 1977.

Orme, William W. "Civil War Letters." *Journal of the Illinois State Historical Society*, July 1930, pp. 246–315.

Patterson, Gerard A. *Debris of Battle: The Wounded of Gettysburg*. Mechanicsburg, Pa.: Stackpole Books, 1997.

Patton, Robert H. *The Pattons: A Personal History of an American Family*. New York: Crown, 1994.

Pemberton, John C. *Pemberton: Defender of Vicksburg*. Chapel Hill: University of North Carolina Press, 1942.

Perry, Mark. *Conceived in Liberty: Joshua Chamberlain, William Oates, and the American Civil War*. New York: Viking Press, 1997.

Pfanz, Donald C. *Richard S. Ewell: A Soldier's Life*. Chapel Hill: University of North Carolina Press, 1998.

Priest, John M. *Into the Fight: Pickett's Charge at Gettysburg*. Shippensburg, Pa.: White Mane, 1998.

Robbins, Peggy. "Peace on Earth, But Not in Vicksburg." *Civil War Times Illustrated*, December 1999, p. 50.

Sandburg, Carl. *Abraham Lincoln*. Vol. 4, *The War Years*. New York: Charles Scribner's Sons, 1939.

Sanders, Jared Young, II. "Diary in Gray: Civil War Letters and Diary of Jared Young Sanders, II," Edited by Mary E. Sanders. *Louisiana Genealogical Register*, 1969, number 4, pp. 300–308; 1970, number 1, pp. 15–22.

Schildt, John W. *Roads from Gettysburg*. Shippensburg, Pa.: Burd Street Press, 1998.

Sherman, William T. *Memoirs of General William T. Sherman*. New York: Appleton, 1913. Reprint, Bloomington: Indiana University Press, 1957.

Slade, Jim, and John Alexander. *Firestorm at Gettysburg: Civilian Voices*. Atglen, Pa.: Schiffer Military/Aviation History, 1998.

Small, Cindy L. *The Jennie Wade Story*. Gettysburg: Thomas Publications, 1991.

Smith, Gene. *Lee and Grant: A Dual Biography*. New York: New American Library, 1984.

Snow, William P. *Lee and His Generals*. New York: Fairfax Press, 1982.

Sorrel, G. Moxley. *Recollections of a Confederate Staff Officer*. Jackson, Tenn.: McCowat-Mercer Press, 1958.

Stackpole, Edward. *They Met at Gettysburg*. Harrisburg, Pa.: Eagle Books, 1956.

Stevens, Joseph E. *1863: The Rebirth of a Nation*. New York: Bantam Books, 1999.

Stewart, George R. *Pickett's Charge: A Microhistory of the Final Attack at Gettysburg, July 3, 1863*. Boston: Houghton Mifflin, 1959.

Stewart, Salome Myers. *The Ties of the Past: The Gettysburg Diaries of Salome Myers Stewart*. Gettysburg: Thomas Publications, 1996.

Strong, George Templeton. *Diary of the Civil War*. New York: Macmillan, 1962. Reprint, Seattle: University of Washington Press, 1988.

Sublett, Charles W. *Fifty-seventh Virginia Infantry*. Lynchburg, Va.: H. E. Howard, 1985.

Swanberg, W. A. *Sickles the Incredible*. New York: Charles Scribner's Sons, 1956.

Symonds, Craig L. *Joseph E. Johnston: A Civil War Biography*. New York: W. W. Norton, 1992.

Taylor, Walter H. *Four Years with General Lee*. New York: Bonanza Books, 1962.

Thomas, Emory M. *Bold Dragoon: The Life of J. E. B. Stuart*. New York: Harper & Row, 1986.

———. *Robert E. Lee: A Biography*. New York: W. W. Norton, 1995.

Trulock, Alice Rains. *In the Hands of Providence: Joshua L. Chamberlain and the American Civil War*. Chapel Hill: University of North Carolina Press, 1992.

Tunnard, W. H. *A Southern Record: The History of the Third Regiment, Louisiana Infantry*. Baton Rouge, La.: W. H. Tunnard, 1866. Reprint, Dayton, Ohio: Morningside Bookshop, 1970.

U.S. War Department. *War of the Rebellion: A Compilation of the Official Records of the Union and Confederate Armies*. Washington, D.C.: Government Printing Office. Series 1, vol. 24, Part 2, 1889; series 1, vol. 27, Part 2, 1889.

Wainwright, Charles S. *A Diary of Battle: The Personal Journals of Colonel Charles S. Wainwright*. Edited by Allan Nevins. New York: Harcourt, Brace & World, 1993.

Walker, Peter F. *Vicksburg: A People at War, 1860–1865*. Chapel Hill: University of North Carolina Press, 1960.

Waugh, John C. *Reelecting Lincoln: The Battle for the 1864 Presidency*. New York: Crown, 1997.

Wert, Jeffry D. *Custer: The Controversial Life of George Armstrong Custer*. New York: Simon & Schuster, 1996.

———. *General James Longstreet: The Confederacy's Most Controversial Soldier—A Biography*. New York: Simon & Schuster, 1993.

Wheeler, Richard. *The Siege of Vicksburg*. New York: Thomas Y. Crowell, 1978.

———. *Witness to Gettysburg*. New York: Harper & Row, 1987.

Wilcox, Charles E. "With Grant at Vicksburg: From the Civil War Diary of Captain Charles E. Wilcox," edited by Edgar L. Erikson. *Journal of the Illinois State Historical Society* (January 1938): pp. 441–503.

Wilson, James Harrison. *Under the Old Flag: Recollections of Military Operations in the War for the Union, the Spanish War, the Boxer Rebellion, etc.*, vol. 1. New York: Appleton, 1912.

Newspapers

Baltimore Sun.

New York Times.

(Washington, D.C.) Evening Star.

INDEX

Alexander, Porter, 289–92, 303–4, 309–12,
  400–401, 403
Anderson, Dwight, 259
Anderson, Nancy S., 259
Anderson, Richard, 203
Anderson Cottage, 11
Angle battlefield, 316, 325–31, 337, 356
Antietam Creek, 63
Archer, James, 207–8, 216
Archer's brigade, 207
Arlington House, 46–48, 50, 52–54, 59
Armistead, Lewis A., 288, 307–9, 314,
  327–29, 333–35
Armistead's brigade, 307, 313, 319, 327–28
Army nurses, 383–85
Army of the Mississippi, 68
Army of the Missouri, 26
Army of the Ohio, 68
Army of the Potomac, 8
  under Hooker's command, 134–35, 161–62
  under Meade's command, 162–67
Army of the Tennessee, 6, 68
Autrey, James, 78

Balfour, Emma, 96, 98–100
Baltimore, martial law declared, 178–79
Barksdale, William, 255
Barlow, Francis, 372–73
Barziza, Decimus, 382

Bayly, Harriet, 216, 240–41
Beauregard, Pierre G. T., 49, 58, 82
Bellows, Henry, 381
Benny Havens's tavern, 281
Big Black River crossing, 100–102
Blacks, in Gettysburg, 135, 160
Blair, Francis Preston, 58
Blair, Montgomery, 8
Bloody Angle, 316, 325–31, 337, 356
"Bonnie Blue Flag," 152
Booth, John Wilkes, 55–56
Bowen, John S., 12, 265, 286–87, 341–42, 346
Brady, Mathew, 369
Bright, Robert, 322–23
Broadhead, Sallie, 135, 138, 139, 157, 197,
  204, 219–20, 240, 261, 263, 274–75,
  339, 348, 350, 375, 380, 383
Brooks, Noah, 6, 9, 10, 406
Brown, Charles, 300, 310–11
Brown, John, 54–55
Buchanan, James, 54
Buckner, Simon Bolivar, 23, 28
Buehler, Fannie, 134–35, 138, 156–58,
  160–61, 214, 218–19, 261, 348, 374
Buell, Don Carlos, 68
Buford, John, 194–96, 198–202, 208–9, 398,
  404
Buford's cavalry, 194–96, 199–201, 208, 209,
  246, 248

Bull Run, 5, 28, 62, 82
Bunch, Mollie, 76–77
Burns, John, 205
Burnside, Ambrose, 5, 63
Butler, Ben, 78
Butterfield, Dan, 247

Cadwallader, Sylvanus, 73, 93, 109, 115–17
Cameron, Simon, 179
Catton, Bruce, 65, 185, 293, 295, 314
Cemetery Hill, 212, 214, 220, 231–33, 235,
    236, 247, 259, 306
Cemetery Ridge, 232, 237, 245, 247, 251, 259
    bombardment of, 295–301, 304, 309, 310
    Meade's headquarters at, 267–68, 296
Chamberlain, Joshua, 229–30, 253–55, 359
Chamberlain's 20th Maine, 229, 253–55
Chambersburg occupation, 151–56, 243
Champion Hill battle, 95–99
Chancellorsville campaign, 5, 6, 65, 140
Chandler, Albert B., 3–4, 400
Chandler, Zachariah, 368
Chesnut, Mary Boykin, 81, 249
Chicago Times, 93
Cincinnati Gazette, 7
Citizen (Vicksburg), 129–30, 265, 390–91
Civilians, *See* Gettysburg, civilians; Vicksburg,
    civilians
Coffin, Charles, 137
Cold Harbor battle, 109
Colville, William, 258, 260
Colville's regiment, sacrifice of, 258
Confederate forces (Army of Northern Vir-
    ginia), 62, 134
    casualties, 140, 302, 306, 330, 332, 370–72
    Cemetery Ridge battle, 314–19, 321–22,
        328
    Lee's invasion plan, 13–14, 66, 95–96,
        138–42, 233
    morale, 140–44, 155
    retreat from Gettysburg, 370–72, 374,
        378–80, 400–408
    surrender at Gettysburg, 330–33
    Union bombardment of, 318–22
Cooper, Samuel, 82
Copperhead antiwar movement, 141
Corinth campaign, 69–70
Corps of Engineers, 34, 36, 45
Couch, Darius, 178, 210
Cowan, Edgar, 178
Crawford, John, 230
Cullum, George, 29–30
Culp, John Wesley, 272

Culp's Hill, 214, 221, 223, 232, 236, 247, 259,
    271, 272, 285, 306, 356
Curtin, A. G., 138, 178
Cushing, Alonzo, 300, 310, 316, 324, 328
Custer, George Armstrong, 9
Custer, Libby, 9
Custis, George Washington Parke, 46, 53

Dahlgren, John, 9
Daily Citizen (Vicksburg), 129–30, 265,
    390–91
Dana, Charles A., 71–72, 74, 86, 93, 115–16,
    165, 173
Dana, N. J., 138
Davis, Jefferson, 23, 52, 59–62, 66, 75, 81–84,
    95, 101, 102, 106, 192, 392–93, 401
Davis, Joe, 207–8
Devil's Den, 214, 251–52
Dickert, August, 404
Dix, Dorothea, 383
"Dixie," 160
Donaldson, Francis, 149, 161, 356
Dooley, John, 147, 152, 276–77, 301
Dooley, Tom, 243, 313, 320, 324, 330, 376–77
Doubleday, Abner, 207–9, 214, 221, 321,
    335
Doubleday's corps, 214
Duff, William, 93

Early, Jubal, 158–59, 223–24, 226, 308
Early's division, 158, 159, 161, 224
Easley, Drewry, 313, 328, 329, 331
Eckert, Thomas, 4–5
Emancipation Proclamation, 5
Eustice, George, 205
Ewell, Richard, 142–43, 151–54, 187–90,
    208–10, 212, 213, 221–24, 226–27,
    230, 235–37, 247, 259, 267, 269, 272,
    306, 352, 403
Ewell's corps, 142, 151–54, 161, 168, 187,
    188, 208, 212–13, 221–24, 227, 247,
    259, 306

Fairfax, John, 167
Falling Waters crossing, 400–405
Farley, William, 183–84
Farragut, David, 78–79, 84, 86
File-closers, 313, 318
Finnessey, William, 326
Fiske, Sam, 150, 165
Floyd, John, 54
Foote, Andrew, 27–28
Foote, Shelby, 266

Forney, John H., 264
Fort Donelson, 28, 29
Fort Henry, 27–28
Fort Humboldt, 22
Fort Mason, 56
Fort McHenry, 377
Fort Sumter, 25, 37, 58, 81, 82
Fort Vancouver, 22
Fortress Monroe, 47, 48, 61, 81
Foster, Catherine, 276
Fourth Artillery, 300, 310, 316, 324
Fourth of July, 9, 12–13, 15, 265, 344, 347–50,
    361, 365, 367–69
Fredericksburg campaign, 5, 63–64
Freeman, Douglas Southall, 190, 204, 236
Fremantle, Arthur J. L., 110, 132, 141, 146,
    152–53, 192, 323, 338
Fry, James, 369
Fuger, Frederick, 324, 333

Gage, Jeremiah, 303
Gardner, Alfred, 300–301
Garnett, Dick, 288, 307–8, 325
Garnett's brigade, 307
General Orders (Lee), 143, 154
General Orders (Meade), 355, 369
Gerlach, Anna, 274
Gettysburg, 8, 13–15, 158–59
    aftermath of battle, 356–59, 374–77,
        383–88
    civilians, 134–35, 138–39, 156–61, 194–97,
        204–6, 214–20, 230, 238–42, 261–63,
        272–76, 339–41, 348–51, 357, 374–77
    Confederate occupation of, 218–20
    relief efforts at, 380–89
Gettysburg Blues militia, 139
Gibbon, John, 267–68, 292–93, 296, 298, 305,
    316, 320, 321
Gibbon's division, 319
Glatthaar, Joseph, 144
Goddard, Charley, 149
Goldsborough, Euphemia, 384–85
Gordon, Lesley, 337
Grant, Jessie, 16–18, 23, 26
Grant, Julia Dent, 19–24, 26, 87–89, 191
Grant, Ulysses S., 6–7, 9, 12–13, 16–31,
        67–75, 80, 83–96, 100–109, 111–12,
        130–32, 174, 191, 227–28, 265–66,
        286–87, 341–47, 362–65, 389–90,
        394–95
    background, 16–26
    drinking problem, 7, 22–23, 25, 27, 31, 71,
        73, 84, 93, 114–17

feud with Halleck, 26–30, 67–70
    "Unconditional Surrender," 28
Greene, Nathaniel, 41
Grierson, Benjamin, 91

"Hail Columbia," 362
Haines' Bluff, 91, 102–3
Halleck, Henry W., 26–30, 67–70, 74–75, 92,
    148, 175, 178, 180, 248, 354–55,
    397–401
Hamer, Thomas, 18
Hancock, Cornelia, 383–84
Hancock, Winfield Scott, 211–12, 220–21,
    257–58, 292, 304–5, 308–9, 321,
    333–35
Hancock's corps, 211, 220, 231, 258
Hardie, James A., 163–64
Harding, Milton, 328–29
Harmon, Amelia, 205–6
Harmon, William, 329, 331
Harper's Ferry arsenal, 54–55
Harrison, Henry, 167–68
Haskell, Frank, 211, 250, 259–60, 293–94,
    296, 298, 316, 334–35
Hay, John, 399, 406
Hearn, Chester, 172
Heth, Henry, 196–97, 201, 203, 212, 270, 276
Heth's division, 196–97, 200, 207, 307
Hill, Ambrose Powell, 13, 187–88, 190, 197,
    200, 203, 208–9, 223–24, 267, 270–71,
    404
Hill's corps, 142, 168, 187, 208, 213, 221, 247,
    271, 306
Hodges, Alphonse, 199–200
Hoke, Jacob, 144, 152, 155
Hollinger, Jacob, 239
Hood, John Bell, 53, 153, 181, 187, 234, 270
Hood's division, 237, 244–46, 251, 306
Hooker, Joseph, 5, 8, 64–65, 134–36, 140, 142,
    146–48, 155, 156, 161–62, 164, 184
Hooker's Retreat (whiskey), 161
Horton, Thomas, 288
Howard, Oliver, 202, 209, 210, 212–13, 231,
    335, 402
Howard's corps, 202, 209, 212–14
Hunt, Henry, 309–10
Hunton, Eppa, 279, 314, 319
Hutter, James Risque, 288, 302

Imboden, John, 347, 370–72, 378–79, 397
Imboden's wagon train, 370–72, 378–80,
    400–408
    Union attacks on, 379, 405

Independence Day, 9, 12–13, 15, 265, 344, 347–50, 361, 365, 367–69
Iron Brigade, 207, 213

Jackson, Andrew, 32, 45
Jackson, Isaac, 107–8, 118, 121, 345, 360, 362
Jackson, Mississippi, campaign, 90–95
Jackson, Thomas (Stonewall), 55, 62, 65, 187–90, 222–24, 226, 236, 307
Jacobs, Henry, 214, 261, 263, 350
Jacobs, Julia, 351
Jacobs, Michael, 158, 205, 261, 263, 340
Jefferson Barracks, 19
Jenkins, Albert, 151–52, 157–58
Jenkins's brigade, 151–52, 157–58
Johnson, Edward, 224, 271–72
Johnson, Samuel, 234, 235
Johnston, Albert Sidney, 52, 82
Johnston, D. E., 303
Johnston, Joseph E., 52, 62, 81–84, 87, 90, 92–95, 100, 102–3, 110–11, 129–33, 141, 227–28, 264, 344, 364–67, 392, 395
  feud with Jefferson Davis, 82–84
Jones, John, 60
Jones, William, 300–301
July 4th, 9, 12–13, 15, 265, 344, 347–50, 361, 365, 367–69

"Kathleen Mavourneen," 309
Kemper, James, 305, 307, 319
Kemper's brigade, 305, 307, 320–22
Kimble, Junius, 277, 332
Kirby-Smith, Edmund, 53

Lane, James, 306
Law, Evander, 251–52
Lee, Ann Carter, 42–45
Lee, Fitzhugh, 53, 278, 379
Lee, Henry (Black Horse Harry), 43, 45
Lee, Light Horse Harry, 41–43, 45, 61
Lee, Mary Anna Randolph Custis (wife), 46–48, 50–53, 59
Lee, Matilda, 41–42
Lee, Robert E., 7–9, 13–15, 21, 134–48, 154–56, 167–68, 175–76, 180–87, 190, 193–94, 203–4, 212–14, 221–27, 232–38, 242–44, 266–67, 269–71, 276–77, 288, 338, 347, 352–54, 369–70, 372–73, 396, 398–401, 403–5
  background and description, 41–66, 145–47
  seeks prisoner exchange, 352
  on Stuart, 146–47, 155, 156, 167, 180–81, 203, 242

welcomed in Maryland, 145–46
Lewis, John, 302, 314
Lincoln, Abraham, 3–11, 13, 15, 26, 28, 30, 31, 39, 63, 66–68, 70, 71, 74, 75, 84, 111–12, 136, 138, 140, 142, 147–48, 161, 162, 166, 179, 355, 364–65, 367–70, 396, 397, 399–402, 406–7
  assassination attempt, 10–11
Lincoln, Mary Todd, 9–11, 39–40
Little, George, 261
Lockett, Samuel, 102, 104–5, 113, 174, 363, 391
Loehr, Charles, 287–88
Logan, John, 341, 362
Longacre, Edward, 281
Longstreet, James (Pete), 13, 20, 21, 62, 142, 145, 146, 154, 187, 188, 190–94, 203, 212, 224–27, 243–47, 251, 255, 257–59, 281–82, 284, 285, 288–92, 295, 305–6, 311–12, 323, 336, 338, 354, 403, 404, 408
  dispute with Lee, 193–94, 224–25, 227, 234–38, 269–71
Longstreet, Louise Garland, 191–92
Longstreet's corps, 142, 168, 187, 203, 212, 225, 226, 235, 244, 257–59, 306
Lord family, 106, 123–27, 169, 171, 346, 359–60, 366, 390, 393
Loughborough, Mary, 89, 95, 97, 106, 112, 125, 127–29, 133, 170, 360, 393
Lutheran Seminary, 158, 200, 205, 213

Marston, Henry, 345
Martin, Rawley, 327
Marvin, Matthew, 149, 229, 299
Mayo, Joseph, 277–78, 301
McAllister, Mary, 216, 218, 240, 261, 348, 350, 351
McClean, Billy, 239
McClean, Robert, 205
McClellan, George, 5, 11, 22, 25, 28, 29, 38, 50, 61–63, 70, 136, 179
McClernand, John, 74–75, 86, 100, 108–9
McClure, A. K., 31
McCreary, Albertus, 158, 160, 197, 205, 215, 219, 239, 262, 275, 340, 349–50, 357, 388
McCurdy, Charles, 159, 197
McDowell, Irwin, 5
McFeely, William, 23
McIlheny, R. F., 196
McLaws, Lafayette, 235–37, 244–45, 270
McLaws's division, 235–37, 244–45, 255, 306

McLean, Moses, 276

McLellan, Ellen, 155

McPherson, James B. (Union corps commander), 108, 109, 341

McPherson, James M. (historian), 73

McRae, Lucy, 126, 129, 346, 360

Meade, George, 8–9, 11, 13–15, 174–76, 178, 181–82, 202, 209–12, 221, 231–33, 244, 246–48, 250–51, 253, 257–59, 267–68, 271, 292–93, 296–97, 309, 352, 365, 369–70
    background, 31–40
    fails to counterattack and pursue, 334–36, 354–56, 372–73, 396–407
    given command, Army of the Potomac, 162–67
    wounded, 38–39

Meade, George, Jr. (son), 33, 164, 292, 396

Meade, Margaretta Sergeant (wife), 34–40, 369

Mexican War, 12, 19–21, 34, 36, 49–50, 80, 82, 188, 191, 278, 281–82

Militia, Union recruitment of, 136–39, 210

Miller, Dora, 90, 98–99, 133, 171

Minnesota Volunteers, 149–51, 165, 177, 228, 298–99, 316, 329–30
    sacrifice of, 258

Moe, Richard, 209

Montford, Mary Elizabeth, 217

Montgomery, Louis, 286, 341, 342

Muskets, improper loading of, 357–58

Myers, Sallie, 135, 157, 204, 215, 241–42, 261–62, 274, 339, 348, 375–76

Oates, William, 252–55

Olmstead, Frederick Law, 381

Ord, Edward, 341

Orme, William, 118–19, 122, 173, 361, 365–66, 396

Osborn, Thomas, 309–10

Parker, Joel, 138

Patrick, Marsena, 161

Patterson, Gerard, 377

Patton, Waller, Tazewell, 278, 288, 301, 327–28, 384

Peach Orchard, 245, 250–51, 255, 256

Pemberton, John C., 11–13, 21, 36, 80–81, 83, 84, 87, 90–95, 97, 98, 100–107, 110–13, 130–32, 172, 227–28, 263–66, 286–87, 341–47, 363, 365–67, 394–96

Pemberton, Martha Thompson, 81

Peninsular campaign, 5, 38, 61–62, 83

Pennsylvania Volunteers, 324–27

Pettigrew, James Johnston, 196–97, 314, 321–22, 405

Pettigrew's division, 213, 276, 307, 321–22

Pickett, George, 13, 14, 145, 191, 234, 270, 278–85, 288–92, 304, 306, 307, 310–13, 319, 320, 322–24, 328, 329, 336–38, 347, 353

Pickett, LaSalle Corbell (Sallie), 282–85, 337

Pickett's division, 243, 266, 271, 276, 306–7, 311–19, 322–24, 328
    as prisoner escort, 353–54

Pierce, Tillie, 157, 159, 195, 204, 217, 238, 262, 274, 340–41, 357, 388

Pipe Creek defense line, 176, 211

Plank, Elizabeth, 206

Pleasonton, Alfred, 183, 208–9, 335

Plummer, John, 177

Pope, John, 5, 62, 68, 183

Porter, David, 86–88, 172, 343, 364–65

Potomac River crossing, 378–79, 403–4

Powell, Robert, 386

Powers, Alice, 230

Quaker guns, 105

Rawlins, John A., 73, 86, 93, 109, 114, 116–17, 391–92

Rawlins, Mary Hurlburt, 391–92

Reynolds, John, 163, 202, 206–7, 210

Reynolds's corps, 202, 206–8

Richardson, John, 332

Richmond Grays militia, 55

Richmond Sentinel, 392

Rifles, 7-shot repeaters, 200–201

Roach, Mahala, 78

Road, Hosea, 345

Rodes, Robert, 208, 223–24, 226

Round Tops, 214, 232, 235, 246–55
    Union signal post on, 244, 247, 253

Sacramento Union, 6

Sap rollers, 120–21

Scales, Alfred, 306

Schwartz family, 376

Scott, Winfield, 49–50, 54, 57–58

Secession, 56–58

Seddon, James A., 93–94, 130–31, 392–93

Seminary Ridge, 205, 212, 213, 221, 224, 232, 247
    bombardment of, 301–3, 309

Seminole Indian wars, 33, 80, 82, 187, 308

Seven Days' battles, 38, 62

Seward, William H., 178
Sherman, William Tecumseh, 7, 24, 69, 75, 85, 86, 91, 92, 95, 100–104, 106–9, 113, 364–65
Shiloh Church battle, 30–31, 68–69
Shotwell, Randolph, 302
Sickles, Dan, 210, 220, 235, 248–51, 256–57, 259
Sickles's corps, 210, 220, 235, 249–51, 255, 256, 259
Sisters of Charity, 380
Skelly, Daniel, 197, 350
Skelly, Jack, 273
Slocum, Henry, 210, 220, 247, 271
Smith, A. J., 286, 341–42
Smith, C. F., 29
Smith, Gene, 44
Smith, J. C., 371
Snow, William P., 82
Snyder, Jacob, 371
Soldiers' Home, 10–11
Sorrel, Moxley, 279, 285, 321, 404
Spessard, Michael, 319, 333
Stannard, George J., 320–22
Stanton, Edwin, 5, 30, 71, 72, 74, 136, 162, 180, 249
"Star Spangled Banner," 229, 362
Stewart, Alexander, 241, 261–62, 274, 375–76
Stewart, George, 337
Stewart, James, 329
Stone, Charles, 10
Stone, Kate, 78
Straight, Albert, 300–301
Stuart, James Ewell Brown (JEB), 13, 51, 54–55, 62, 136, 142, 146, 150, 155, 156, 167, 177, 181–86, 203, 225, 242–43, 246, 266, 380, 405
    confrontation with Lee, 242
Stuart's cavalry, 184–86, 225, 242–43, 246, 266
Sturtevant, Wesley, 277
Sumner, Edwin V., 52
Swanberg, W. A., 256
Swords, J. M., 129, 390

Taneytown, Union headquarters at, 175, 208–9, 231
"Taps," 247
Taylor, Henry, 151, 177, 229, 260, 273–74, 299, 305, 330, 359
Taylor, Isaac, 228–29, 260, 273, 259
Taylor, Walter, 221–22, 266, 336
Taylor, Zachary, 297

Telegraph office, War Department, 3–8, 11, 136, 177–78, 368–69, 399–401
Thunder barrels, 117–18
Timberlake, John, 332
Trimble, Isaac, 141, 143, 155–56, 223, 236, 366
Tunnard, Willie, 113, 118, 120, 121, 130, 169, 174, 360, 362, 394

Underground Railroad, 158
Union forces (Army of the Potomac),
    call for volunteers, 136–40, 148
    casualties, 214–20
    failure of leadership, 5, 8–9, 63, 136, 162, 401–7
    morale, 140, 176, 277, 287–88
    retreat at Gettysburg, 214–16
University Grays militia, 303
U.S. Christian Commission, 381–83
U.S. Sanitary Commission, 380–83

Van Dorn, Earl, 53
Vicksburg, 6–7, 11–13, 67, 77–80, 83–84
    civilians, 79, 123–30, 169–71, 265–66, 346, 359–60, 366–67, 389–91, 393
    defenses, 104–8
    description, 6, 75–78
    Grant's battle plan for, 67, 72, 74–75, 100
    naval bombardment of, 78–79
    occupation by Union forces, 389–91
    promises of relief, 110–11, 129–33, 227, 264, 367
    siege, 99–100, 109–33, 172–74, 227, 263–64
    surrender, 264–65, 285–87, 341–45, 360–67, 394–96
    truce for burial parties, 112–13
    Union attacks on, 104–8, 132–33
Vicksburg Whig, 87
Vincent, Strong, 229, 253

Wade, Jennie, 272–73
Wainwright, Charles, 356
Warren, Gouverneur K., 14, 253
Warren, Mary, 351
Washburn, W. M., 120
Washburne, Elihu B., 25, 30, 70
Washington, D.C., defenses, 180
Washington Star, 368
Watson, Samuel, 384–85
Webb, Alexander, 324–27
Weed, Thurlow, 178
Welles, Gideon, 365, 406–7

Wertz, John, 262
Western Union, 4
Whistler, James Abbott McNeill, 51
White, Luther, 359
White House, 9–10
Wilcox, Cadmus, 306
Wilcox, Charles, 85, 107–8, 119, 122, 361
Wilderness campaign, 64–65

Williamsport crossing, 378–79, 403–4
Wilson, John, 363
Winter, Philip, 159
Wise, George, 131–32
Wittenmyer, Annie, 89
Worth, William, 21
Wright, Ambrose, 290–91
Wright, James, 149, 316